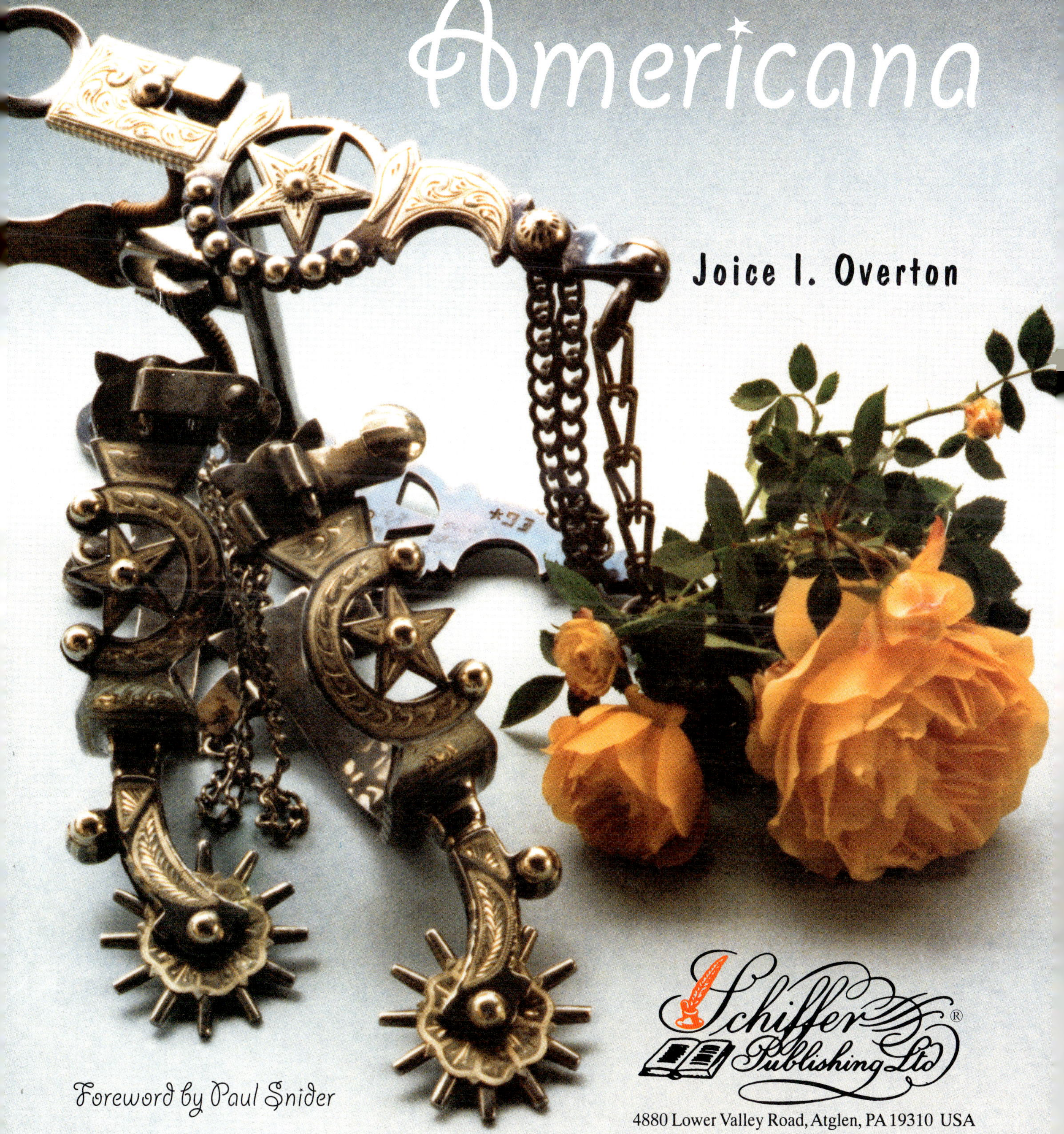

Cowboy Americana

Joice I. Overton

Foreword by Paul Snider

Schiffer Publishing Ltd®
4880 Lower Valley Road, Atglen, PA 19310 USA

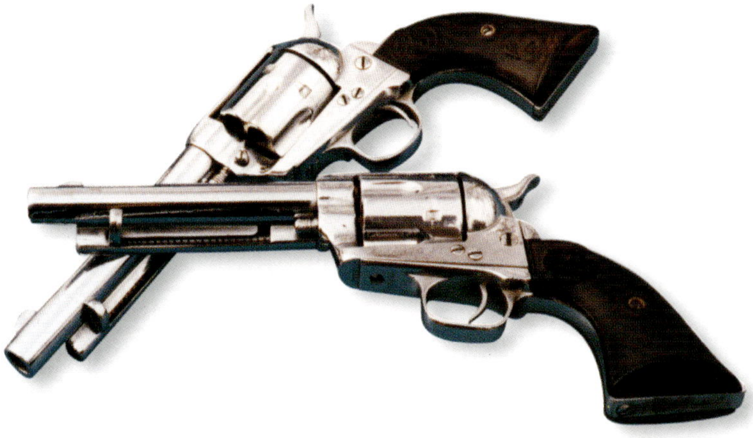

Library of Congress Catalog Card Number: 00-106198

Designed by Bonnie M. Hensley
Cover Designed by Bruce M. Waters
Type set in DomBold BT/Korinna BT

ISBN: 0-7643-1255-3
Printed in China
1 2 3 4

Published by Schiffer Publishing Ltd.
4880 Lower Valley Road
Atglen, PA 19310
Phone: (610) 593-1777; Fax: (610) 593-2002
E-mail: Schifferbk@aol.com
Please visit our web site catalog at **www.schifferbooks.com**

In Europe, Schiffer books are distributed by Bushwood Books
6 Marksbury Avenue Kew Gardens
Surrey TW9 4JF England
Phone: 44 (0) 20-8392-8585; Fax: 44 (0) 20-8392-9876
E-mail: Bushwd@aol.com
Free postage in the UK. Europe: air mail at cost.

This book may be purchased from the publisher.
Include $3.95 for shipping. Please try your bookstore first.
We are always looking for people to write books on new and related subjects.
If you have an idea for a book please contact us at the Atglen, PA address.
You may write for a free catalog.

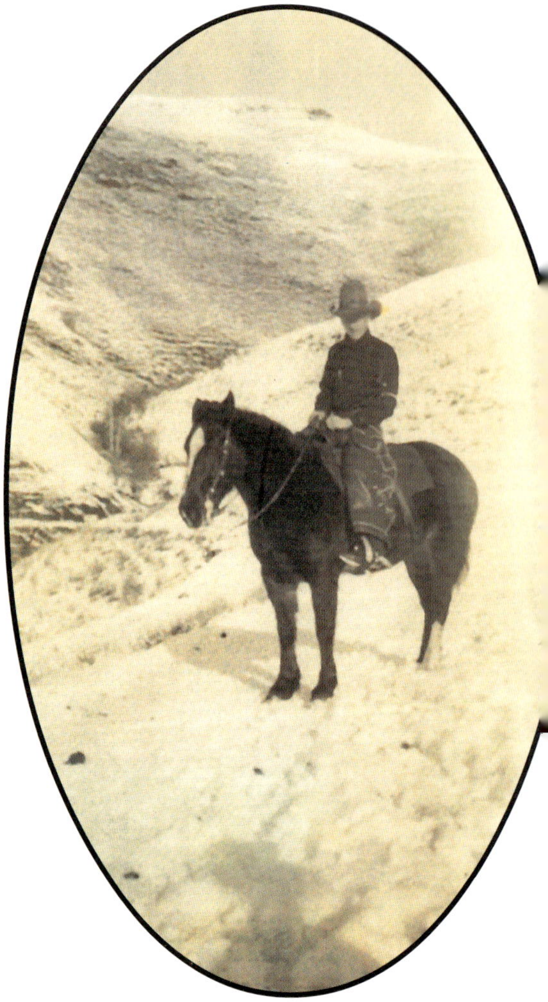

Tom Qualey on Spark Plug.

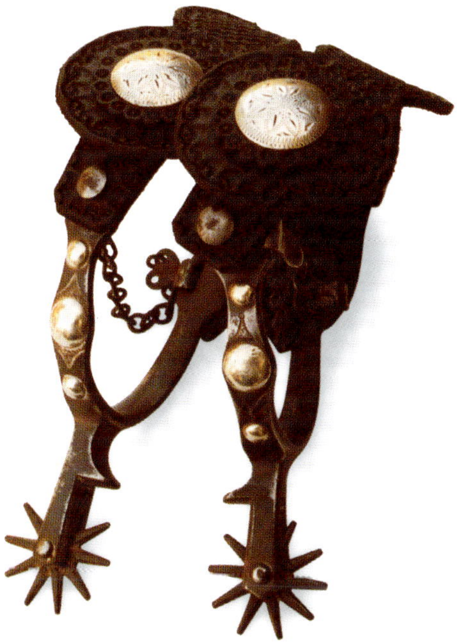

Dedication

This book is dedicated to the people in my life who patiently played a part in helping me to learn to walk again. With God's help and theirs, I have accomplished this three times in my life. To my mother for the first time; to Miss Abondroth (Abby), my physical therapist, who never let me stop trying after two years in the hospital with Polio as a child; and to Dr. Kopp, who "nailed" me back together to put me back on my feet most recently. The words "thank you" will never be enough.

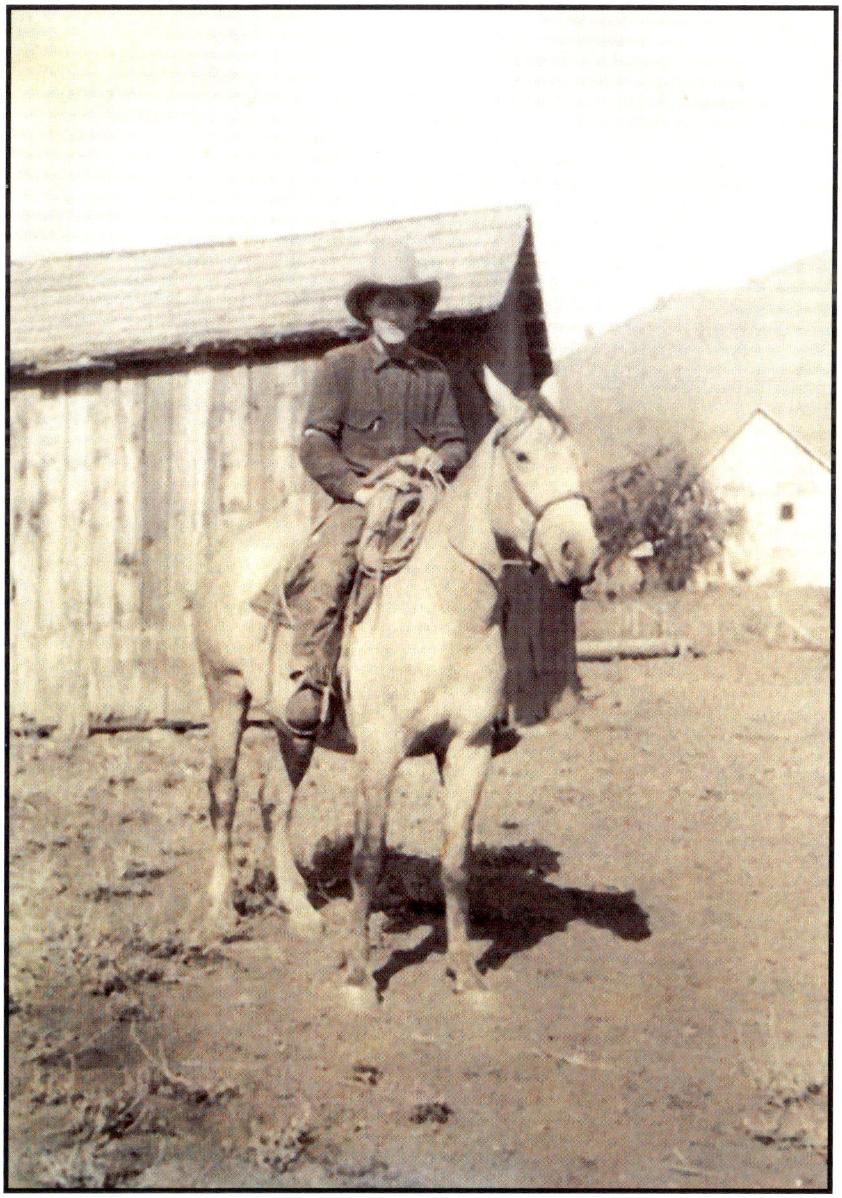

Young Tom Qualey in front of the bit and spur making shop

Acknowledgements

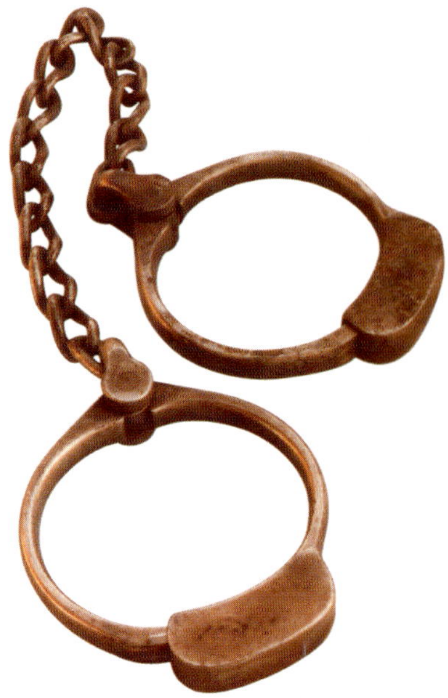

I thank all the wonderful people who were kind enough to help me with the production of this book; without them it would have been impossible. My heartfelt thanks go to:

Paul and Marlene Snider, friends who have never failed us, and to whom we wish the very best of God's blessings in all that they ever do.

Jack Snider, you were great and I sure appreciate the help.
Ron and Sharon Mailloux, dear friends who have enriched our lives immensely.

Eve Morgan, you made my gun chapter possible, and I will always count you as a friend.

Bob and Judy Bertsch, our old time friends, and a special thanks to you, "Jude," for all that "note taking" and extra support.

R.C. and Marvin Bales, how very much we enjoyed our visits together!
Mr.and Mrs. Gene Myers, for all your generous help I am grateful.

Wade Brumley, a great guy and I wish you all the best life has to offer.
Mr. and Mrs. Gene Christopher. Bless you for your gentle kindness to us; I appreciate your help.

Ira and Betty Cochran, the Code of the West still lives on at their ranch! We loved our time with you and I am grateful.

And special thanks to my kids, Barb Rider and Paul Rider, for "riding shotgun" with me.

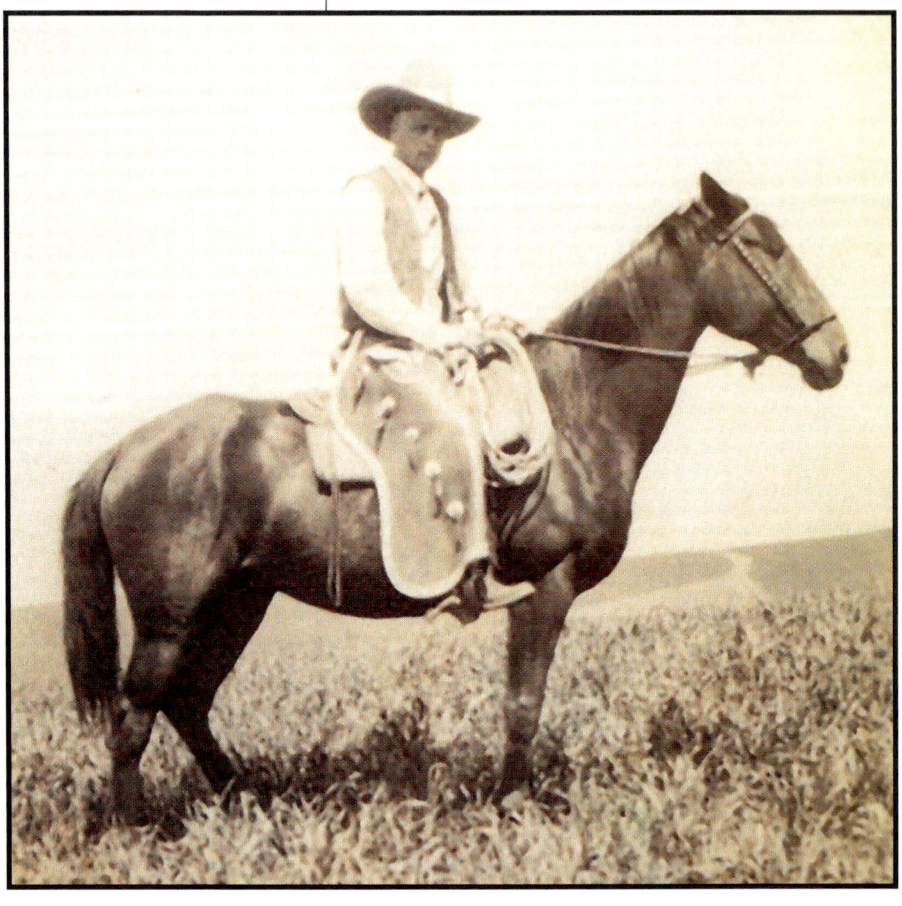

Nels Qualey on Penny-Ante

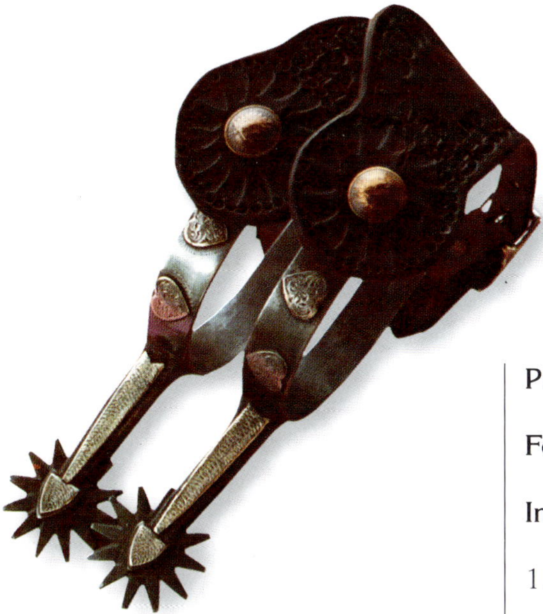

Contents

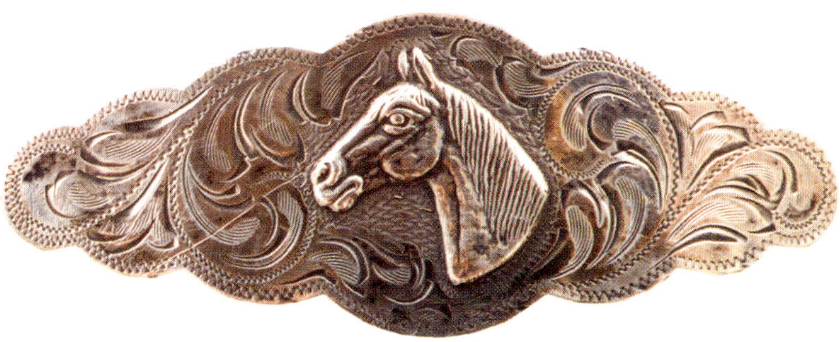

Preface

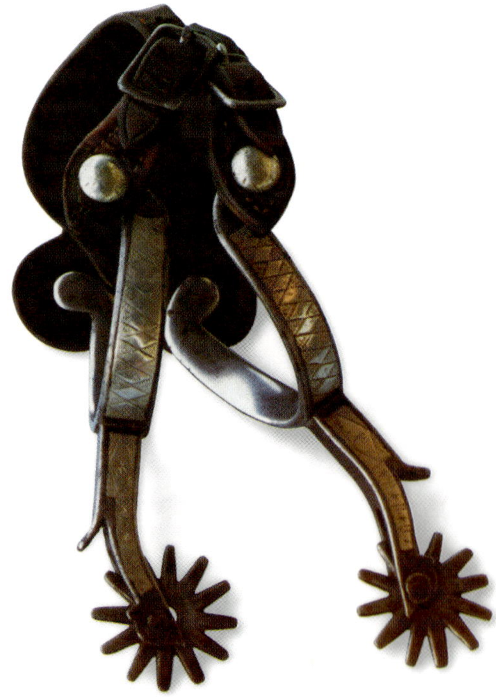

Recently, a gentleman from France contacted me to purchase my books. Even though the money exchange and shipping costs were very high, he was most anxious to receive the information. I dug out my old French/English dictionary and, though it took quite some time and much correspondence on both our parts, we finally accomplished the transaction and he was very happy. He made me aware of the world-wide interest in the American cowboy more than ever. Perhaps that experience has "lit the candle" for my decision to put together this book, for nothing is more gratifying than being able to share one's love of cowboy collectibles with others, far and wide, who also appreciate their history and beauty.

Since so many Native Americans were horsemen *par excellence* long before there *was* a cowboy, I have tried to include items from their part of the history also. It is one way I can give them the honor and tribute they so richly deserve.

With the advent of the new Millenium, we should all recognize the inevitable fact that cowboy Americana, like so many other parts of history, is rapidly disappearing and moving farther behind us every day. All the more reason, then, for books like this to be made available.

It is my sincere wish that the items portrayed here bring you pleasure and that each fact I present will trickle down, like tiny grains of sand, to future readers. I have tried to be honest and correct regarding items; wherever I have failed, I beg your forgiveness and understanding. The information is sometimes sketchy, and there is a massive variety to cover. Enjoy the pursuit of your own cowboy Americana!

About the values placed in this book

I have tried to reconcile values and keep a close eye on some of the Western auctions continually, so I feel that the values here are fair. However, I must allow that each collector has had a say in the value he or she places on their own items, and therefore, among the many other factors, these too, are factored in. I have long-since learned that no single value placed on any single item will satisfy everyone, and so of course there will always be disagreements about the actual value of an item. We all must be able to view *values placed, as values estimated,* and I think that says it all.

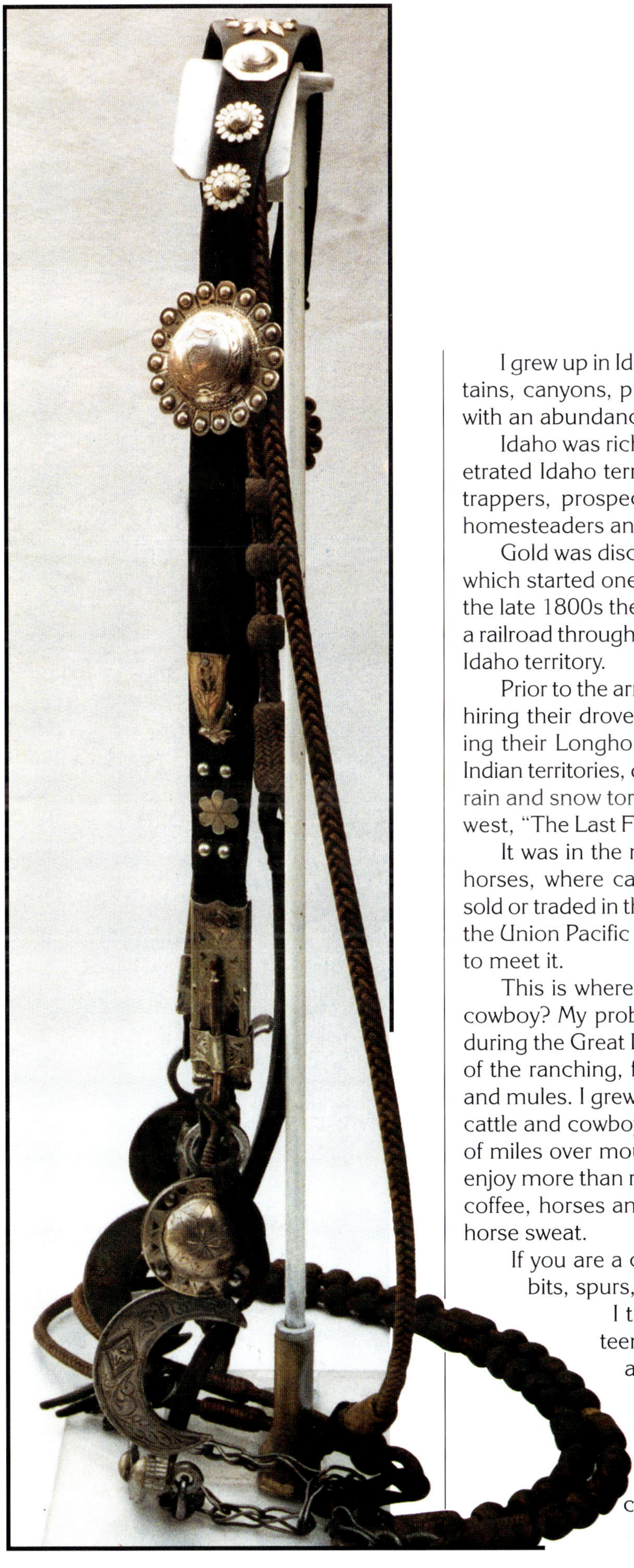

Foreword

by Paul Snider

I grew up in Idaho, a state that abounds with vast wilderness, mountains, canyons, prairies, deserts with pristine rivers and lakes, a state with an abundance of wildlife and birds.

Idaho was rich with early western heritage. The first explorers penetrated Idaho territory on their way to the Pacific, followed by the fur trappers, prospectors, Indian wars, notorious outlaws, gunfighters, homesteaders and cattle ranchers.

Gold was discovered in 1860 by a prospector named John Pierce, which started one of the largest gold rushes in our nation's history. In the late 1800s the Union Pacific Railroad started laying track, pushing a railroad through the northwest, reaching the Pacific as it went through Idaho territory.

Prior to the arrival of the Union Pacific, Texas cattle ranchers started hiring their drovers, assembling their equipment, horses and gathering their Longhorn cattle for cattle drives which took them through Indian territories, deserts, mountains and crossing rivers. The sun, dust, rain and snow torturing them for their 1500 mile journey to the northwest, "The Last Frontier."

It was in the northwest, already populated with free roaming wild horses, where cattle ranches were established supplying beef to be sold or traded in the settlements, army posts, and mining camps. When the Union Pacific arrived in the northwest, the cattle industry was here to meet it.

This is where I was raised. Is it any wonder that I wanted to be a cowboy? My problem; I was born fifty years too late, or was I? Born during the Great Depression, as a young boy, I remember the majority of the ranching, farming, and transportation being done with horses and mules. I grew into adulthood, surrounded with horses and mules, cattle and cowboys. Over the last sixty years, I have ridden thousands of miles over mountains and wilderness trails. There is nothing that I enjoy more than rocky trails, camp smoke, good company, side boiled coffee, horses and mules, "squeaky" saddle leather and the smell of horse sweat.

If you are a cowboy, you must love cowboy equipment, saddles, bits, spurs, reatas, chaps, boots, hats, Winchesters, and Colts.

I traded for my first single action Colt when I was sixteen years old, which was the beginning of my collecting all cowboy equipment, including the "firearms that won the West," a hobby that I have enjoyed over the last forty years.

The year was nineteen hundred and thirty seven, in a two-story frame house, on a snowy day in December, in a little settlement named Indian Valley,

Idaho, located in the head waters of the Weiser river. Bill and Leona Hunsucker were blessed with a little girl, who they named Joice. She grew up in the beautiful valley of rich grass, surrounded by big timber teaming with wildlife, the Weiser River full of Rainbow trout and Salmon;, and the rich grass meadows full of cattle. At the age of nine, after a severe bout with polio, Joice moved to Baker, Oregon, the center of Oregon's great cattle country. Baker has since been re-named Baker City. Joice, at the age of fifteen, received her first rifle, a .22 caliber Winchester single shot, given to her by a friend. Joice saved her money and bought a second rifle, a Remington Competition .22 caliber, which weighed just over thirteen pounds. Joice joined the John Day Rifle Club, sponsored by the NRA, and shot competition with the rifle team.

When Joice grew into adulthood, she was very successful in the Western Music field, writing and recording music under the label of Gibson Girl Publishing. With her desire and yearning to return to her roots, so deep in cowboy country, Joice wrote a book entitled *Cowboy Bits and Spurs*, published in 1997, which became the written authority on all bit and spur collecting. Joice followed it with another book, entitled *Cowboy Equipment*, published in 1998. Both were smashing successes. After years of research, traveling thousands of miles for hundreds of interviews, and using her own wealth of knowledge, Joice has written a third book, entitled *Cowboy Americana*.

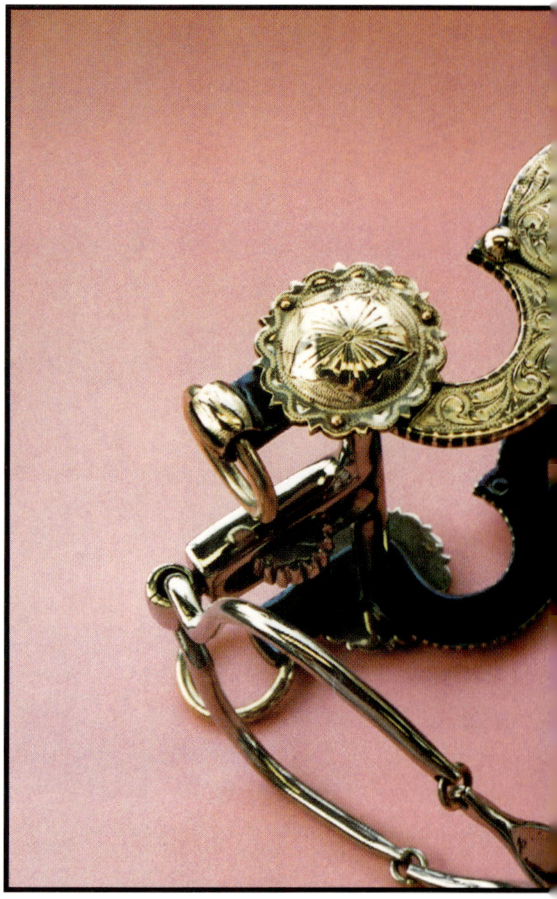

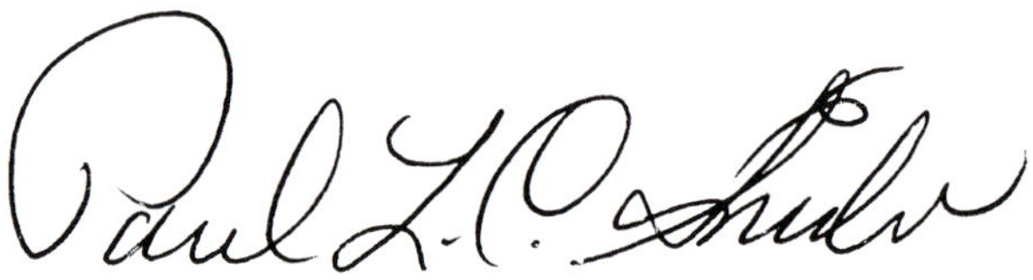

Paul Snider

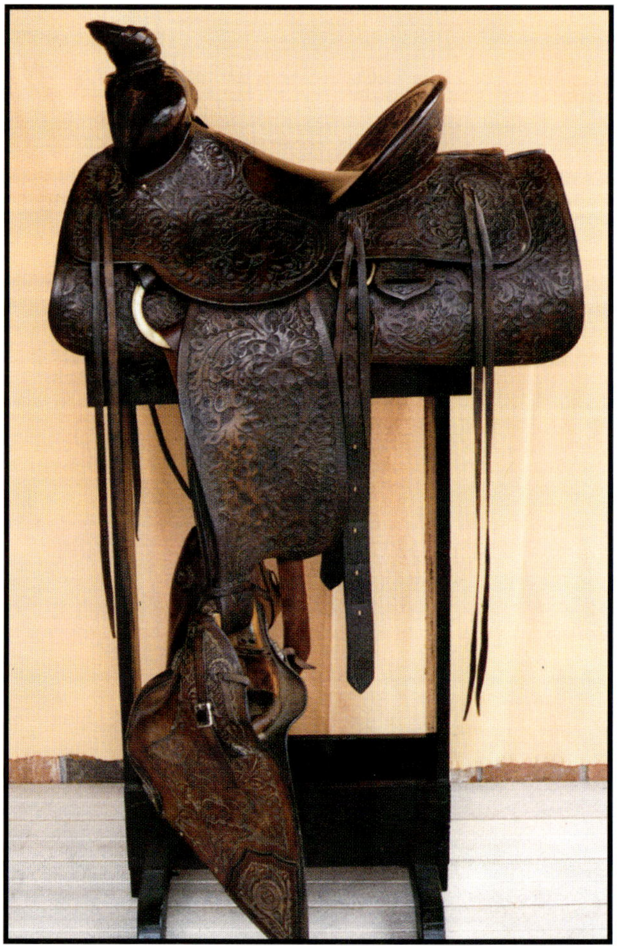

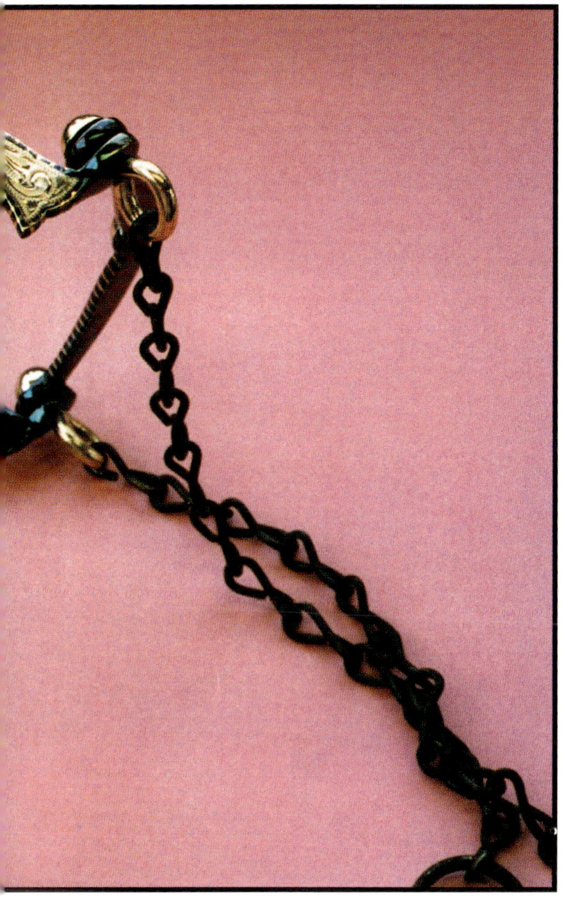

Introduction

While doing research for this book, a friend of mine loaned me a small, leather bound book, written by Harry Carr in 1935 and printed by Angelus Press, Los Angeles, California. It is titled *To Will Rogers, Vaya Con Dios* and has an introduction by the world-famous film star, William S. Hart. That introduction reads as follows:

> Bill, if there was a ladder long enough, some of us fellers that aint good enough to go nohow, would be climbin' up there to see you an' say hello. An' maybe Bill, we might get a chance to see the little chap that wears your brand, that you told Charlie Russell to give a big kiss to when he seen him, an' Bill, maybe some of us no accounts might get a chance to kiss the little cowboy too. We all send our lovin' goodbyes, Bill, and we all hope to see you again....after a spell. Your friend, Bill Hart.

While I realize this tribute to Will Rogers, written shortly after he died in 1935, is somewhat sad, I pass it along to my readers anyway. The old master cowboys mentioned in Hart's introduction were each famous for their own special and separate accomplishments. Will Rogers was the great cowboy humorist and trick roper, William S. Hart was one of the first American cowboy film stars, and Charlie Russell the wonderful cowboy/Indian artist. Now that alone should be reason enough to include the words in my book's introduction, but that is still not the main reason for it being here.

Throughout the history of the American cowboy (and including every modern-day one I ever knew personally), there has been an ambiance about them and their (for lack of a better word) humbleness that is difficult to describe. This bit of writing from the past, you might say from one cowboy to another, portrays that genuine humbleness better than any other I have come across. I never quite figured out why almost all cowboys have this shy and honorable virtue of a humble attitude, but it is still evident in the working cowboys of today, and the competing rodeo hands. I have a theory that it has its roots in the old words, "...the code of the west, where a man's on honor to be his best."

Chapter One

Bits

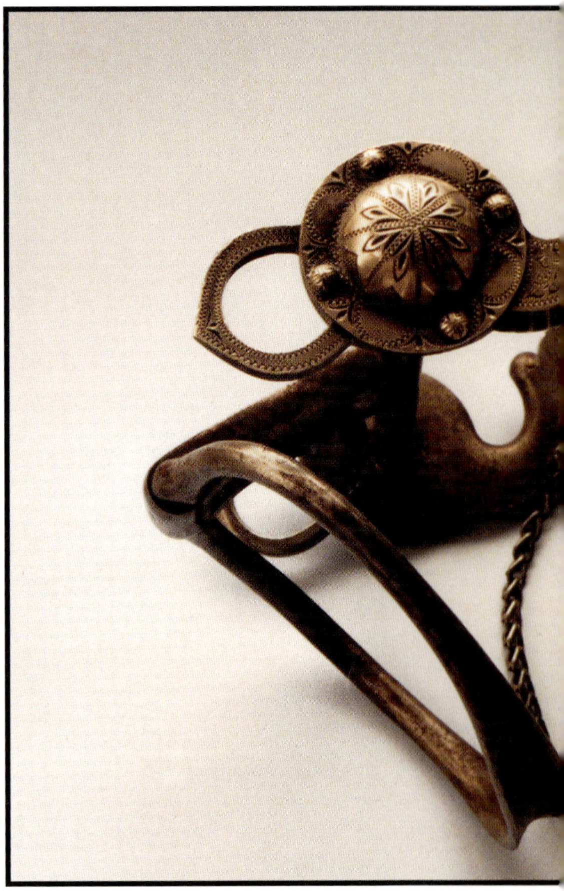

Tom Qualey's items have taken on a recent surge of interest in the bit and spur collector circle and this silver mounted ring bit is an example of his outstanding work. This bit was sold at the Cody, Wyoming, auction in 1998 and brought $12,000 *Courtesy Ron and Sharon Mailloux. $12,000 to 14,000*

"The way to a horse's heart"

Buying a fine old silver mounted collectible bit today can be compared to walking into a real estate office and placing a down payment on an executive style home. Some bits are fetching tremendous amounts at Western auctions around the country lately. Of course it depends on the bit itself and many other varying factors, but some have certainly brought a goodly amount.

The old silver mounted, hand made bits seem to have a certain charm all their own that cannot be compared to any other cowboy collectible. There is such wide variances in the style, maker, mouthpiece, age, area made, etc. that each old bit is almost like a story told in book length. Also, they each carry a certain mystical complexity that no other item does.

There are many books written on saddles and spurs, but the choices for books on bridle bits exclusively seem to be few. These are a few I have found informative and cover the subject somewhat: *Early California Reinsmen* by Ed Connell, *Bridle Bits of the West* by Gil Babcock and Bud Hildenbrand, *Californios* by Jo Mora, and my own *Cowboy Bits and Spurs* which deals in depth on the subject. There are more, but generally they are quite difficult to locate.

It almost seems that one must be schooled in reining techniques and bit usage from some "great grandfather" who had been a natural reinsman all his life, or simply never gain the special knowledge and skill. It helps to have in your family ancestry such a teacher who has handed the skills down with "hands-on" practical teaching. I have been witness to the training and breaking of horses to carry spade bits and chilenos, years ago when Mr. Overton was still doing it as it had been handed down to him by his ancestors. It is incredible that once trained, these "spade bit" horses respond to the bit by a simple "rolling" of the reins between one's fingers. They will "turn on a dime and give you change," as the old timers say. A good cutting horse is quite often broke to a spade bit, and they are truly magnificent to watch.

It is a sad fact that the true, old California-style bit reinsman is a dying breed. Few men actually have full comprehension of the use of a spade bit or a chileno today. And even more rare is the horse that was broke to carry these old style bits.

No wonder, when we view old silver-mounted California style bits, we fall all over ourselves to own them, for they speak loudly of our Southwestern history and old cowboys and Vaqueros of the past. While it may sound trite to repeat, it can still be said of these old bits: "If they could only speak, what stories they could tell!"

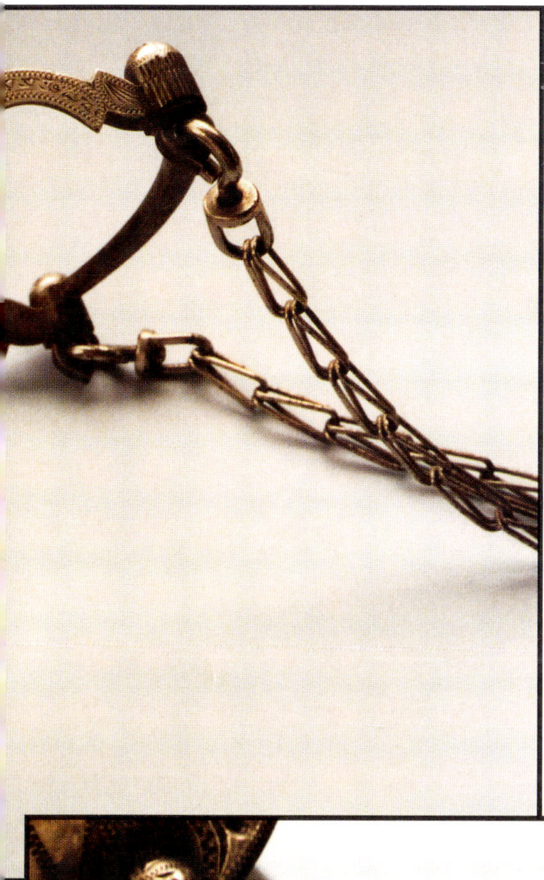

The variety of bits that follows represent different styles and makers and some unique bits of various values and ages. In these times, finding antique bridle bits to photograph is sometimes a tall order. They used to be available for sale in antique stores around the country and in second-hand stores, but recently they are scarce. Happy bit collecting!

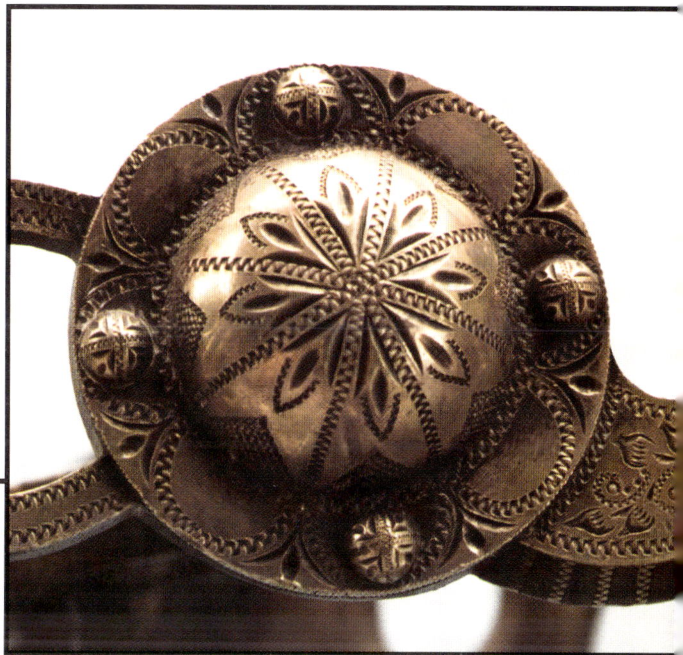

Close up detail of the concho on the Tom Qualey's ring bit.

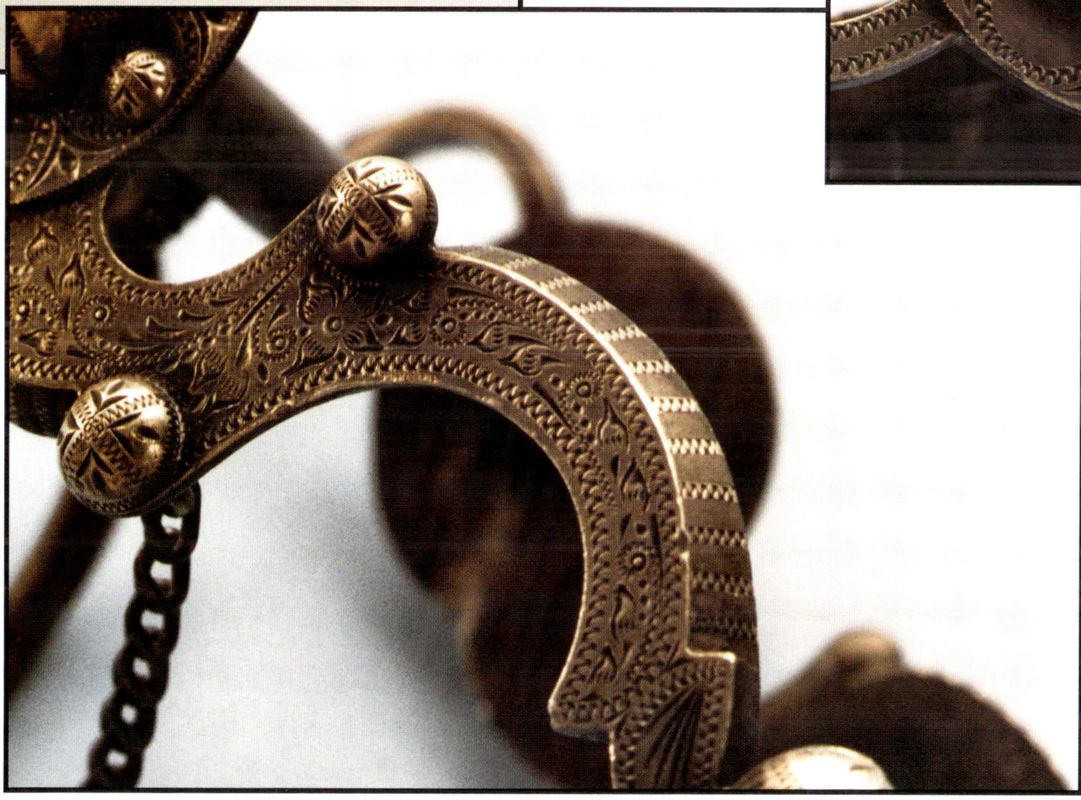

Detail of the most excellent work in Tom Qualey's ring bit.

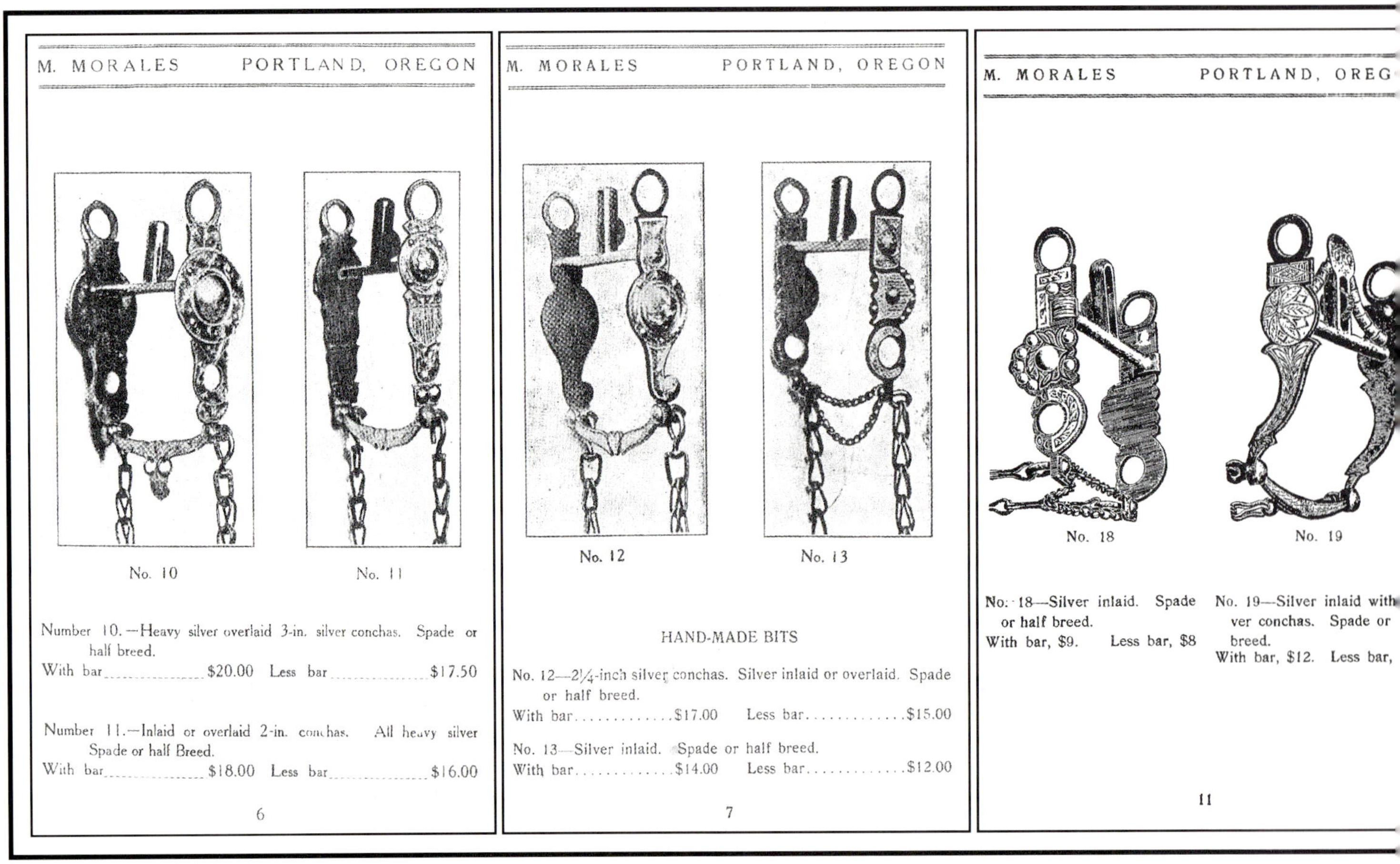

M. MORALES PORTLAND, OREGON

No. 10 No. 11

Number 10.—Heavy silver overlaid 3-in. silver conchas. Spade or half breed.
With bar............... $20.00 Less bar............... $17.50

Number 11.—Inlaid or overlaid 2-in. conchas. All heavy silver Spade or half Breed.
With bar............... $18.00 Less bar............... $16.00

6

M. MORALES PORTLAND, OREGON

No. 12 No. 13

HAND-MADE BITS

No. 12—2¼-inch silver conchas. Silver inlaid or overlaid. Spade or half breed.
With bar............ $17.00 Less bar............ $15.00

No. 13—Silver inlaid. Spade or half breed.
With bar............ $14.00 Less bar............ $12.00

7

M. MORALES PORTLAND, OREG

No. 18 No. 19

No. 18—Silver inlaid. Spade or half breed.
With bar, $9. Less bar, $8

No. 19—Silver inlaid with ver conchas. Spade or breed.
With bar, $12. Less bar,

11

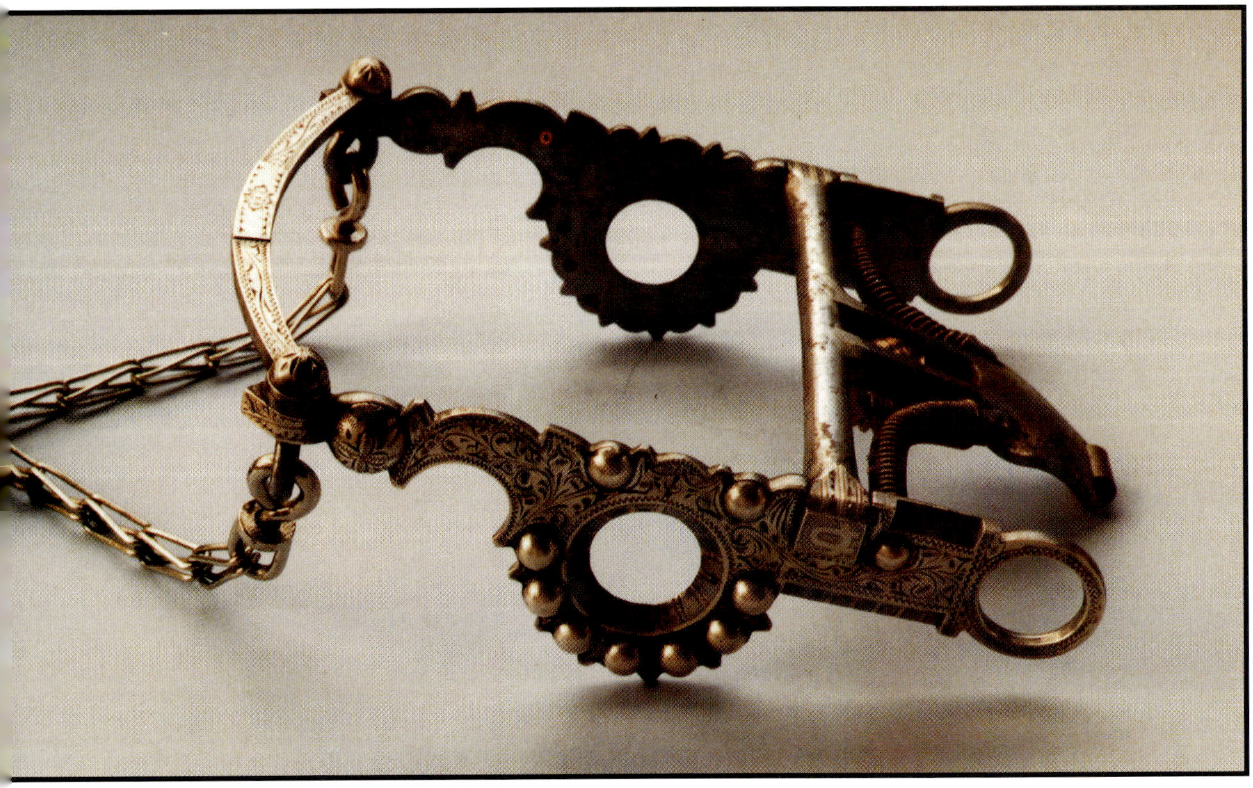

June 23, 1999 at Cody, Wyoming, another fine piece of Tom Qualey's work came through the auction there. This fine Santa Barbara spade has detail that is hard to find and a finish that excels all others. *Courtesy Ron and Sharon Mailloux. $10,950 to 12,500*

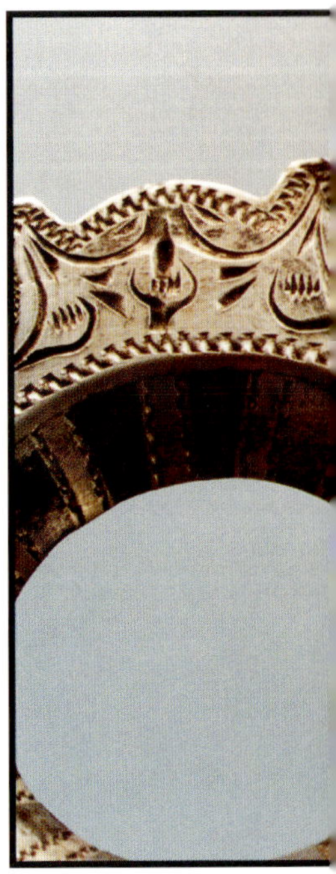

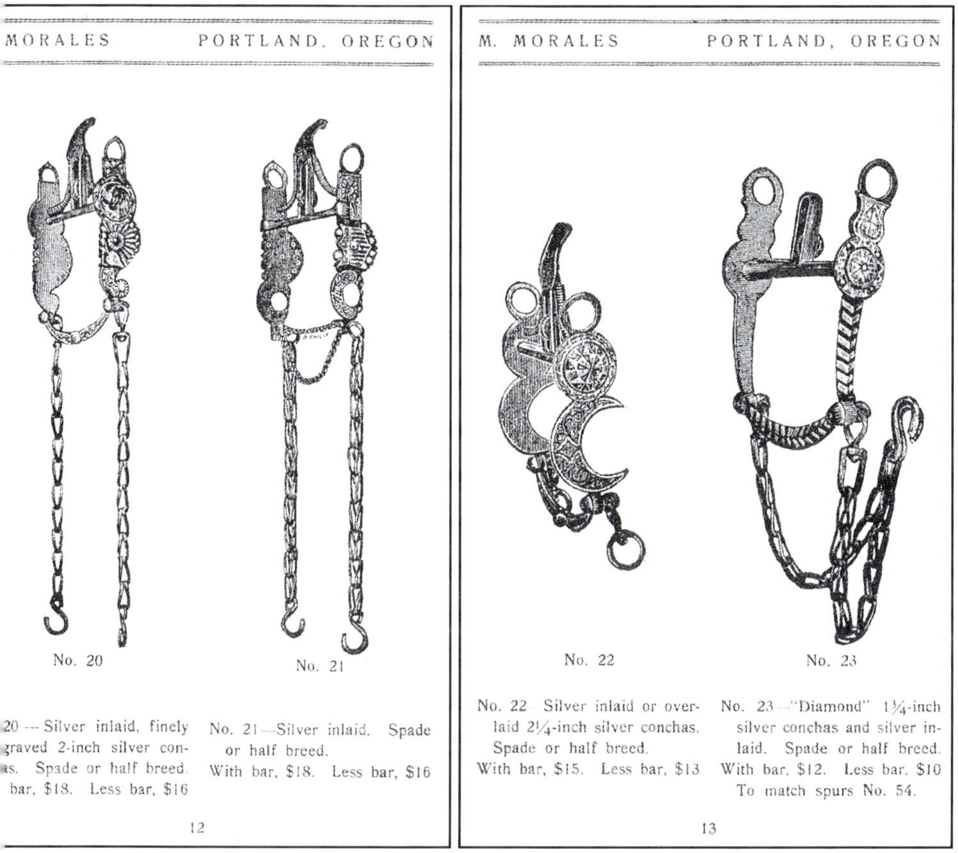
MORALES PORTLAND, OREGON

No. 20

No. 21

20 — Silver inlaid, finely graved 2-inch silver con-as. Spade or half breed. bar, $18. Less bar, $16

No. 21—Silver inlaid. Spade or half breed. With bar, $18. Less bar, $16

12

M. MORALES PORTLAND, OREGON

No. 22

No. 23

No. 22 Silver inlaid or overlaid 2¼-inch silver conchas. Spade or half breed. With bar, $15. Less bar, $13

No. 23—"Diamond" 1¾-inch silver conchas and silver inlaid. Spade or half breed. With bar, $12. Less bar, $10 To match spurs No. 54.

13

The Mike Morales catalog from 1900 illustrates the prices then current for some of the bridle bits contemporaneously collected and displayed.

Detail of the Santa Barbara spade bit showing also Tom Qualey's identifying mark.

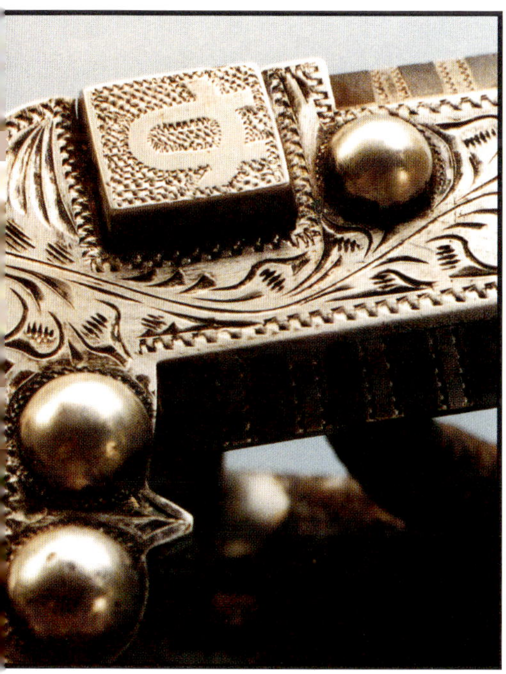

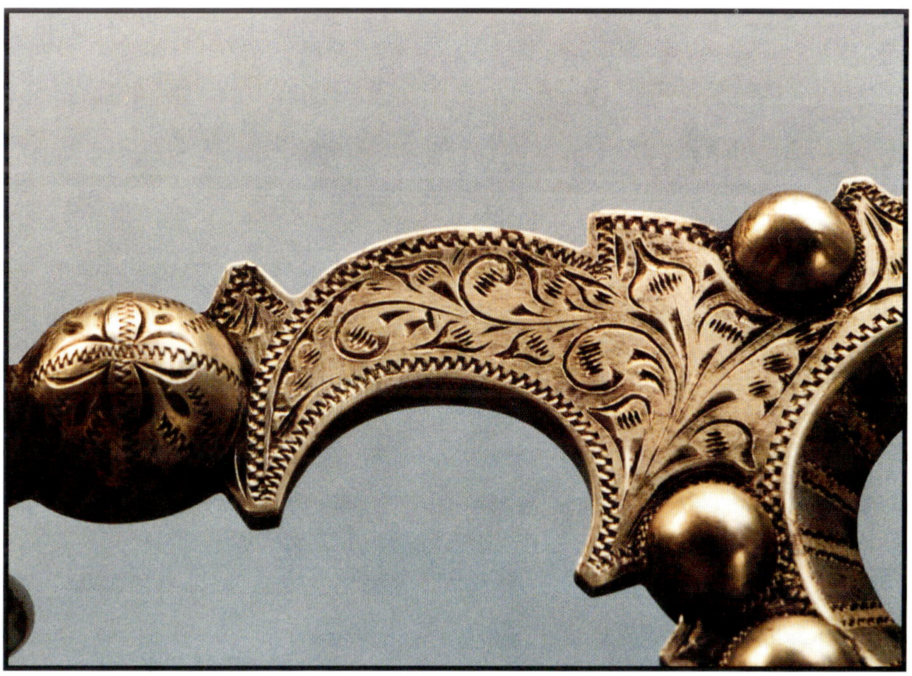

Another detail of the workmanship on Qualey's spade bit.

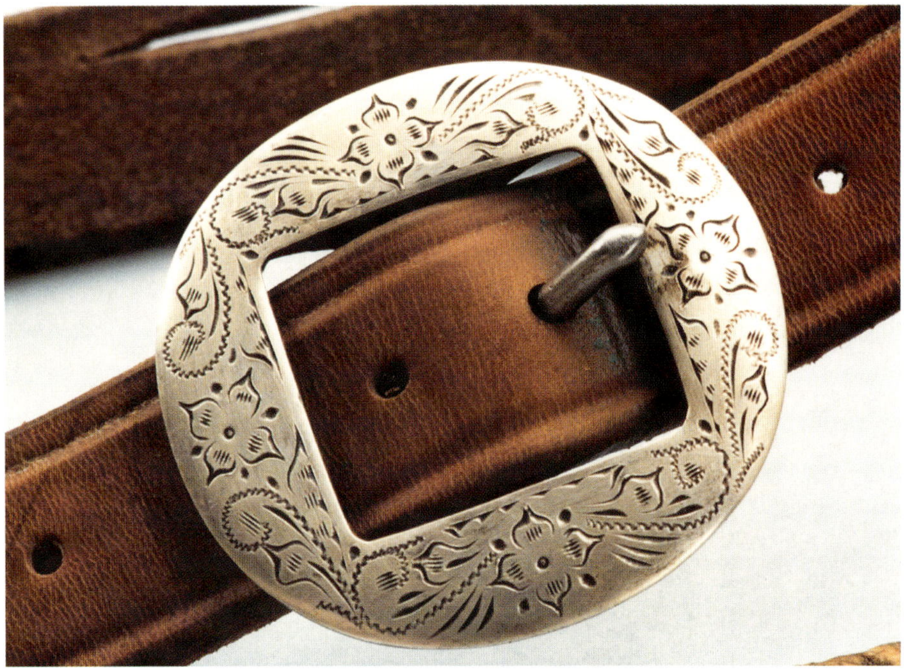

Tom Qualey also made all of the silver work on the headstall with which the Santa Barbara spade was outfitted.

Silver concho on headstall of Qualey's spade bit.

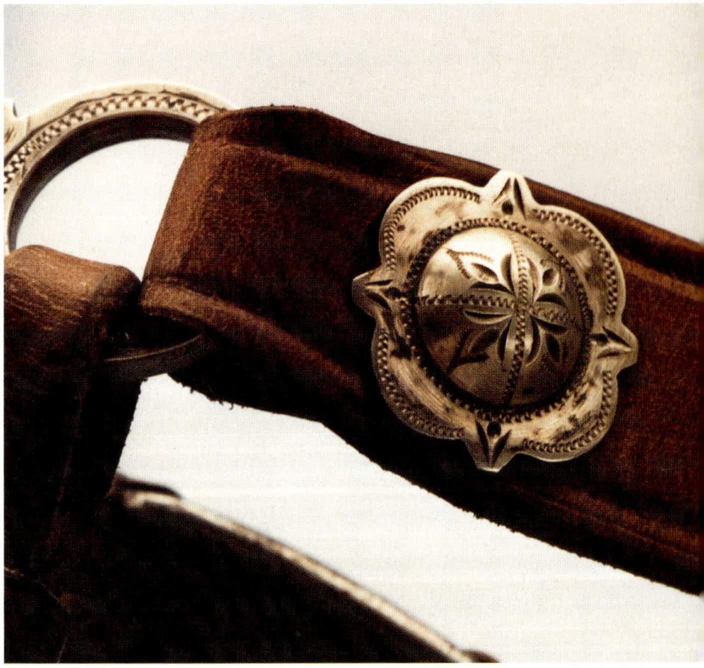

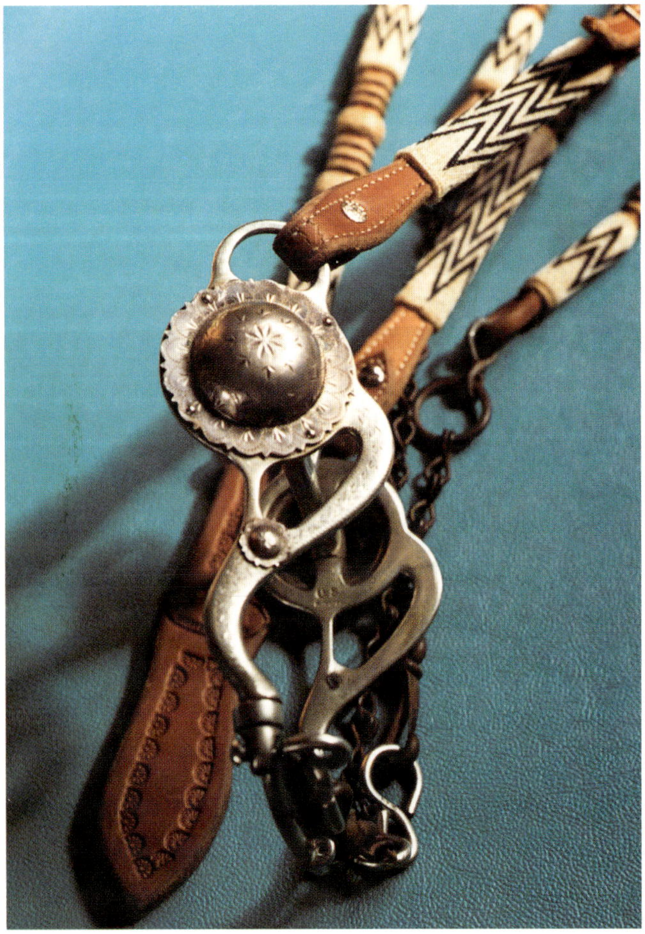

Visalia "Humane" bit is outfitted with one of the nicest sets of horse hair braided reins. *Courtesy Ron and Sharon Mailloux. $1500 to 1800*

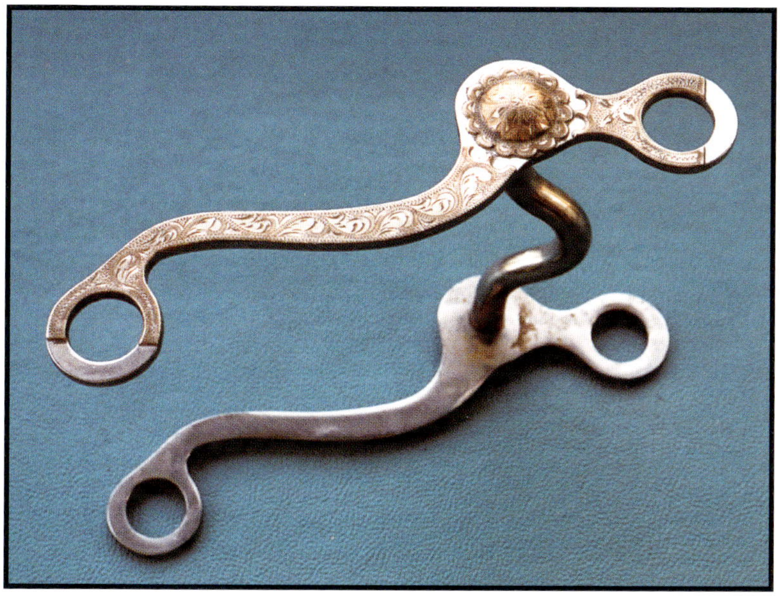

Marked "Crockett" the bit is a nice low port, long shanked using type with elegant silver overlays. *Overton collection. $350 to 500*

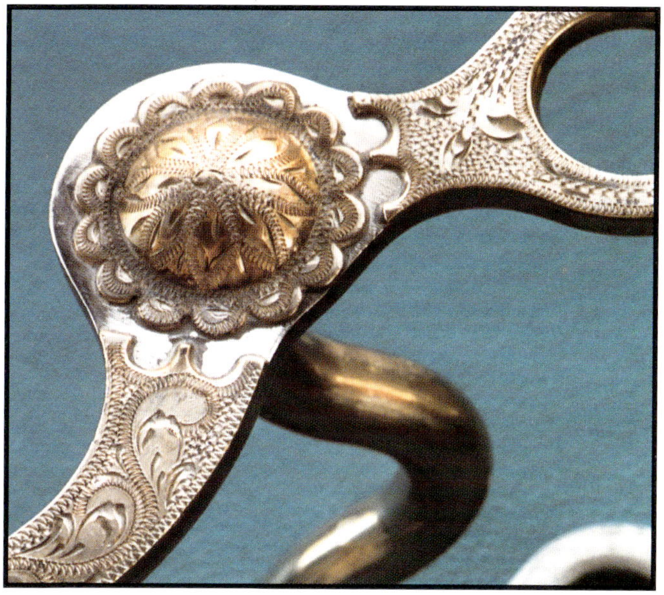

Detail of the previous Crockett bit.

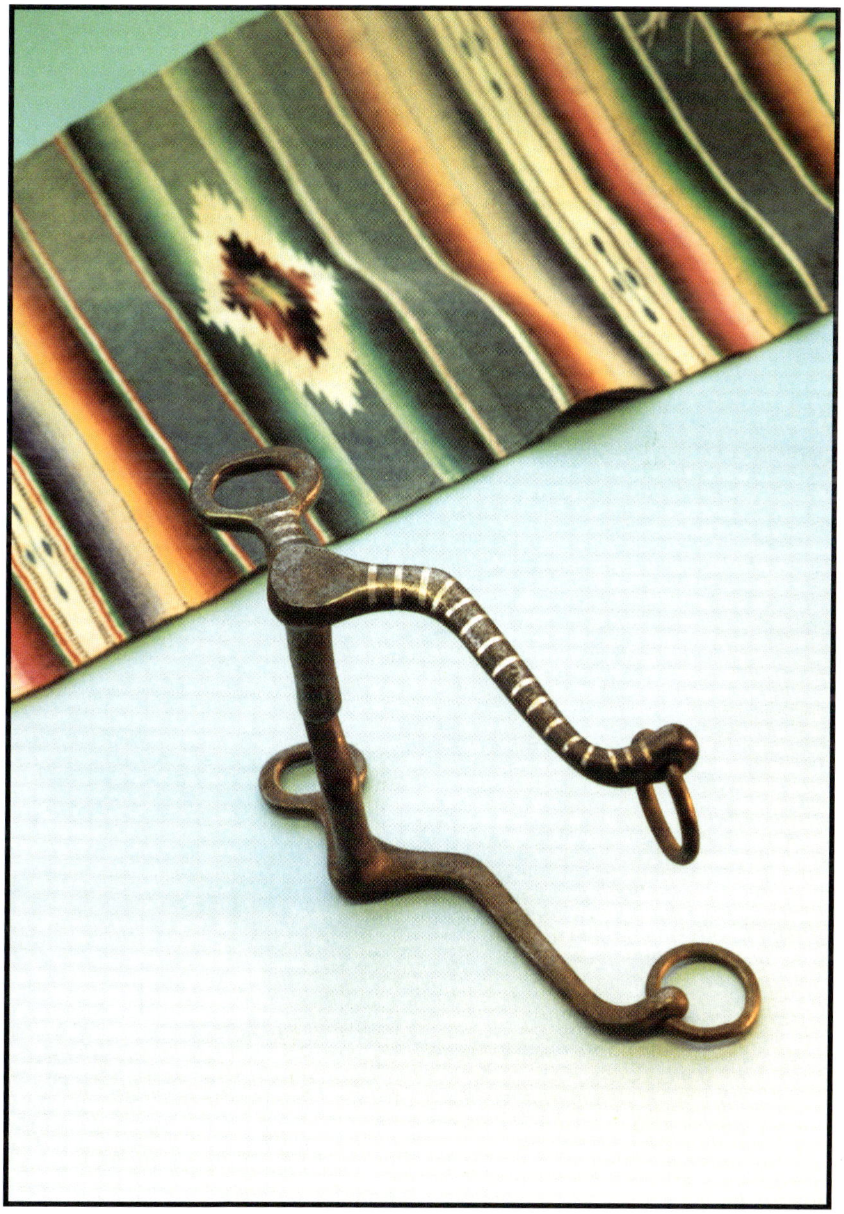

Low port, short shanked bit, it has been silver inlaid. Unmarked, it is most likely a North and Judd. *Courtesy Wade Brumley. $75 to 100*

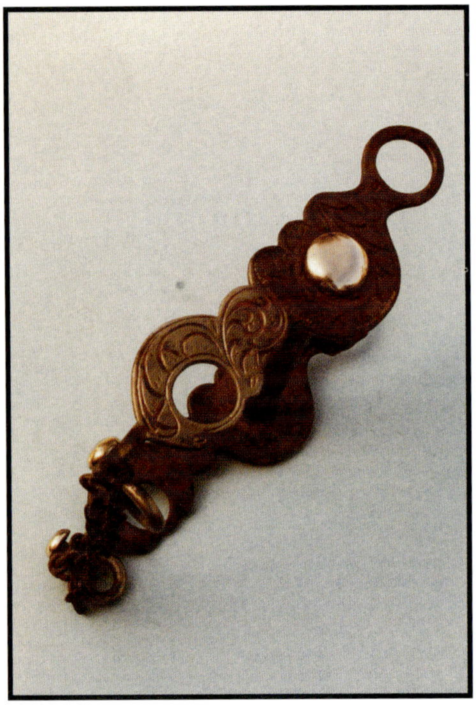

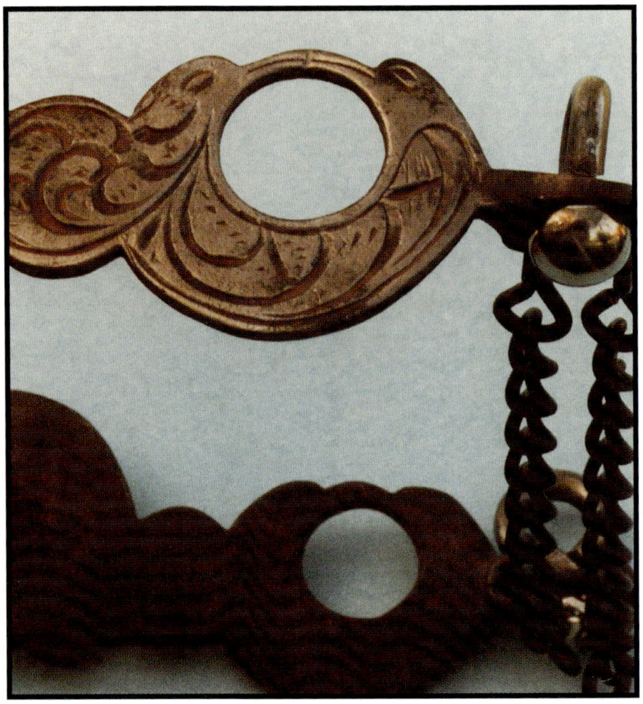

Detail of the classic "Kissing Birds."

Kissing Bird bit with one silver spot, and chased iron on the remainder. *Courtesy R.C. and Marvin Bales. $250 to 350*

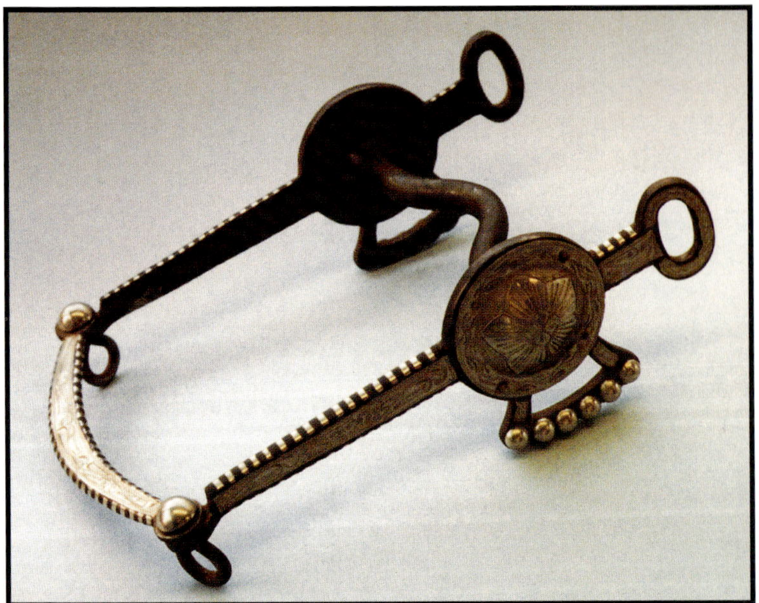

Bit is unmarked but a very beautiful old "Los Cruces" and it has overlays and inlays throughout. *Private collection. $450 to 650*

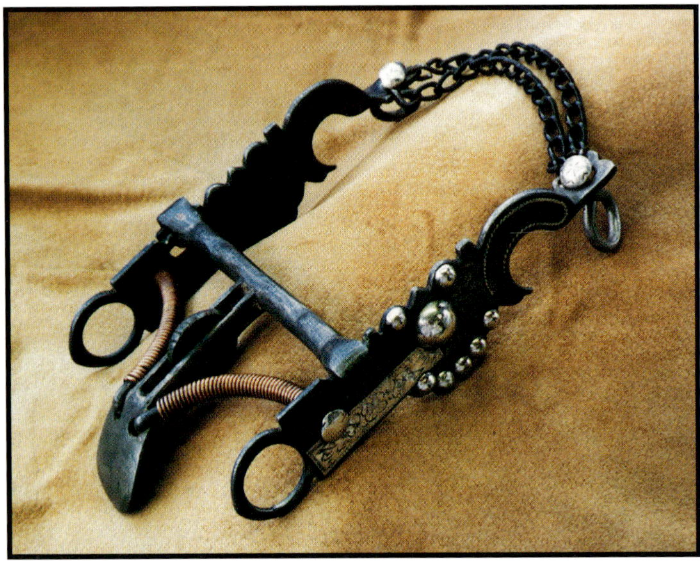

As seen in the 1897 Maine and Winchester catalogue, the bit is a spoon spade, single bird's head design. *Overton collection. $500 to 750*

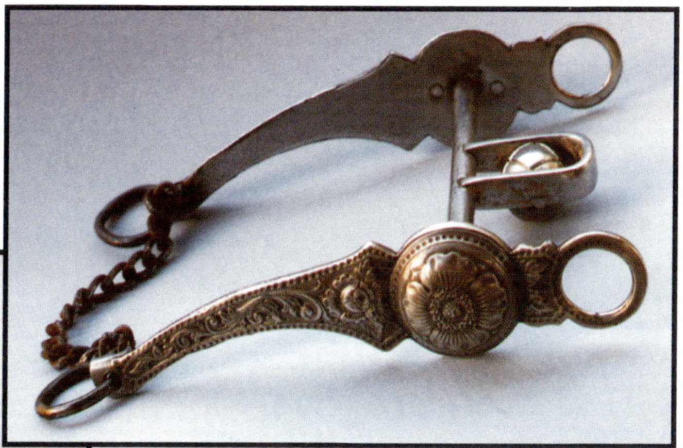

Made by E. Bohlin of Hollywood, California, this bit is a half breed mouth piece and one of the more beautiful designs ever done. *Private collection. $1200 to 1500*

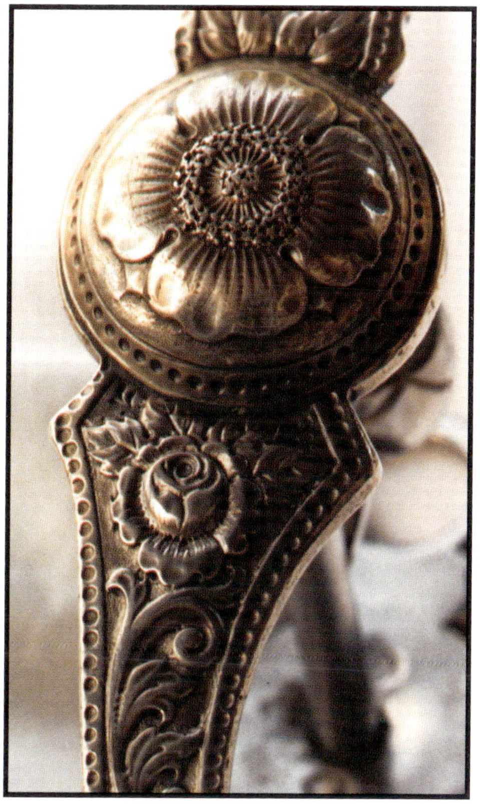

Detail of the Bohlin roses on the half breed bit.

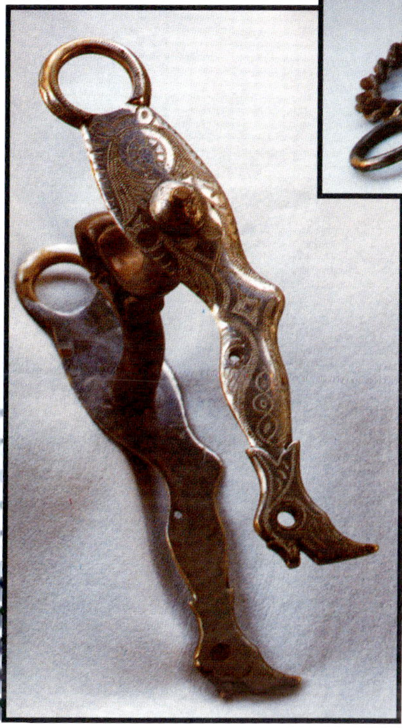

Lady leg Mexican made bit with silver inlays. *Private collection. $200 to 300*

Mike Morales spade bit with nice old 1920's brass spot headstall. The spade bit is in good condition is "quality par excellence." *Courtesy Gene Christopher. $1000 to 1200*

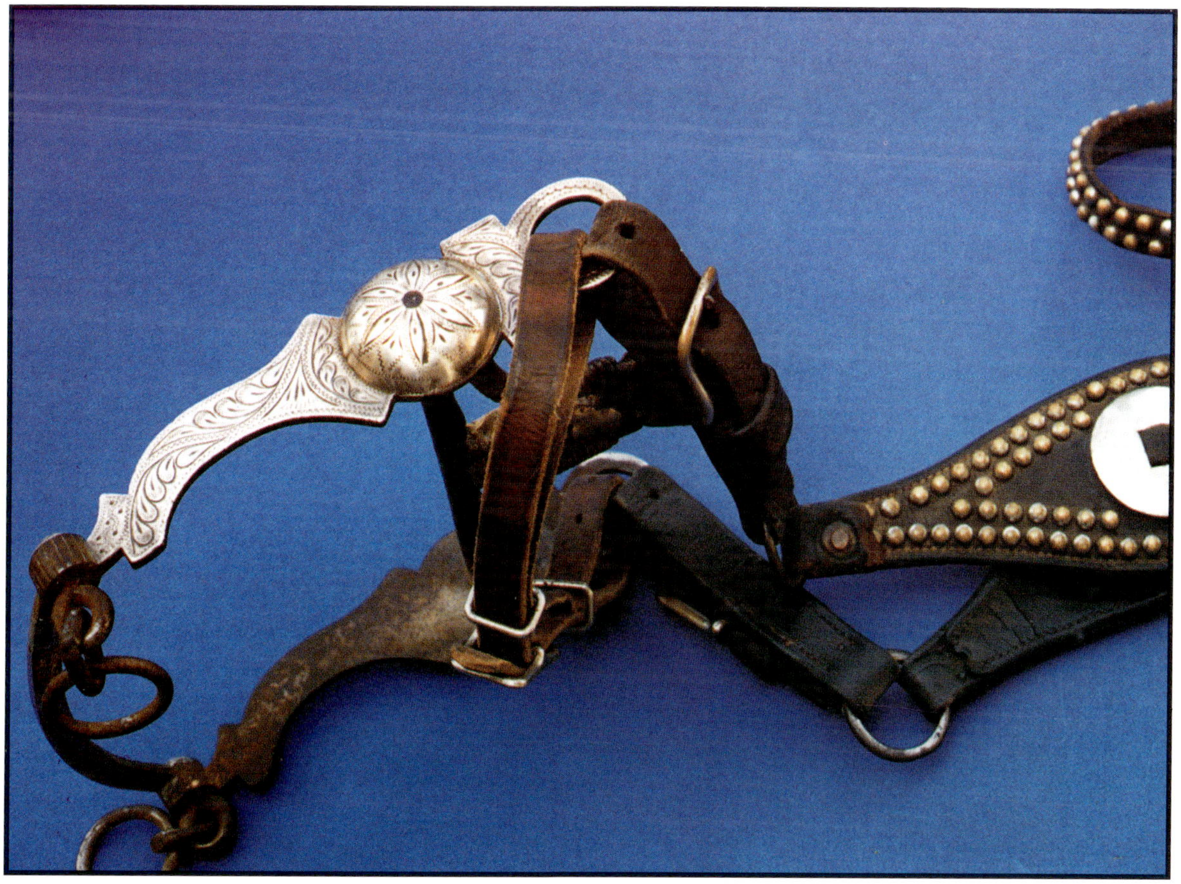

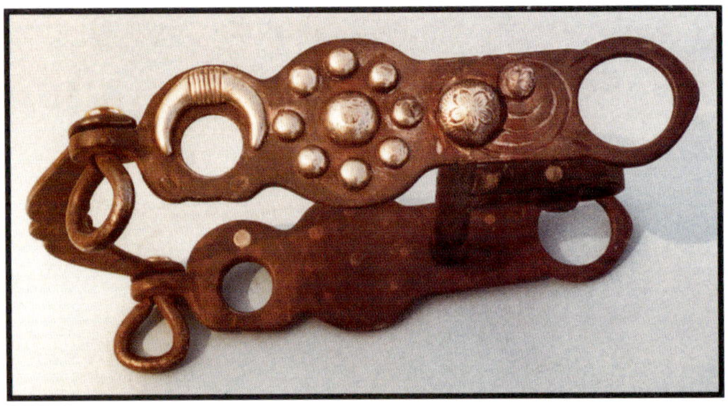

Old kissing bird bit with silver overlays and spots. *Courtesy R.C. and Marvin Bales. $200 to 250*

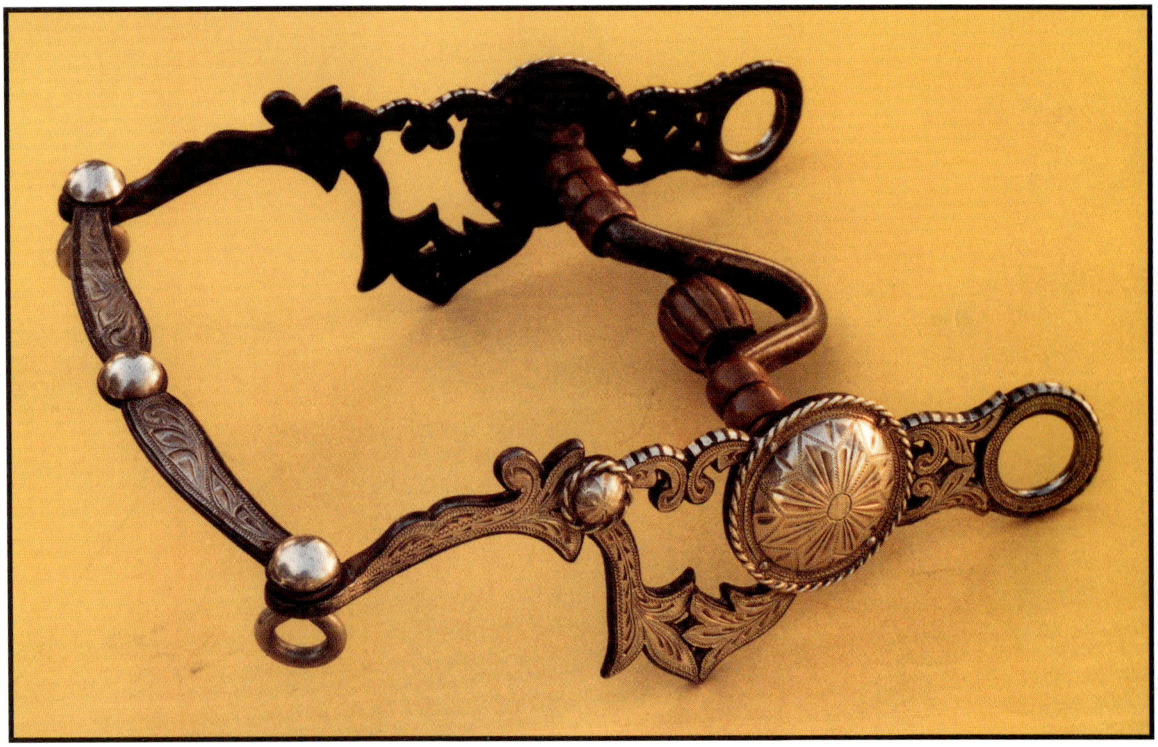

This beautiful rendition is attributed to "D. Vogt" but is unmarked. *Courtesy R.C. and Marvin Bales. $875 to 1000*

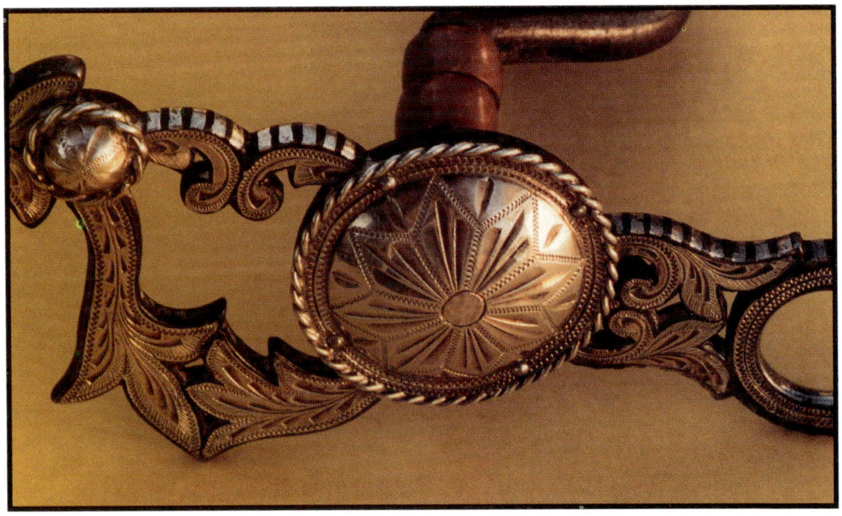

Detail of the "D.Vogt" bit.

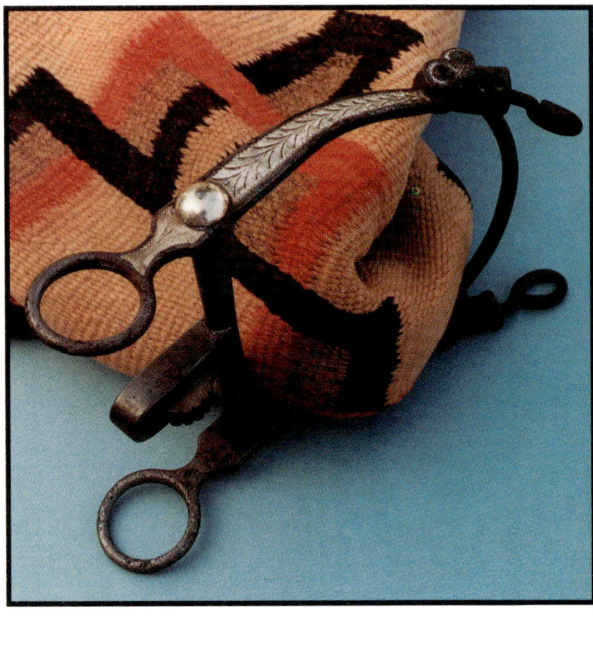

August Buermann is the maker of this bit in very fine condition. *Courtesy R.C. and Marvin Bales. $200 to 300*

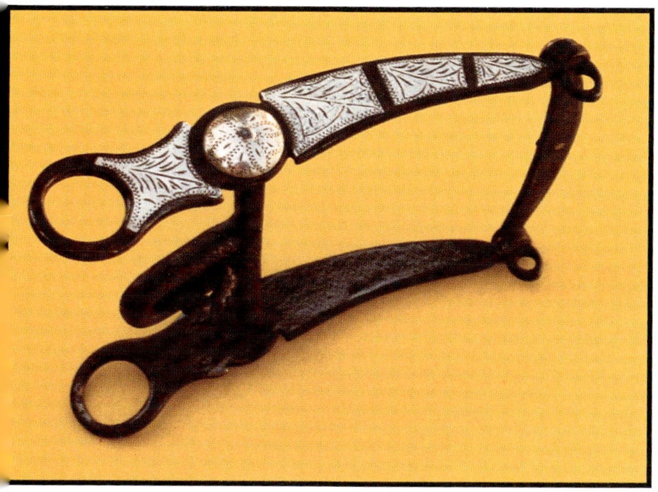

Mike Morales is the maker of this half breed bit in excellent condition. *Courtesy R.C. and Marvin Bales. $1000 to 1200*

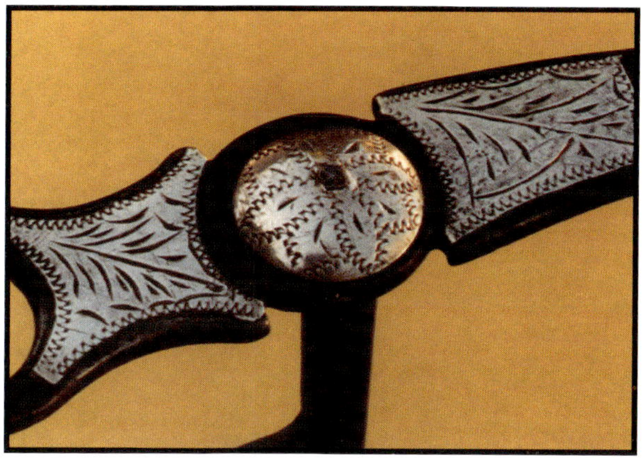

Detail of the Morales half breed bit.

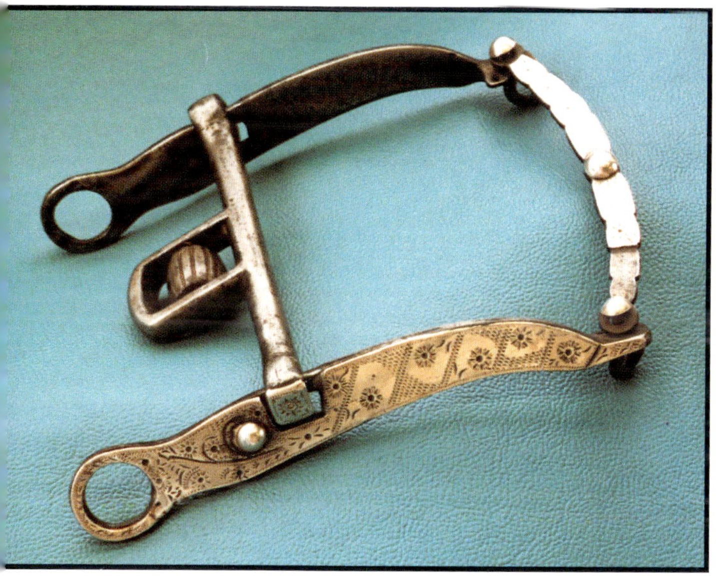

Prison-made Banana Cheek plates with silver overlays attributed to the Boise, Idaho State Penitentiary. It has seen some wear. *Courtesy R.C. and Marvin Bales. $300 to 500*

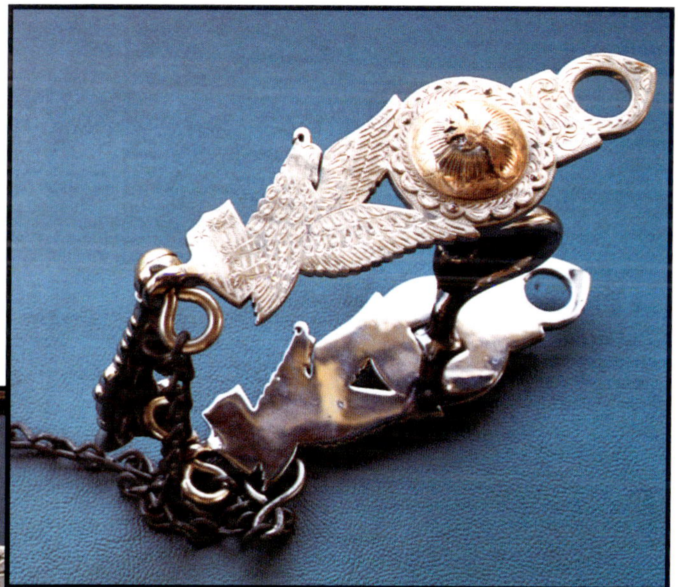

Eagle bit has a Mona Lisa mouthpiece and a small golden eagle on the top of the large concho. It makes a beautiful bit with even the slobber bar bearing the eagle design. *Overton collection. $1000 to 1500*

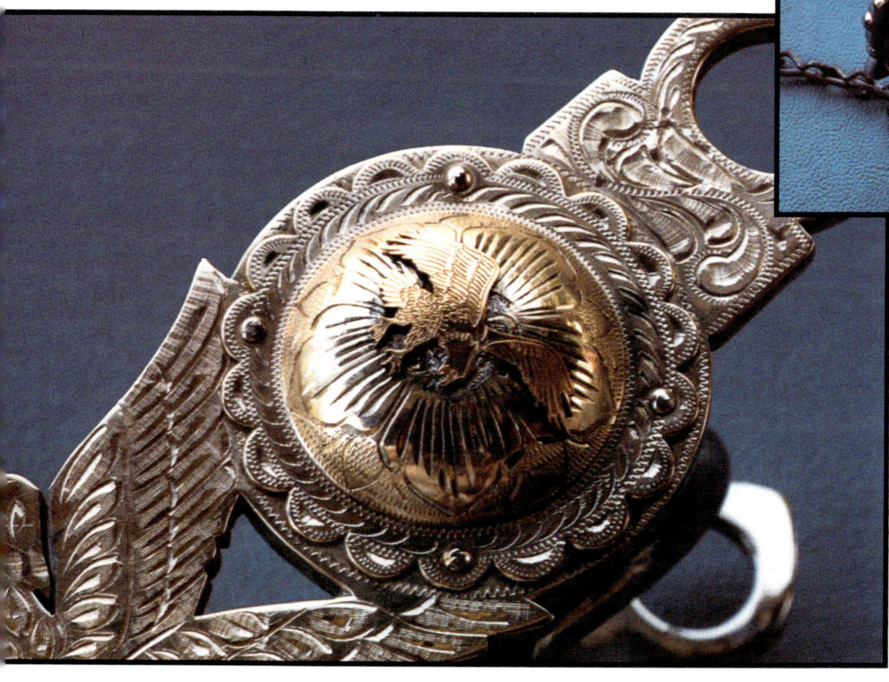

Detail of small golden eagle on top of the concho.

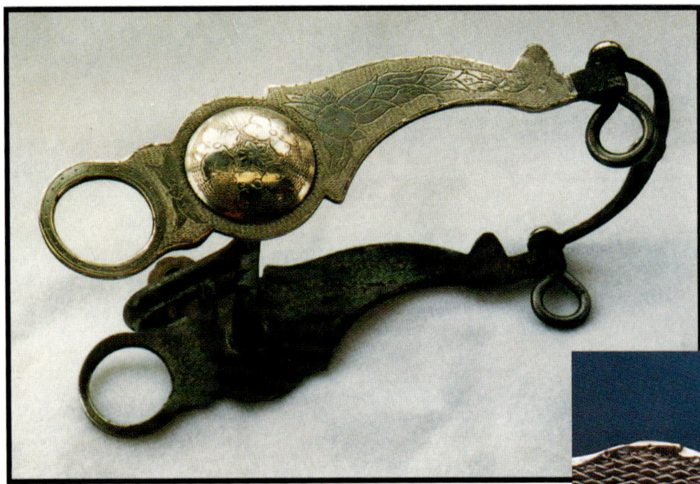

The bit is a Walla Walla , Washington prison-made bit and beautiful in its overall interpretation. *Overton collection. $700 to 900*

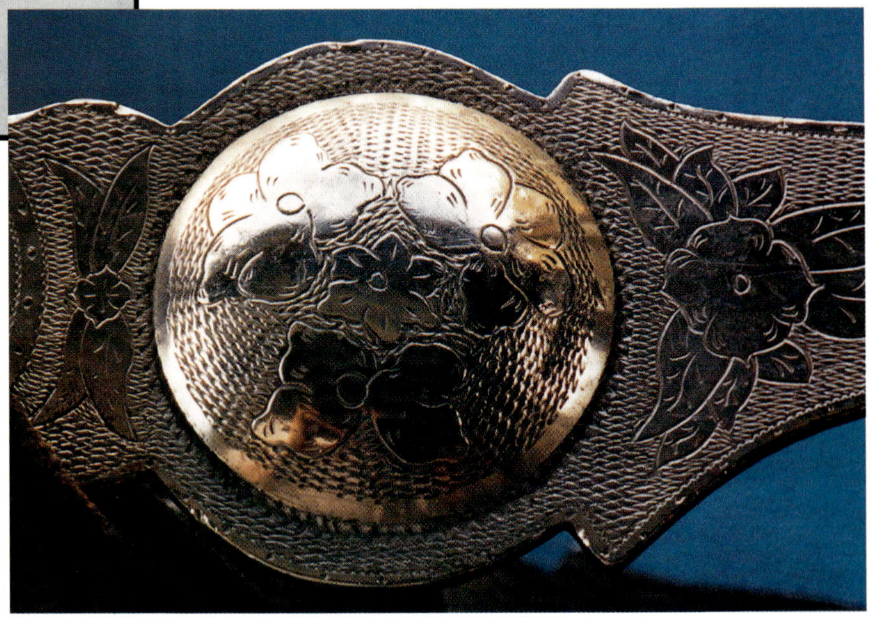

Detail of the engraving on the Walla Walla bit.

Marked "B.A. Day," the pistol bit has a "frog" mouthpiece. *Overton collection. $400 to 500*

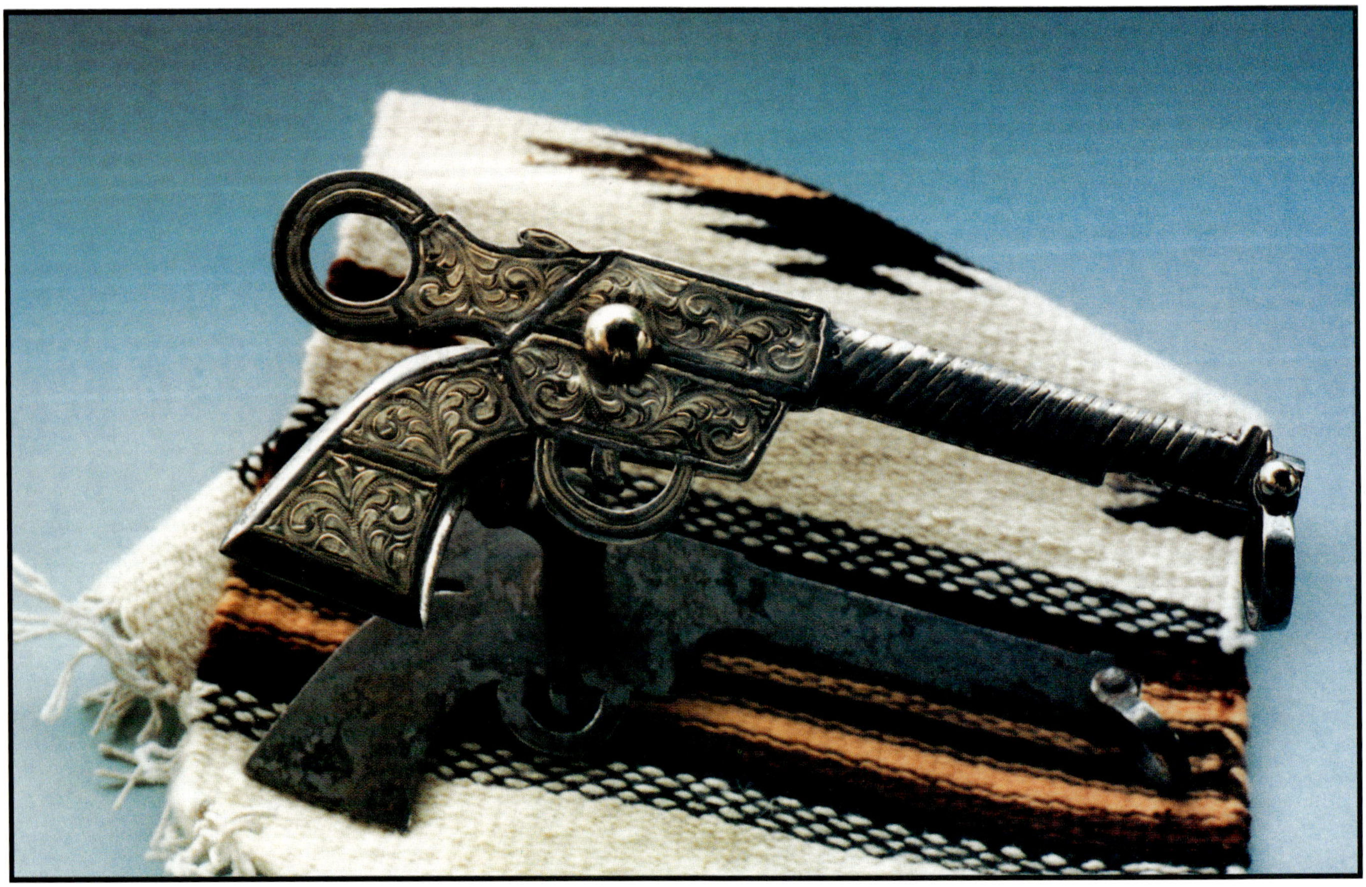

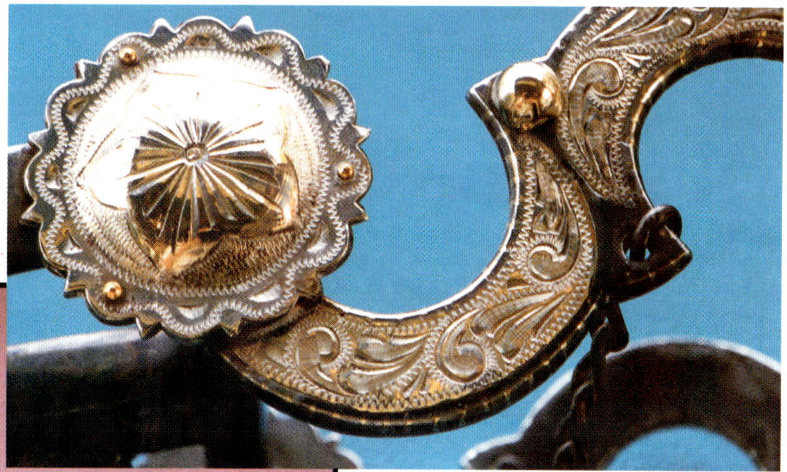

Detail of silver work on the ring bit.

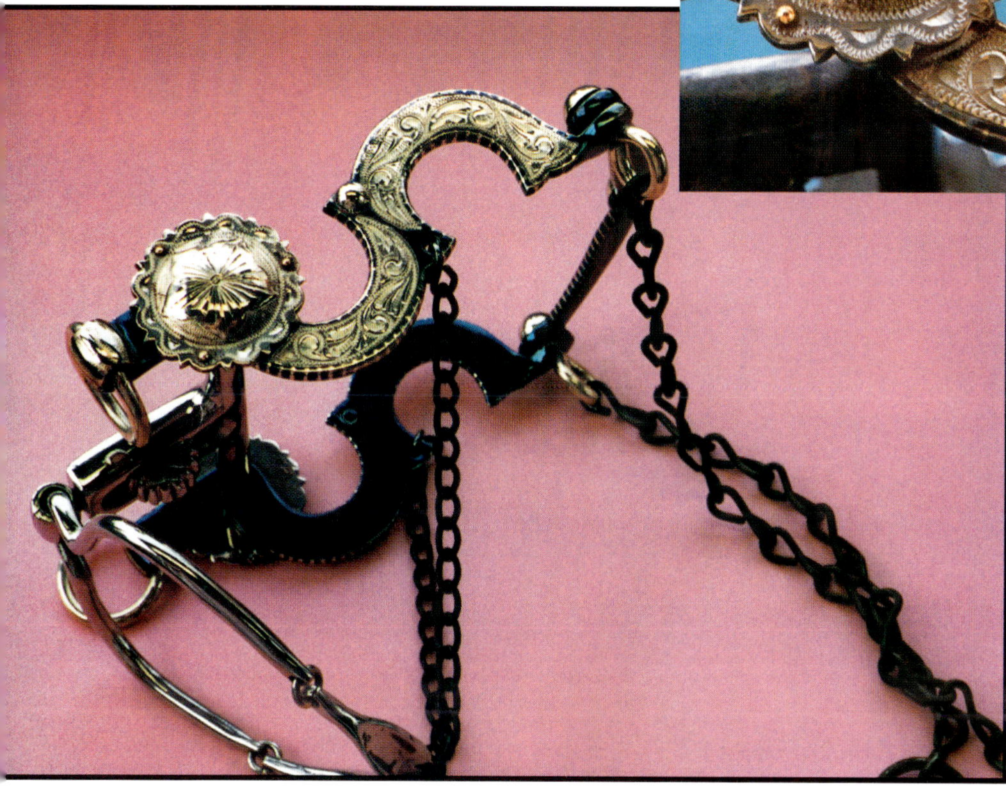

Beautiful contemporary ring bit made in the traditional style. Ring bits are rare in any time frame and are a collectible field all their own. *Overton collection. $300 to 500*

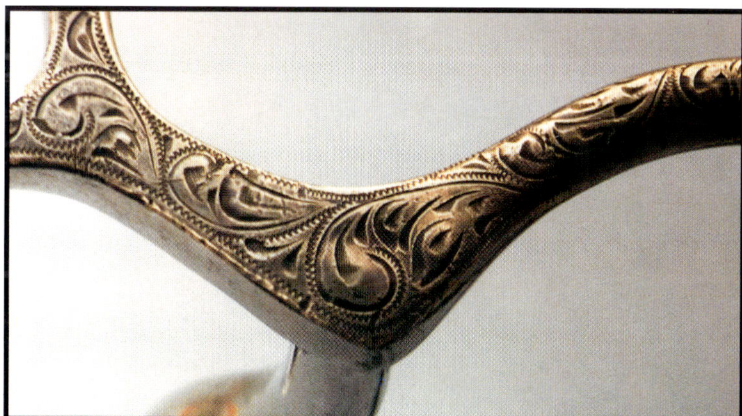

Detail of the silver overlaid Fleming bit.

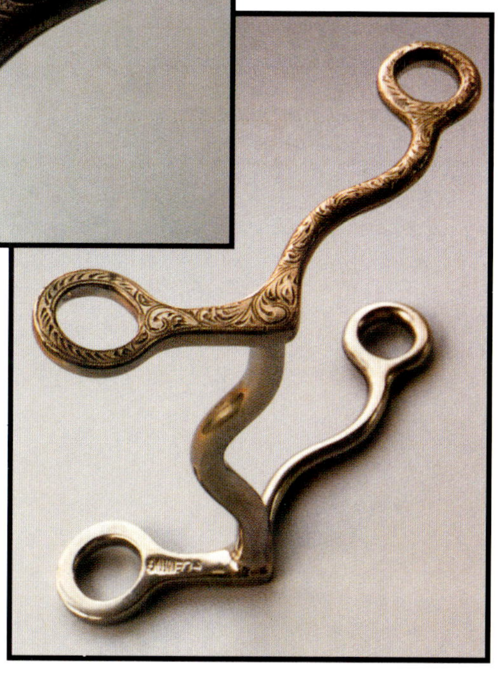

Silver overlaid bit is stamped "Fleming," so is to be considered a very excellent and collectible bit. *Private collection. $325 to 500*

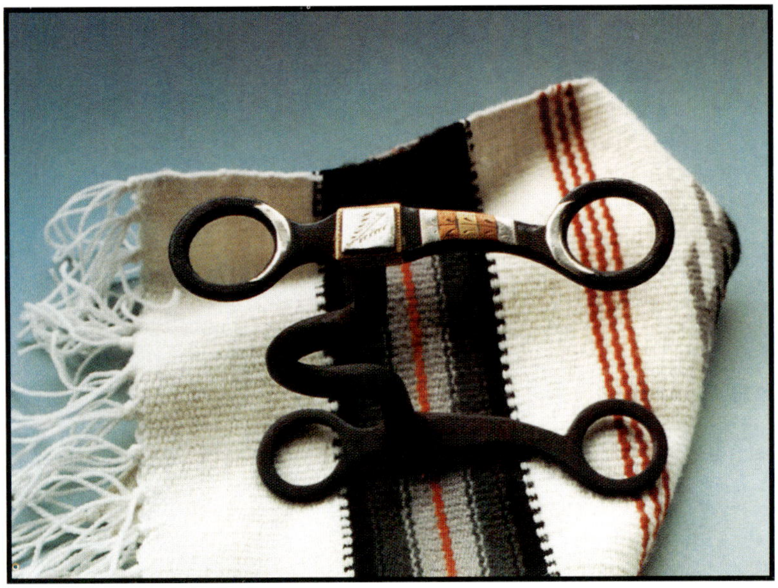

Very nice old McChesney grazer bit with multi-metal overlays and inlays. *Overton collection. $400 to 600*

Bit is marked "Ricardo" and made with a most unusual "sweet" mouthpiece which enables the user to add a little sugar or honey to the hollow bar of the port and, by way of two holes, it can gradually seep out into the horse's mouth. *Overton collection. $450 to 550*

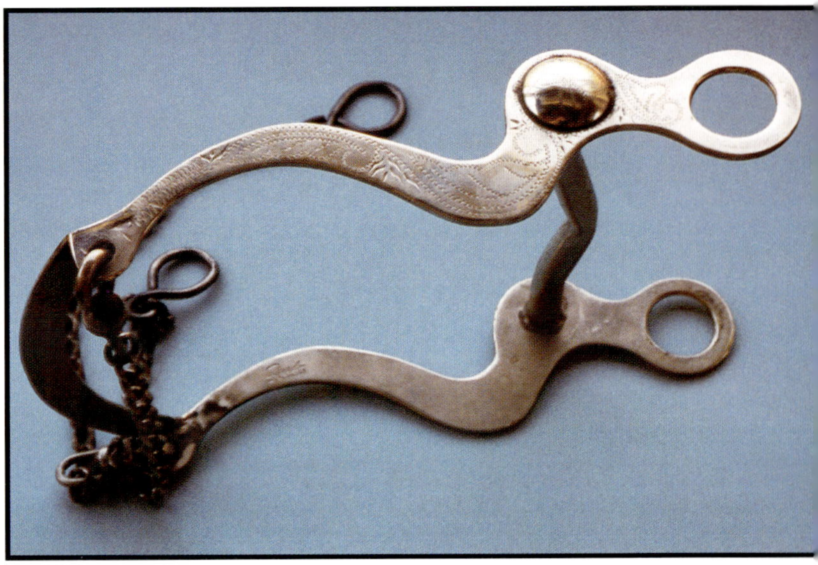

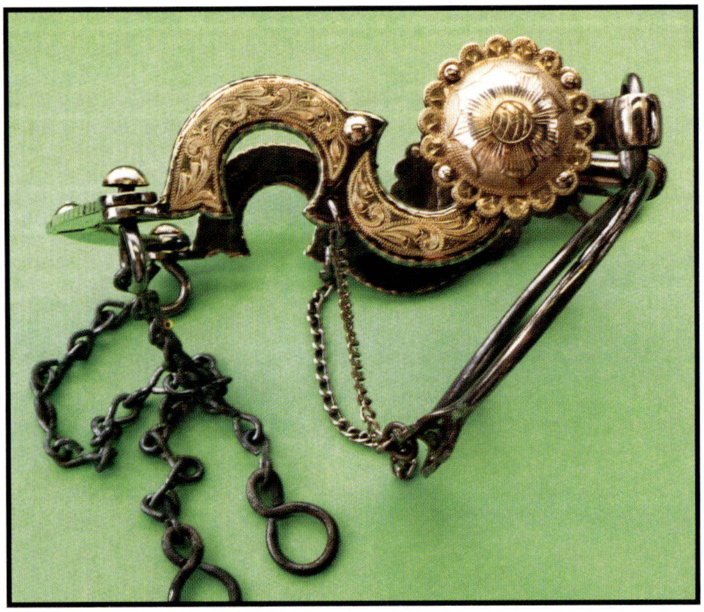

Contemporary ring bit rendered in the traditional style and with very beautiful silver overlays. *Overton collection. $300 to 500*

Detail of workmanship on silver ring bit.

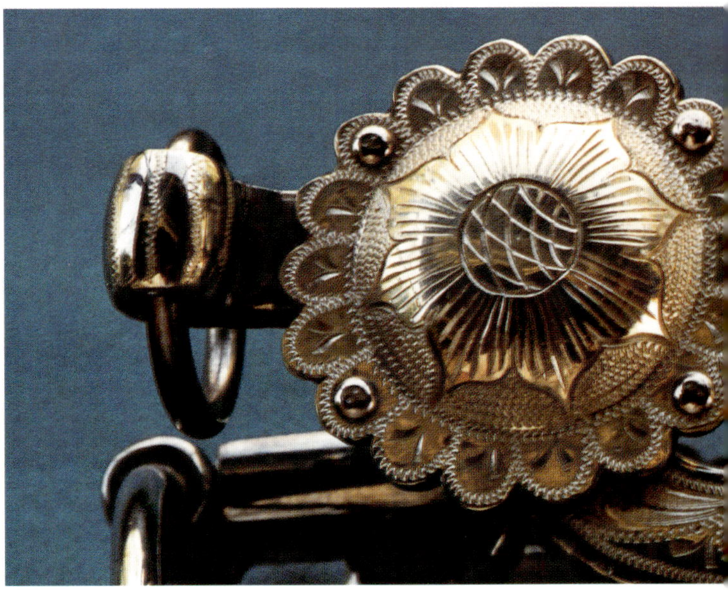

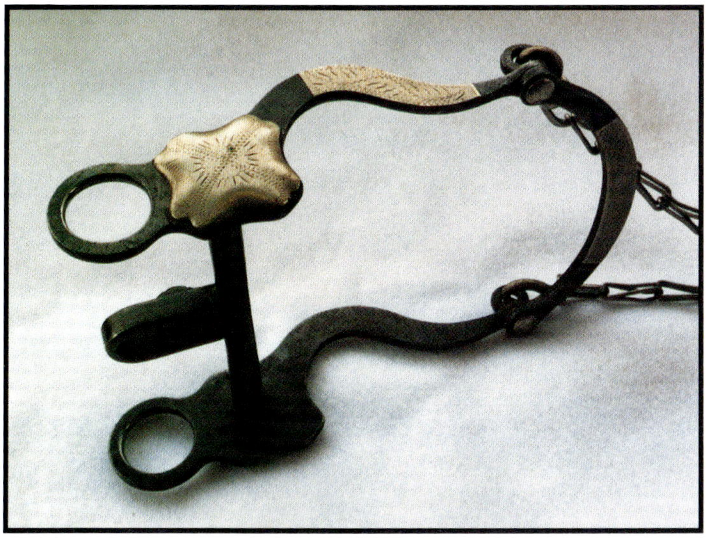

Marked "Crockett," the bit has a four leaf clover designed concho and silver overlay. A very nice half breed bit. *Overton collection. $325 to 425*

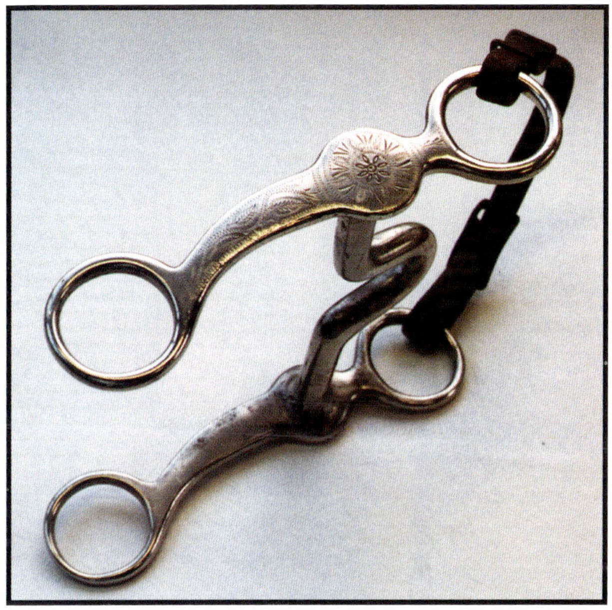

Marked with Buermann's "Star Steel Silver," the bit is finely finished and in excellent condition. *Overton collection. $400 to 600*

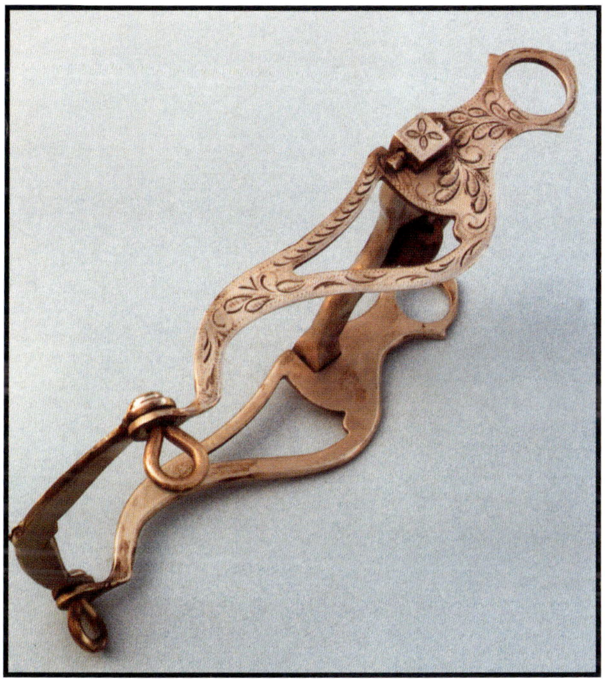

Nice old unmarked bit, it is a loose jaw. *Courtesy R.C. and Marvin Bales. $275 to 325*

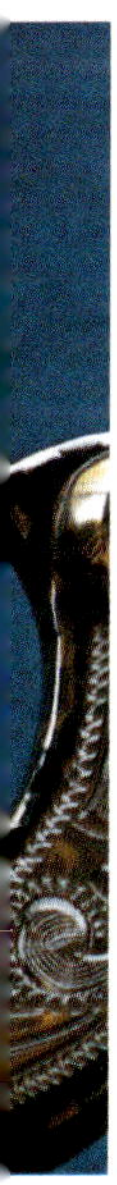

Single flying bird bit of chased metal. It has seen a few better days, and most likely could tell great stories if it could only speak. *Courtesy Wade Brumley. $100 to 125*

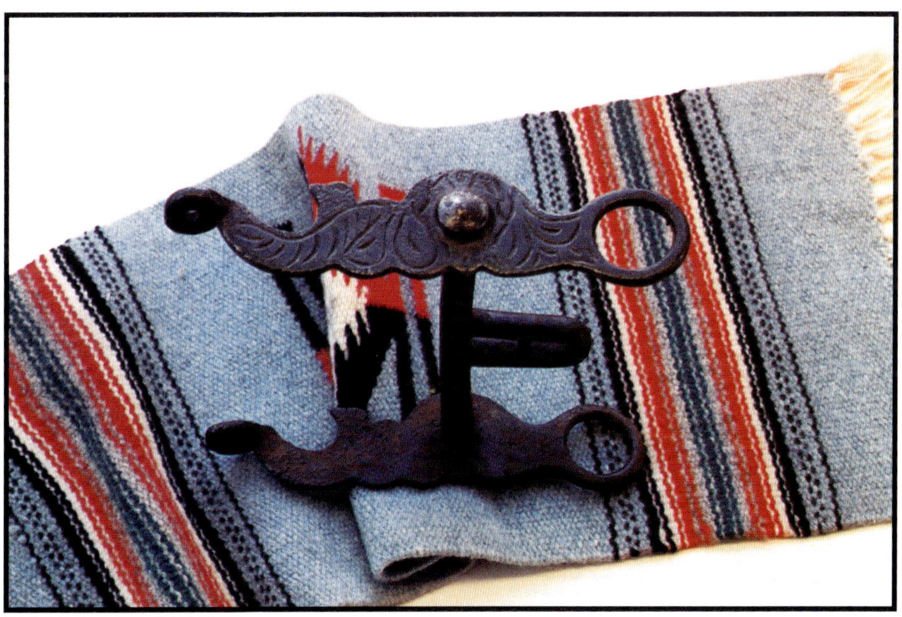

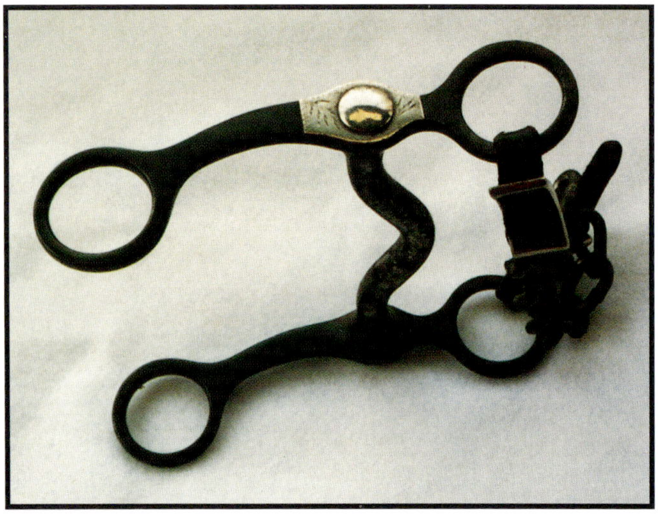

McChesney grazer bit with silver overlays and a low port mouthpiece. *Overton collection. $350 to 400*

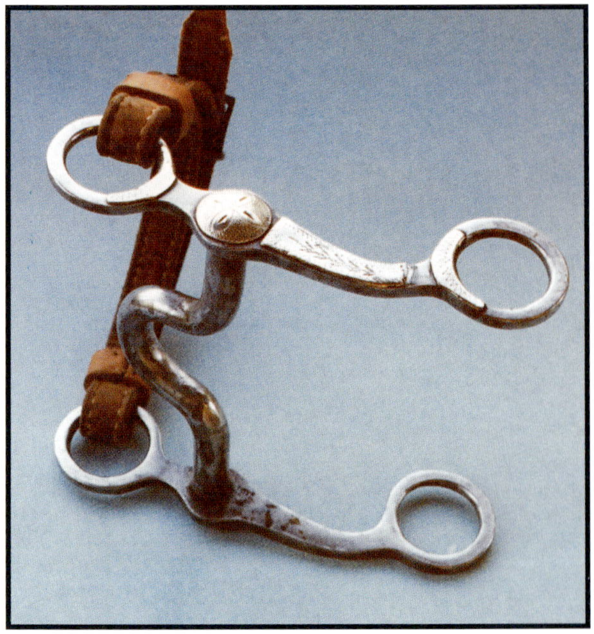

Marked "Crockett," the little grazer bit is a nice usable bit and any cowboy would love it, even today. *Overton collection. $200 to 300*

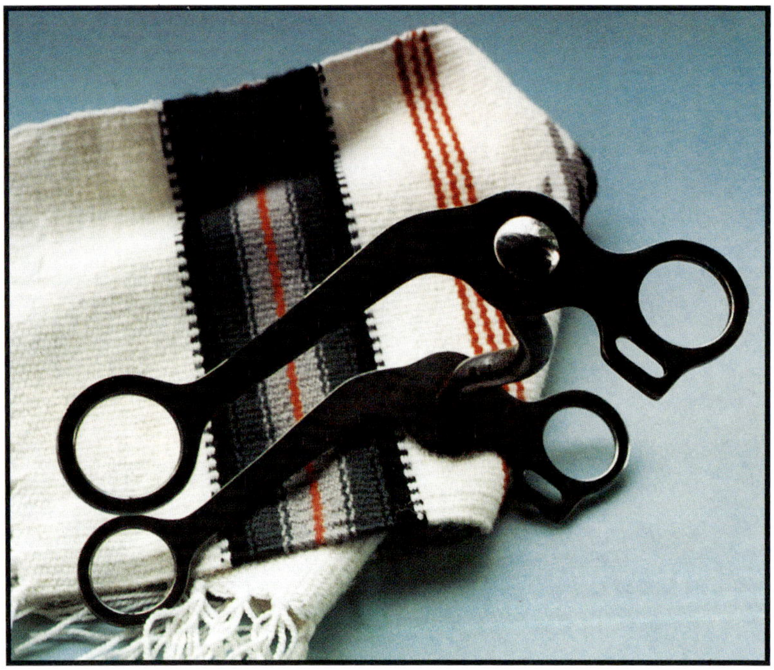

This Crockett long shanked low port bit sports one silver spot. *Overton collection. $300 to 400*

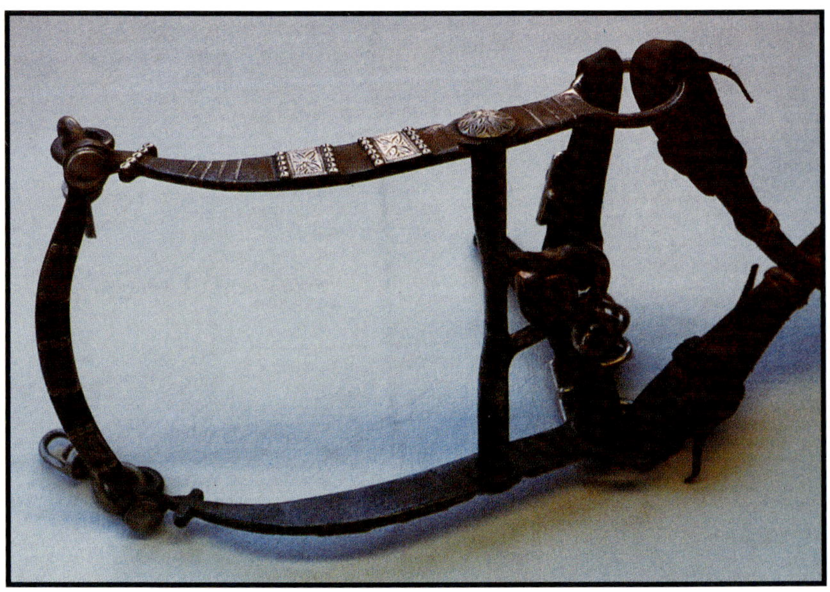

Nice old shop-made half breed bit with some silver overlays and inlays. *Private collection. $350*

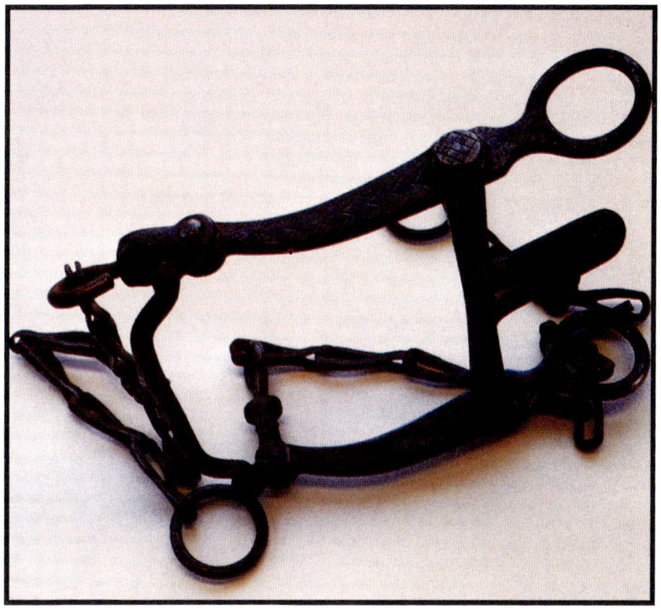

Old half breed bit with chased metal and in good condition. *Courtesy Wade Brumley. $100 to 150*

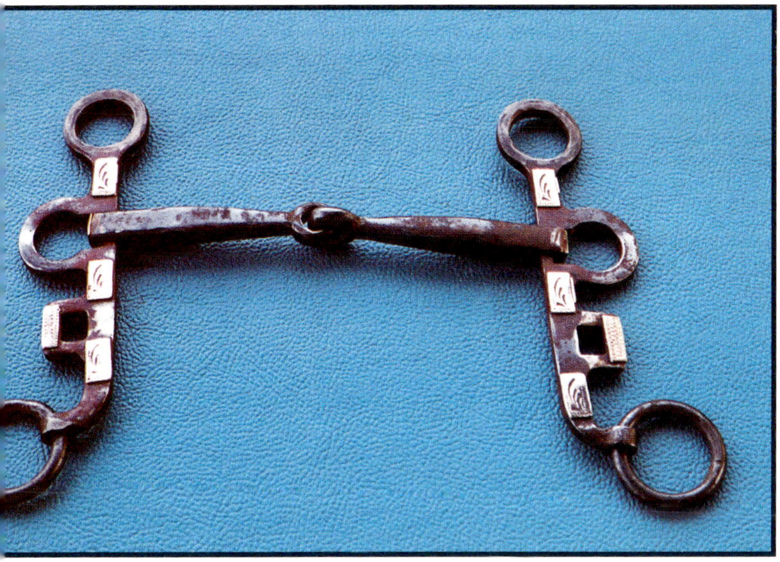

Argentine snaffle bit, one of the nicest, is well made and silver overlaid. *Overton collection. $100 to 150*

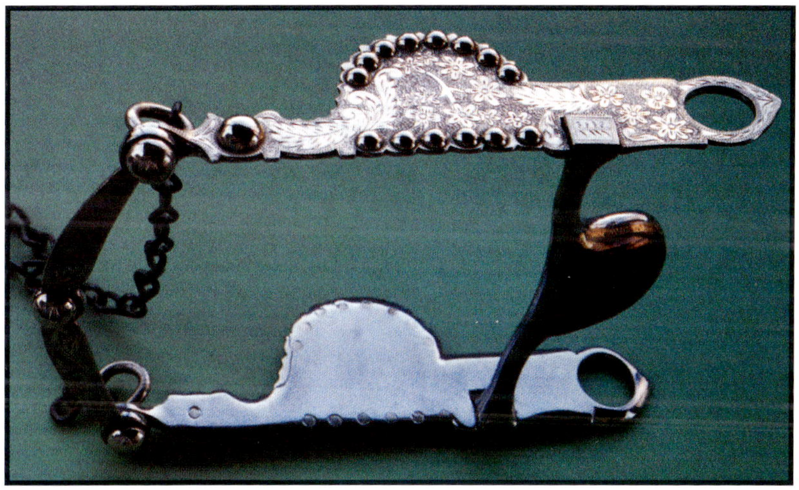

Beautiful floral engraved bit attributed to Vogt, but unmarked and unknown. On one side of the cheek plates there are 14 flowers, on the other cheek plate, only 13. *Overton collection. $500*

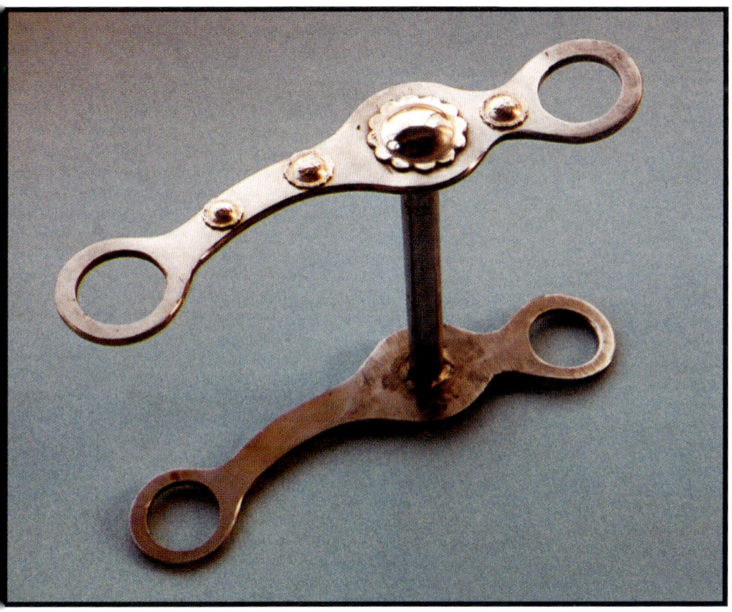

Hand made grazer bit; it is a very useable, honest little bit with three small silver conchos and one large one. *Overton collection. $150 to 200*

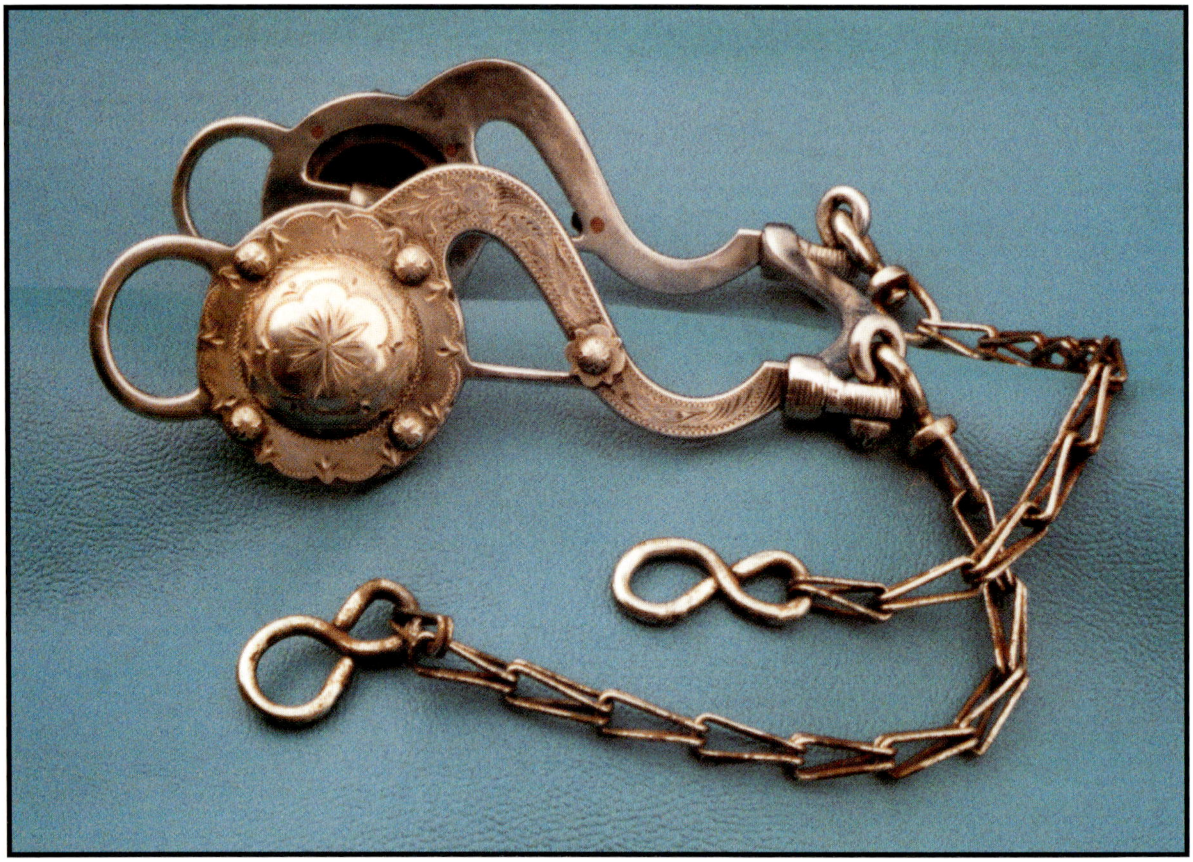

Loose jawed bit marked on left inside cheek "Qualey," and on inside slobber bar "WSR." It is a very lovely bit and has all of the "Qualey" quality of beautiful engraving evident throughout. *Courtesy Paul and Marlene Snider. $6500 to 7500*

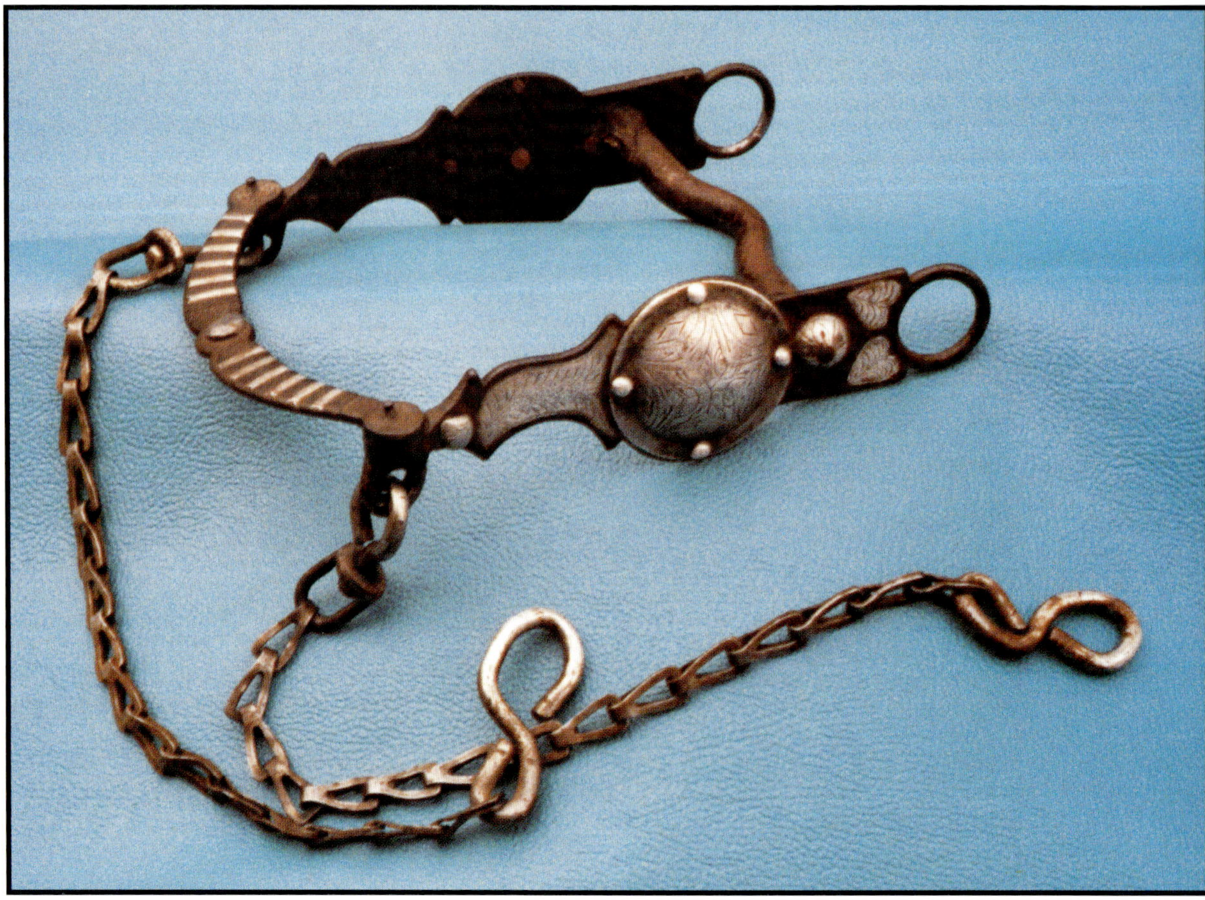

Marked on inside slobber bar "Qualey Bros," then on outside "Joseph, Idaho." The small conchos are missing from the slobber bar, but otherwise in good condition. It is, perhaps, one of the early items made. *Courtesy Paul and Marlene Snider. $5000 to 7000*

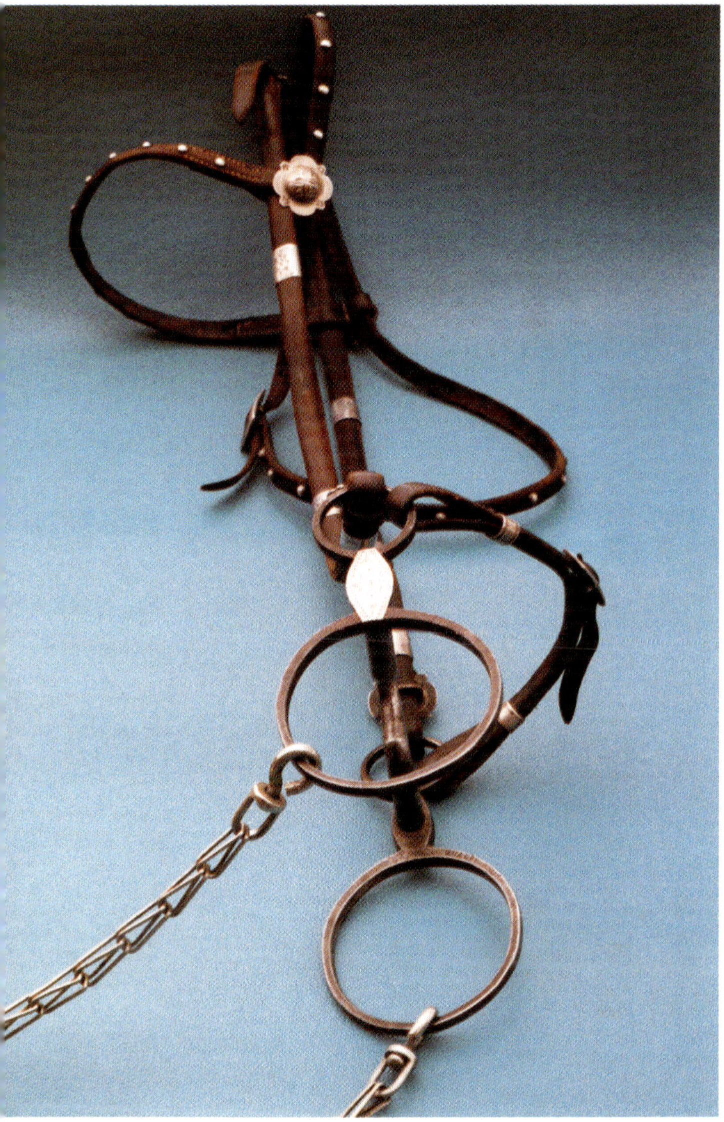

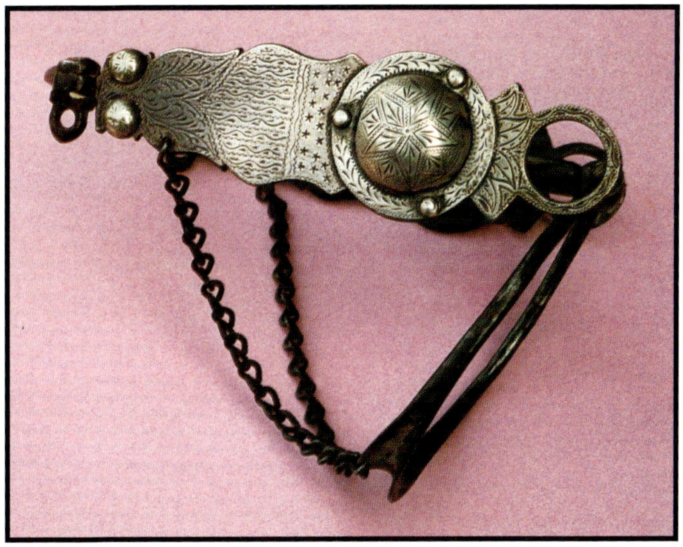

Mike Morales is the maker of this fine ring bit, bearing a patriotic shield and large engraved concho. Ring bits are rare and difficult to find as most of them had to be custom ordered years ago. *Private collection. $1200*

"Qualey Bros." globe bit with a Qualey Bros. headstall and all silver work on the headstall also done by Qualey Brothers. *Courtesy Paul and Marlene Snider. $2500 to 3500*

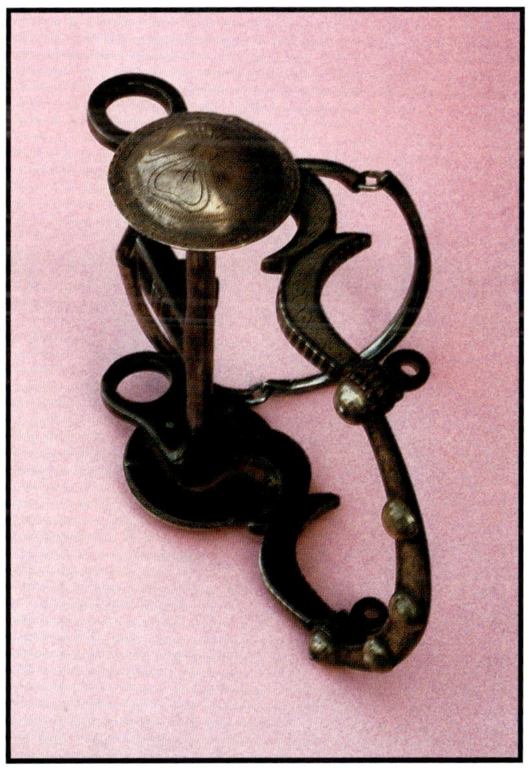

Sterling silver unmarked ring bit made in Mexico. It is in quality condition. *Courtesy private collector. $700 to 1000*

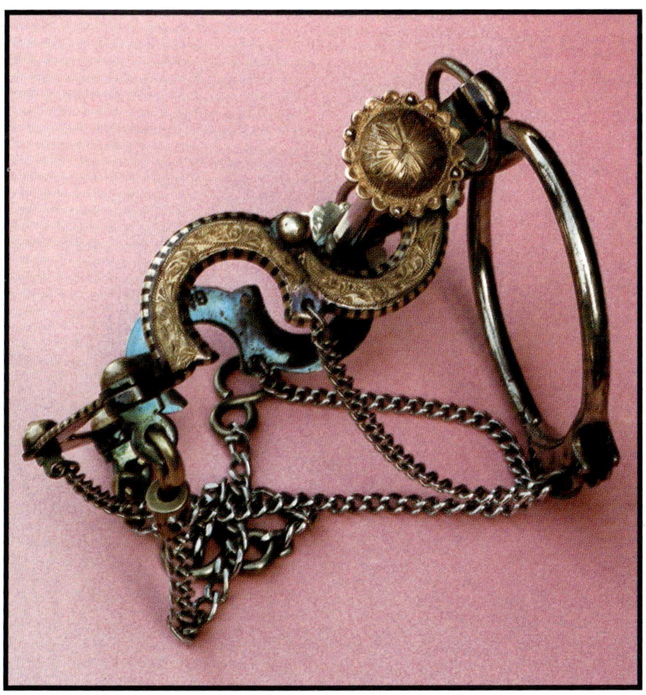

Garcia contemporary ring bit, it is a lovely rendition .
Courtesy private collector. $300 to 500

Chapter Two

Spurs

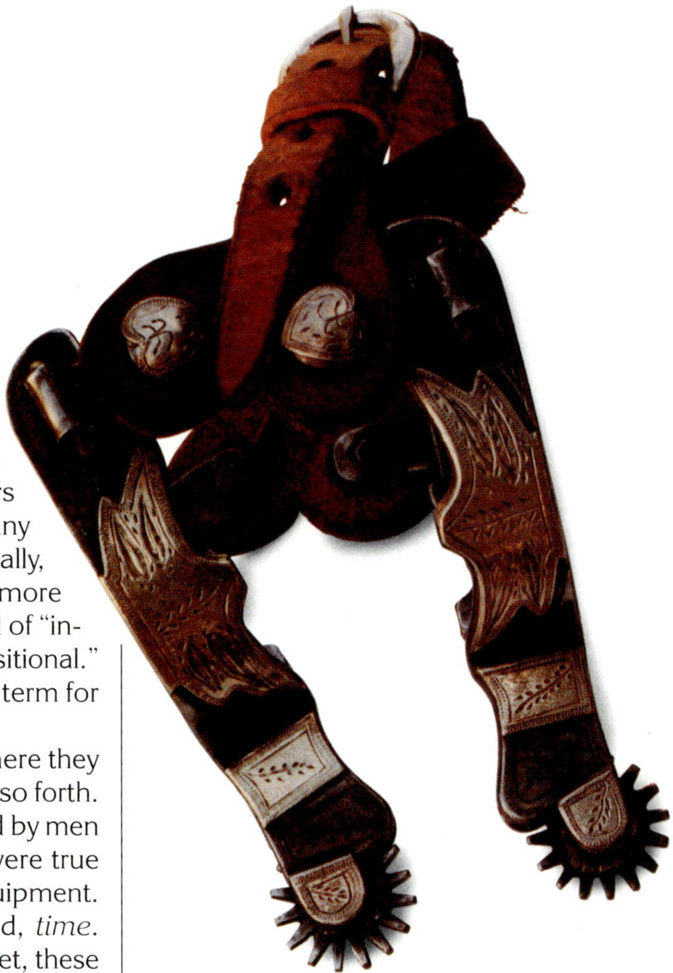

"A little horse encouragement"

We trace the introduction of spurs to America to the arrival of Hernando Cortez in the 1500s. Some of the early *Espaula Grande* spurs had rowels that exceeded six inches, and one can't help wondering just how a man ever wore them, much less used them or mounted a horse with them on his boots. However, it seems evident that the evolution of spurs designed in America spread rapidly. Before long there were many styles being made, and the end of the big rowels came gradually, but surely. Between the end of the "huge rowel era" and the more sensible and usable ones we see today, there flourished a kind of "in-between" style spur with large rowels, sometimes called "transitional." I have always maintained that "transitional" was too general a term for these spurs and I am glad it is no longer being used.

Quite early, spur styles took on the names of locations where they were made, i.e California drop shanks, Great Plains style, and so forth. Especially fascinating are prison-made spurs that were created by men in penitentiaries across the country. Many of these makers were true artisans who created beautiful spurs with generally poor equipment. The creative factor probably can be summed up in one word, *time*. While men in the trade were manufacturing for the mass market, these men behind bars were slowly, impeccably creating spurs that could take months to build, rather than days.

Possibly prison made, these spurs have a very unique construction and most unusual shank. They are very finely finished and have a nice feel. *Courtesy R.C. and Marvin Bales. $1500 to 2000*

Many old catalogs are currently reproduced that portray early spurs which were available, by mail or otherwise, to the public. It is a good idea for today's collectors to acquire as many of these as they can get to become familiar with spurs made in the 1800s and early 1900s. More can be learned from early catalogs than from any other source. Interested people can learn a great deal from other collectors by joining the National Bit Spur and Saddle Collectors Association at Post Office Box 3035, Colorado Springs, CO 80934.

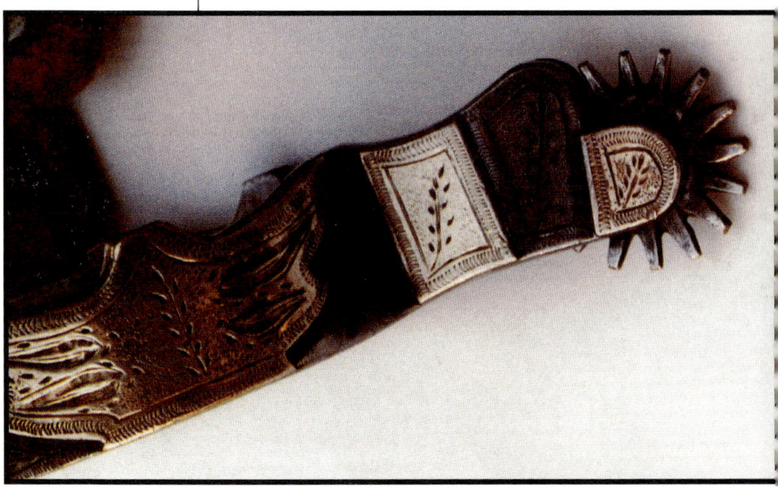

Detail of spurs showing unusual shank.

M. MORALES PORTLAND, OREGON

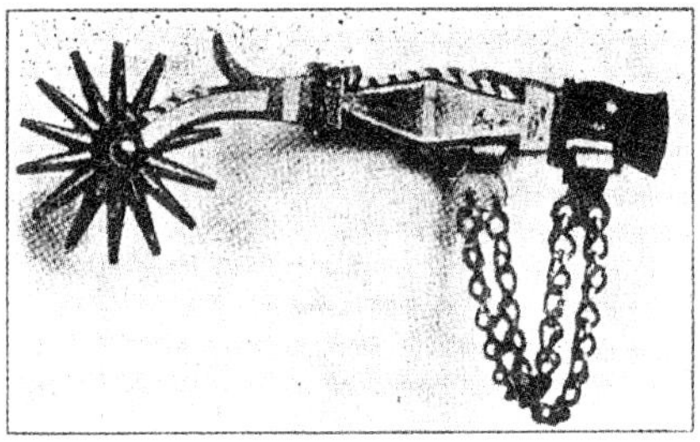

No. 55

To match bit No. 14. Silver inlaid, nicely finished.
Price, per pair.....................................$9.00

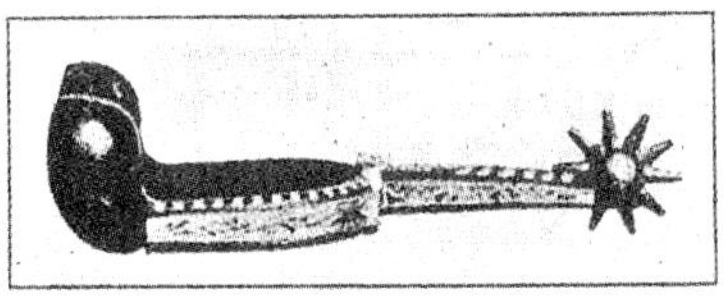

No. 56

Silver inlaid, fine finish, per pair.....................$9.00

20

M. MORALES PORTLAND, OREGON

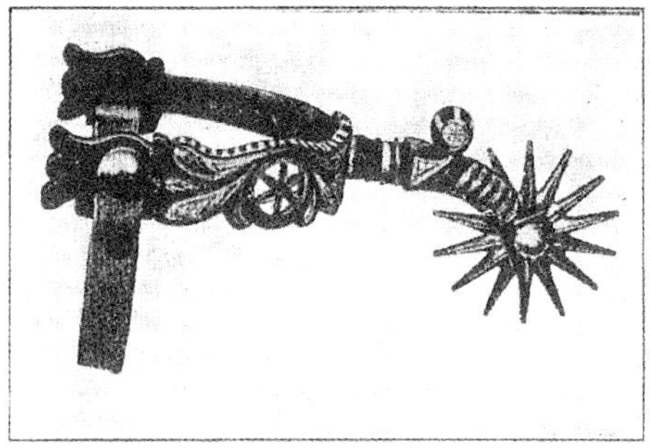

No. 57

Silver inlaid, very showy, per pair....................$25.00

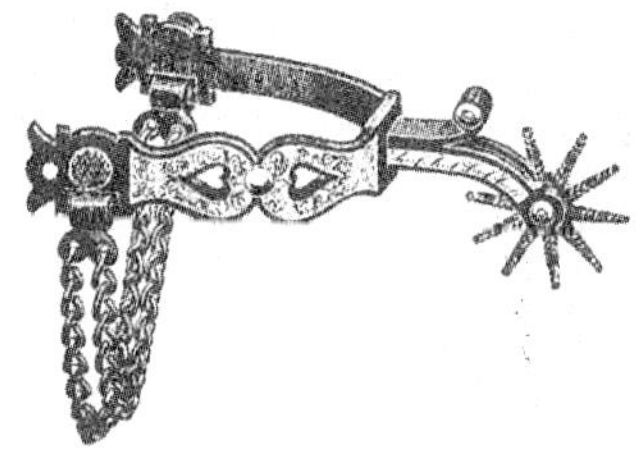

No. 58

Open work, silver inlaid, per pair.....................$14.00

21

M. MORALES PORTLAND, OREGON

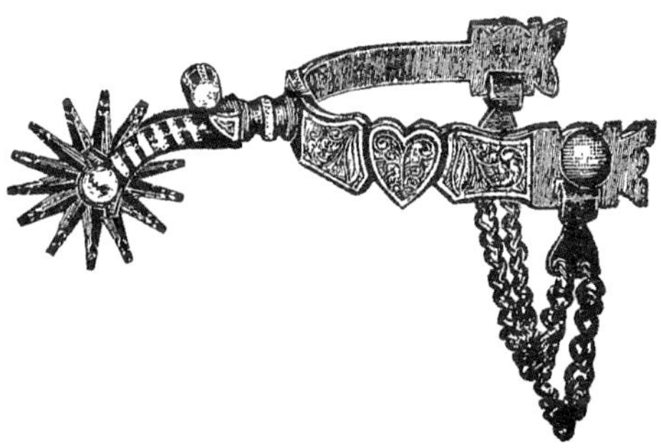

No. 59

Silver inlaid, very nicely engraved, per pair...........$14.00

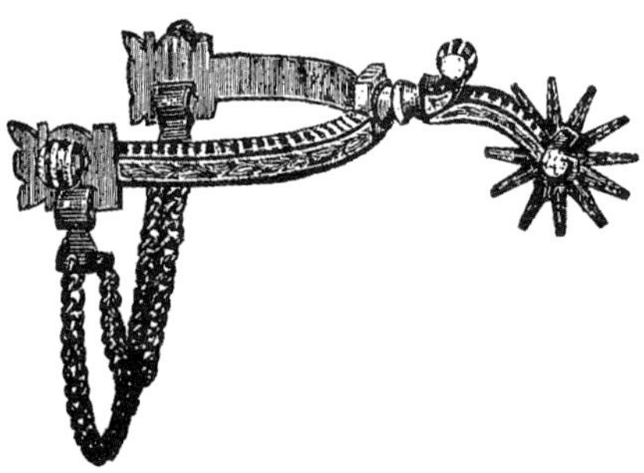

No. 60

Silver inlaid, price, per pair.........................$12.00

22

M. MORALES PORTLAND, OREGON

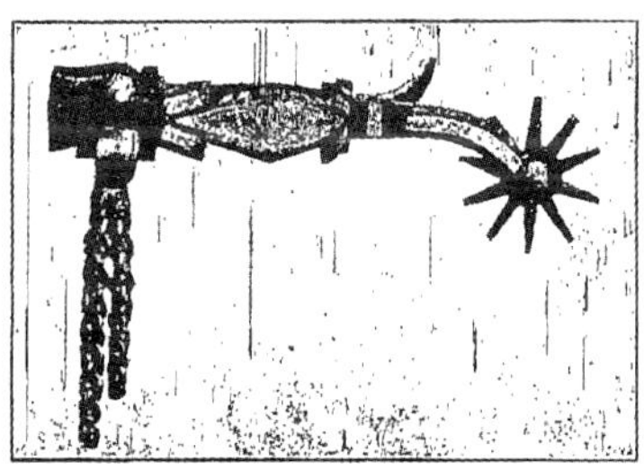

No. 61

Silver inlaid, price, per pair.........................$8.50

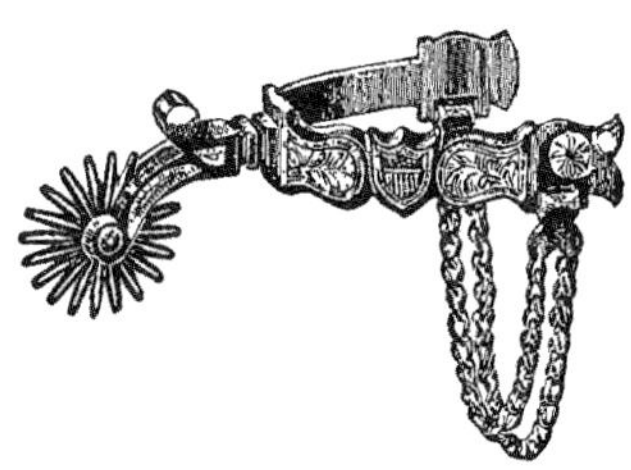

No. 62

Silver inlaid, fine engraving, per pair................$13.50

23

The Mike Morales catalog from 1900 illustrates the prices then current for some of the spurs contemporaneously collected and displayed.

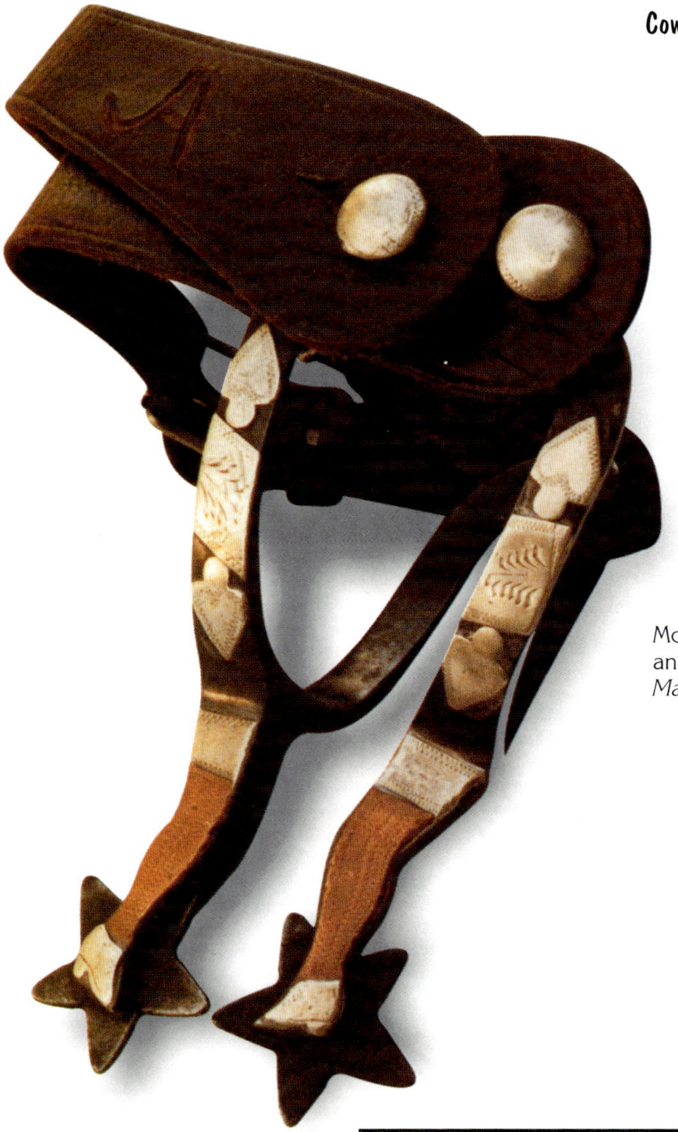

McChesney lady legs in excellent condition and have old leathers. *Courtesy R.C. and Marvin Bales. $1500 to 2000*

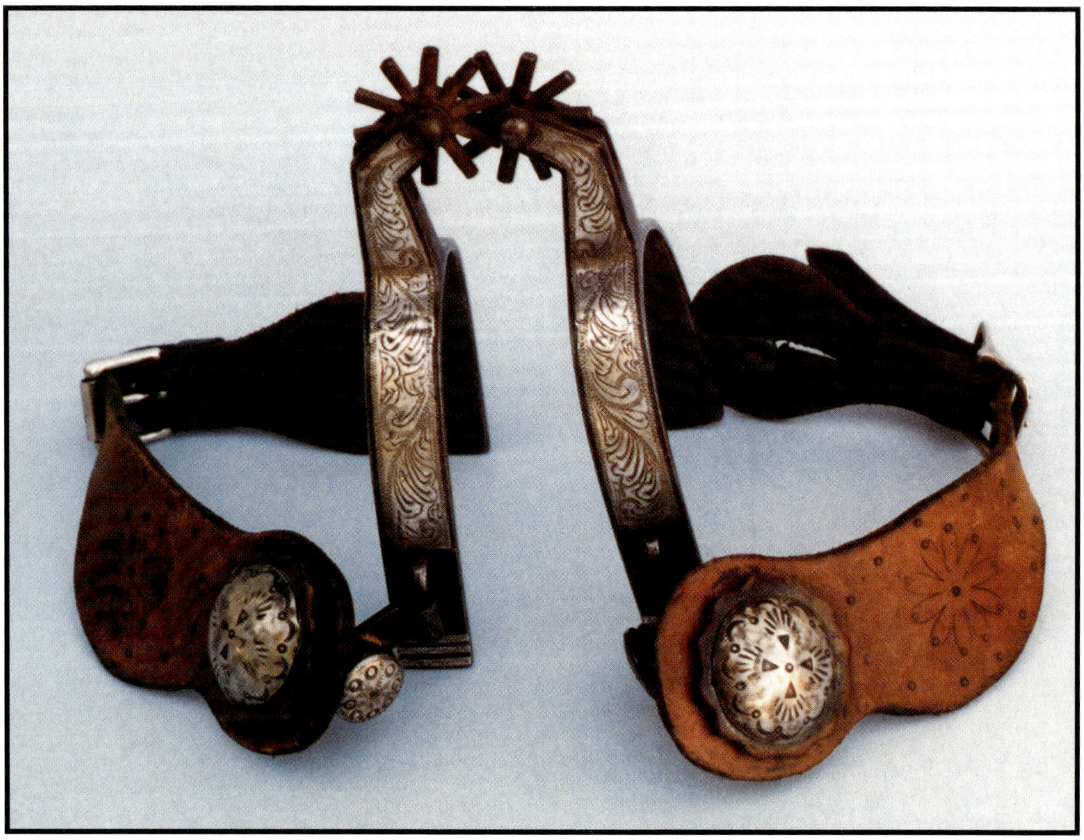

Garcia Saddlery, Salinas, California is the maker of these fine spurs. They are silver mounted with nice large silver conchos on the spur leathers. *Courtesy Ron and Sharon Mailloux. $1300 to 1700*

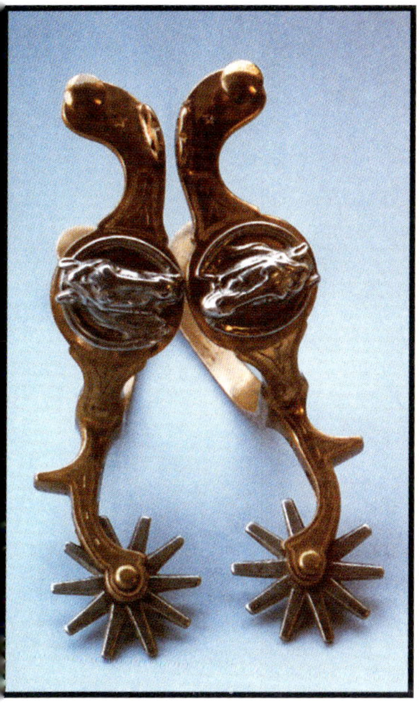

Very nice old Hercules Bronze "horse heads" marked with August Buermann's star mark. *Private collection. $550*

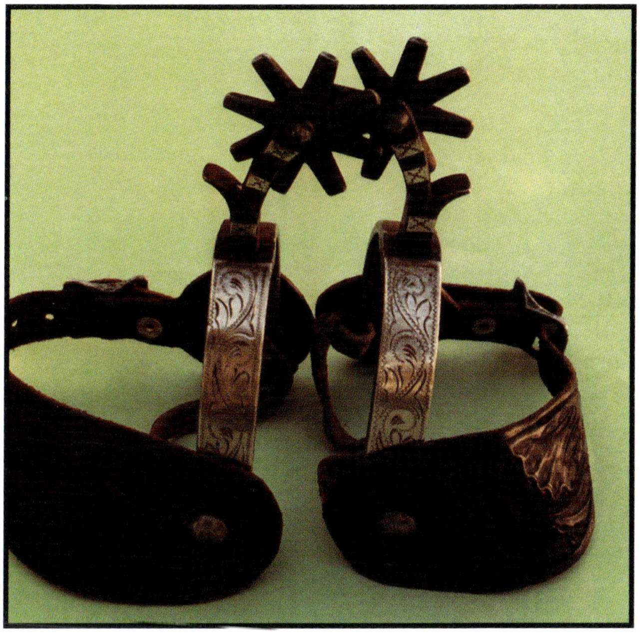

Made in the penitentiary at Boise, Idaho, these prison-made spurs are very well made and in fine condition. *Courtesy R.C. and Marvin Bales. $1500 to 2000*

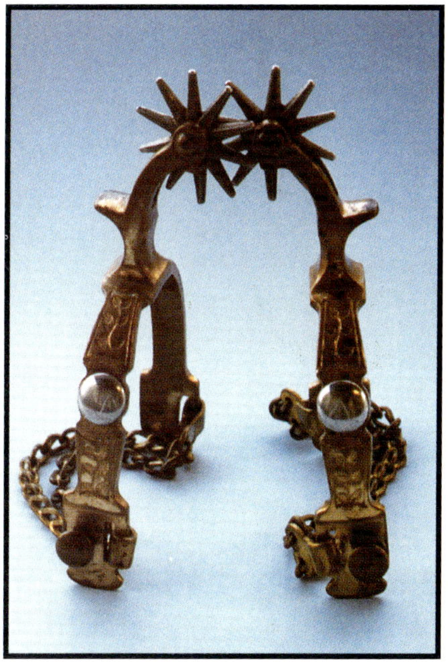

Hercules Bronze spurs are chased metal with a single spot, made by August Buermann. *Private collection. $650 to 750*

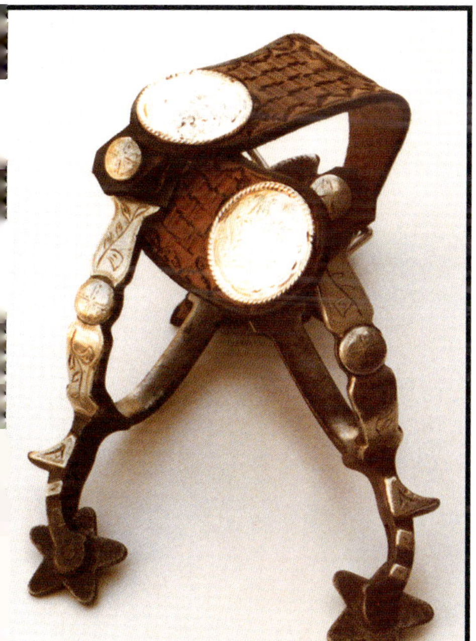

North and Judd silver mounted spurs with star rowels; they have nice leathers with contemporary conchos in silver. *Courtesy R.C. and Marvin Bales. $1200 to 1500*

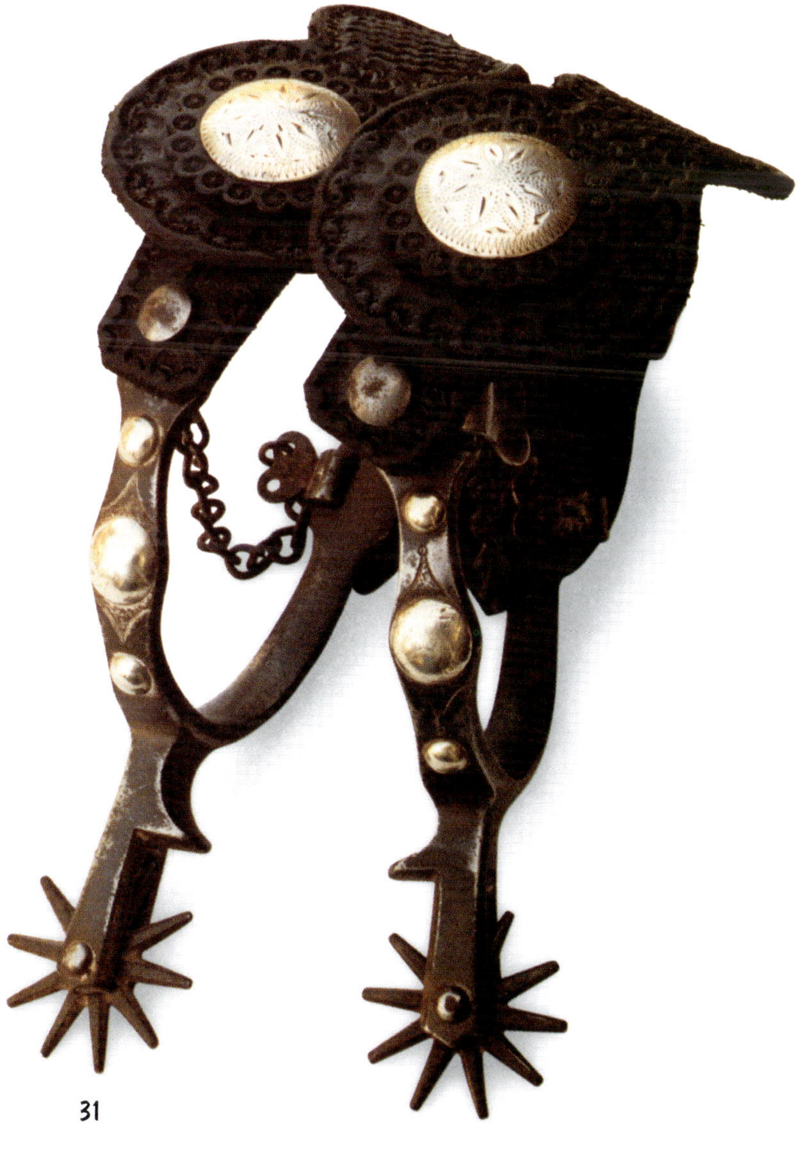

North and Judd "three spot" spurs, they have nice leather with a silver concho. *Courtesy R.C. and Marvin Bales. $250 to 300*

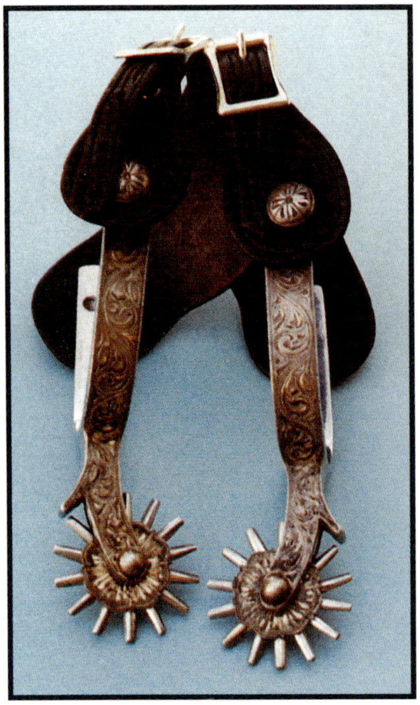

Les Garcia spurs are "parade" dress-up quality, sterling silver overlay and rowel guards. *Courtesy R.C. and Marvin Bales. $ 1200 to 1500*

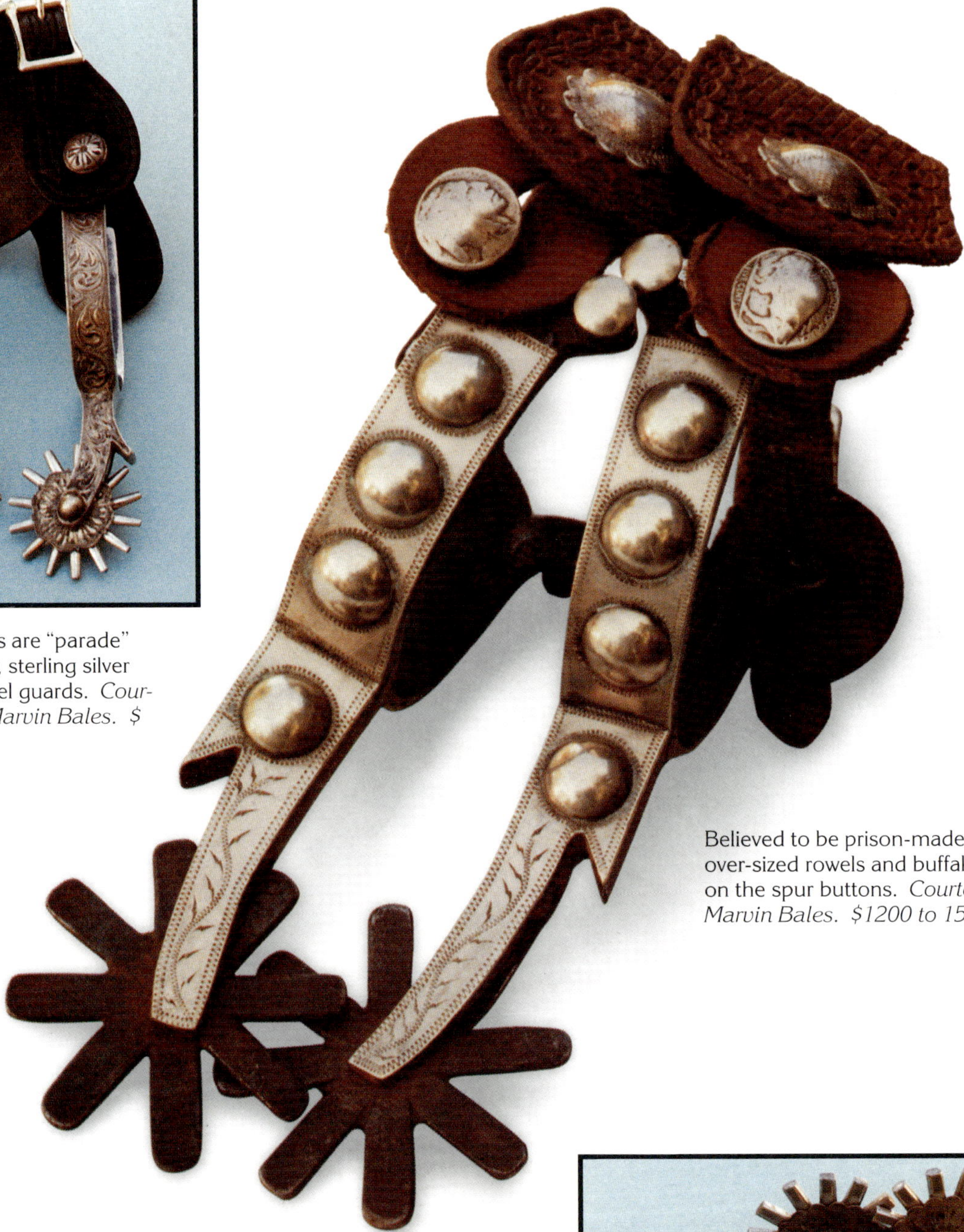

Believed to be prison-made, these have over-sized rowels and buffalo head nickels on the spur buttons. *Courtesy R.C. and Marvin Bales. $1200 to 1500*

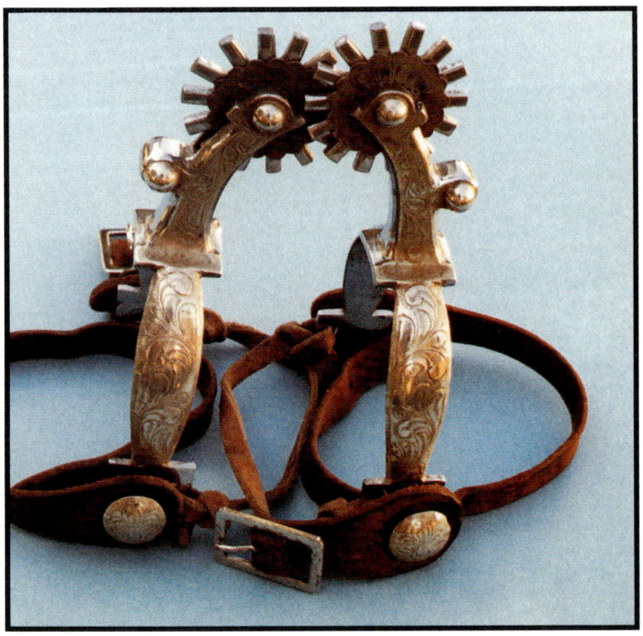

These unmarked spurs are excellent in construction with sterling silver overlays. *Courtesy R.C. and Marvin Bales. $1000 to 1200*

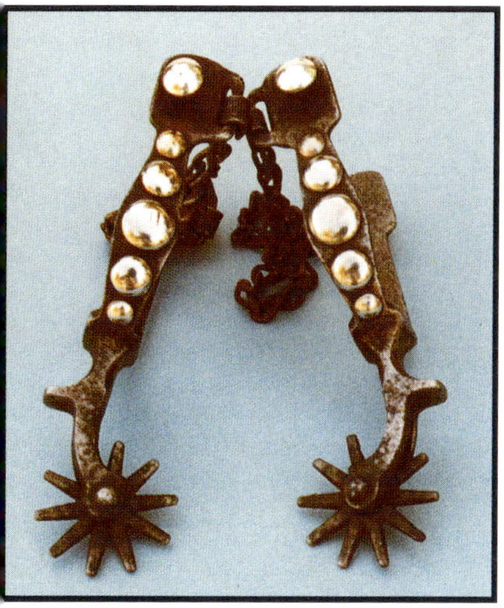

A pair of nice old "five spots," these are most likely by North and Judd. *Courtesy R.C. and Marvin Bales. $300 to 500*

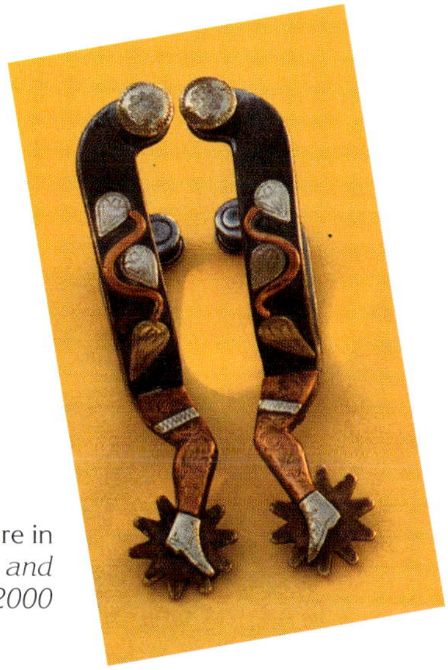

McChesney gal legs, the spurs are in pristine condition. *Courtesy R.C. and Marvin Bales. $1500 to 2000*

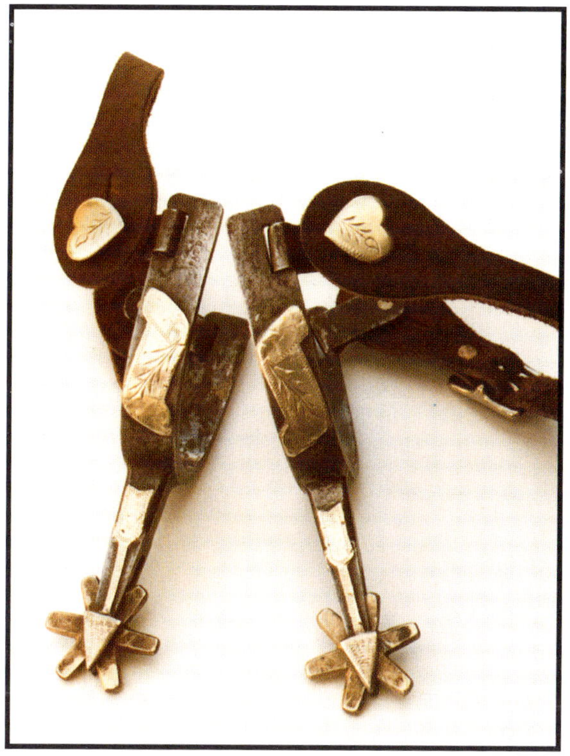

Buermann "scroll" spurs with an arrow shank; they appear on page 12 of his #35 catalogue, patent number 2054. *Courtesy R.C. and Marvin Bales. $700 to 800*

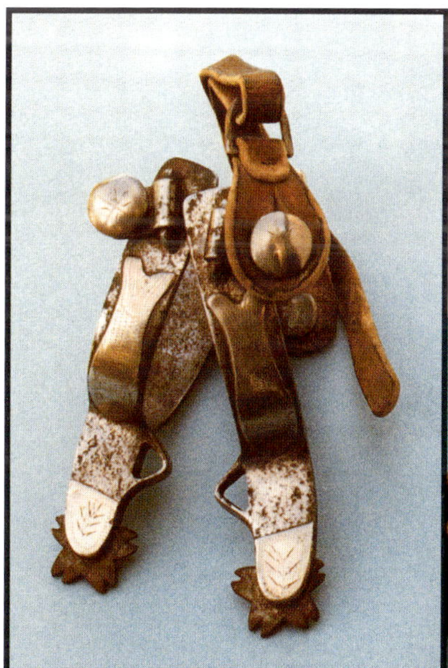

Attributed to Crockett or possibly Kelly Bros., these spurs are unique in that they have a fish on the side. They are the old-time "bronc" spurs. *Courtesy R.C. and Marvin Bales. $600 to 800*

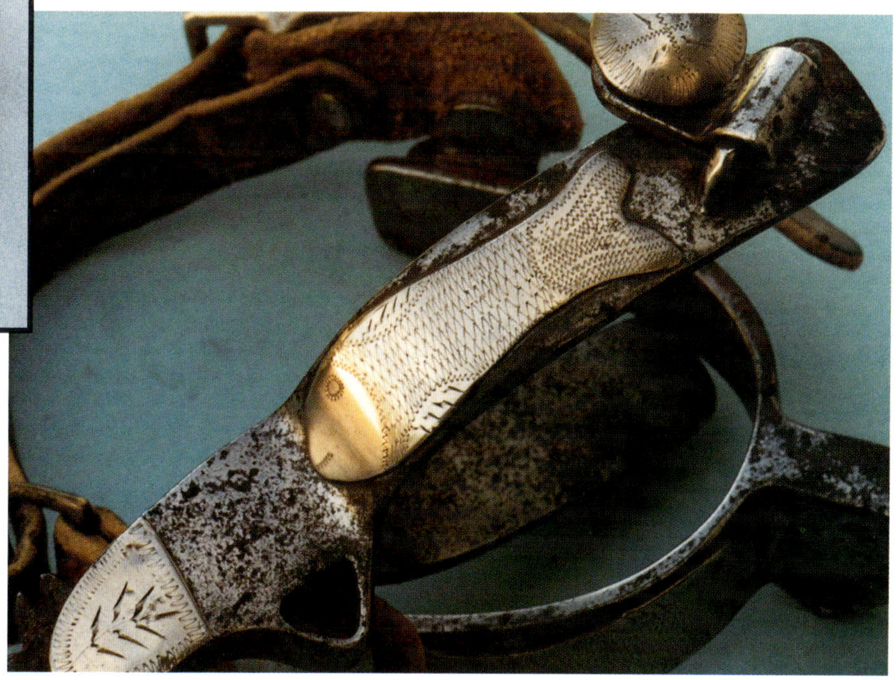

Detail of the fish spurs.

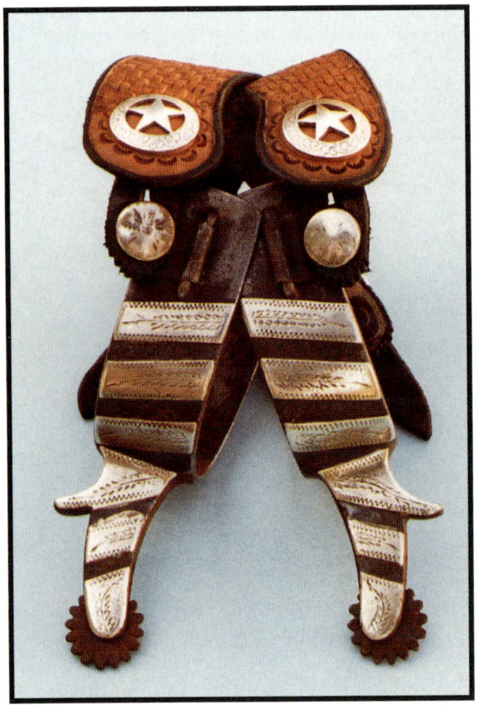

Johnny Mullins spurs made by Crockett; they are in excellent condition with contemporary leathers and Texas star conchos. *Courtesy R.C. and Marvin Bales. $1200 to 1500*

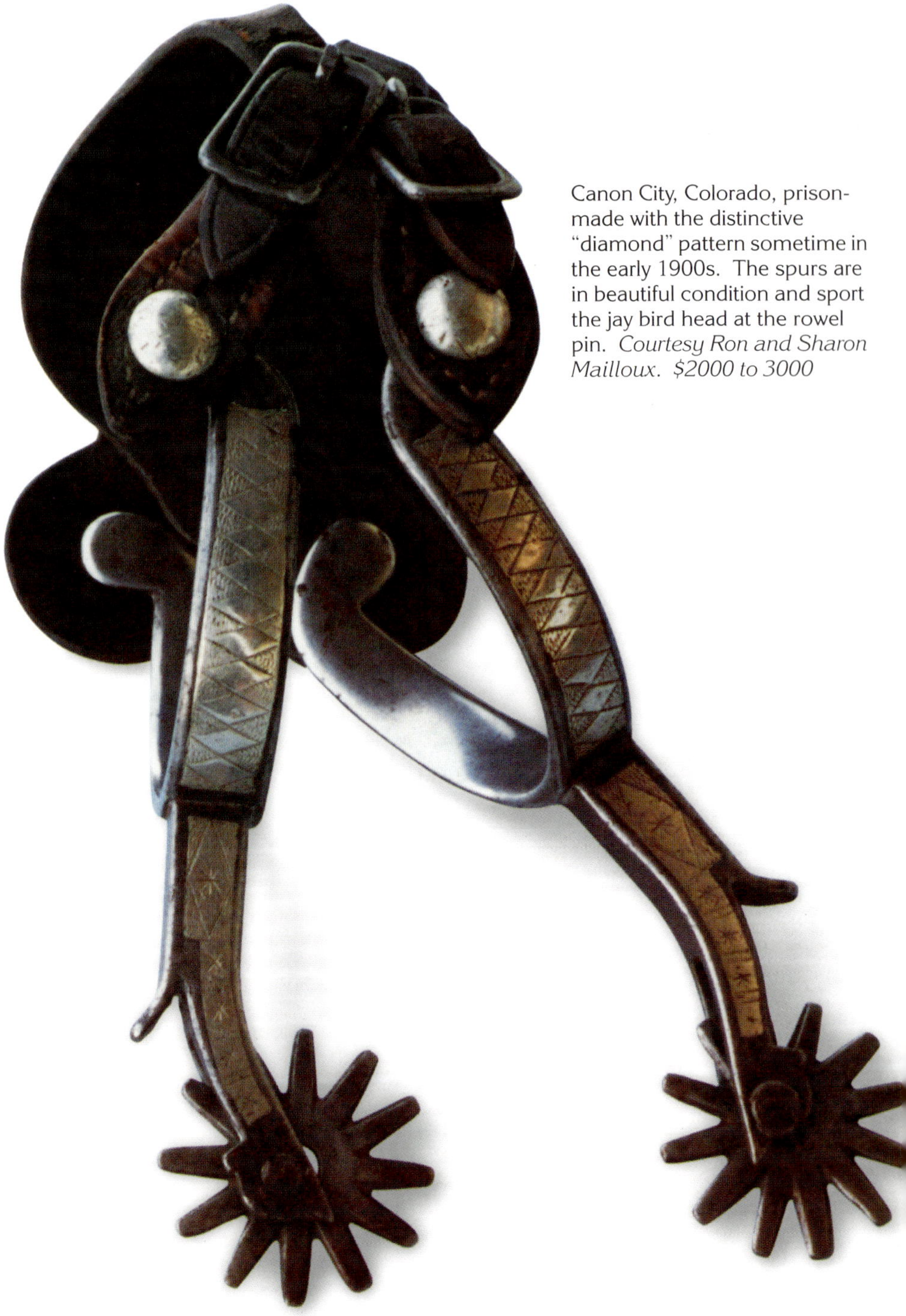

Canon City, Colorado, prison-made with the distinctive "diamond" pattern sometime in the early 1900s. The spurs are in beautiful condition and sport the jay bird head at the rowel pin. *Courtesy Ron and Sharon Mailloux. $2000 to 3000*

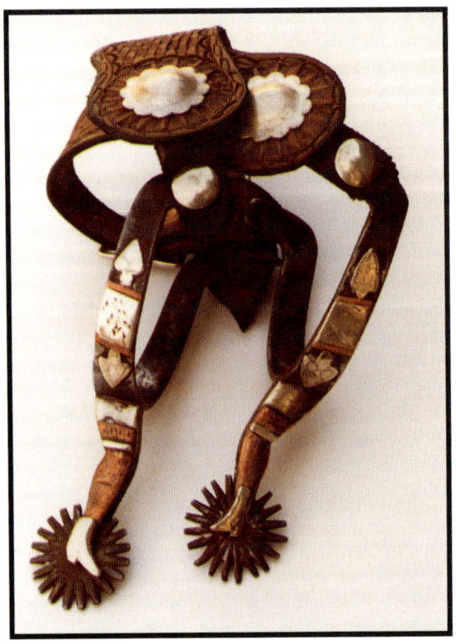

McChesney "lady legs" with twenty-point rowels and sterling conchos on the leathers. *Courtesy R.C. and Marvin Bales. $1500 to 2000*

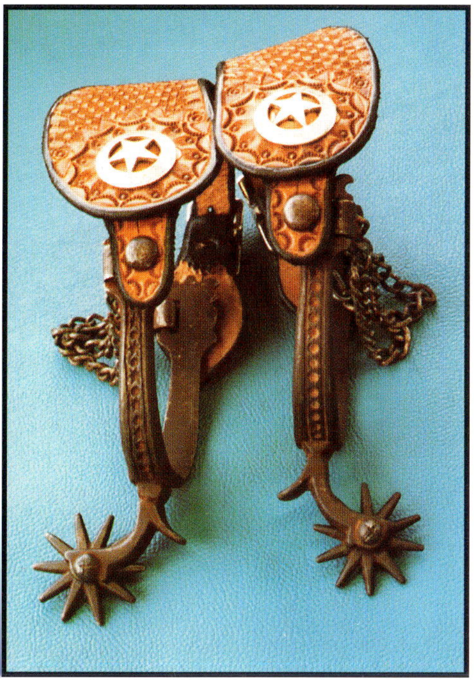

Chased iron California style drop shanks, the spurs are marked "A.B." with a star and were made by August Buermann. *Overton collection. $450 to 550*

Made by R.B. Dunbar of Shaniko, Oregon, the spurs were made in the early 1900s, possibly 1910. Mr. Dunbar was purported to have been a successful sheep herder during the heyday of Shaniko. The spurs are one-of-a-kind and in very fine condition with original leathers and conchos. *Courtesy Ron and Sharon Mailloux. $3000 to 3500*

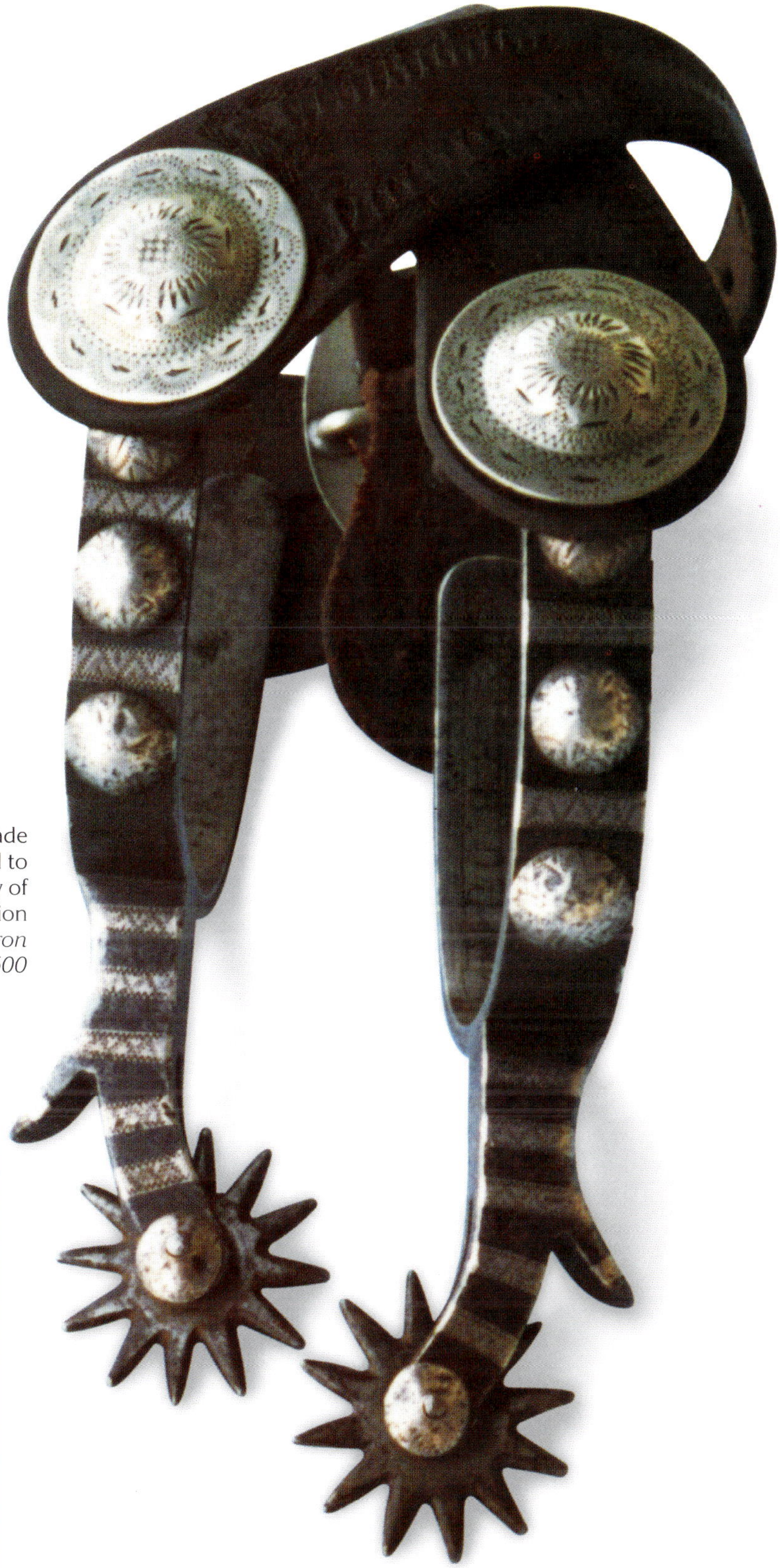

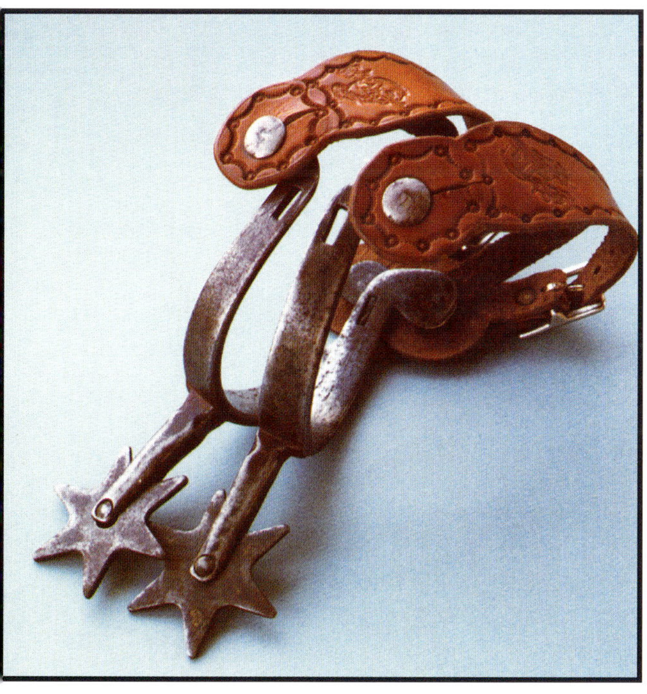

The large holes in the center of the rowel, made at the time the rowel was made, and the fact that the spurs came from Gainsville, Texas, indicate they are possibly by Bass, or at least a protégé of his; however, until more is learned about them they will be valued accordingly. *Overton collection. $500 to 600*

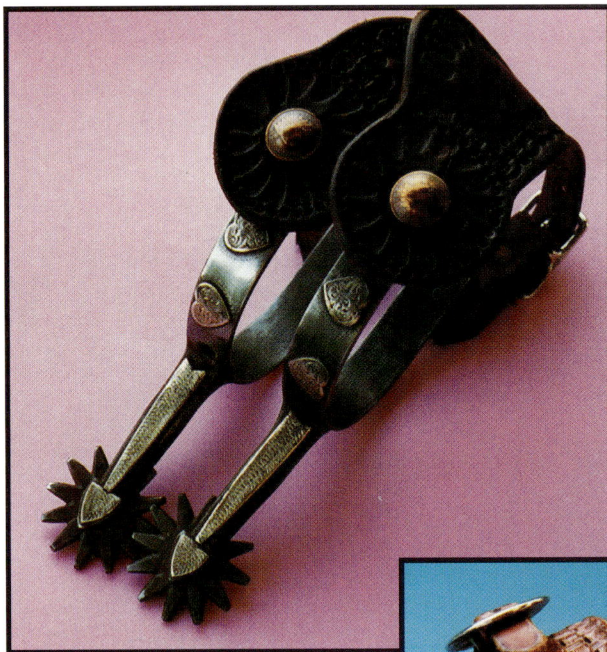

With straight shanked arrows, the spurs are hand made with Indian head pennies on the spur buttons and hearts on the heel bands. Unmarked, but very nice construction. *Overton collection. $300 to 500*

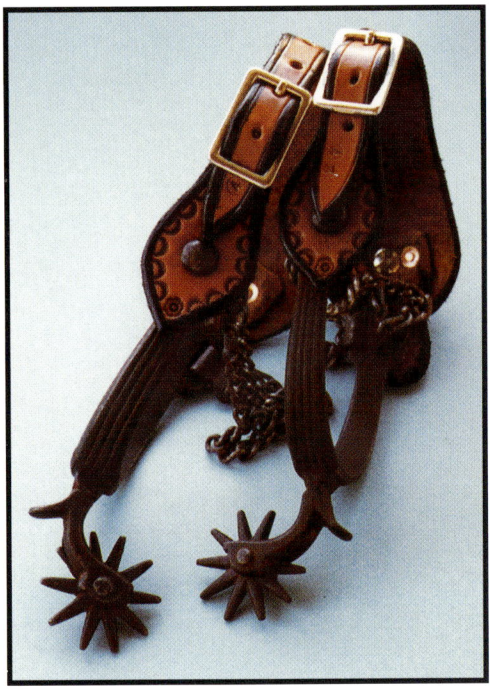

Chased iron spurs made by Buermann are in nice condition for their age. Nice hand made leather spur straps and original old heel chains. *Overton collection. $400 to 500*

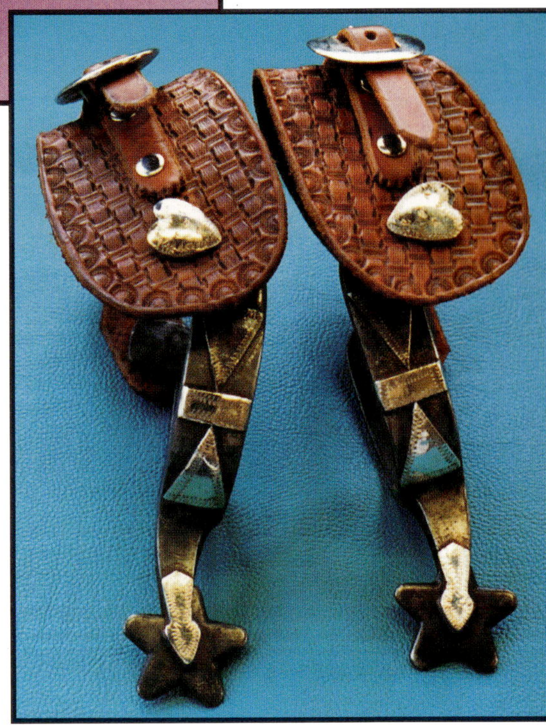

Everyday working type spurs with "buckaroo" straps and sterling silver mounted design. The buttons are silver hearts. *Overton collection. $350 to 450*

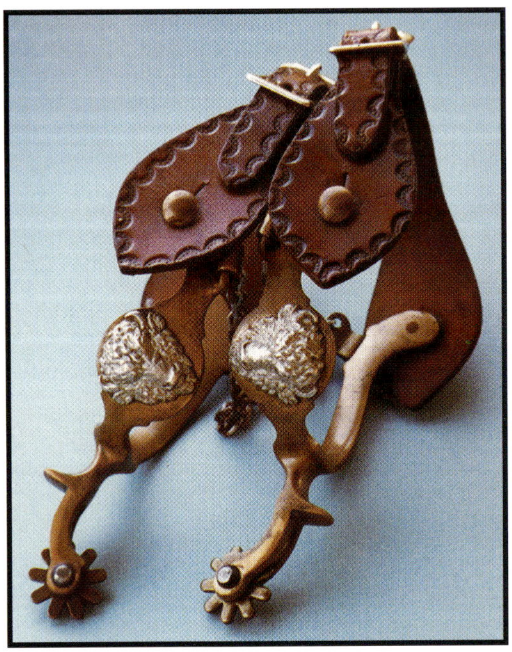

North and Judd, Hercules Bronze buffalo head spurs the leathers were original to the spurs and to the person who had purchased the spurs many years ago. *Overton collection. $300 to 500*

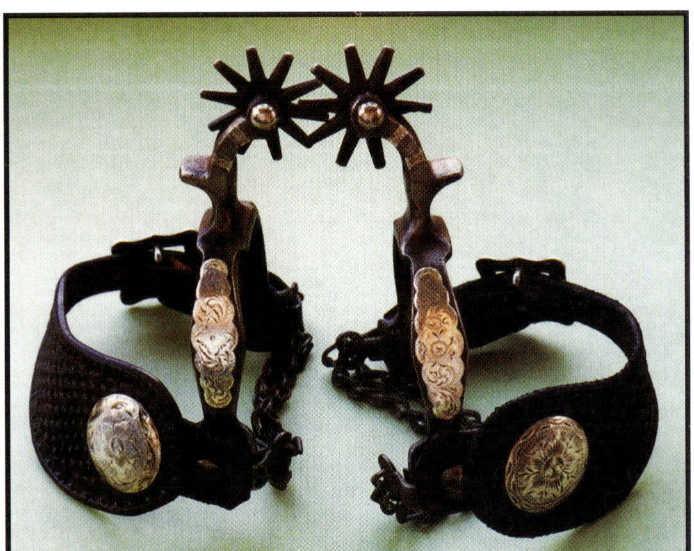

Silver mounted California drop shanks are by North and Judd with a sterling silver overlay. *Overton collection. $400 to 600*

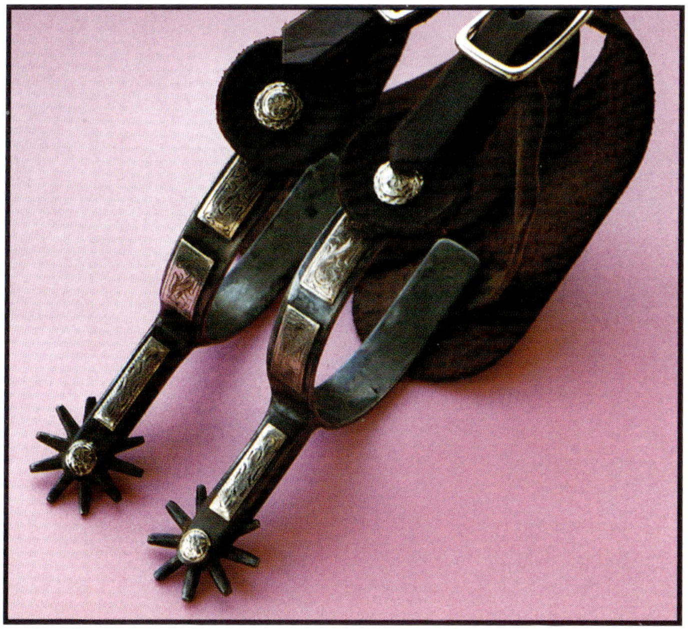

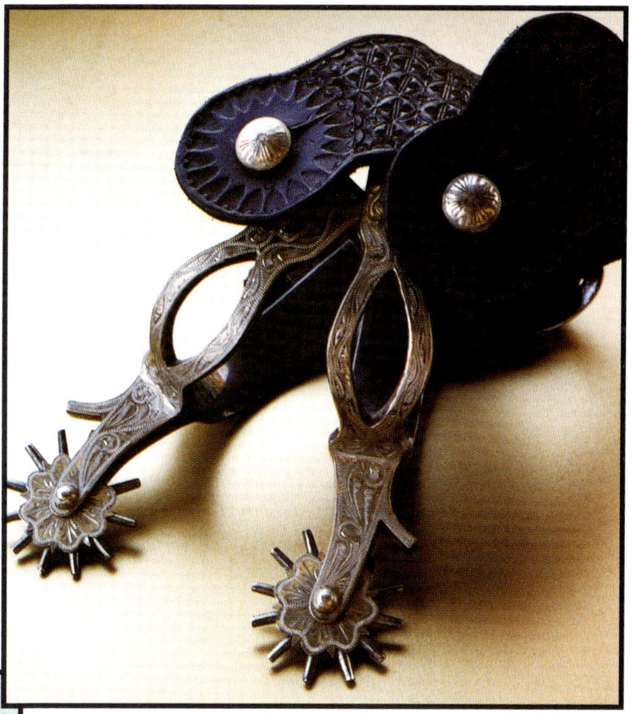

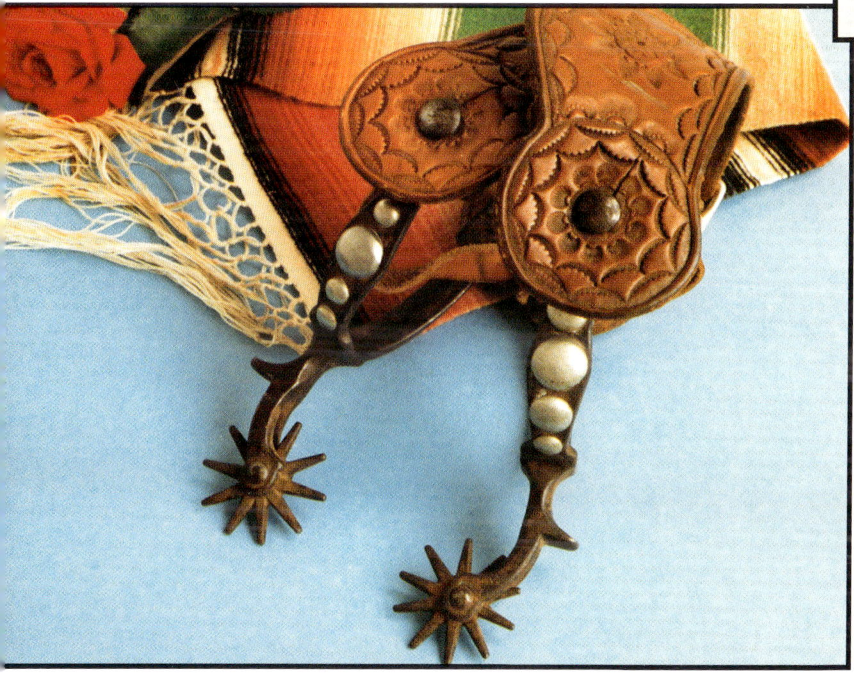

Top left: Straight shanked hand made spurs with sterling silver overlays, unmarked, they are "cowboy friendly" and very useable. *Overton collection. $400 to 500*

Top right: The spurs have silver overlay in an exquisite design and are attributed to A. Tiejien. *Overton collection. $400 to 500*

Left: North and Judd spurs, patent marked 1911, with "five spots" and in excellent condition. *Overton collection. $800 to 850*

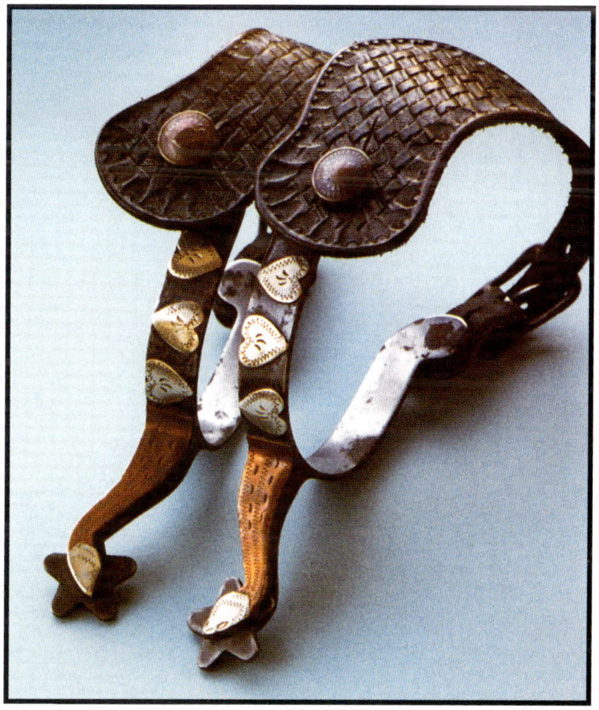

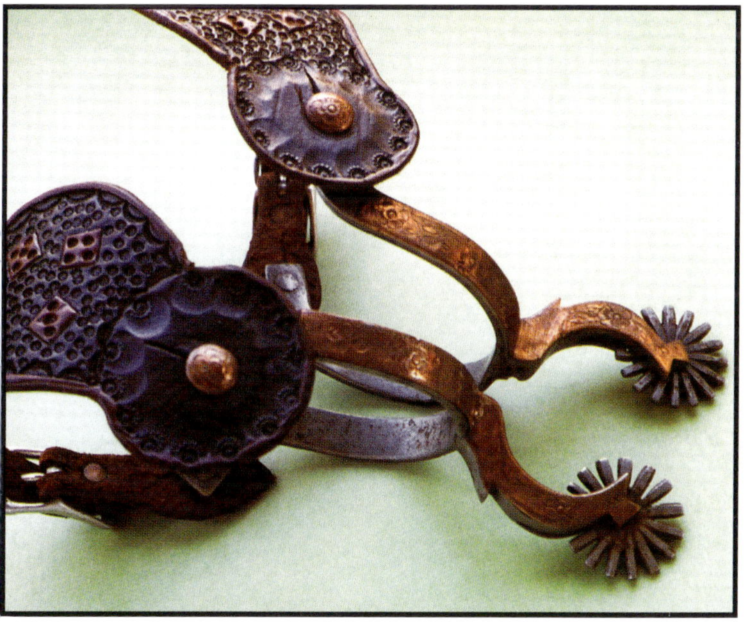

Center right: McChesney is the maker of these fine "goose heads" spurs. They are in excellent condition with old matching Indian head pennies. *Overton collection. $1000 to 1200*

Left: Unusual copper mounted "peacock head" spurs are unmarked, but certainly an interesting pair and quite collectible. *Overton collection. $500 to 700*

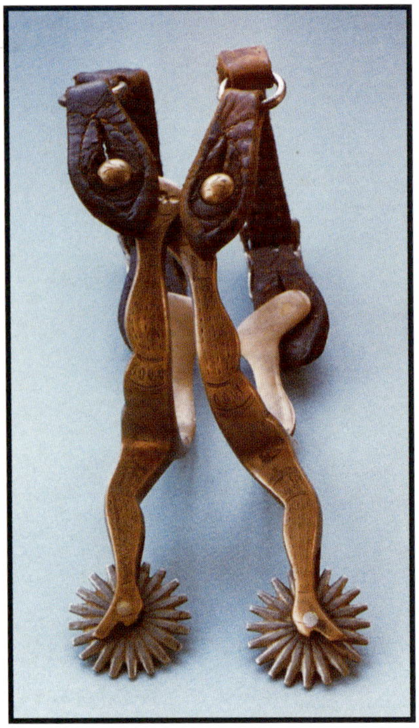

Hercules Bronze double mounted "lady leg" spurs made by Buermann and well marked. They sport what appears to be original leathers. *Overton collection. $800 to 900*

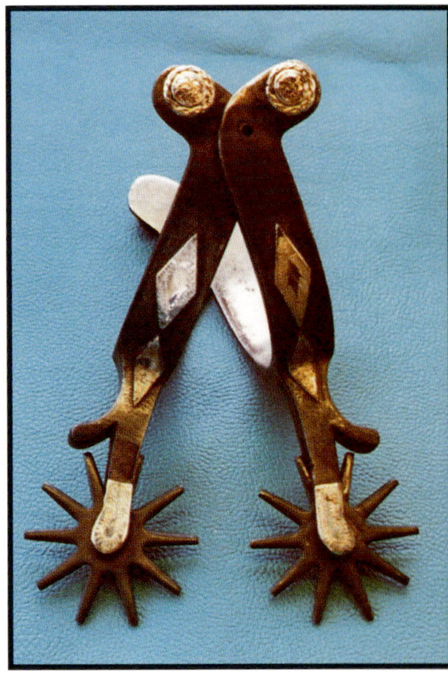

Marked "Crockett," these are in good condition. *Courtesy Bob and Judy Bertsch. $175 to 200*

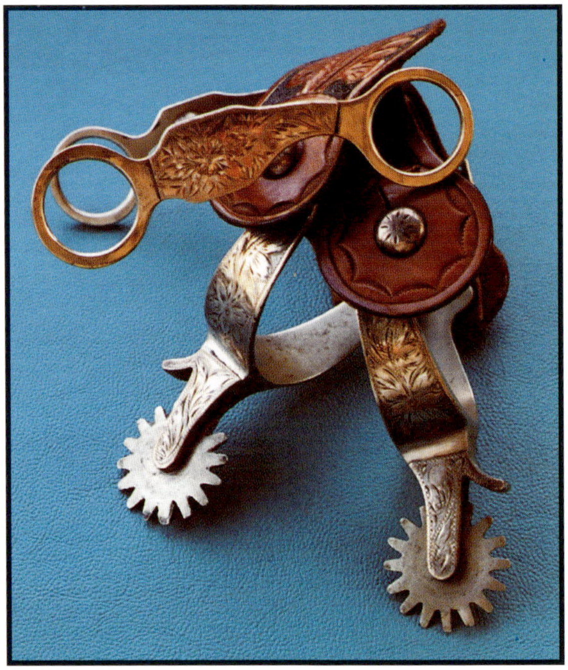

Three-piece set of spurs and matching bit, all marked "Ricardo." It is very rare to find a three-piece set by one maker that matches perfectly; it took a very long time to put this set together. *Overton collection. $1800 to 2000*

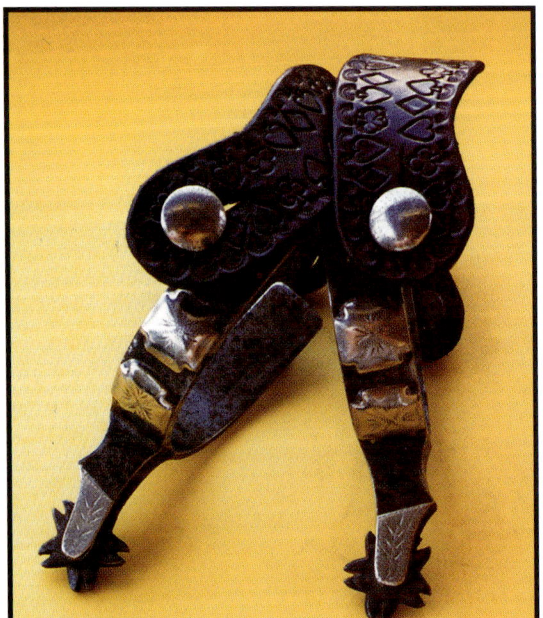

Crockett is the maker of these "four leaf clover" spurs. They are found in a 1946 Keyston Brothers catalogue on page 65, item #1361m, that sold back then for $9.30! *Overton collection. $600 to 800*

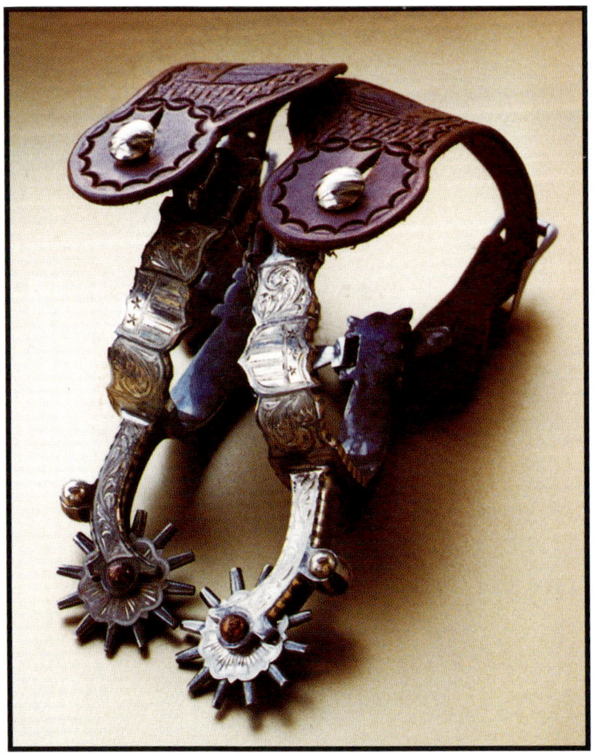

Unmarked contemporary patriotic spurs with U.S. shields tooled by hand into the matching leathers. *Overton collection. $500 to 700*

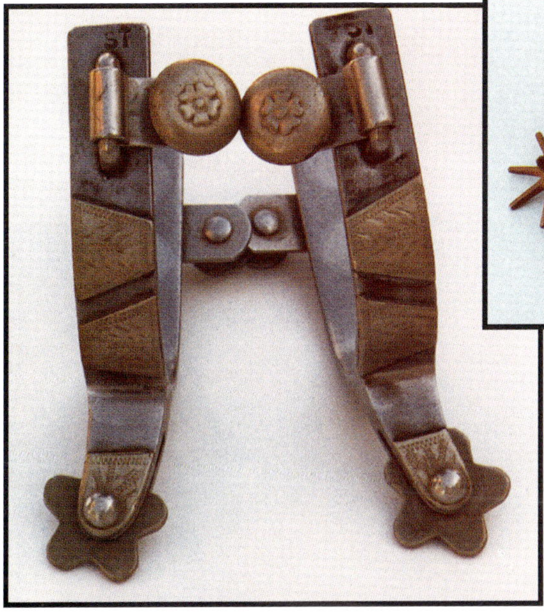

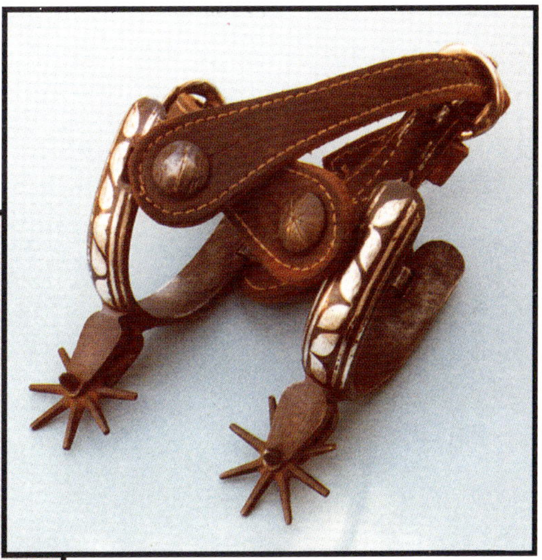

Child-sized, older pair of Mexican Charro spurs, these are finely finished and not the usual "tourist souvenir," as so many are. *Courtesy R.C. and Marvin Bales.* *$150 to 175*

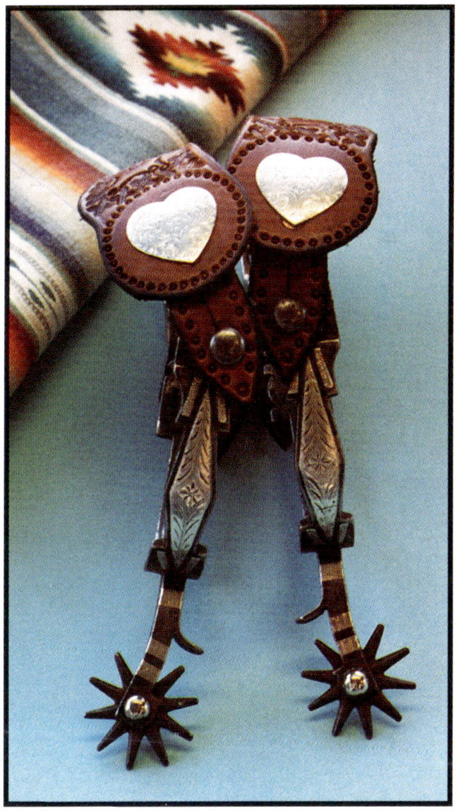

Marked "Crockett, these were purchased at Hamley and Company, Pendleton, Oregon, in the early 1960s *Courtesy Bob and Judy Bertsch.* *$175 to 200*

Spurs attributed to Mike Morales in pristine condition. They have heart conchos, which are most likely a contemporary addition on newer leathers. *Courtesy R.C. and Marvin Bales.* *$600 to 800*

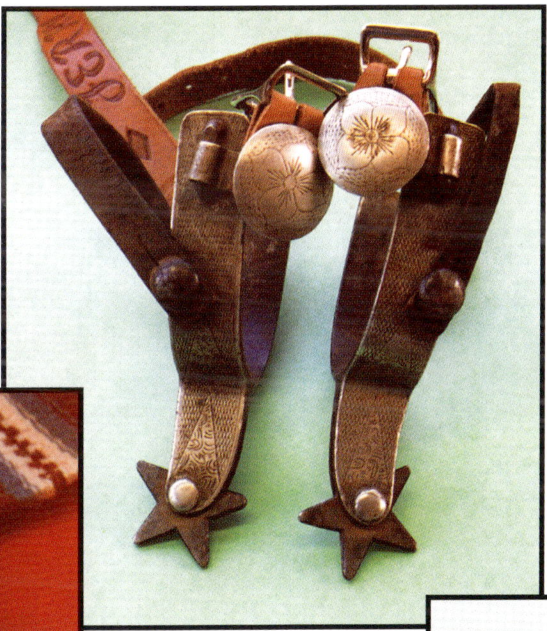

Prison-made spurs, very likely from the Washington State Penitentiary at Walla Walla, Washington, they are in excellent condition and one-of-a-kind. *Private collection.* *$400 to 500*

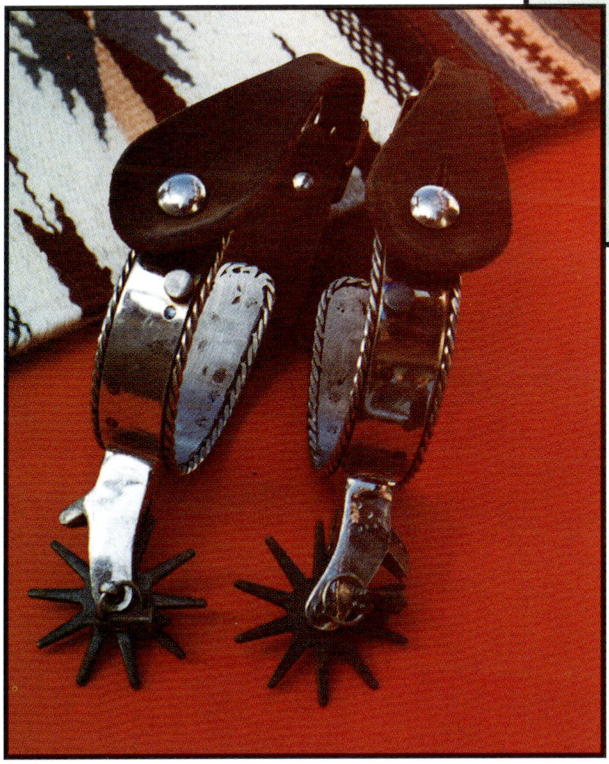

Contemporary spurs made by Bob Christopher, these are unique and very nicely finished. *Courtesy Gene Christopher.* *$125 to 175*

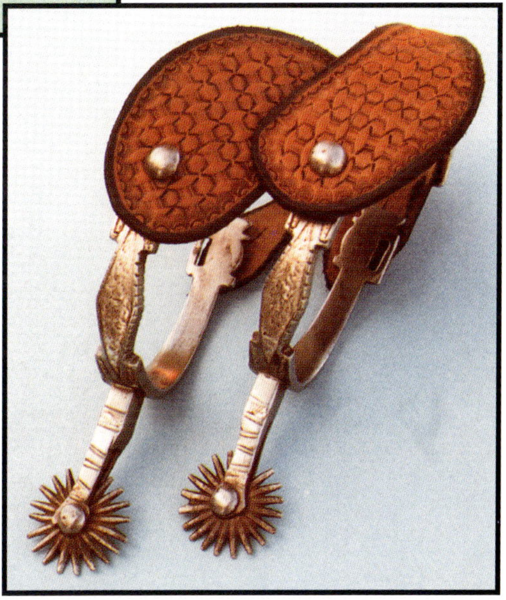

Unmarked spurs, attributed to Mike Morales, are in excellent condition with newer hand-stamped leathers. *Courtesy R.C. and Marvin Bales.* *$550 to 650*

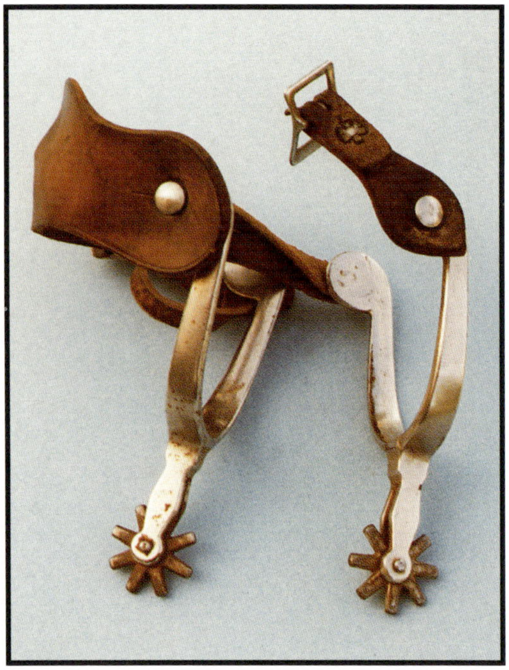

North and Judd spurs of a simple style and in very nice condition. *Courtesy R.C. and Marvin Bales. $125 to 150*

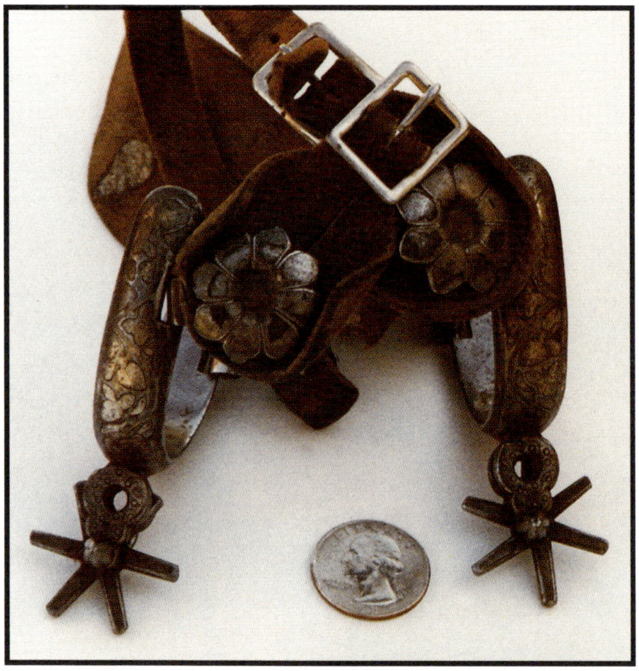

Charro spurs they have gold and silver overlays and are Mexican made. *Courtesy Bob and Judy Bertsch. $150 to 200*

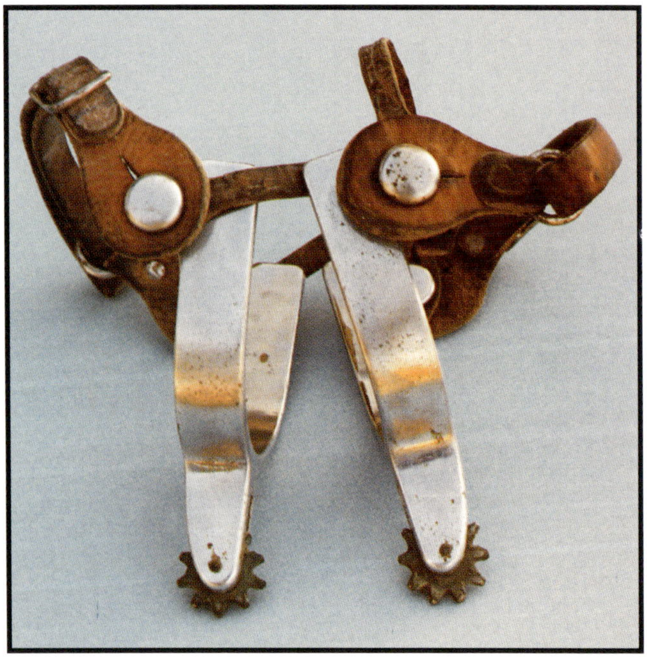

The spurs are marked "Roy" and were made in Texas. These are bronc spur design and would be considered fairly contemporary, at least within the past thirty years. *Courtesy Schiffner Military Museum, George and Margaret Schiffner. $125 to 150*

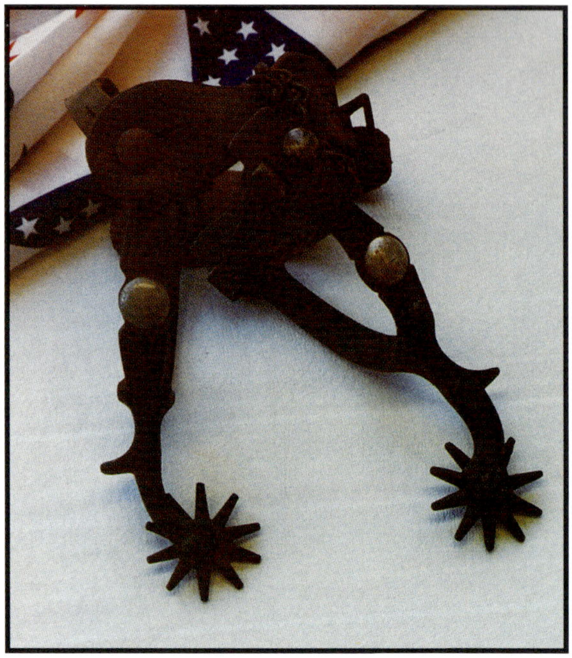

Very old "One Spots" made by August Buermann. *Private collection. $250*

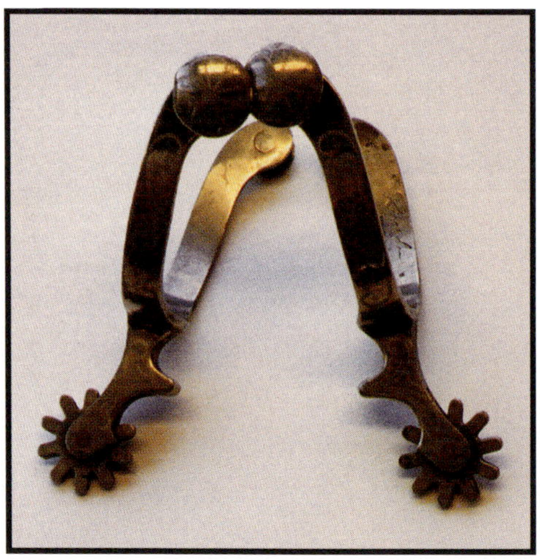

Marked "Ricardo" inside heel band, the spurs were most likely lady spurs. *Courtesy Wade Brumley. $150 to 200*

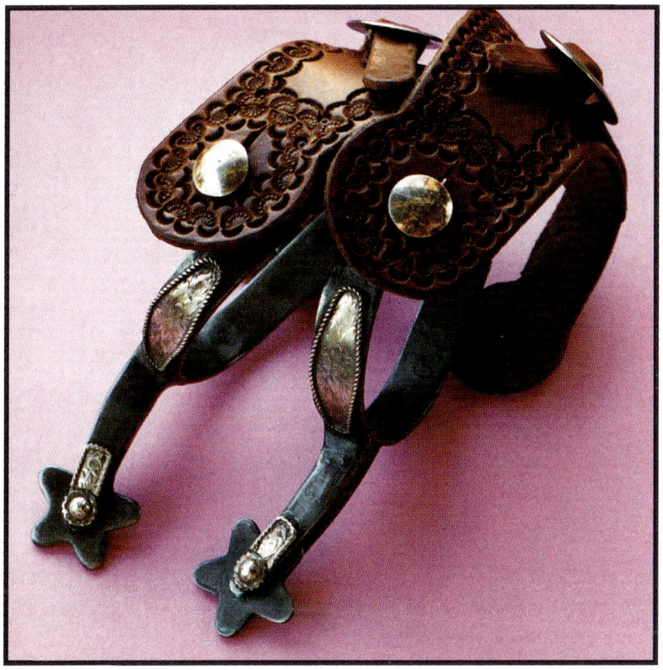

Hand forged silver mounted drop shanks with "Buckaroo" leathers and five point rowels. *Overton collection. $500 to 900*

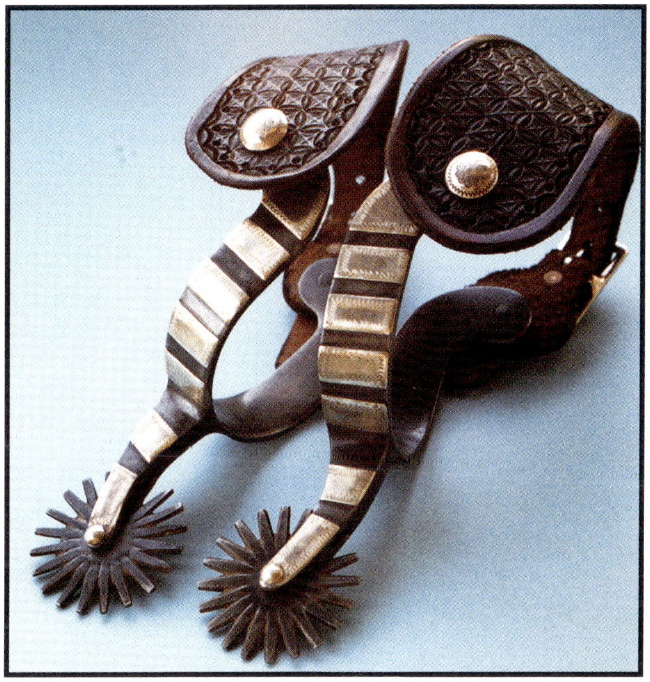

Marked with a "W/O" under spur button the spurs have nice silver overlays and twenty point rowels. *Overton collection. $275 to 350*

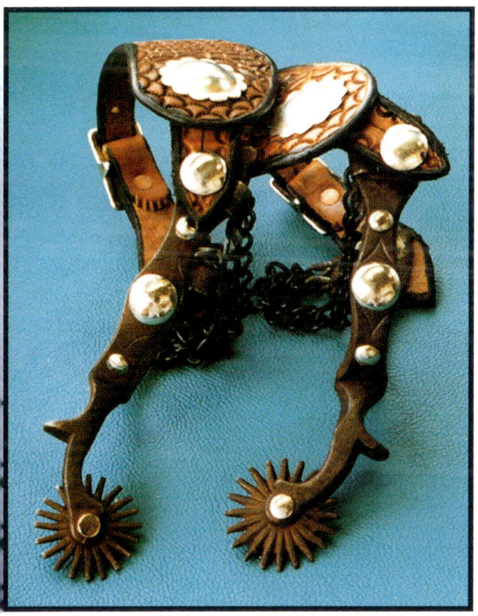

North and Judd "Three Spots" they are in very nice condition with contemporary leathers and silver conchos. *Overton collection. $300 to 450*

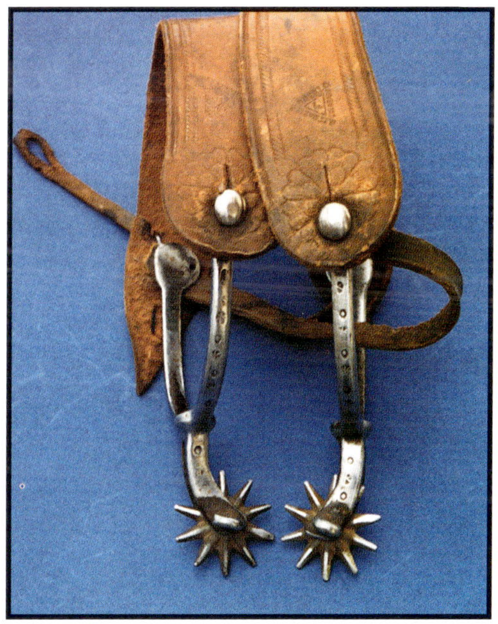

The old original leathers have the "R.T. Frazier" cartouche on them and the spurs are lady spurs made by August Buermann. *Courtesy Gene Christopher. $500 to 600*

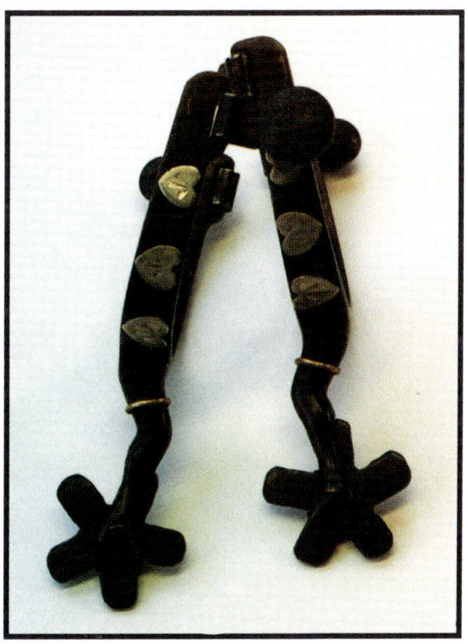

Spurs are Lady Legs and are unmarked but attributed to McChesney, though they are in an unpolished state, they are in very nice condition with old rowels. *Courtesy Wade Brumley. $400 to 500*

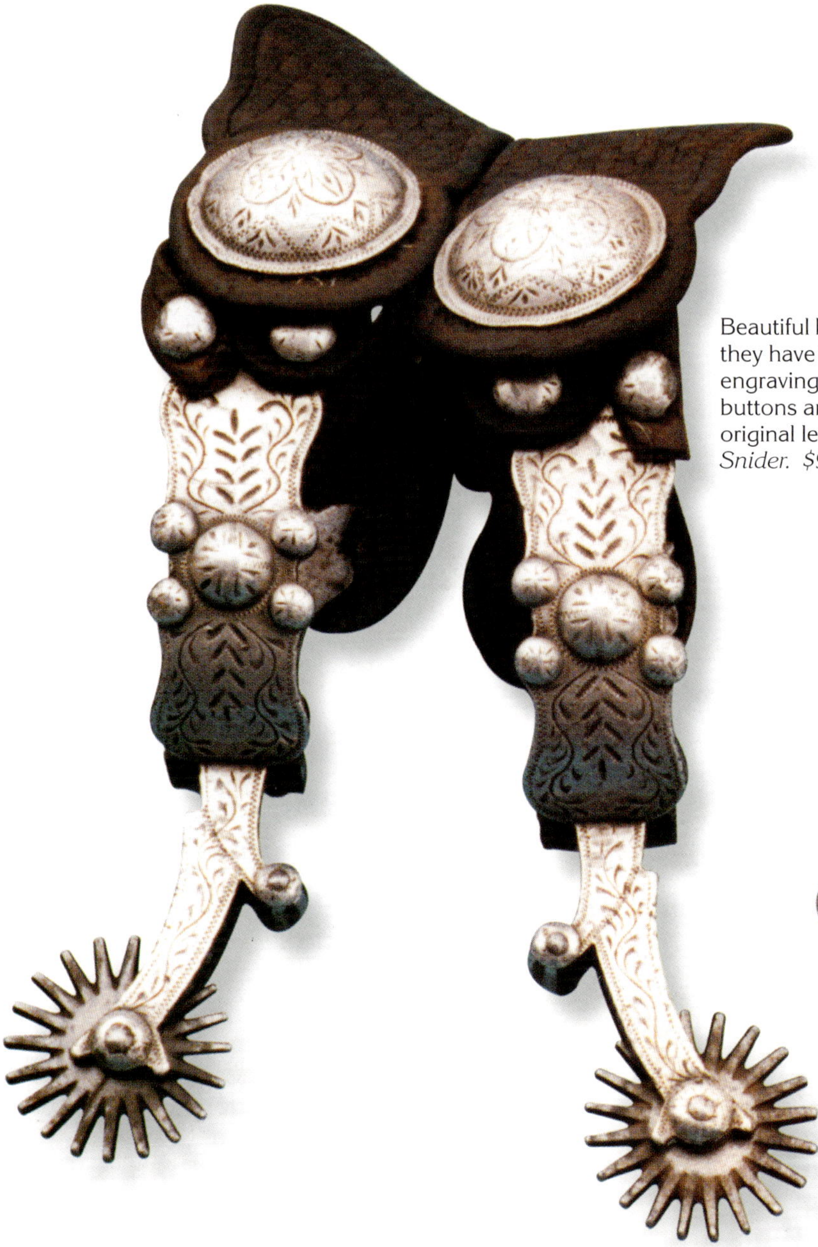

Beautiful hand made spurs marked "Qualey Bros" they have twenty point rowels and fine detailed engraving. In excellent condition they have double buttons and large Qualey made conchos on the original leathers. *Courtesy Paul and Marlene Snider. $9000 to 11,000*

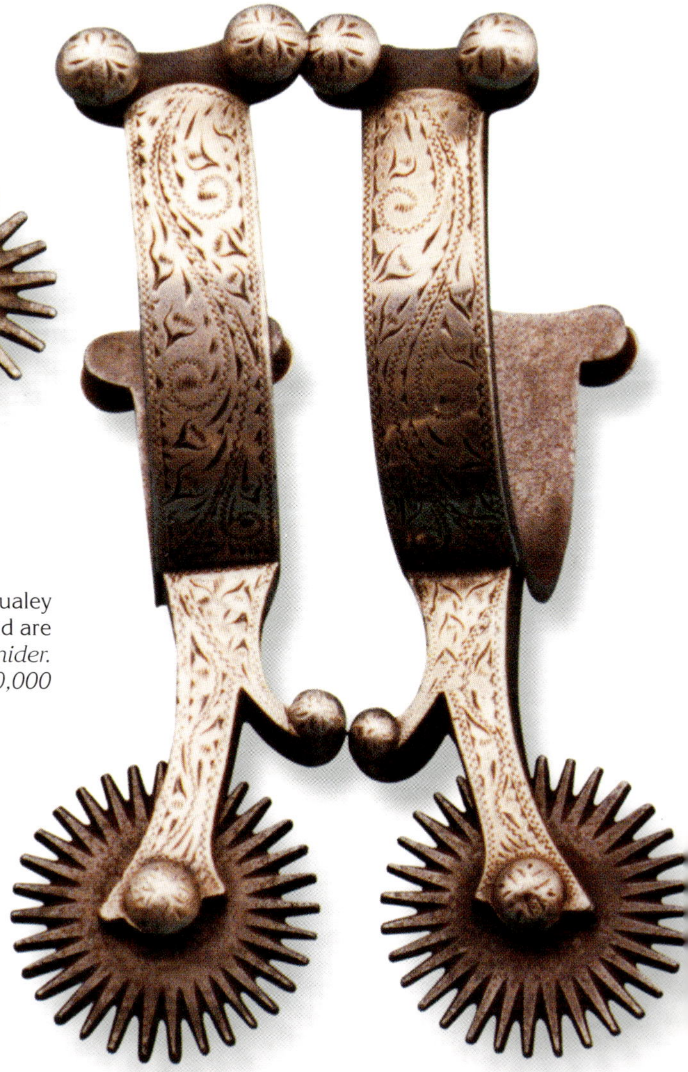

Another pair of exceptional quality spurs made by "Qualey Bros" they have thirty point rowels and double buttons and are in pristine condition. *Courtesy Paul and Marlene Snider. $8000 to 10,000*

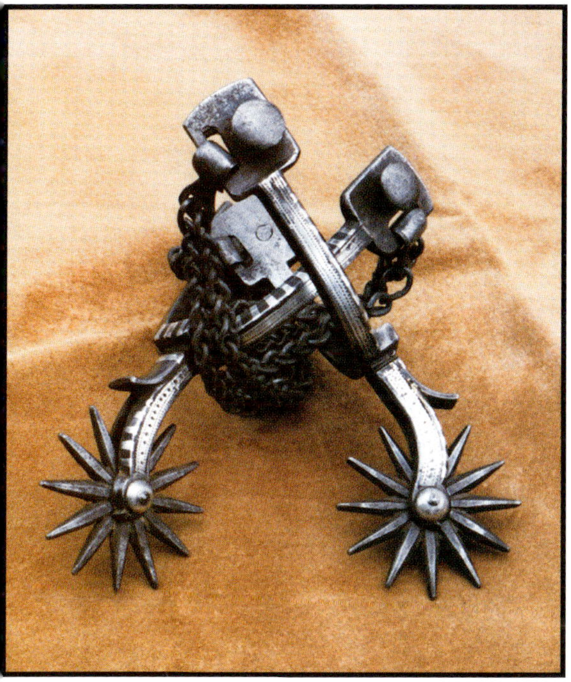

Un-marked, they have exquisite silver inlays and large unique rowels most likely hand made in the 19th century or at best, the early part of 20th century. *Courtesy Paul and Marlene Snider. $1500 to 1700*

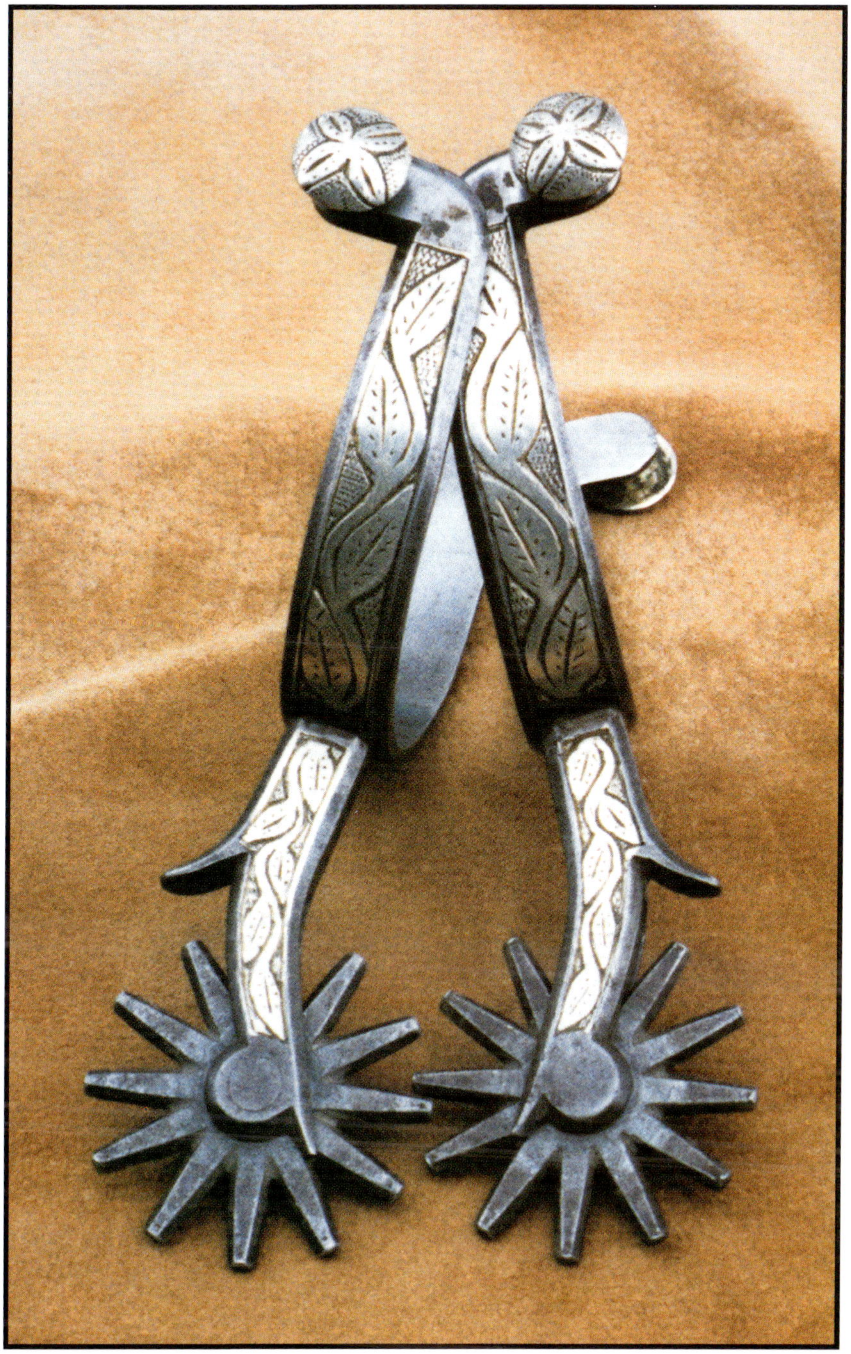

Very Classic Canon City spurs with leaf and vine pattern that seems to occur quite regularly in Canon City, Colorado prison made items. The spurs are in excellent condition and numbered with #9781. *Courtesy Paul and Marlene Snider. $6000 to 7000*

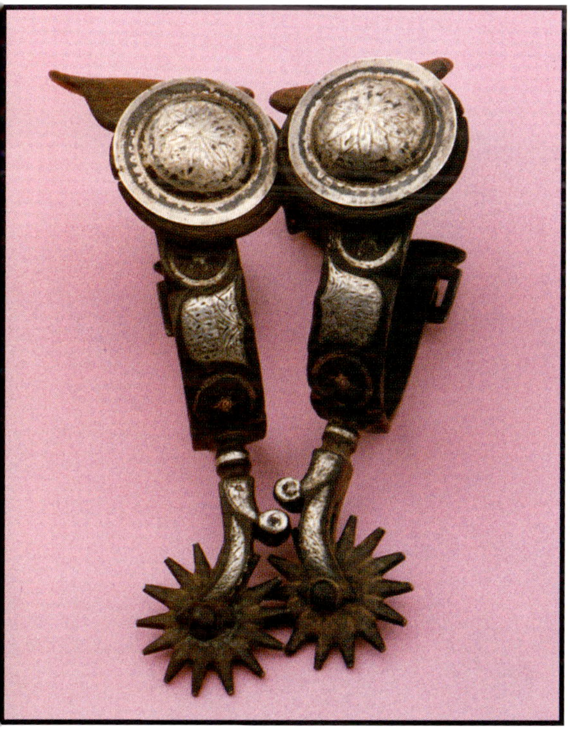

Although un-marked the spurs are attributed to L.D. Stones outlet which would make them current to the mid or late 19th century. They have a patriotic shield on the heel band and large silver conchos on leathers. *Courtesy Paul and Marlene Snider. $3500 to 4500*

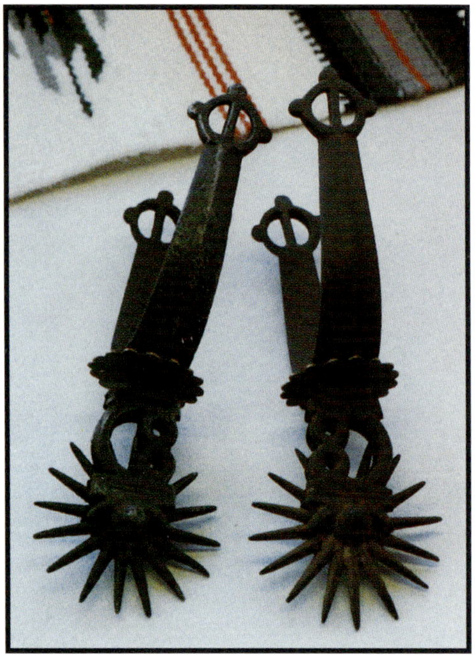

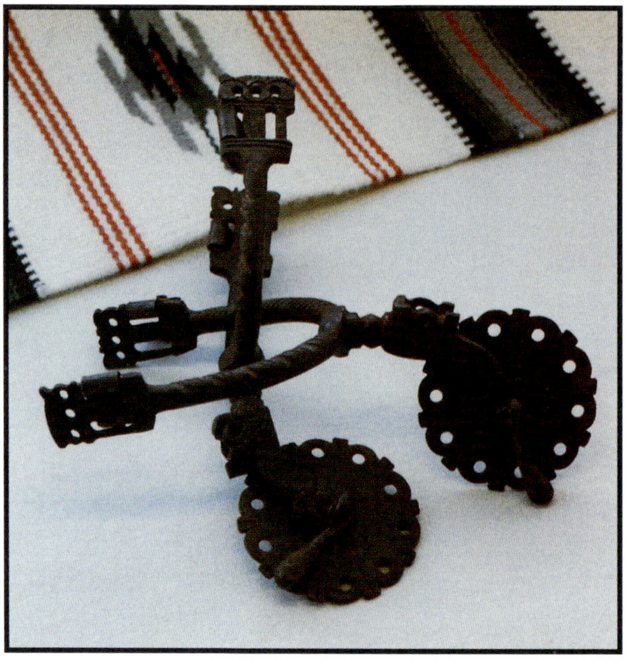

Another Spanish colonial type pair of spurs with single *pajedos* and large round rowels. The twisted metal on heel band is typical of early Spanish made spurs. *Courtesy Wade Brumley. $800 to 1500*

Quite possibly Spanish colonial, they are reminiscent of style and type and are in very good condition. *Courtesy Wade Brumley. $800 to 1200*

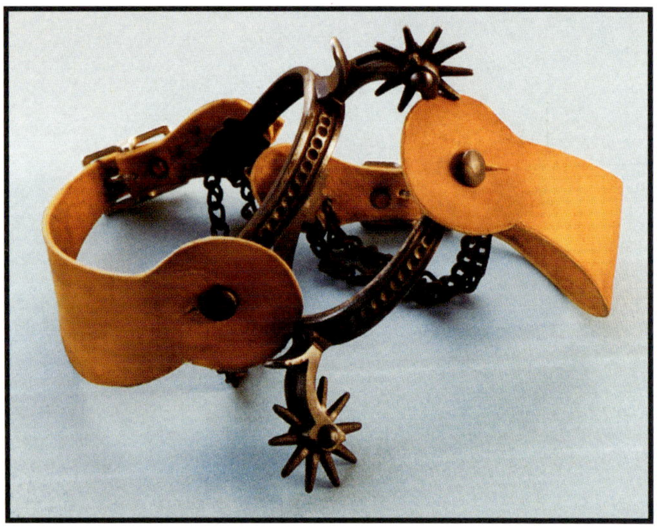

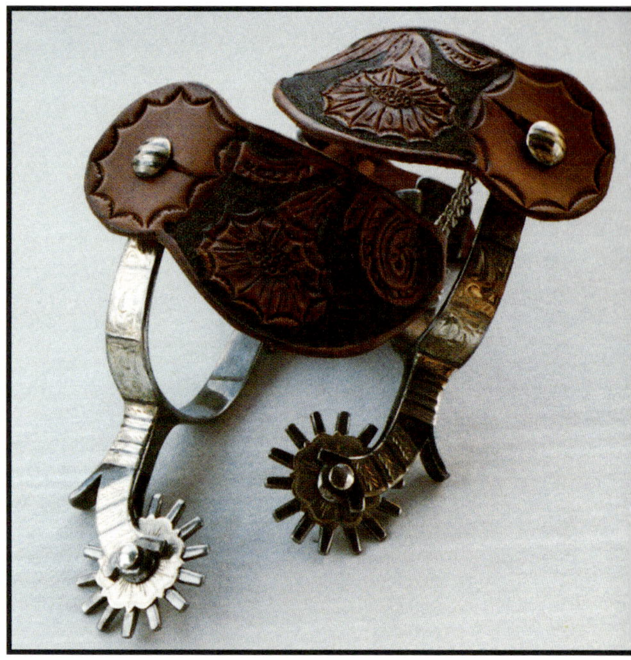

August Buermann is the maker of these little iron spurs. They are perfectly honest in their presentation and have simple iron chased design. *Overton collection. $350 to 400*

Marked "EG" they are considered contemporary in appointment yet they are reminiscent of early styles with a unique hand tooled pair of leathers they make an attractive pair. *Overton collection. $400 to 475*

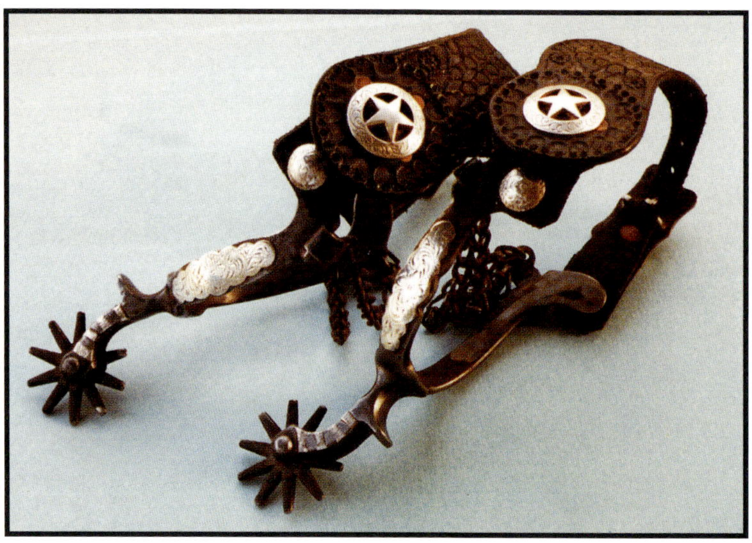

North and Judd blanks they have been silver mounted and are quite attractive with Texas star conchos on leathers they make a very beautiful pair. *Overton collection. $500*

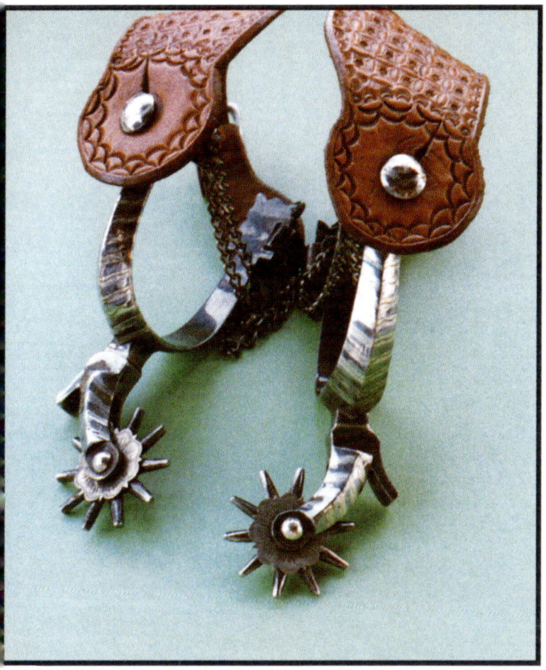

The spurs are made by Les Garcia making them somewhat contemporary but with very lovely silver inlays and rowel guards. Hand tooled leathers. *Overton collection. $400 to 450*

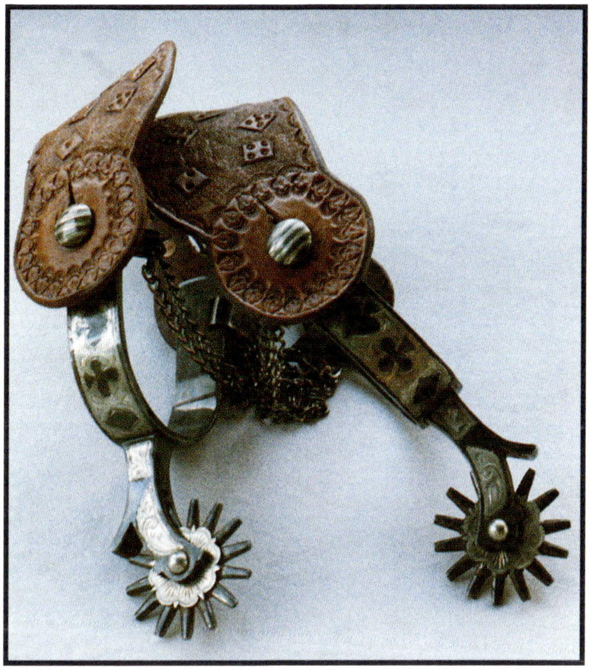

Spurs are un-marked "Card Suits" and are very nicely done. With "Gamblers Dice" on the spur leathers they make a very attractive pair. *Overton collection. $375 to 425*

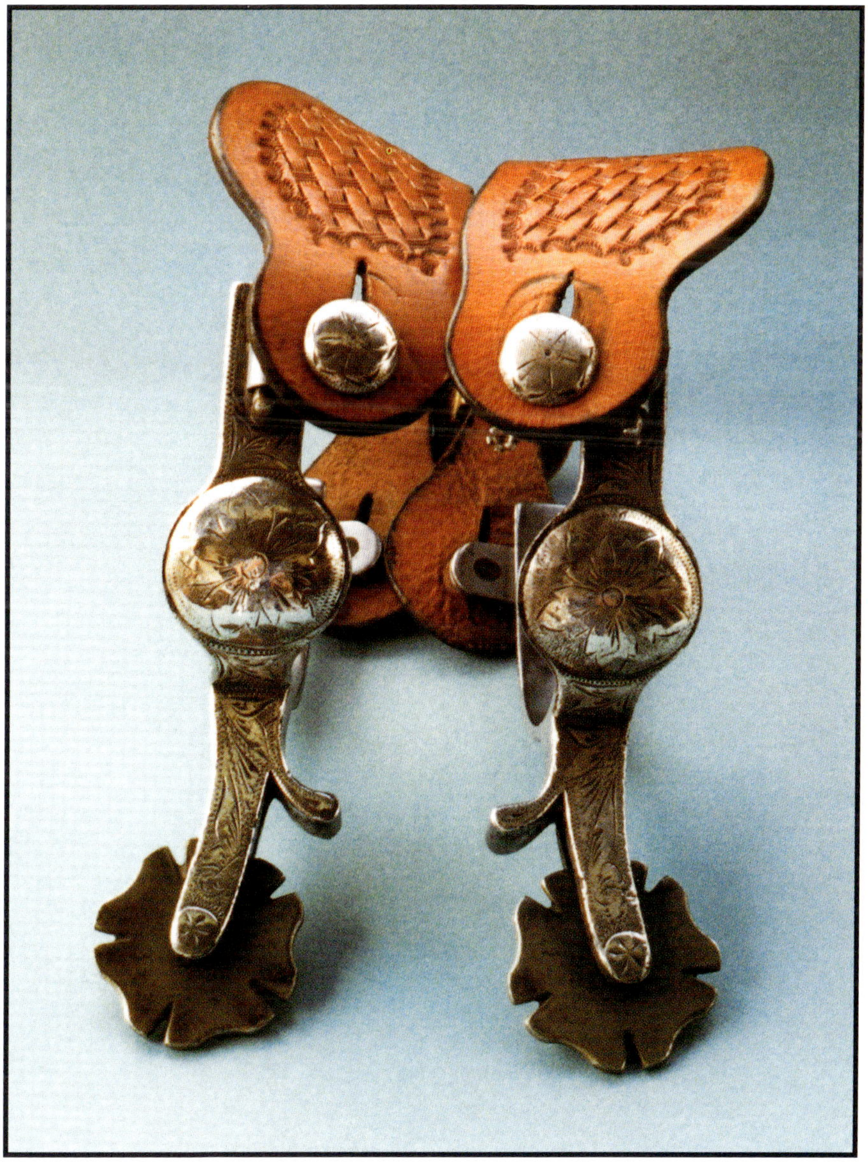

Crockett Parade spurs with cloverleaf rowels and newer leathers, they have seen some wear but are in good shape otherwise. *Courtesy R.C. and Marvin Bales. $1500 to 2000*

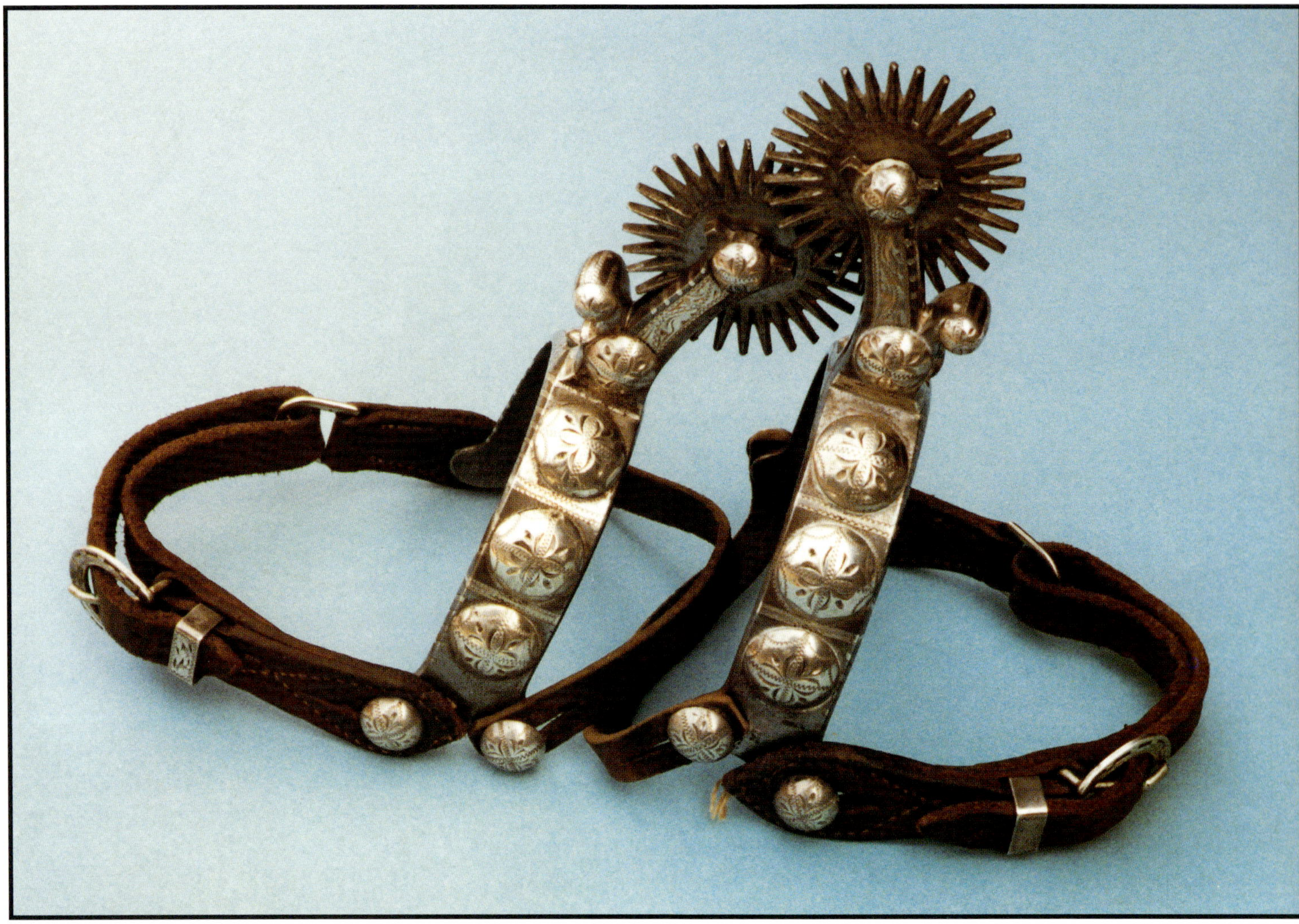

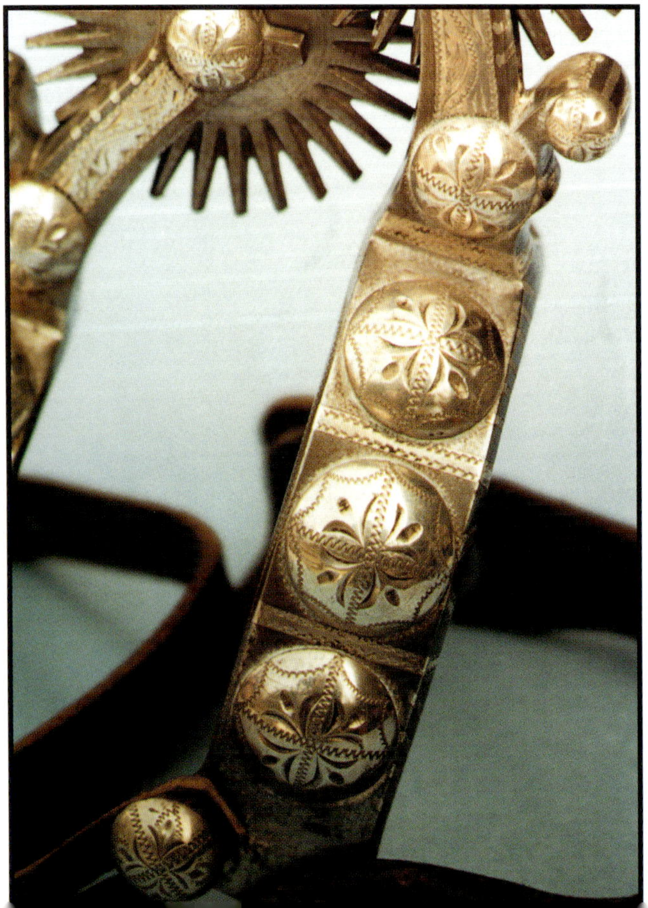

Qualey spurs with the Cheyenne double buttons and thirty point rowels, they are in pristine condition and a lovely pair to behold. Made in the early 1950's, and very collectible today because of the name. *Courtesy private collector. $12,000 to 15,000*

Detail of the very excellent workmanship on the Qualey spurs.

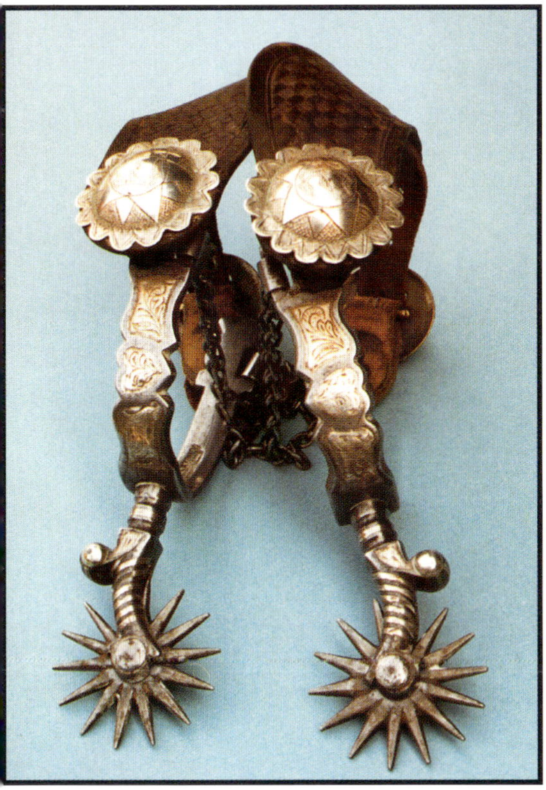

G.S. Garcia, Elko, Nevada, is the maker of these fine spurs, c.1920. The spurs are sporting original leathers and have fourteen point rowels. *Courtesy private collector. $8000 to 9000*

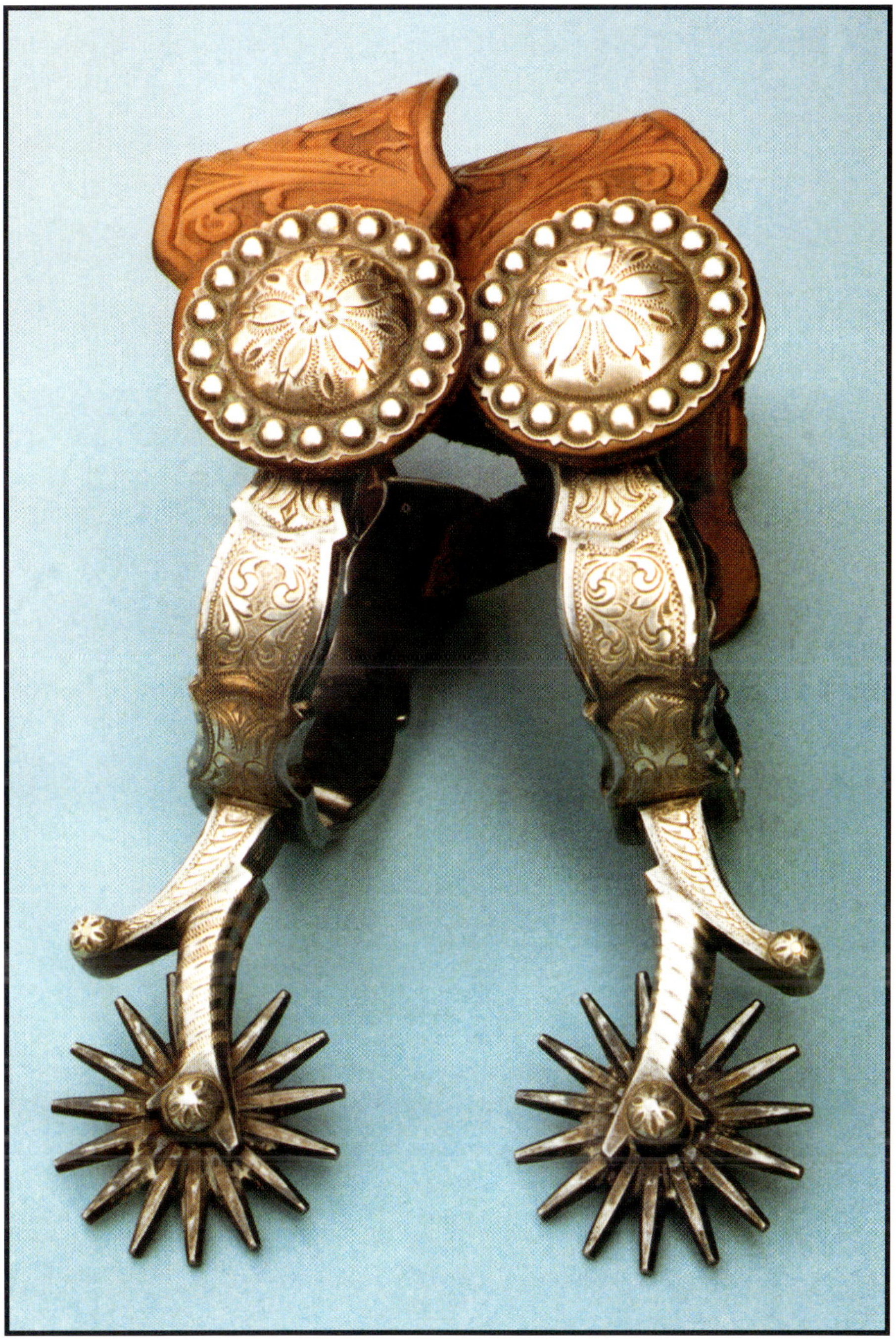

R.W.Graham is the maker of these very beautiful spurs. It is purported that he learned the trade alongside Qualey brothers. The spurs are double marked and have sixteen point rowels. They are also purported to be his last pair made. We bow with reverence to the very talented man. *Courtesy private collector. $12,000*

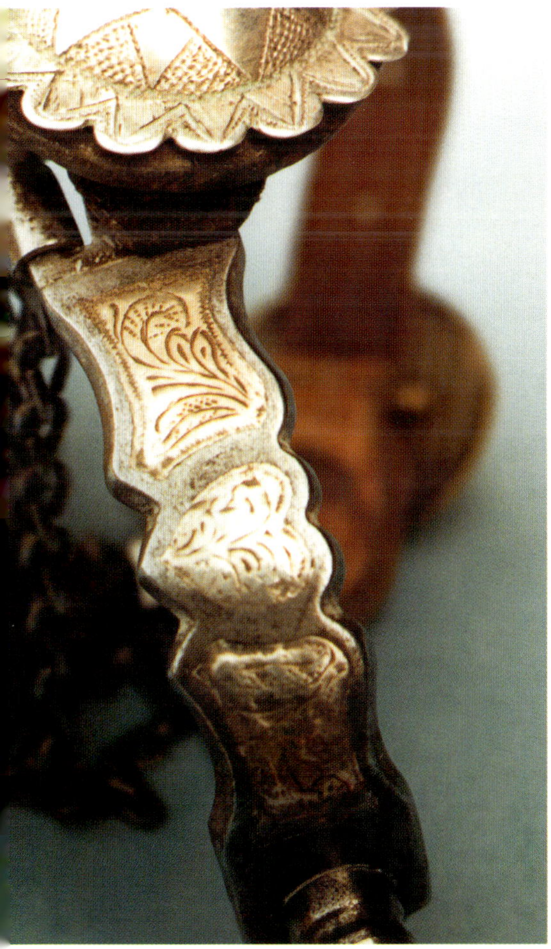

Detail of G.S. Garcia spurs and heart on the heel bands.

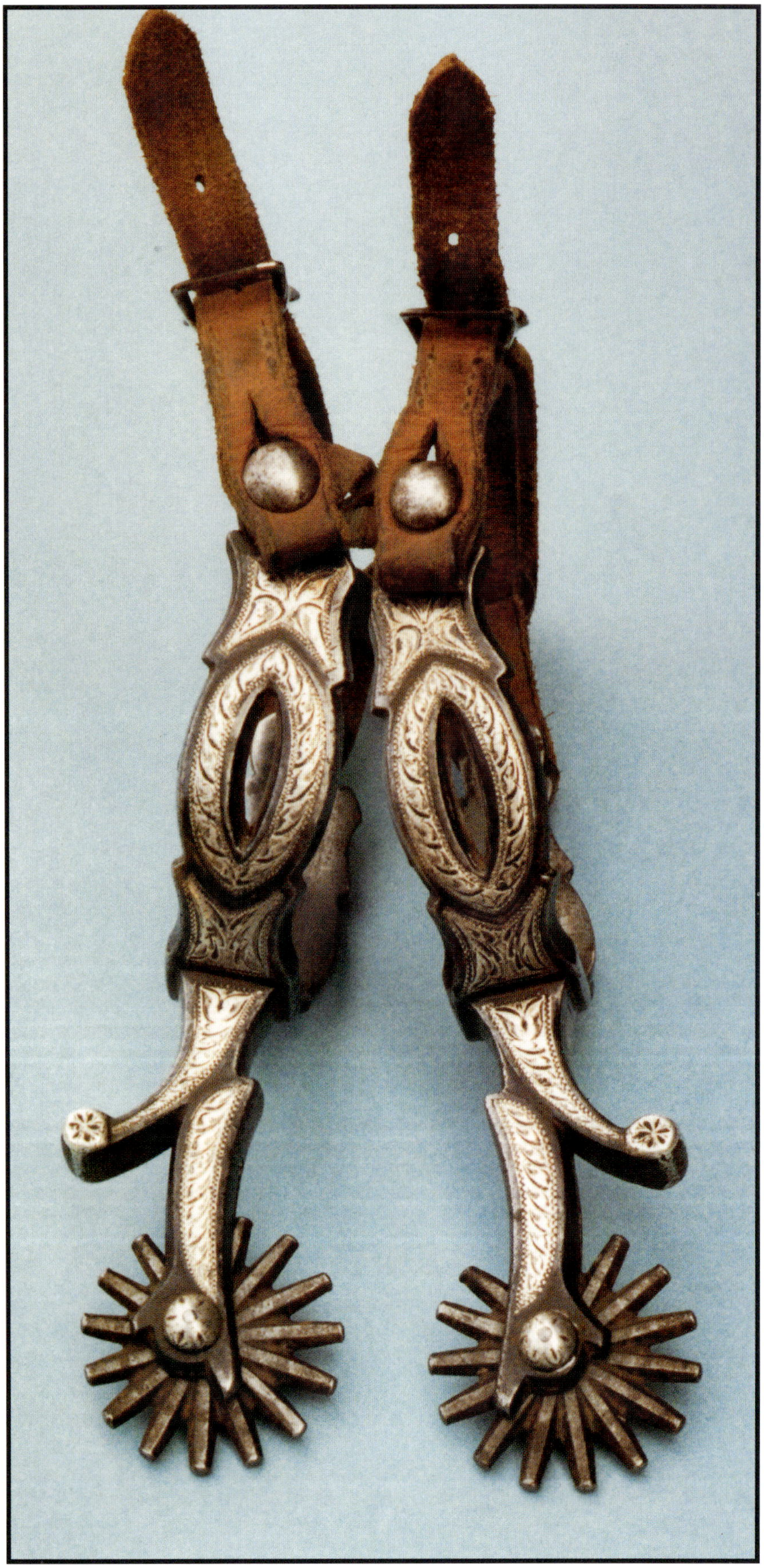

R.W. Graham also made these spurs. They are double mounted sterling silver and fourteen point rowels. *Courtesy private collector. $10,000*

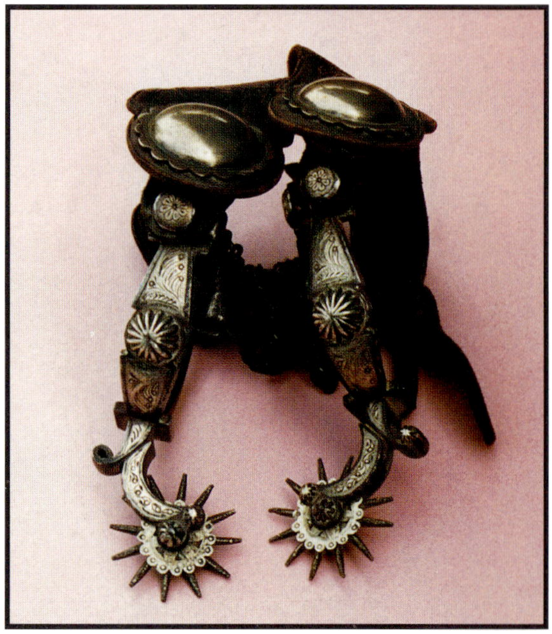

Un-marked, but the spurs are excellent and are made with fine delicate engraving and design. With Jello-mold conchos on the heel bands and twelve point rowels, they are California style drop shanks from another century. *Courtesy private collector. $4000 to 4500*

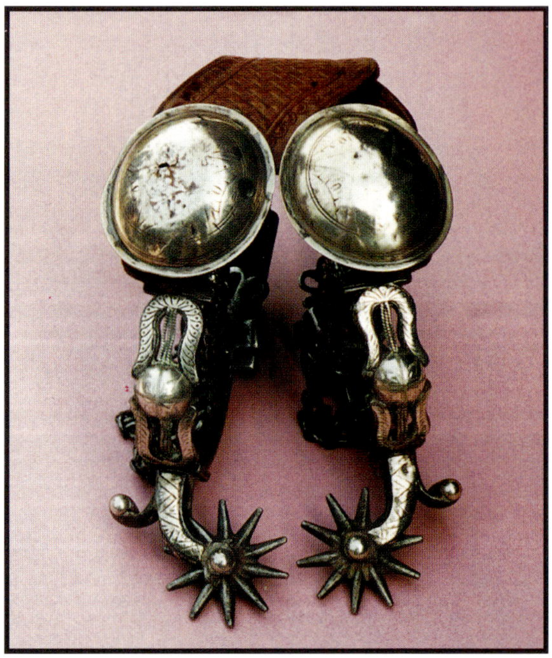

The spurs supposedly arrived in Walla Walla, Washington in 1852 and were owned by the banker there. They are un-marked but they are beautifully rendered with most unique "Harps" with silver wires for strings in center. *Courtesy private collector. $4500 to 5000*

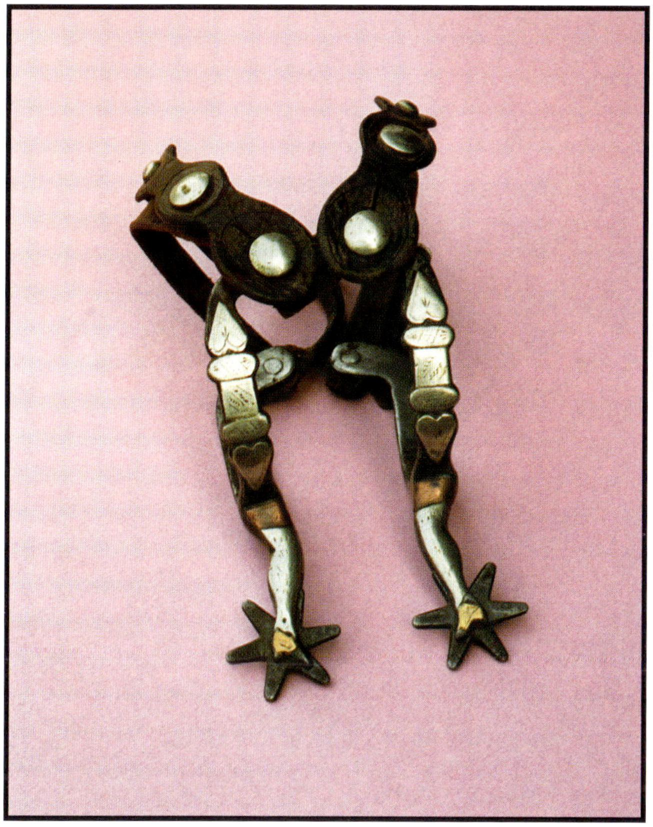

McChesney is the maker of these lady legs, though they have seen some wear, they are still in very good condition. *Courtesy private collector. $900 to 1100*

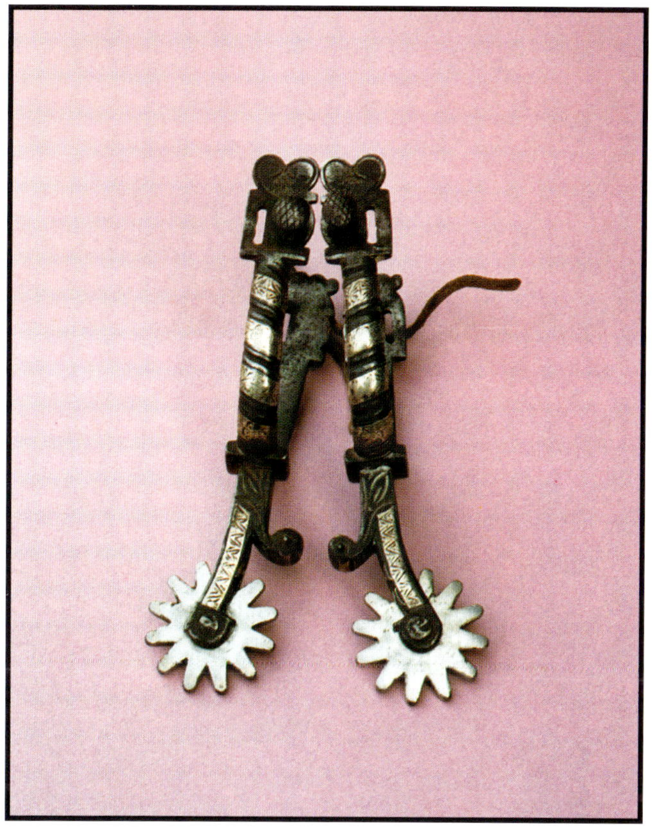

August Buermann is the maker of the spurs and on opposite side they have silver card suits. A most appealing pair in spite of replaced rowels. *Courtesy private collector. $200 to 300*

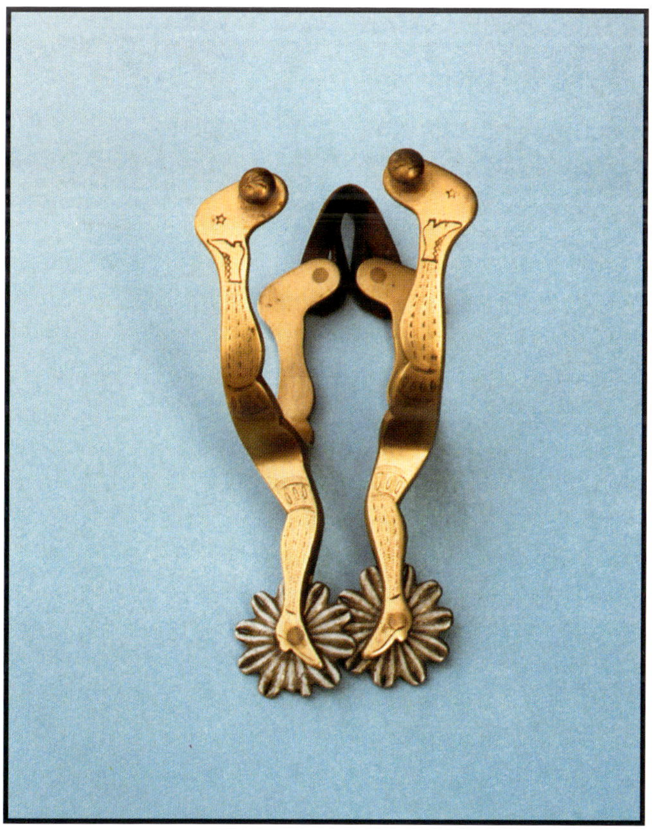

Hercules Bronze the spurs are August Buermann's and are in pristine condition. *Courtesy private collector. $400 to 475*

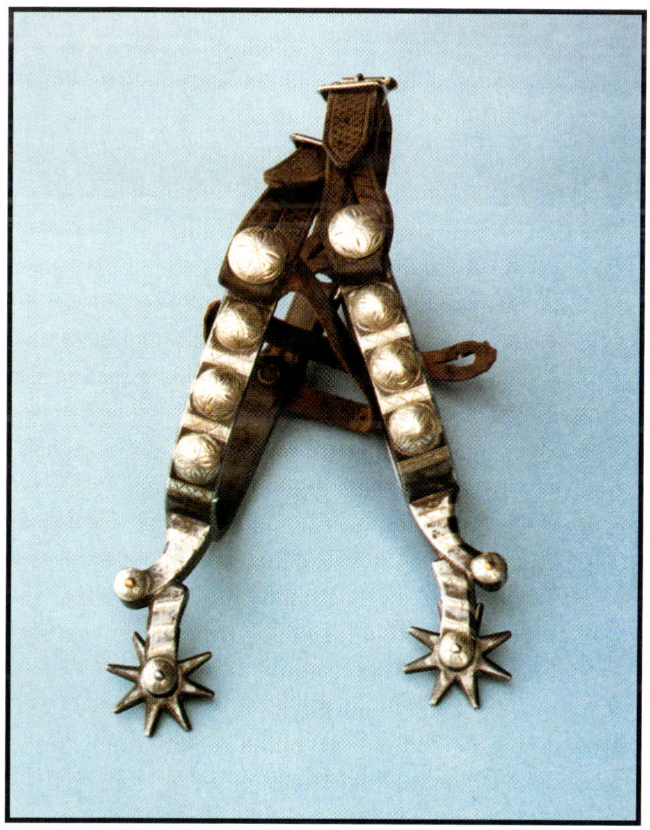

The spurs are un-marked but are attributed to a fellow who was a sheepherder? Nothing more seems to be known. They are excellent workmanship. *Courtesy private collector. $1600 to 1800*

Chapter Three

Native American

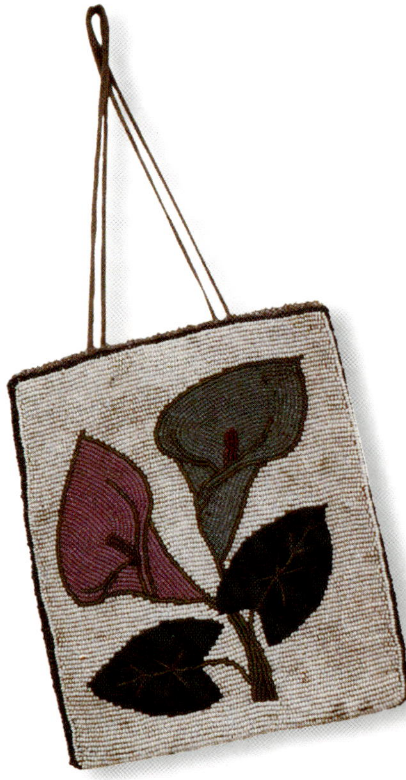

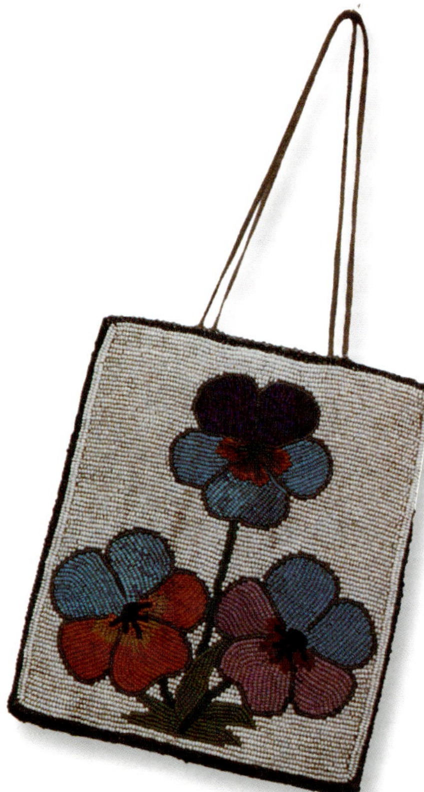

"Cowboys and Indians"

The beauty of colorful items that are unique to Native American cultures is highly appealing. Many of the items cowboys used in their line of work came to them through their interrelations with Native Americans. Some are directly related to their use of horses.

Cornhusk bags

Cornhusk bags were made by Native Americans of the Pacific northwestern plateau and are unique to that area, for they are found nowhere else in North America. Though they are most often referred to as "Nez Perce cornhusk bags," many different tribal groups in the area made them.

At their onset, these were utilitarian bags used to gather and store edible roots, which were a staple food to all the plateau people. They were often used as part of the ritual exchanges made when a marriage took place. The groom's family generally furnished horses, leather, dried fish, and meat; the bride's always included twined bags filled with dried roots and berries, along with other beadwork and baskets. The ritual of gift exchange was seemingly simple, yet it served as the basis of a strong marriage for the couple, since the family members were off on the right foot with each other in the giving and receiving of gifts. The exchanges were always made with the other family's counterparts: the groom's aunt traded a gift with the bride's aunt, and so forth.

Sometime after 1875, the use of root foods declined, as roots became more difficult to obtain. Euro-American farmers plowed root fields, and between the changing of topography and perhaps localized weather patterns, roots were not so available. The sizes and shapes of the twined bags began to change. Large, deep bags were no longer widely needed. Though still used for food purposes, they also were used to hold personal belongings on long journeys and generally hung over a "squaw" saddle; therefore, *these bags actually represent the first saddle bags in existence!*

Since it was the women who traditionally had been both bag weavers and root gatherers, it was only natural that they would adapt the bags to other functions. Soon they began to carry them in much the same way that non-Indian women would carry a handbag. Before long, the bags were brightly decorated in multiple color schemes, and finer twine was being used. These changes took place gradually in Plateau culture, most likely between the time span of about 1850 and 1900.

If you have any knowledge of the northwest Plateau region, you soon learn that these Native Americans lived on fish from the Colum-

Opposite page:

Top: Cala lillies on a white background with pansies on the reverse make this lovely bag unique and most desirable. *Courtesy Ron and Sharon Mailloux. $1000 to 1500*

Bottom: Reverse of the calla lilly bag.

bia River valley and were gatherers, not farmers by tradition. The Nez Perce people were not corn planters. You may rightly ask how the Nez Perce obtained the cornhusks for the bags they wove. This mystery was solved for me when I learned that even though the techniques of the actual weaving never changed, the materials have. The earliest bags were woven entirely of Indian hemp (*Apocynum cannabinum*) and some were decorated with designs of false embroidered beargrass (*Xerophyllum tenax)*. Since Euro-American settlers came to the Plateau in the early nineteenth century, introducing agriculture to the area as early as 1826, corn (*Zea mays)* was grown from that time on. Indian weavers may have recognized the husks of corn as being quite useful, and certainly the husks were not used for much by those who grew corn. One can only assume that the corn husks were salvaged and/or gleaned by Native Americans in the Plateau region early in the nineteenth century. One cornhusk bag with false-embroidered cornhusk designs was collected by Henry Spalding during his tenure as a missionary to the Nez Perce between 1836 and 1847. It is one of the earliest examples known.

By 1870, the introduction of wool yarn by early settlers brought a new material to the bags being woven. Analine-dyed yarns became common and available. With these facts in hand, it becomes easier to date a cornhusk bag. Although some may not like to admit it, these bags preceded the cowboy's saddle bags and military bags, so we have Native Americans to thank for this helpful innovation, among many others.

Moccasins

A few beaded moccasins are included here because, in a strange and distant way, they also tie in with the equipment bought and used by early frontier cowboys. In the Time Life book entitled *The Cowboys*,there are photos of an early frontier Montana cowboy-turned-cattle baron and his Shoshone Indian wife, Aubony. The lady raised nine of their own children and two of his dead brother's. She was a full blood Shoshone and from the photo provided you can be sure that *this cowboy's wife wore moccasins.*

Gauntlets

Beaded gauntlets are another helpful item from Native American origin that carried the cowboy through many tough labors. The gloves were durable, warm, and often kept his arms from being scratched; therefore they were another invaluable item of equipment. Of course, the gloves he was able to procure for his work usually were not beaded originally. But when he found beaded ones available to him through trade with a Native American woman, he seldom passed them up. Since many people still do not understand the value of them, some even have been reported being used to dig in the garden!

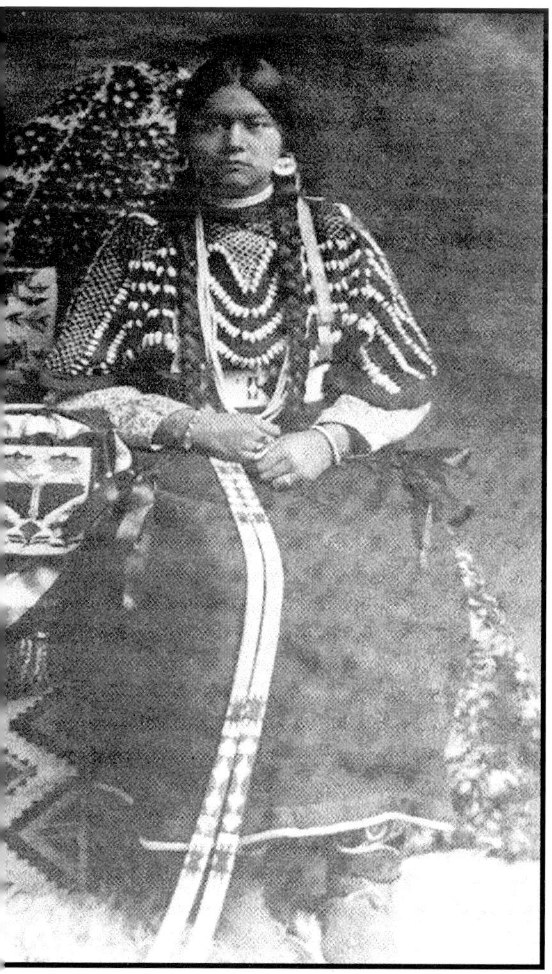

Nez Perce maiden with beautiful bags and ornamented dress. Most of the bags were created with a verso/recto effect, in that both sides were decorated with designs that varied somewhat. *Photo courtesy Ron and Sharon Mailloux.*

This bag is unique with a small extra pocket at the bottom. Note the flag and swastika designs used jointly, which is rare. *The swastika was quite often used in the 19th century by Native Americans. Courtesy Ron and Sharon Mailloux.* $5500 to 6000

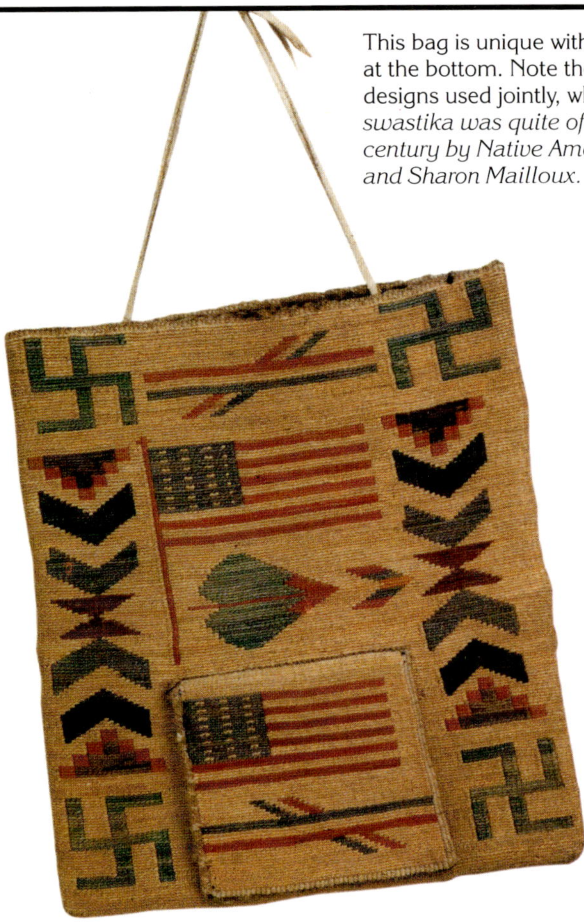

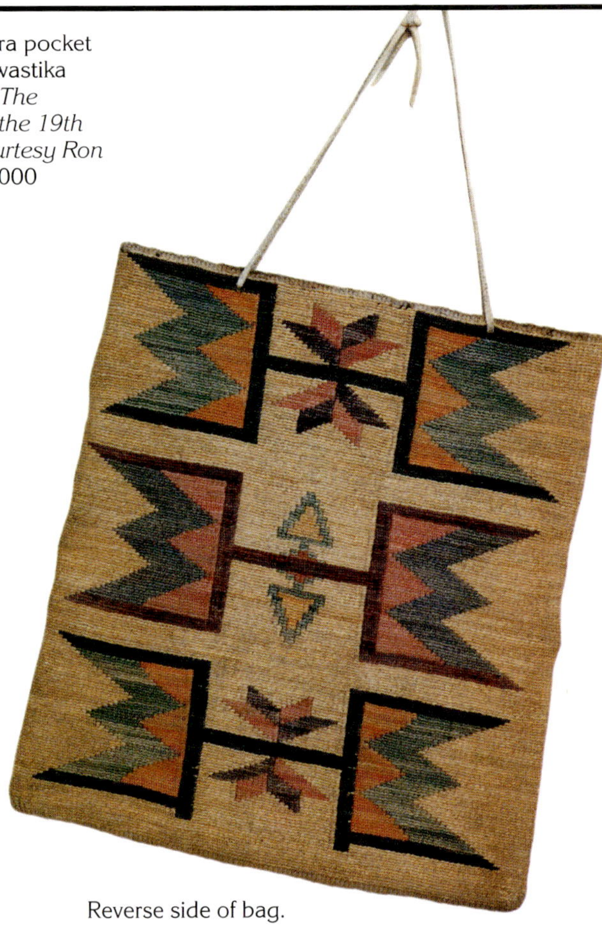

Reverse side of bag.

Extra large corn husk bag rare to find in such fine condition. *Courtesy Ron and Sharon Mailloux. $5000 to 5800*

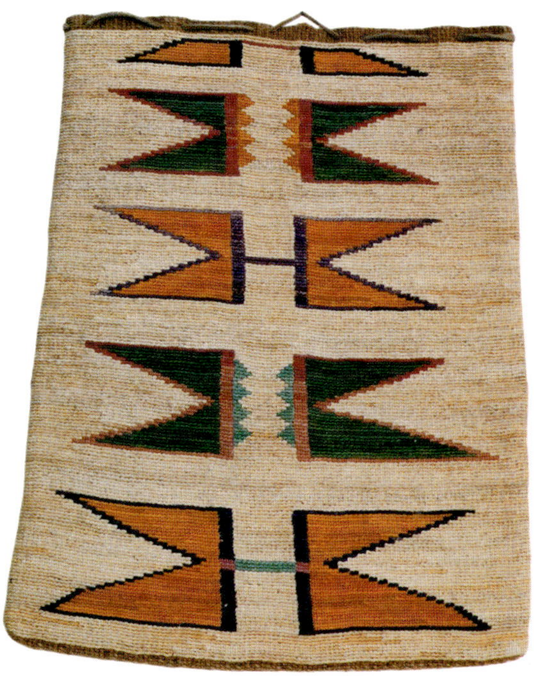

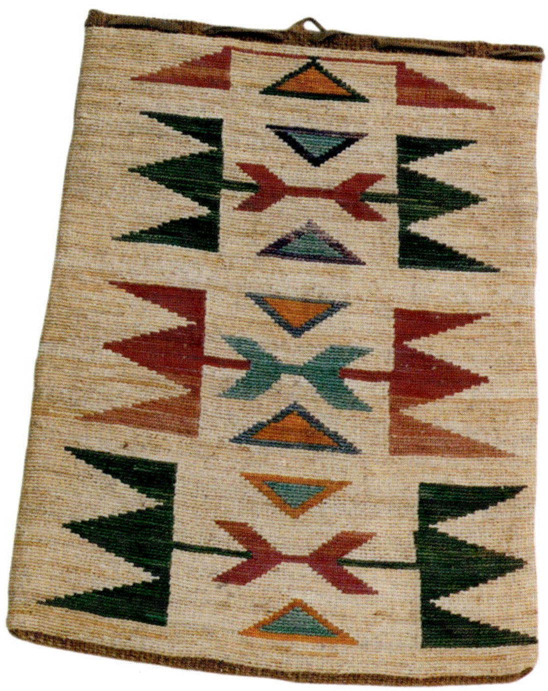

Reverse side of bag.

Extra large corn husk bag with beautiful geometric design. *Courtesy Ron and Sharon Mailloux. $4500 to 5000*

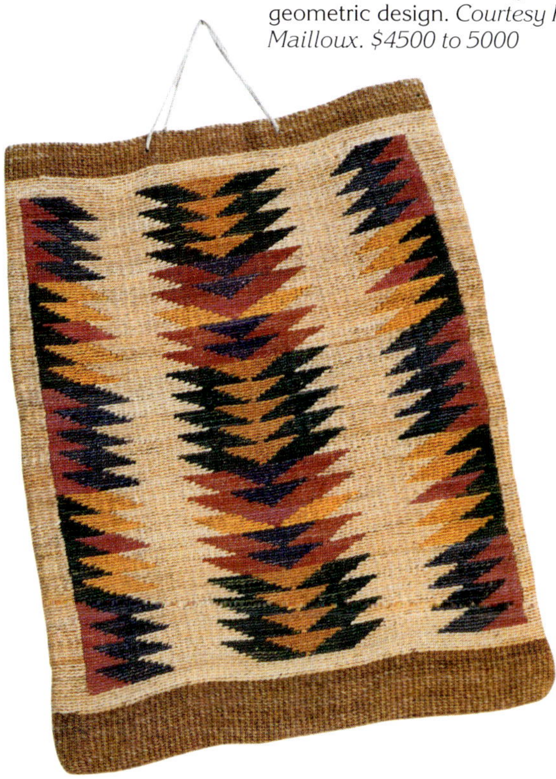

Reverse side of bag.

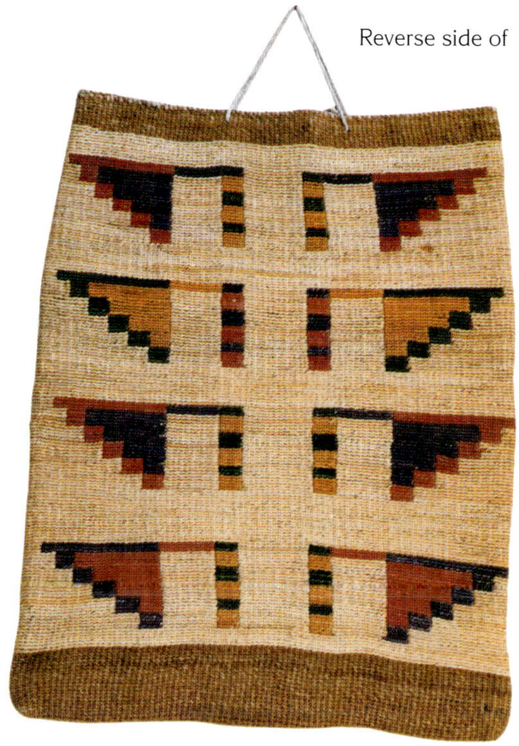

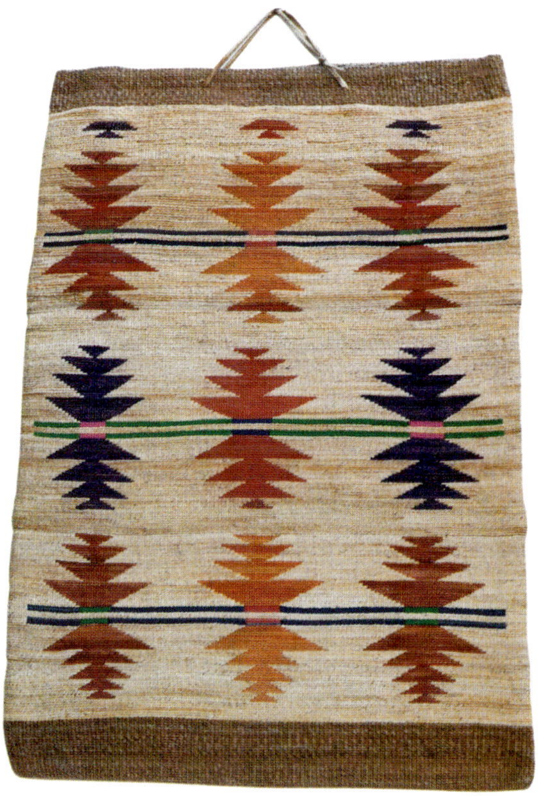

Reverse side of bag.

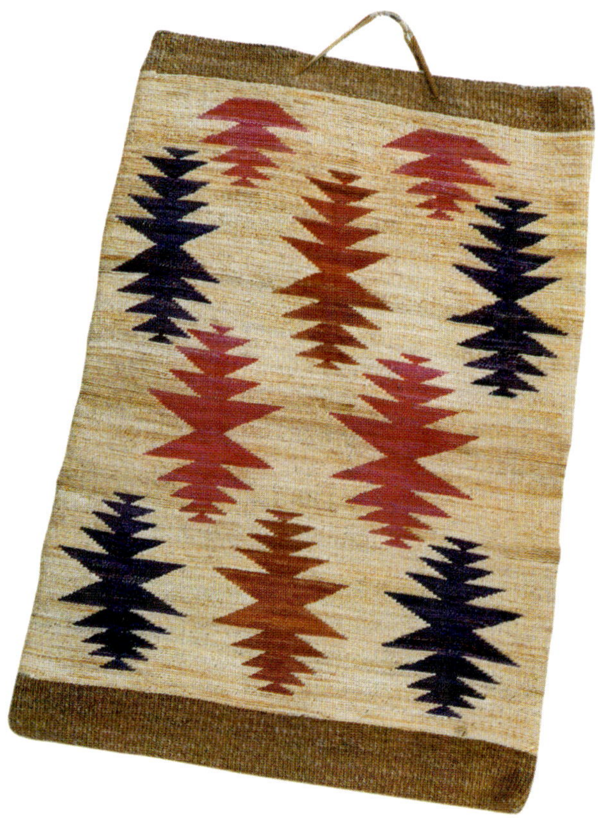

A very large, old and beautiful corn husk bag in pristine condition. The larger ones are usually older. *Courtesy Ron and Sharon Mailloux. $4000 to 5000*

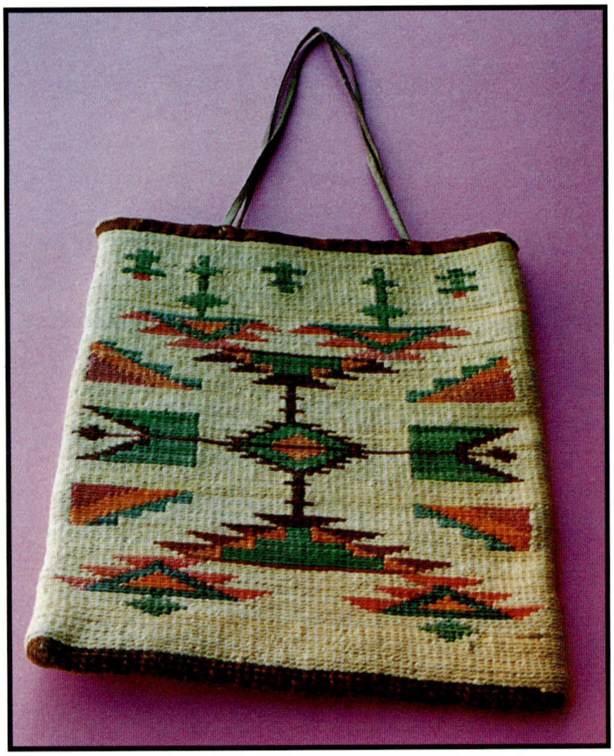

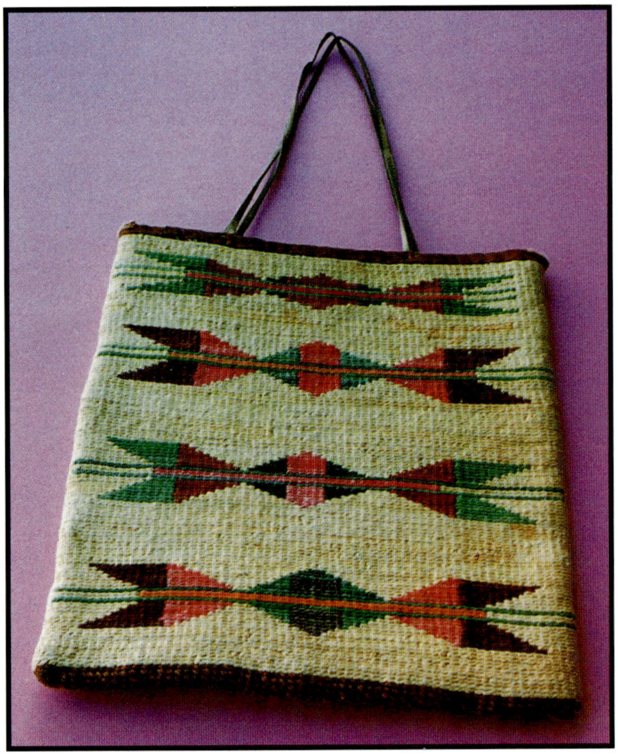

Reverse side of bag.

This lovely bag, woven with a pastel design, is especially graceful and attractive. *Courtesy Ron and Sharon Mailloux. $800 to 1000*

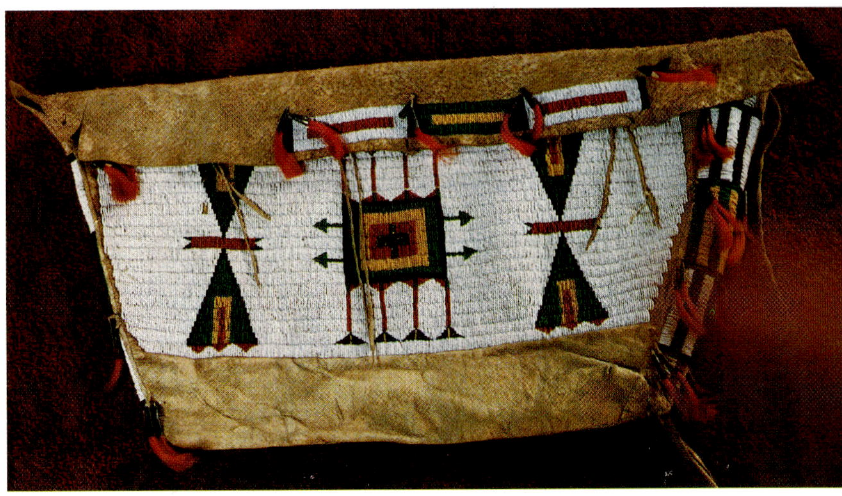

This bag is approximately 18" by 34" and beaded with "lazy squaw" stitching. Bags of this size were often called "possible" bags, since they held almost anything possible. *Courtesy Ron and Sharon Mailloux. $3000 to 5000*

A most unusual design with peacock and butterfly on a large and perfectly beautiful bag. *Courtesy Ron and Sharon Mailloux. $800 to 1200*

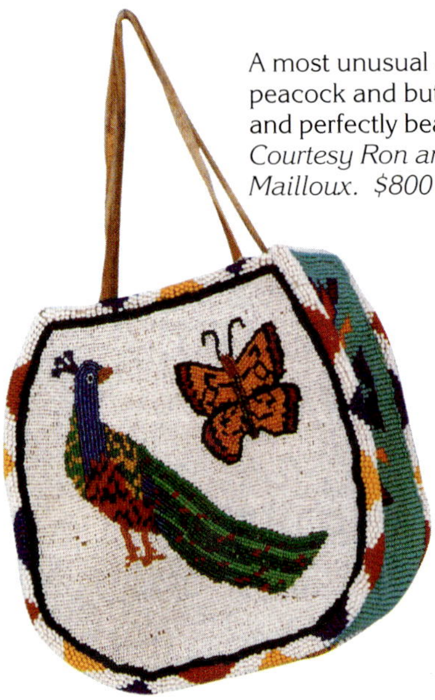

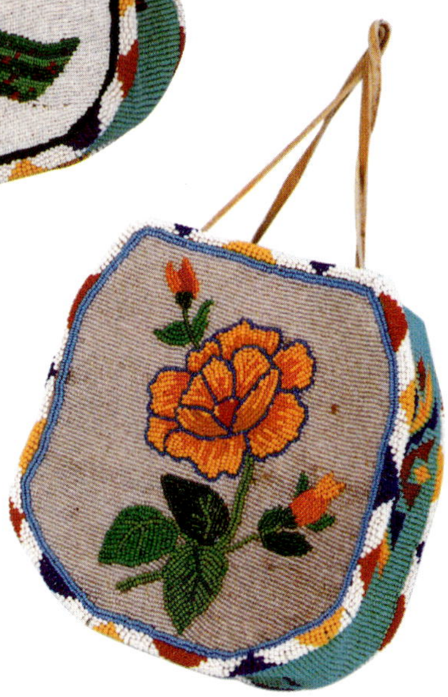

Reverse side of the peacock bag.

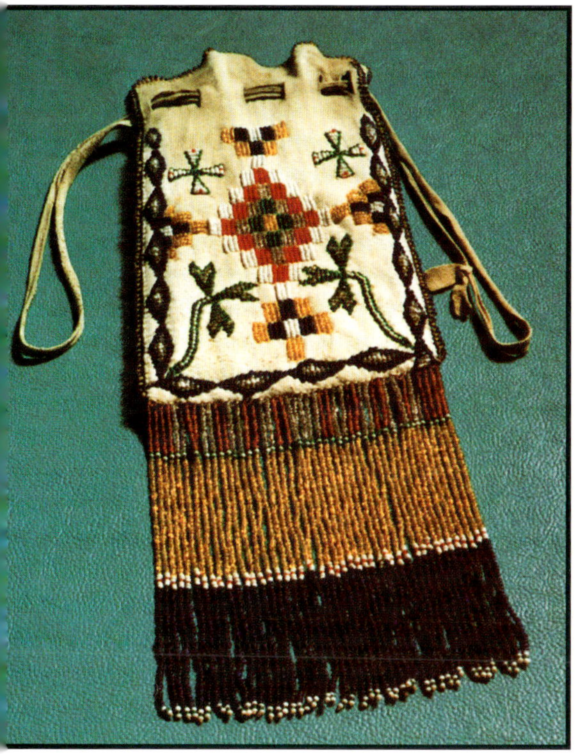

A very rare example of Apache beadwork in a long, fringe-trimmed bag with verso/recto designs, c.1904. *Courtesy Ron and Sharon Mailloux. $400 to 500*

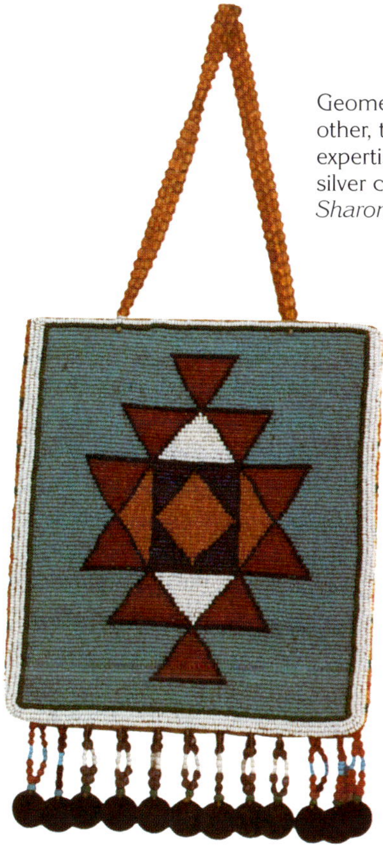

Geometric on one side and roses on the other, this bag was finely beaded with great expertise. The fringe is larger beads with old silver coins dangling. *Courtesy Ron and Sharon Mailloux. $1000 to 1500*

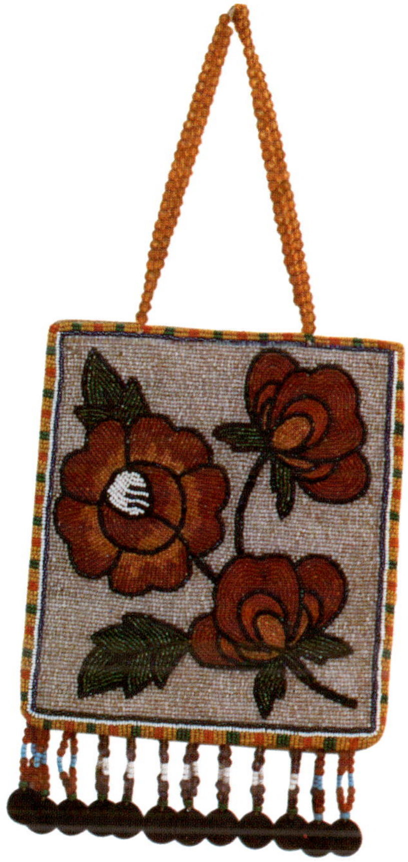

Reverse side of coin-trimmed bag.

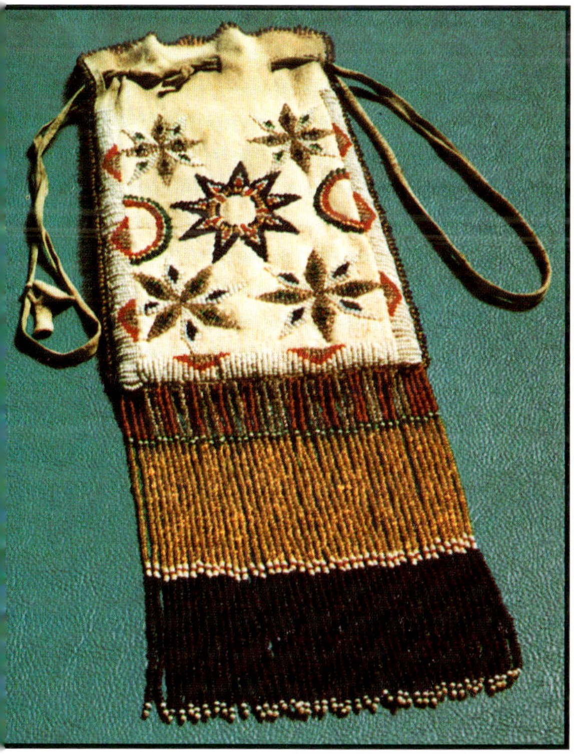

Reverse side of Apache beaded bag.

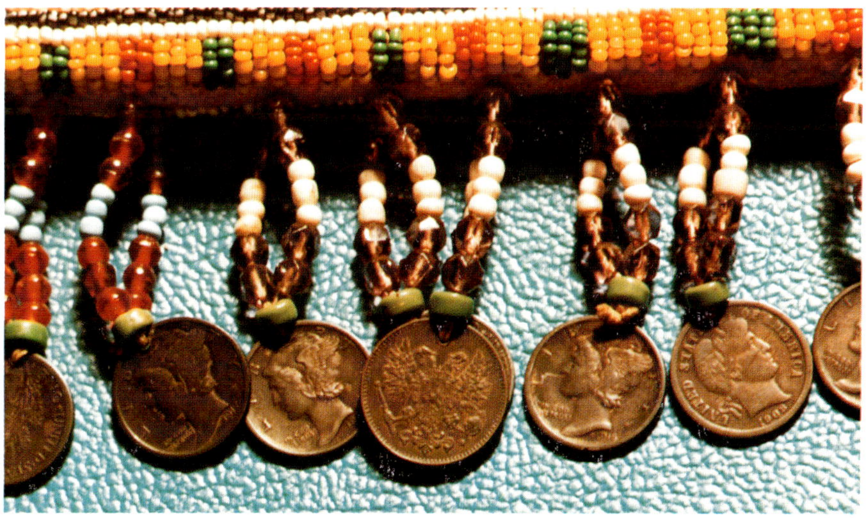

Detail of old coins on the bag.

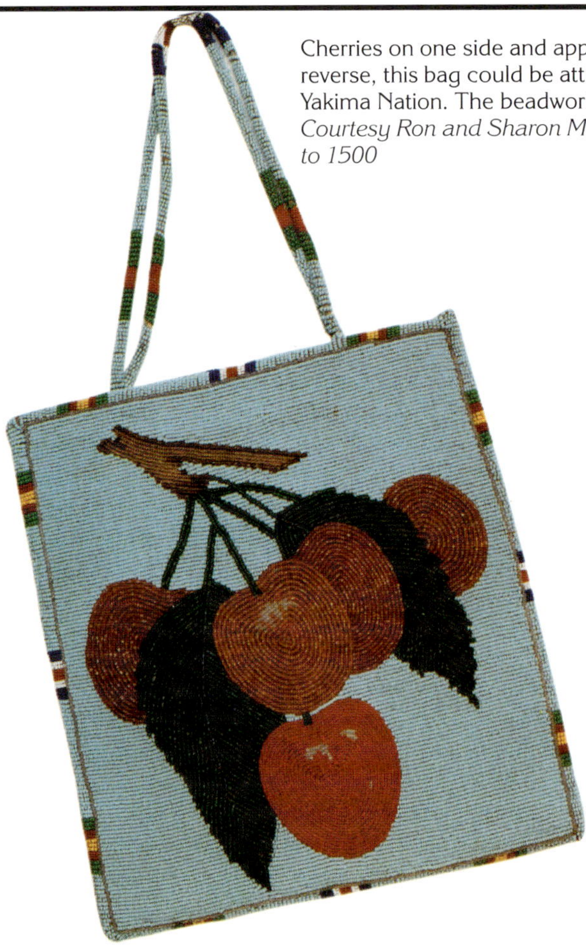

Cherries on one side and apple design on reverse, this bag could be attributed to the Yakima Nation. The beadwork is finely done. *Courtesy Ron and Sharon Mailloux. $1000 to 1500*

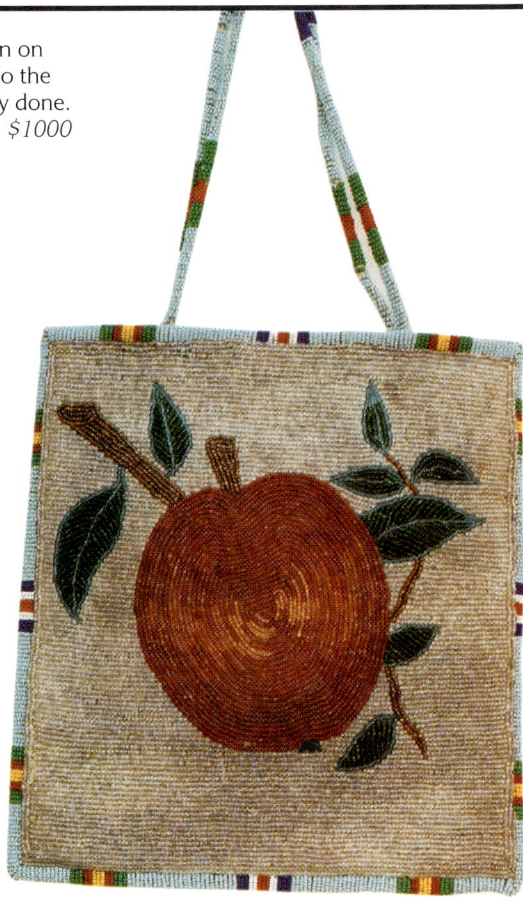

Reverse side of the cherries bag.

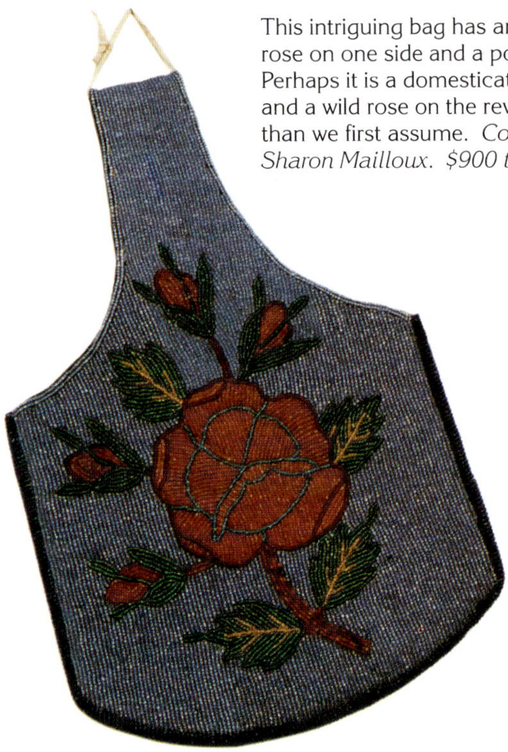

This intriguing bag has an unusual shape with a rose on one side and a poppy on the reverse. Perhaps it is a domesticated rose on one side and a wild rose on the reverse, depicting more than we first assume. *Courtesy Ron and Sharon Mailloux. $900 to 1400*

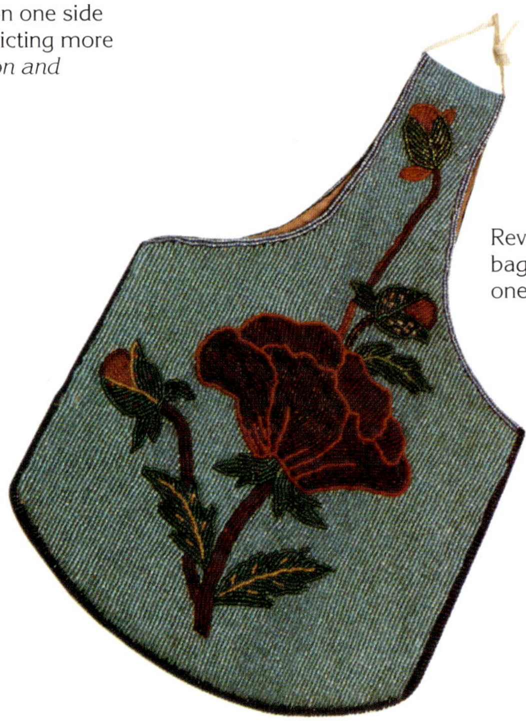

Reverse side of the rose bag showing the "wild" one.

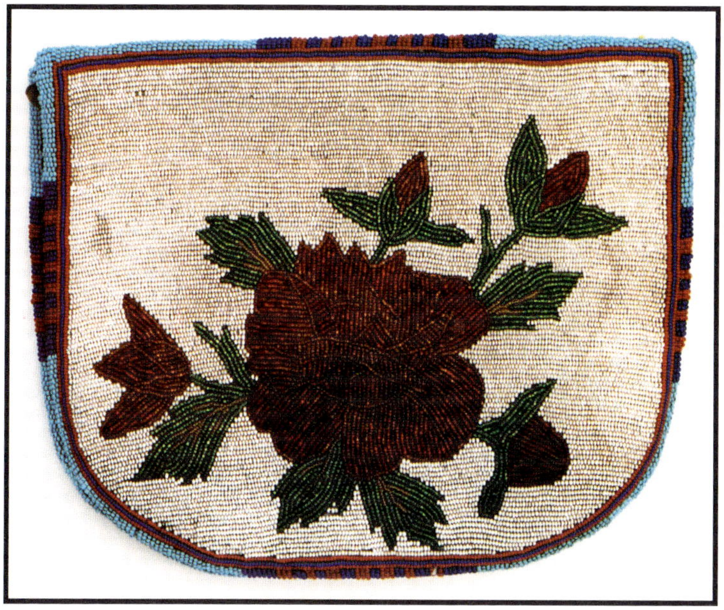

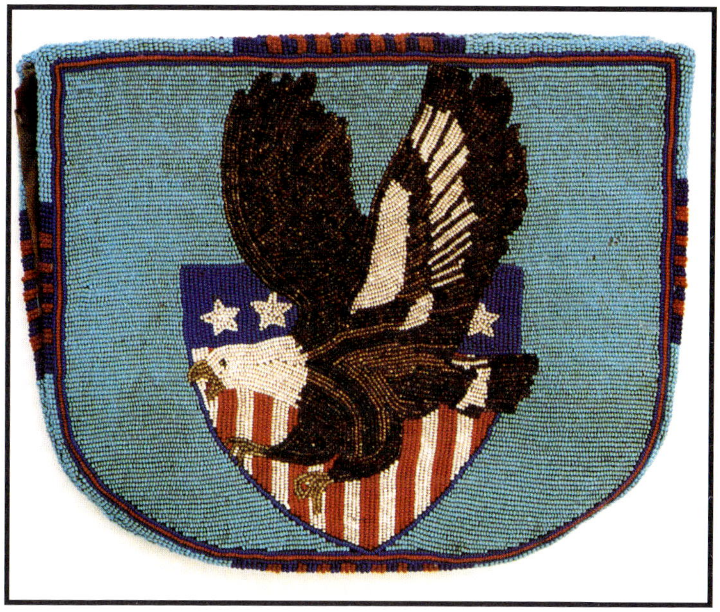

This fully beaded bag depicts an American Beauty rose on one side and an eagle with the American crest on the other. *Courtesy Ron and Sharon Mailloux. $1500 to 1800*

Reverse of the rose bag.

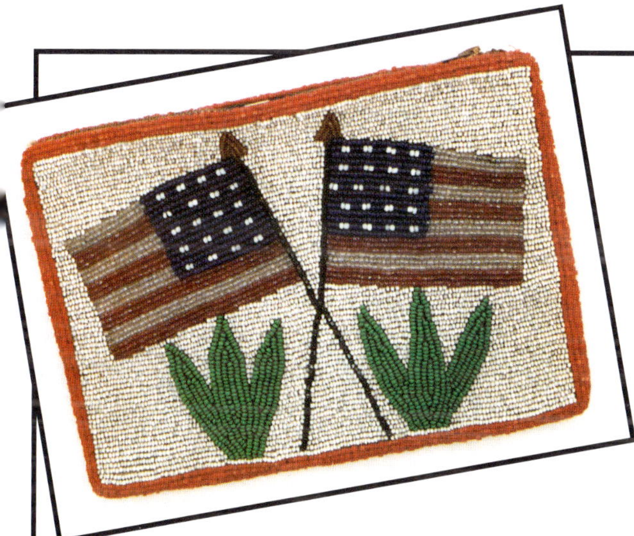

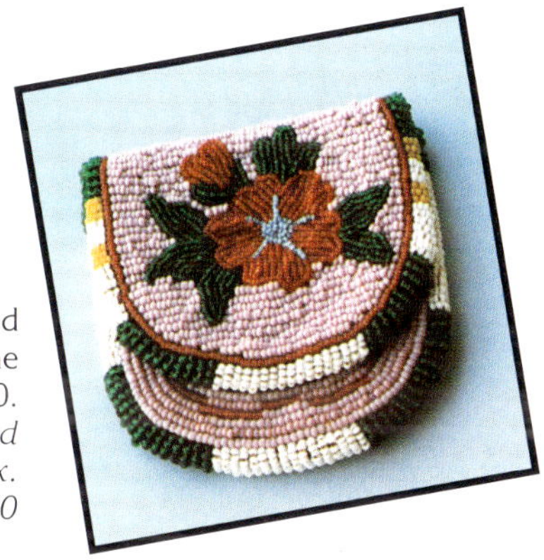

Watch pouch beaded and attributed to the Nez Perce, c. 1900. *Courtesy Ron and Sharon Mailloux. $300 to 600*

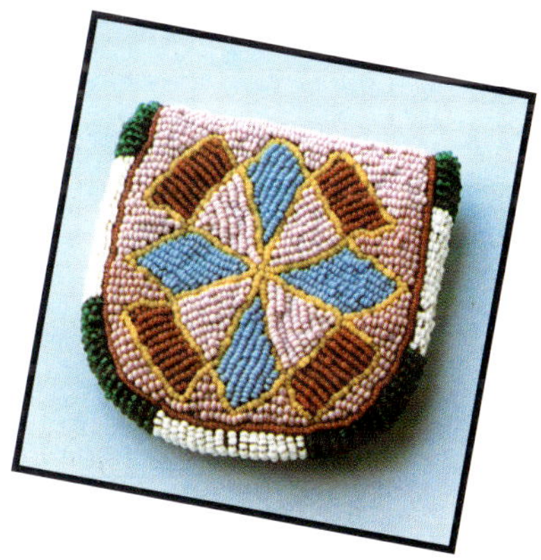

Back of the watch pouch.

Two American flags on the front and an American crest on the reverse, this lovely bag is wonderfully patriotic. *Courtesy Ron and Sharon Mailloux. $1500 to 1700*

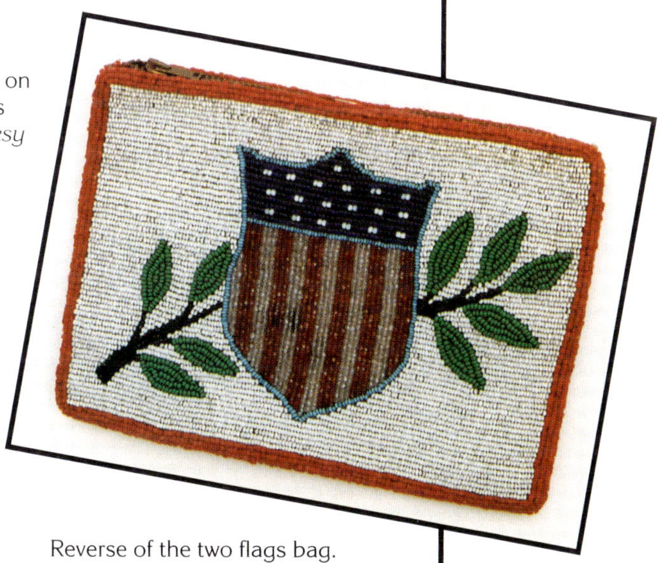

Reverse of the two flags bag.

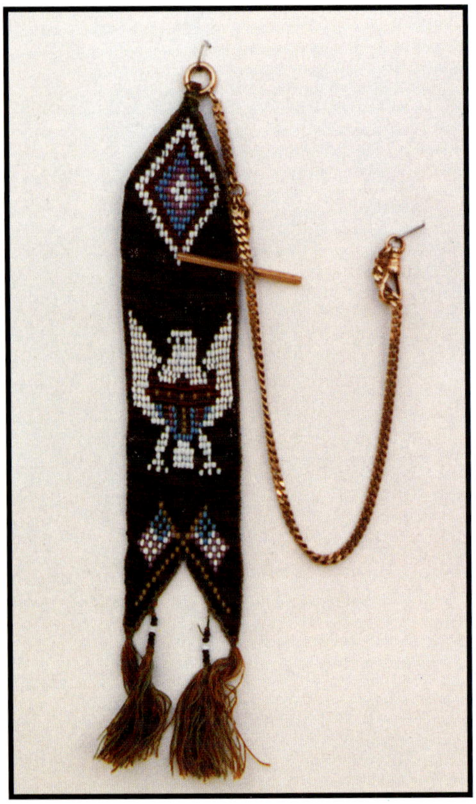

Loom-beaded watch fob, c. 1905 to 1915. *Courtesy Ron and Sharon Mailloux. $200 to 300*

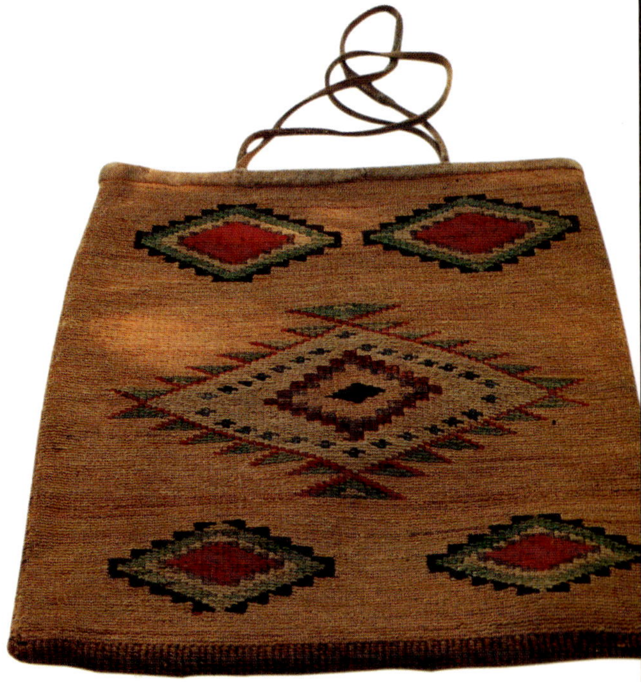

Wonderful old corn husk bag with stunning yarn overlays and designs. *Courtesy R.C. and Marvin Bales. $900 to 1200*

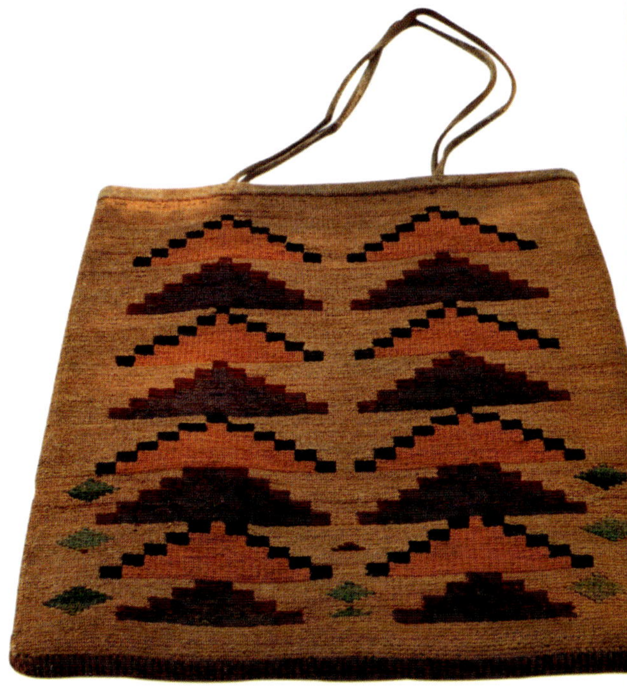

Reverse of the bag.

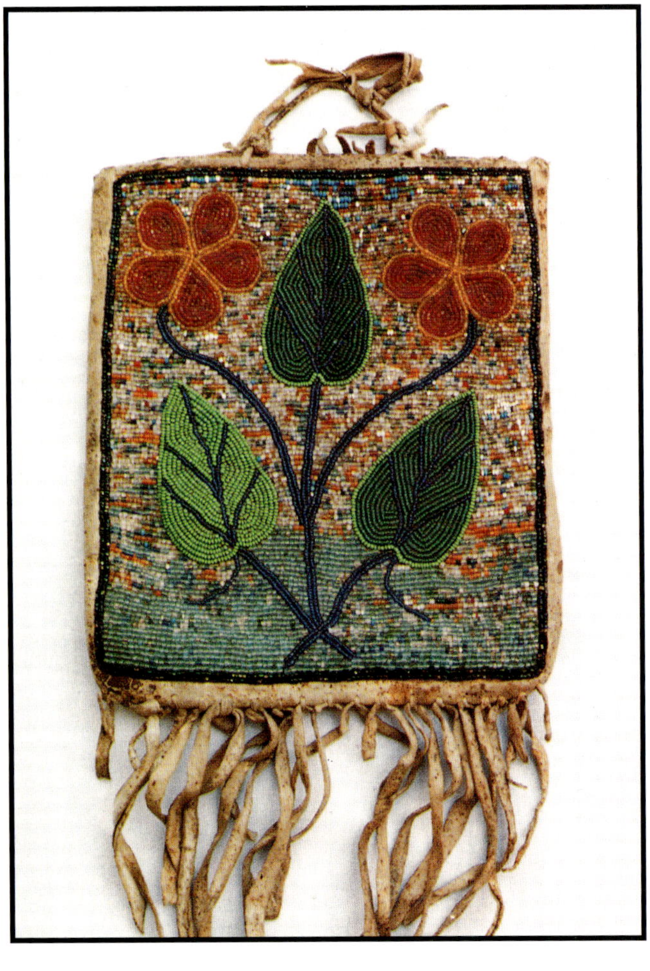

A very old, one-sided bag showing wonderfully worked ancient beads and some wear. *Courtesy private collector. $600 to 750*

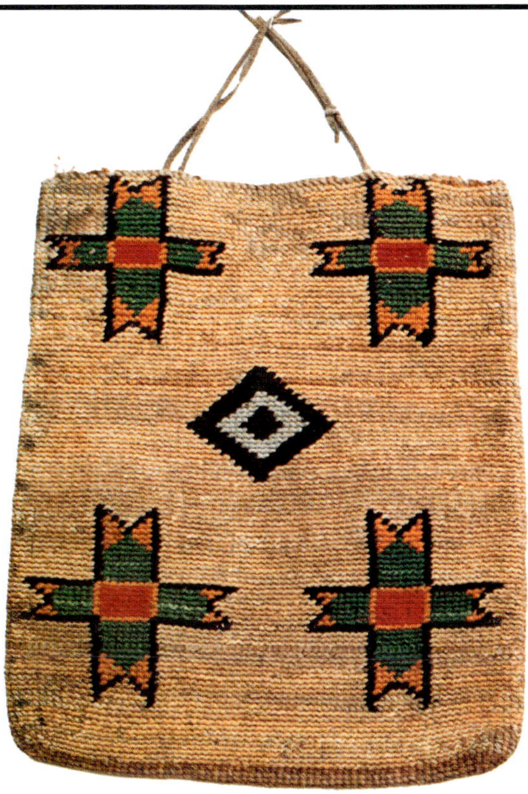

Very old Nez Perce corn husk bag with geometric designs and showing some wear. *Courtesy private collector.* *$550 to 650*

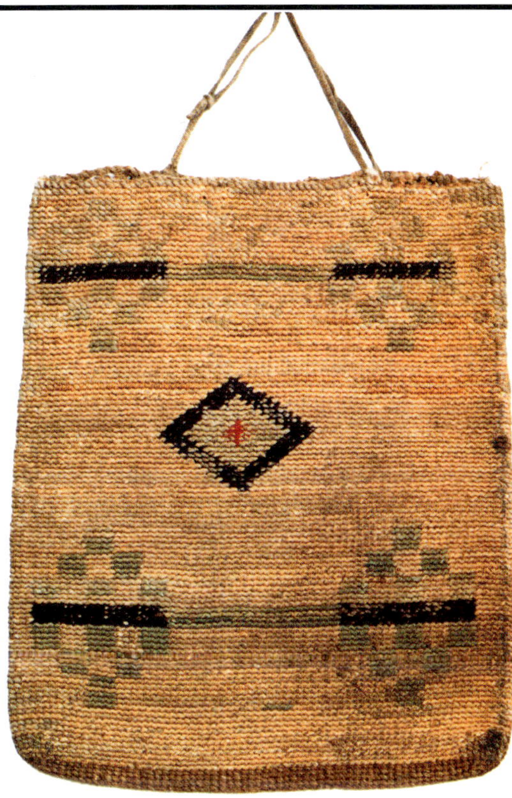

Reverse of the old Nez Perce bag.

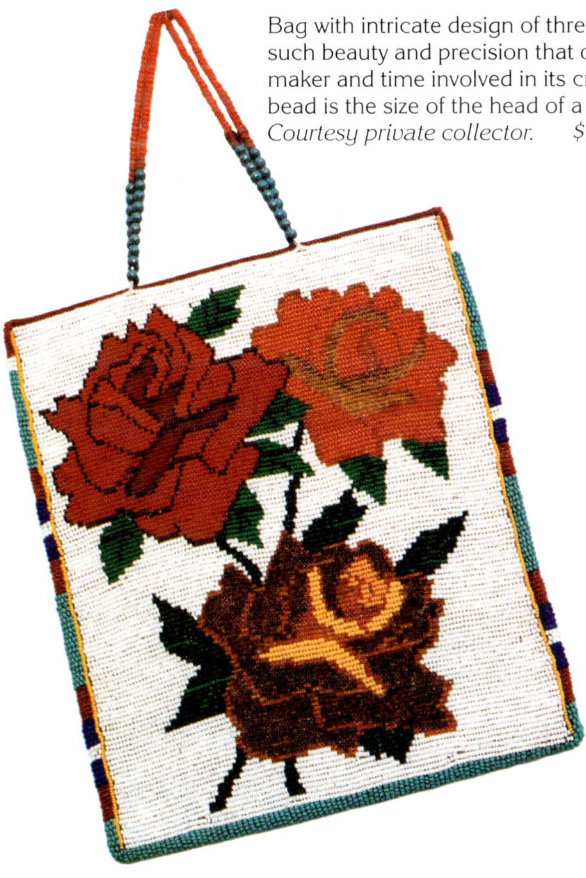

Bag with intricate design of three roses made with such beauty and precision that one must admire the maker and time involved in its creation. Each tiny bead is the size of the head of a straight pin. *Courtesy private collector.* *$675 to 750*

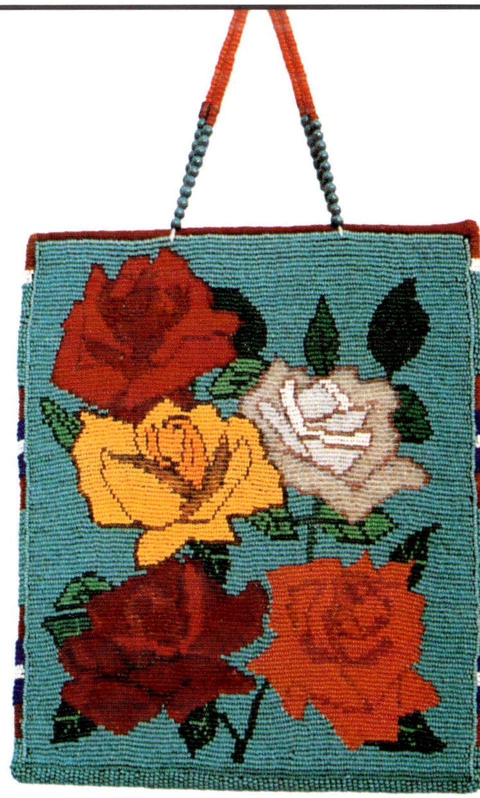

Reverse of the three roses bag.

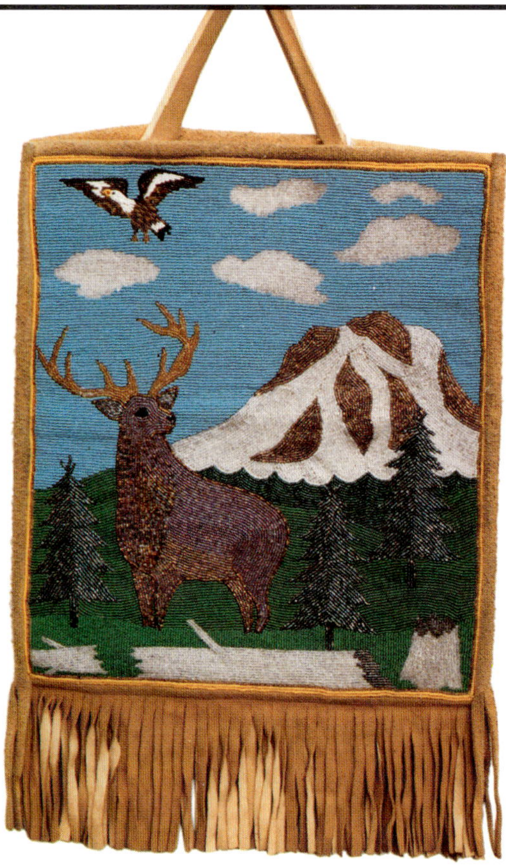

This large bag is unusual in that it has only one side ornamented; the reverse is plain deerskin. It was patiently worked to depict the elk, or Wapiti, and the flying eagle. *Courtesy private collector. $650 to 800*

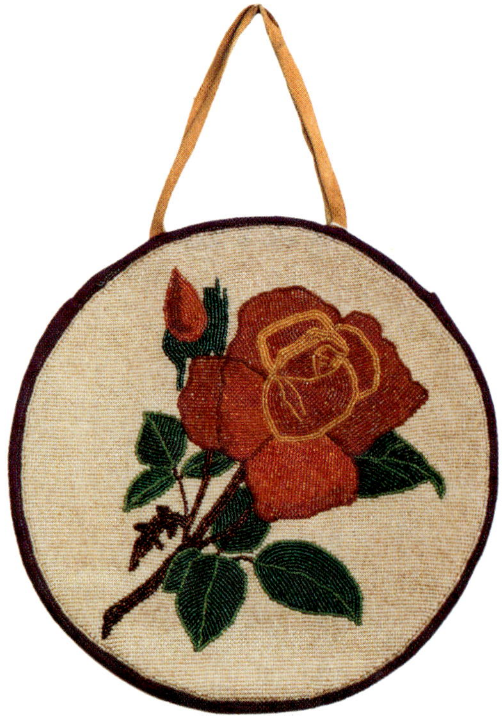

An unusual single-sided, round bag beaded with a large American Beauty rose and a single bud on a cream-colored background. *Courtesy private collector. $325 to 425*

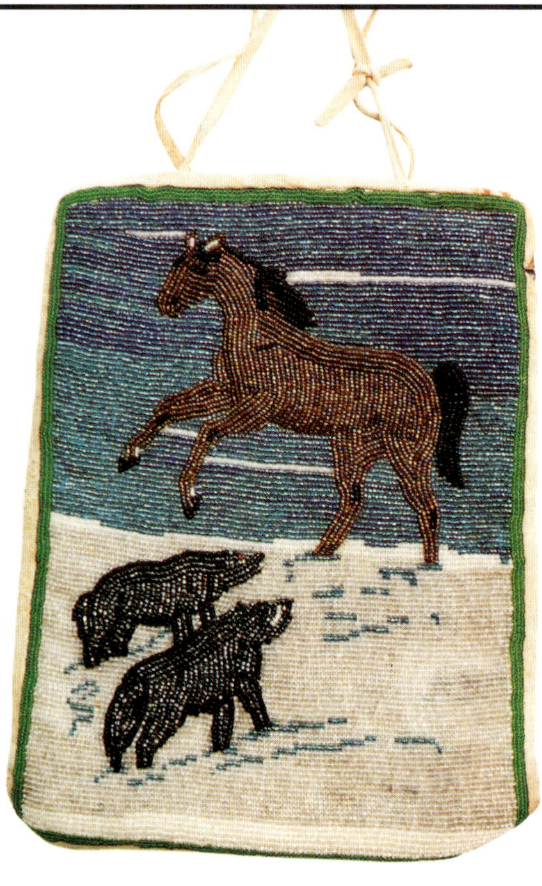

The bags almost exclusively portray a form in nature or a geometric design. This very large and beautifully worked, single-sided bag shows a horse and bears. *Courtesy private collector. $465 to 600*

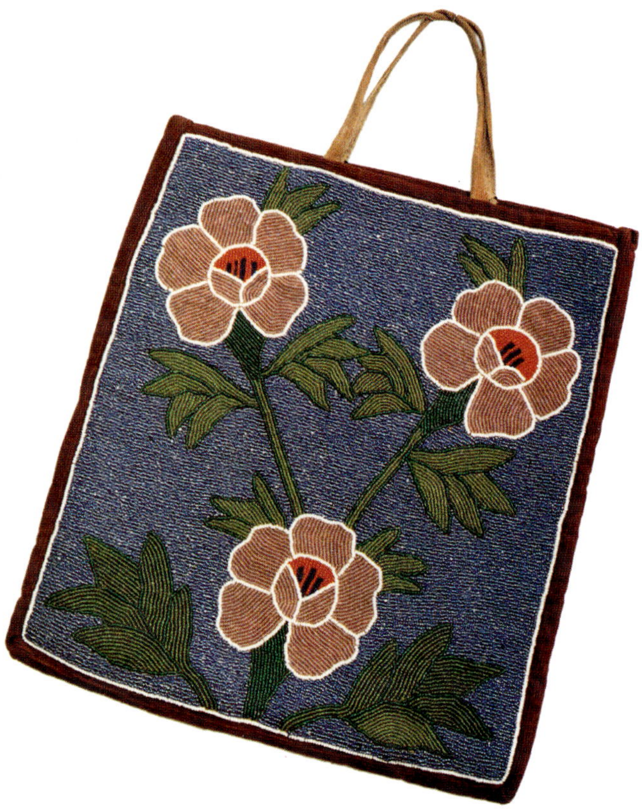

Three open roses on a purple background decorate this lovely single-sided beaded bag. *Courtesy private collector. $675 to 700*

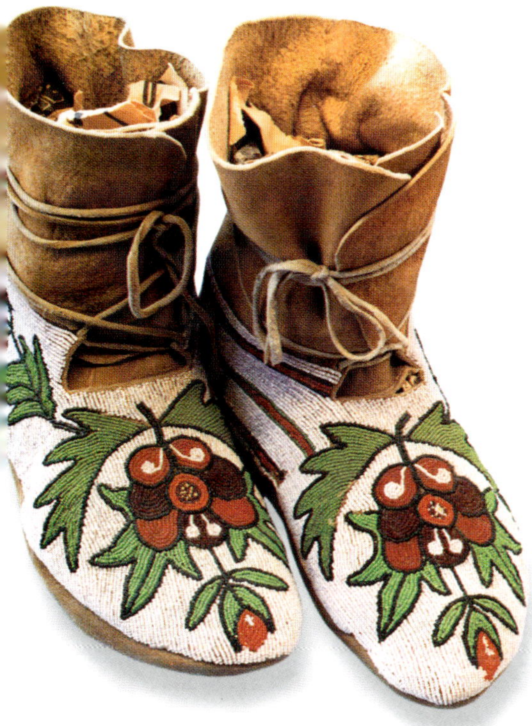

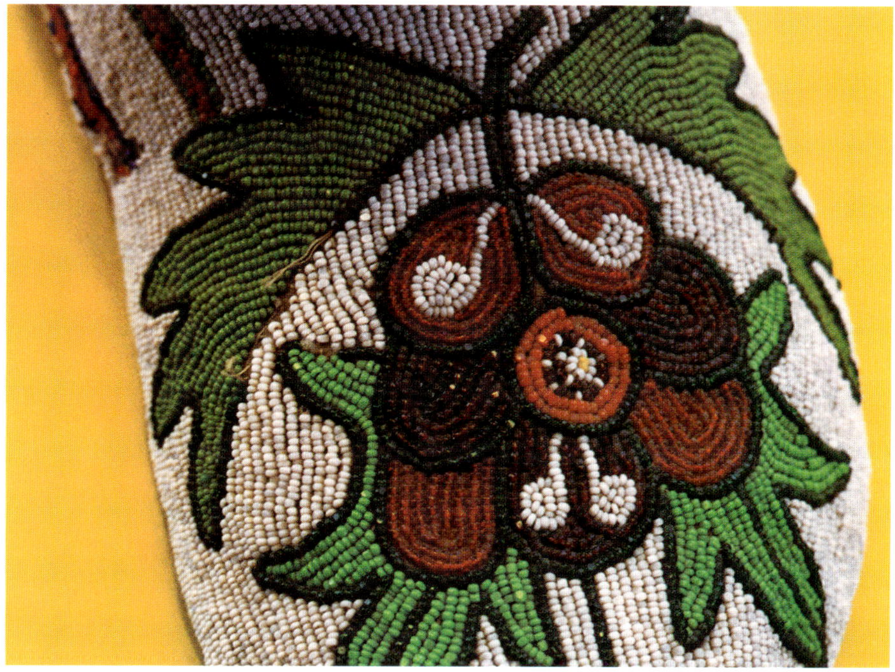

Detail of beading on the tall mocs.

This unworn pair of "tall mocs" are in excellent condition and are finely worked on what appears to be elk hide. They would have been a very serviceable pair. *Courtesy private collector.* *$1300 to 1500*

These tall elk hide moccasins are made in the traditional wrap style and beaded with a floral design. *Courtesy private collector. $1300 to 1500*

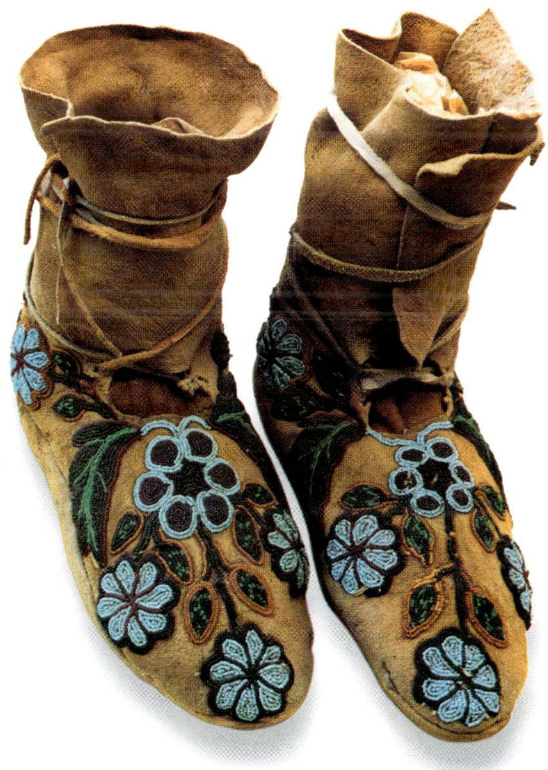

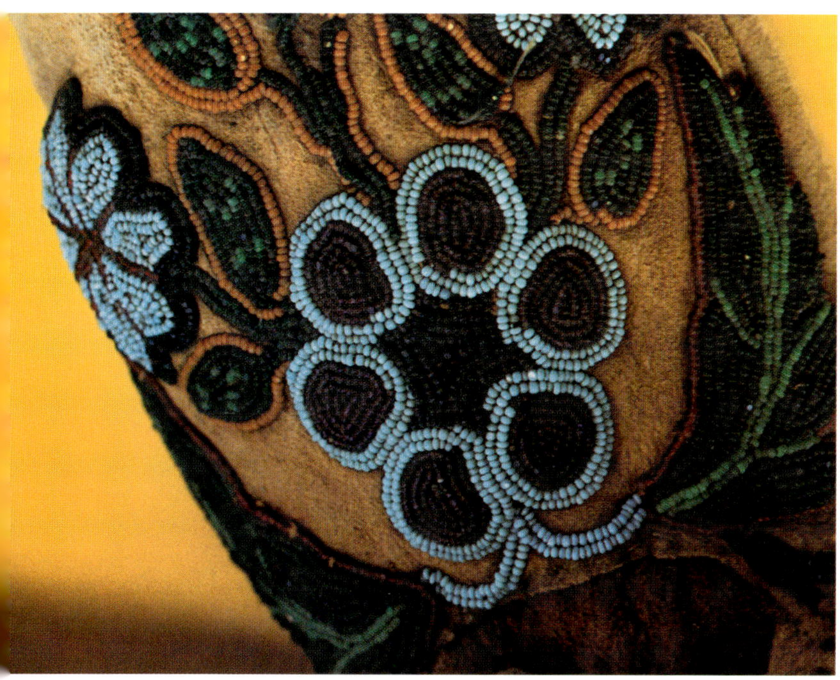

Detail of the toe beading on the moccasins.

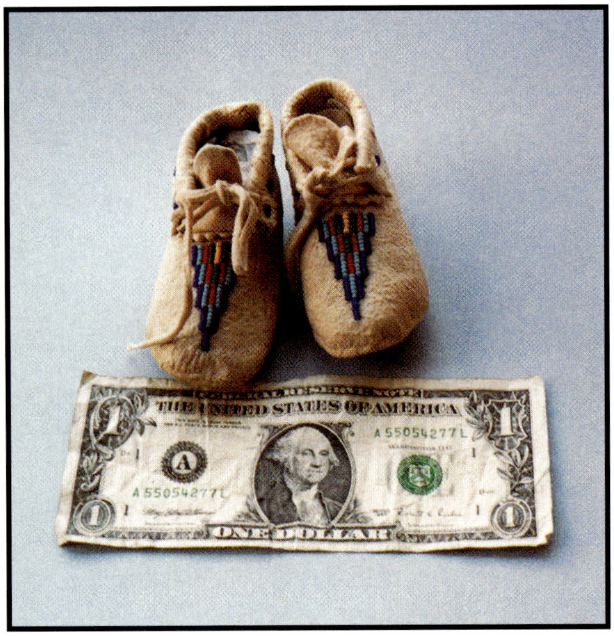

Most likely these were made for a new baby. *Courtesy private collector. $95 to 110*

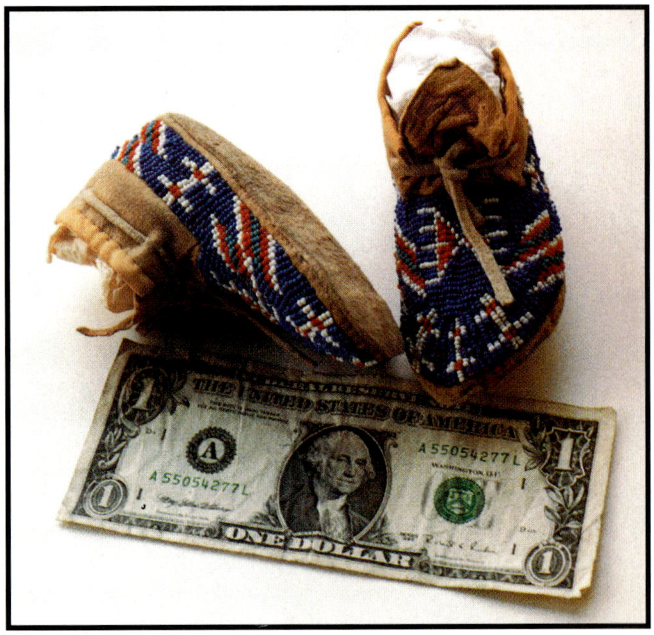

Very old and superbly beaded, these most likely were made for a new baby. *Courtesy private collector. $225 to 275*

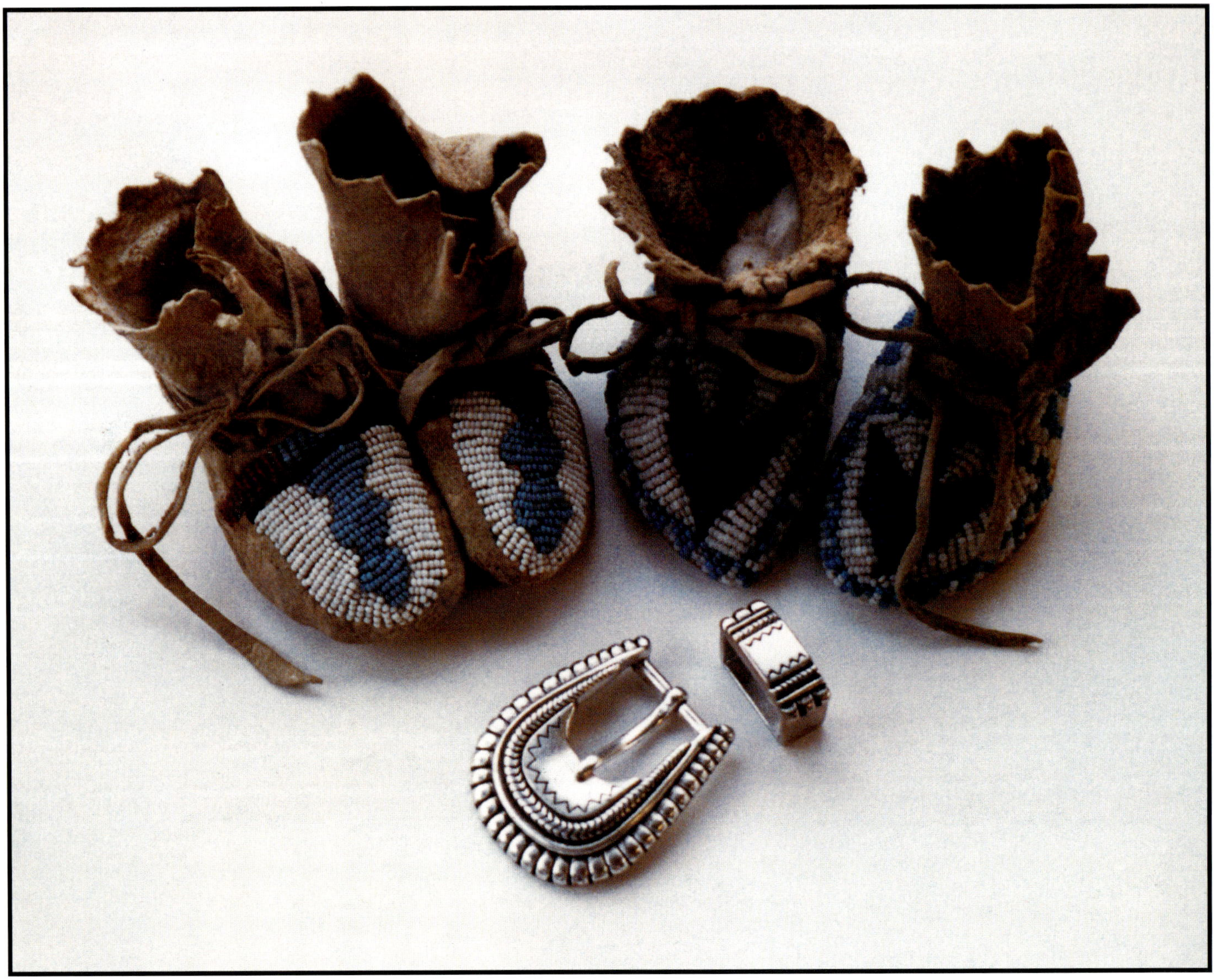

These rare and valuable baby mocs have toes the size of a belt buckle. *Courtesy private collector. $500 to 800 each*

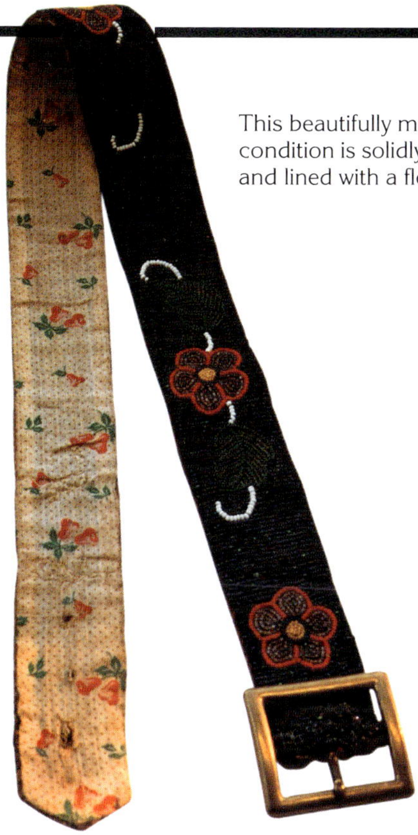

This beautifully made belt in excellent condition is solidly beaded on the outside and lined with a floral calico. *$35 to 55*

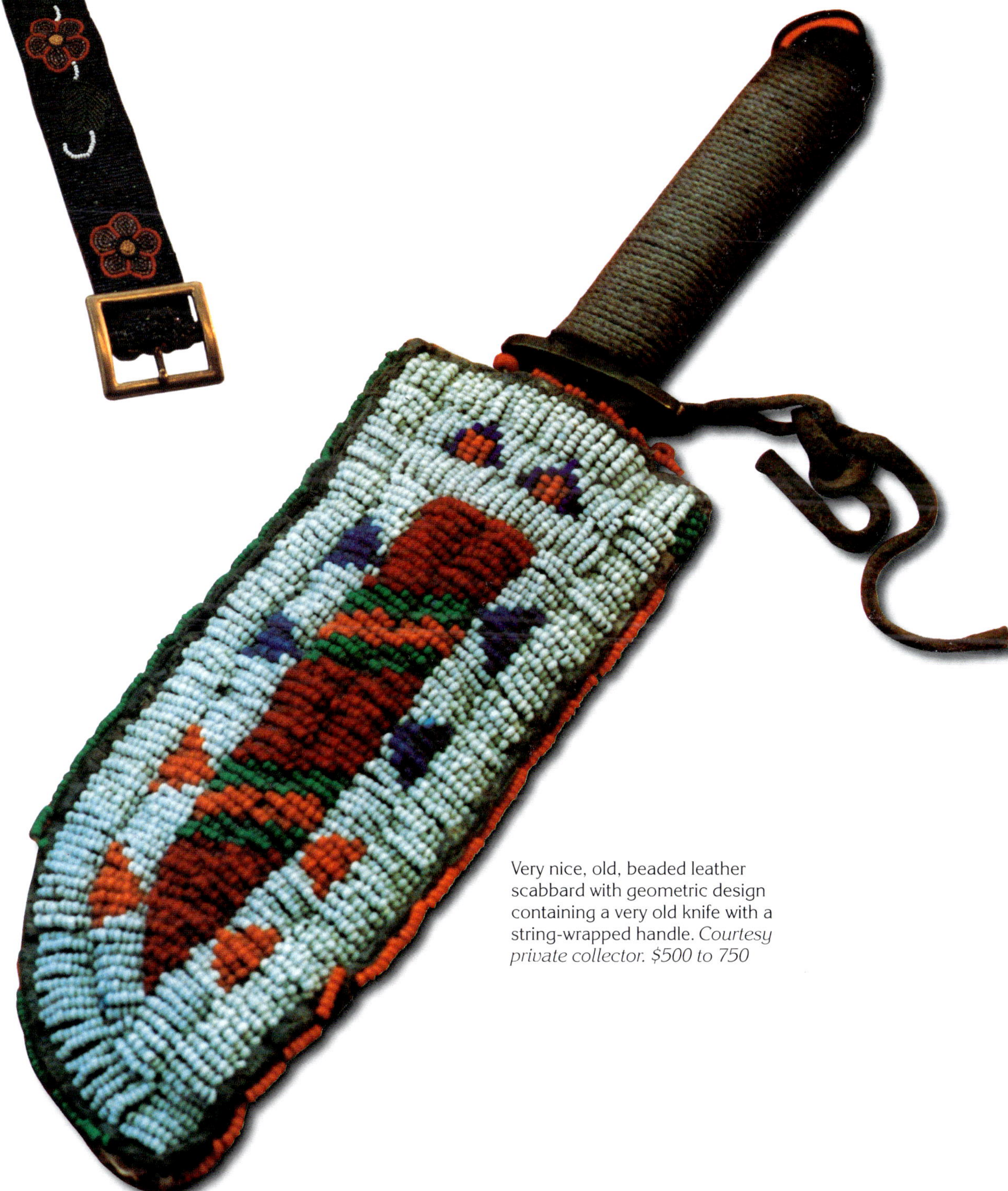

Very nice, old, beaded leather scabbard with geometric design containing a very old knife with a string-wrapped handle. *Courtesy private collector. $500 to 750*

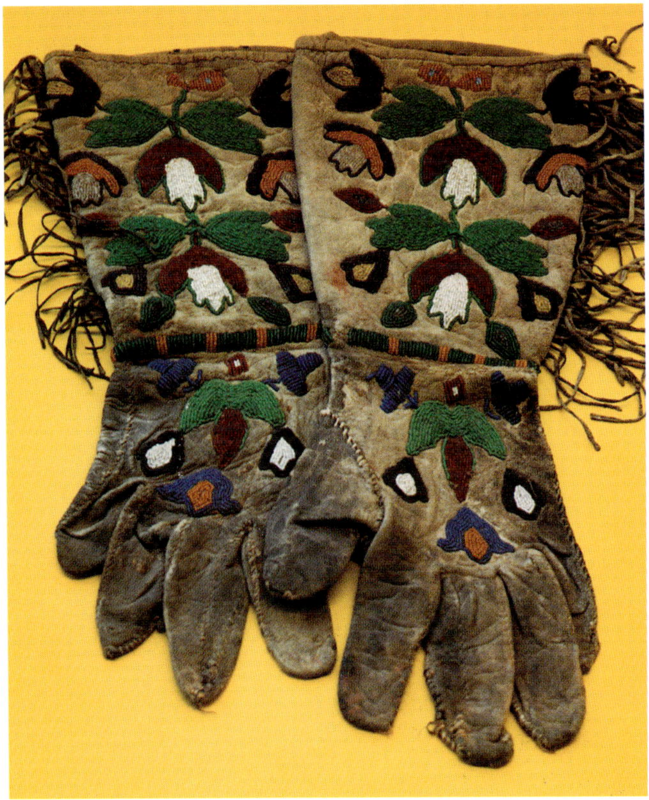

A pair of very old beaded gauntlets showing wear, but the beadwork has outlasted the leather parts. *Courtesy private collector. $800 to 900*

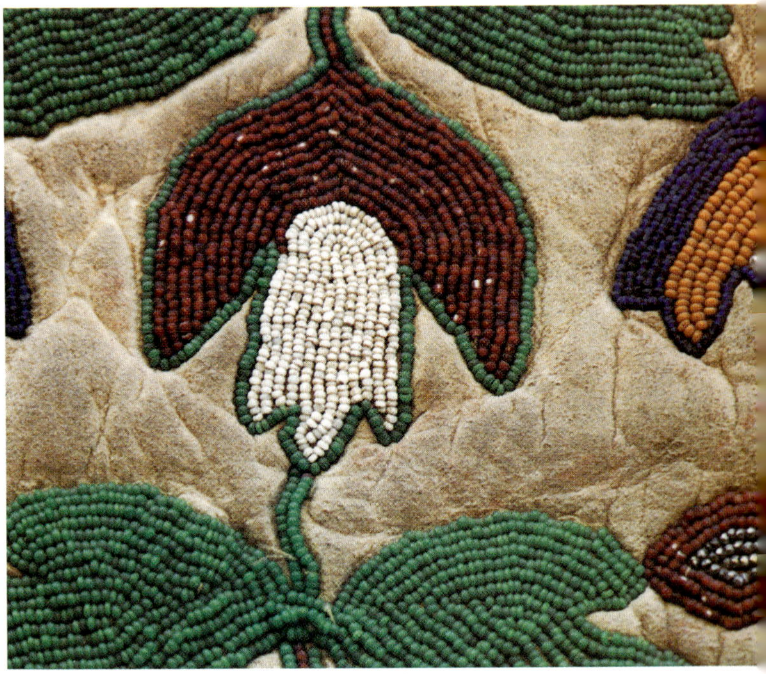

Detail of the beaded gauntlets.

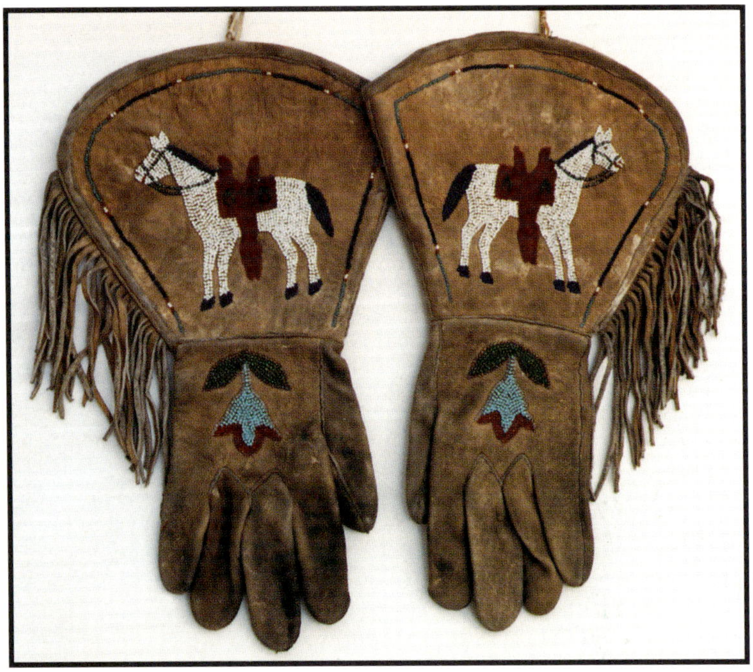

Exceptional beadwork on this pair of gauntlets show they have been worn, but they are in excellent condition throughout. *Courtesy Ron and Sharon Mailloux. $2000 to 2500*

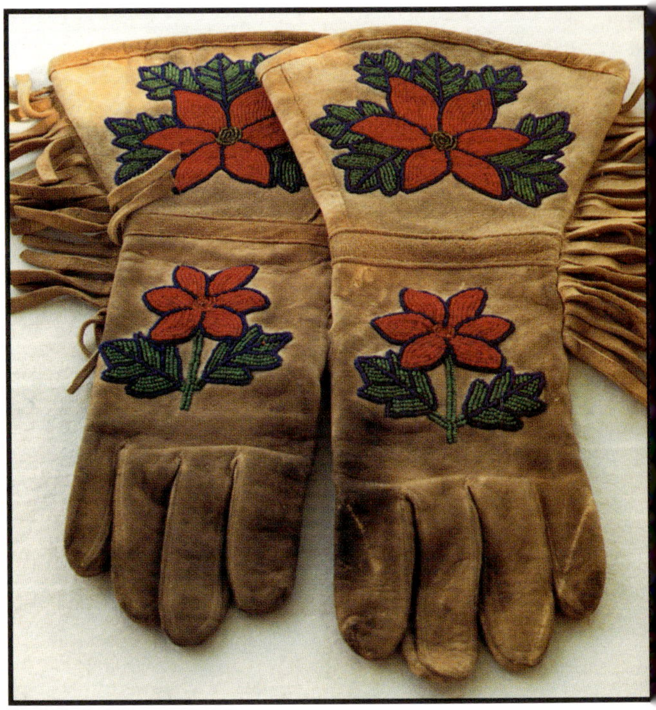

Beaded with red flowers and green leaves, this pair of beaded gauntlets are attractive and in excellent condition but show some use. *Courtesy of R.C. and Marvin Bales. $1200 to 1500*

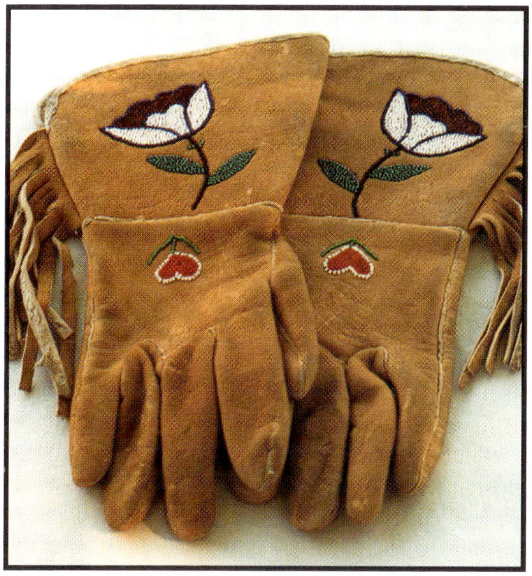

These gauntlets appear to be made of elk hide with simple beading. They are in excellent condition and would be a very serviceable pair. *Courtesy R.C. and Marvin Bales. $500 to 600*

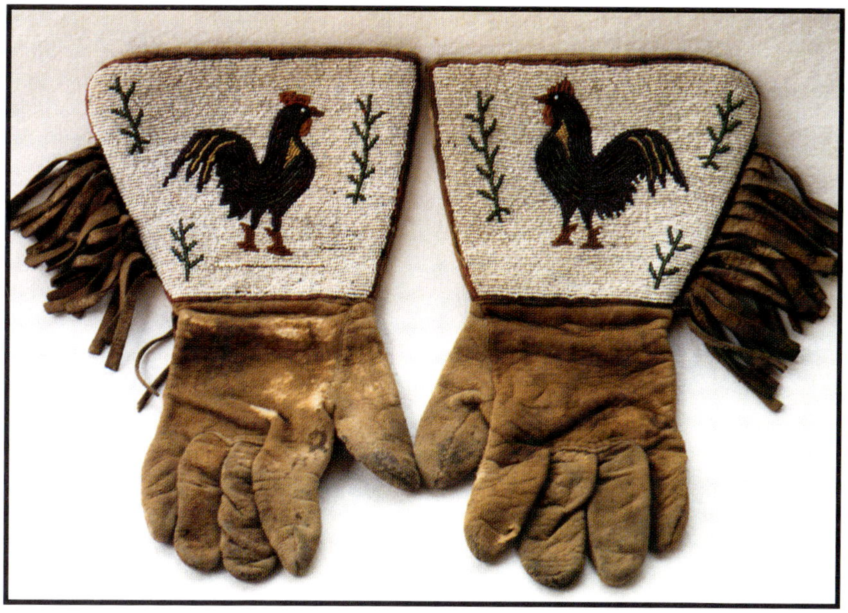

Probably the most interesting pair of beaded gauntlets in this group, these are constructed of very soft elk hide. A Native American woman spent a lot of time readying the leather and more time doing superb beading. They are a wonderful collectible. *Courtesy Ron and Sharon Mailloux. $850 to 1200*

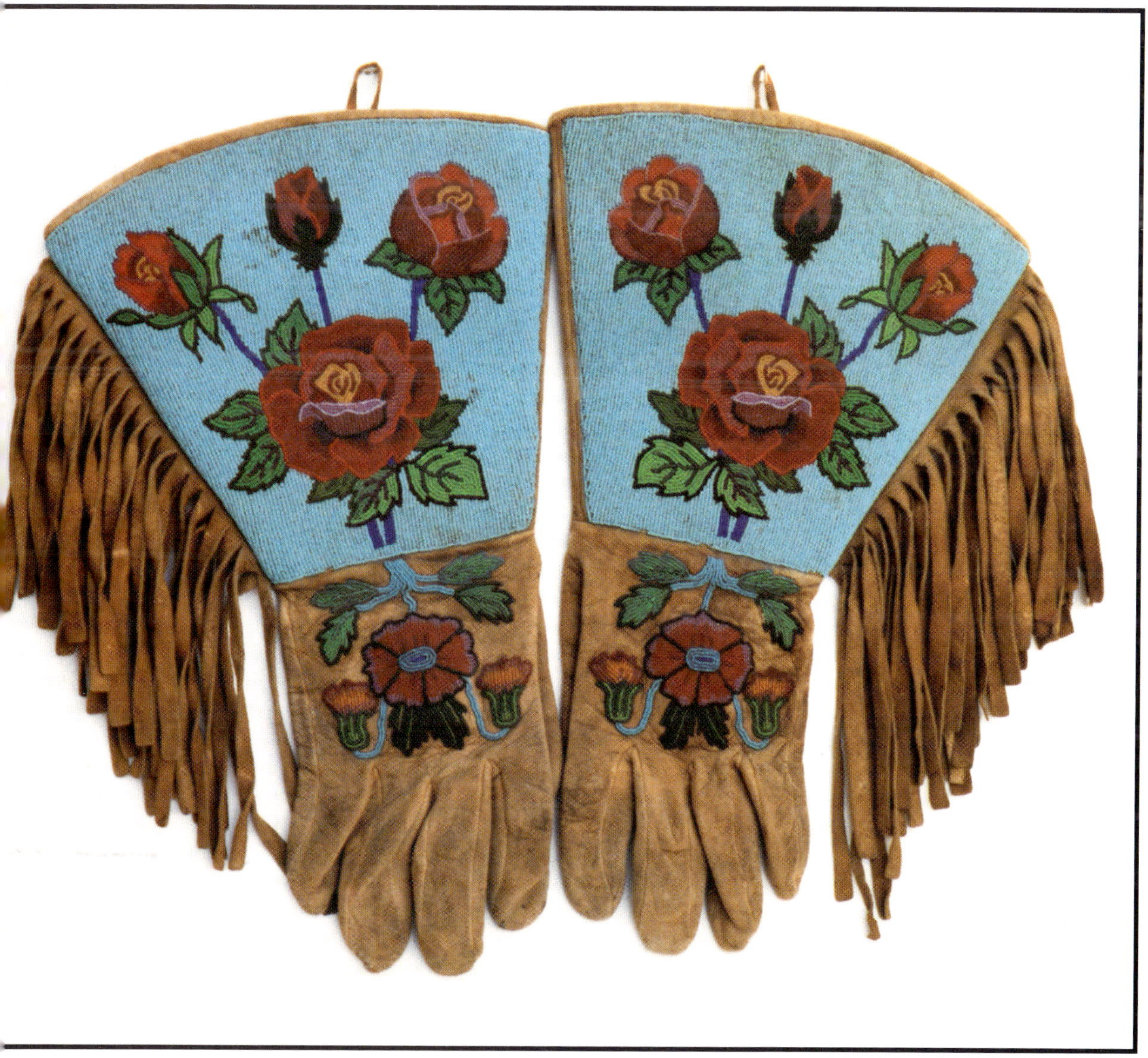

This pair of most beautiful beaded gauntles with blue background are strikingly attractive and so well beaded that one wonders how such precision can be managed with so many tiny beads. The red roses are brilliant and life-like. *Courtesy Ron and Sharon Mailloux. $3000 to 3500*

Chapter Four

Saddles

"Rocking Chairs for cowboys"

Saddle trees

The heart of a saddle is a saddle "tree," the form that the leather is shaped over. A good tree is usually made of wood covered with rawhide. Innovations lately include trees made from fiberglass or other materials, however the really good saddle makers prefer rawhide covered wooden trees.

Saddle trees can take on recognizable and highly commercial personalities of their own, just as do the finished saddles. A knowledgeable "saddle man's" first question will almost always be, "what kind of tree does it have in it?" Saddle trees have a way of becoming famous, as do the saddle makers. Some popular trees of the 1800s were the Missoula, Portland, Stones Improved, White River, Taylor, and others. Speaking in a more contemporary vein, the more notable trees of the current era include the Wade Roper, Form Fitter, Pro-Roper, Ellensburg, Tipton, Cutting Horse, Bowman Roper, Association, etc.

Saddles can sometimes successfully hide a broken tree inside, and one must approach buying an old saddle with some caution. If a horse has ever gone down and rolled over with a saddle on, the wooden tree may be broken. Unless one specifically checks for this, the broken tree can go unnoticed. While a broken tree inside a saddle may not always affect its exterior beauty, it certainly will affect its use, and therefore becomes a serious factor. A good way to test for a broken tree is to place the saddle between your knees while it rests with its rear on the floor. Squeeze your knees. If the saddle moves, it may possibly have a broken fork. Grasp the horn with one hand and the cantle with the other hand and pull together to see if the cantle is loose.

Restoration tips

Old saddles quite often are found in terrible disrepair because of neglect or various other causes. However, a saddle can generally be "brought to life" again if one knows a few simple steps to follow. Here are the best tips to successfully bring a dried out saddle to life. Begin with a good cleaning with a soft brush and/or sheep's wool saturated with liquid glycerin saddle soap. After thoroughly cleaning the saddle and letting it dry, soak a piece of genuine sheep's wool (it can be purchased at any leather supply store) in pure Neatsfoot oil, and rub the saddle down with that. Your saddle should already begin looking better and taking on some new flexibility. Finally, hand rub it with liquid Neat-

F. A. MEANEA, CHEYENNE, WYOMING

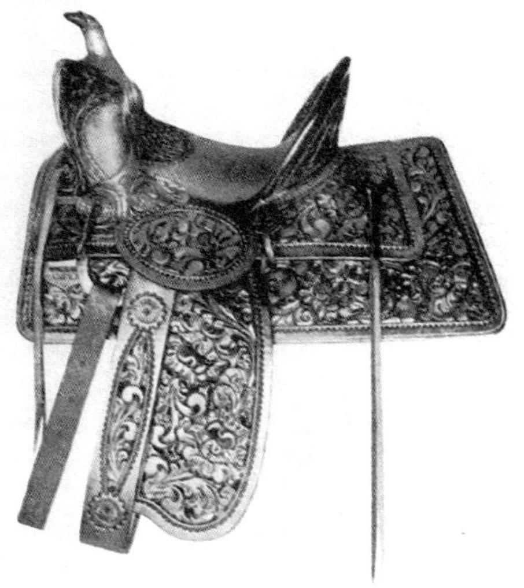

No. 14 FULL RAISED HAND-STAMPED SADDLE

Tree, 15-inch Nelson; 14-inch Swell Fork; Skirts, 15 x 30 inches; bark tan wool sheepskin lined, hand-stitched; **Stirrup** leathers, 3-inch, double at stirrup end; Stirrups, any shown in cut on page 24, except No. 1, which cost $3.00 extra; closed housing; back cantle raised **stamp**; Cinches, cotton front, heavy web flank. Single, double or three-quarter rig, same price. Above cut shows the three-quarter rig. Weight, 37 to 40 lbs. Price $100.00

CATALOGUE AND PRICE LIST

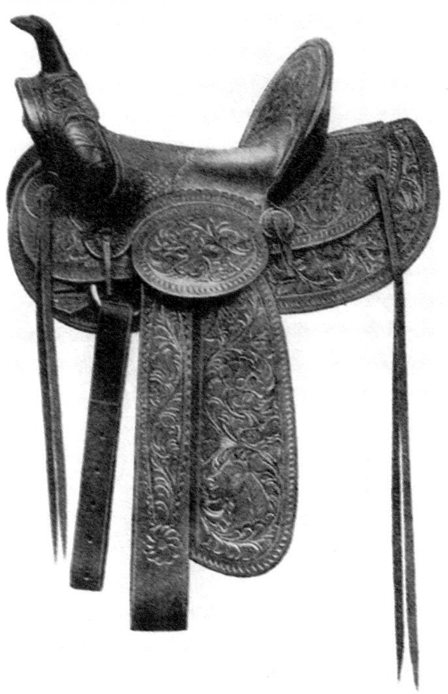

No. 16 FULL RAISED HAND-STAMPED SADDLE

(14-inch extra swell fork)

Tree, 14-inch Portland; Skirts 27 inches long; bark tan wool sheepskin lined; hand-stitched stirrup leathers, 3-inch, double at stirrup end; Stirrups, any shown on page 24, except No. 1, which cost $3.00 extra; closed housing; back of cantle raised stamp; Cinches, cotton or angora hair; made single, three-quarter or double rig; same price. Above cut shows three-quarter rig. Weight, 35 to 38 lbs. Price $100.00

Lac or leather lacquer. Your saddle will now look the best it can for its age and abuse.

Storage

If you wish to store your saddles, keep them in a very dry atmosphere. To prevent moth and mice damage, take an old cotton sock, fill the toe with moth balls, and hang it on the horn or under the saddle rack close to the sheepskin lining. You can keep them undamaged year after year with this method. Happy saddle collecting!

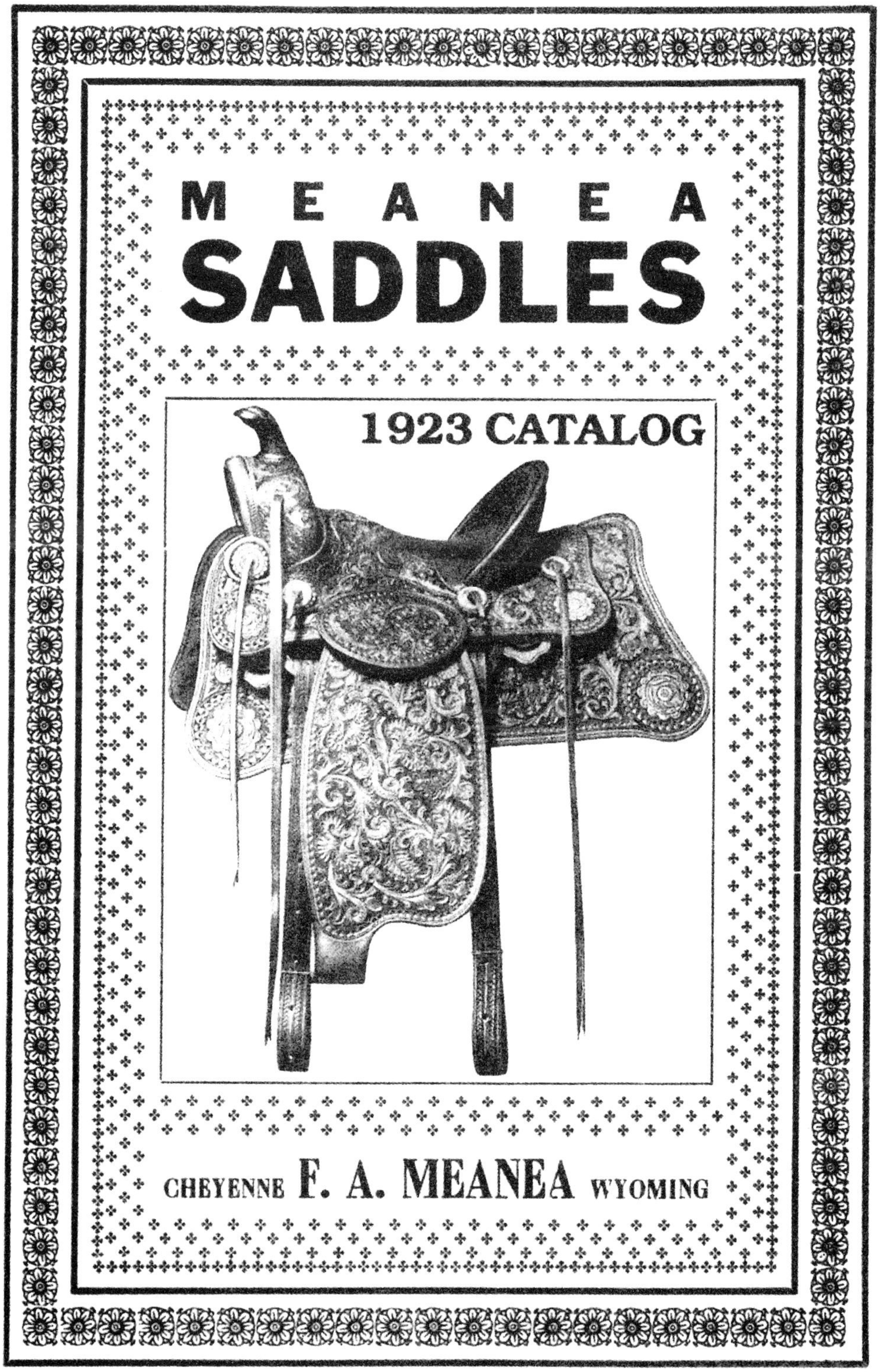

The Meana Saddles catalog from 1923 illustrates the prices then current for some of the saddles contemporaneously collected and displayed.

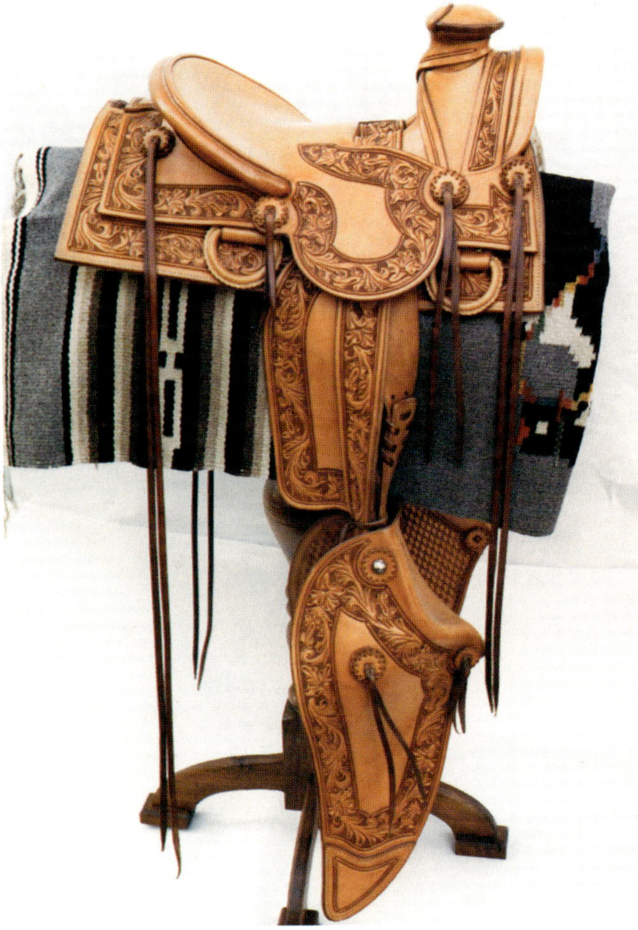

Small, ¾-size youth saddle, hand made by Dave Miller. It features Sam Stagg rigging (1860-1900), Texas-style square skirts, and "Applehorn" slick fork. Back jockeys are laced, early Cheyenne roll, (or low cantle), with a full double rigging (rim fire) and bull nose tapaderos. The saddle has been displayed only and never on a horse. The style is circa 1880. *Courtesy Ron and Sharon Mailloux. $3500 to 4500*

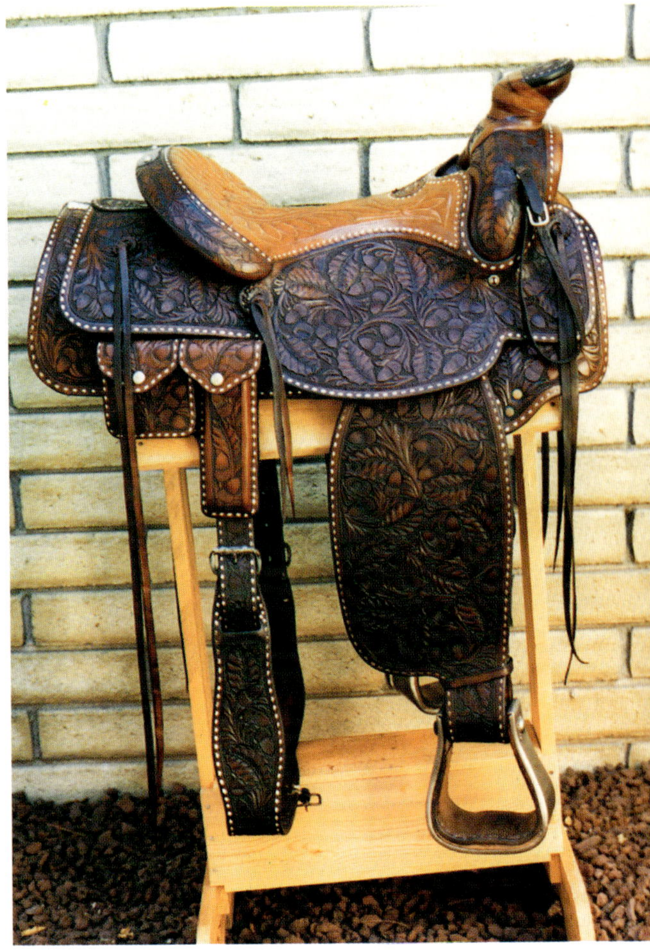

Buck stitched Garcia Saddlery, Salinas, California. The beautiful saddle in pristine condition has extra pockets built onto rear cinch strap. It has very attractive German Silver covered stirrups, with elegant Acorn pattern tooled into the saddle it presents itself as one of a kind and highly collectable. *Courtesy Ron and Sharon Mailloux. $3000 to 4000*

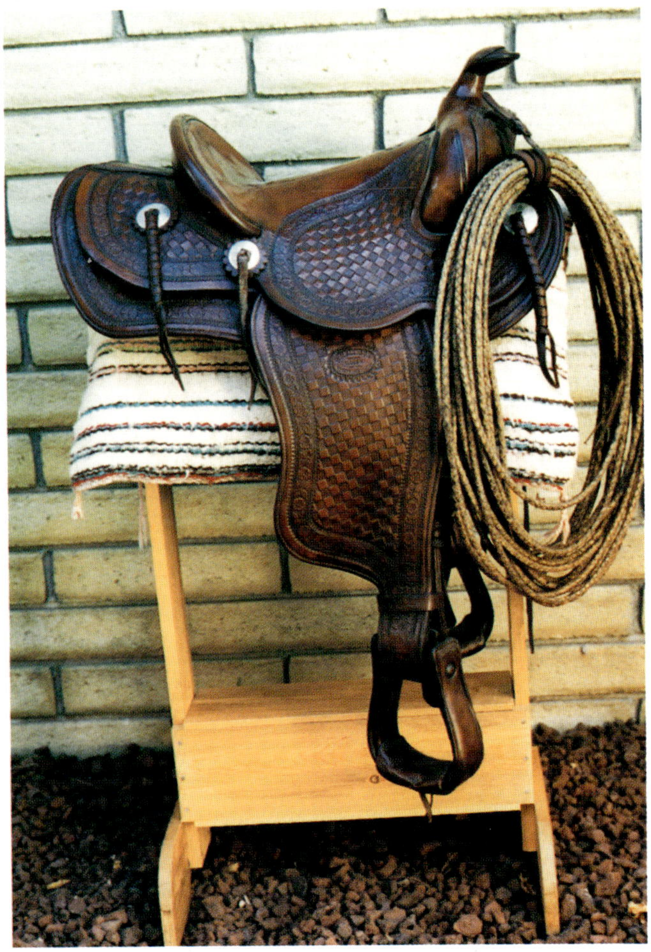

The maker is W.D. Allison of Montrose, Colorado, c. 1930. This round skirted saddle is a fine example of a good working man's saddle. It is excellent in construction with a solid hard leather seat and a sharp cantle. It has leather bound stirrups and the last thing you can say about it folks is; it's what every Cowboy dreams about owning. It carries a rawhide reata. *Courtesy of Ron and Sharon Mailloux. $2000 to 3000*

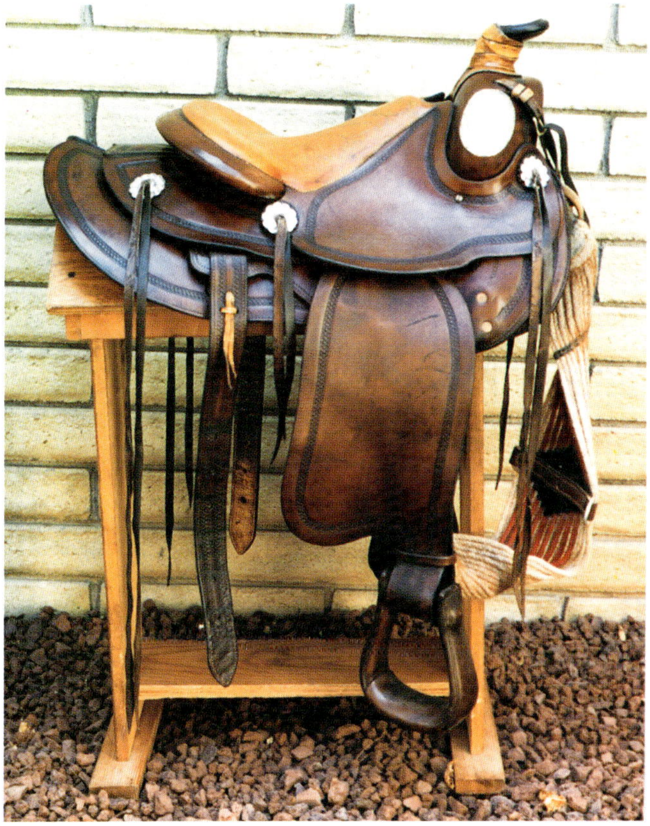

E.V. Horn of Walla Walla, Washington is the maker of this fine saddle, c. 1960's, it has sterling silver on the horn and six sterling silver conchos, plus sterling silver on the forks. Round skirted with double rigging and beautiful tooled border tooling, it sports a glove leather seat. *Courtesy Ron and Sharon Mailloux. $2000 to 3000*

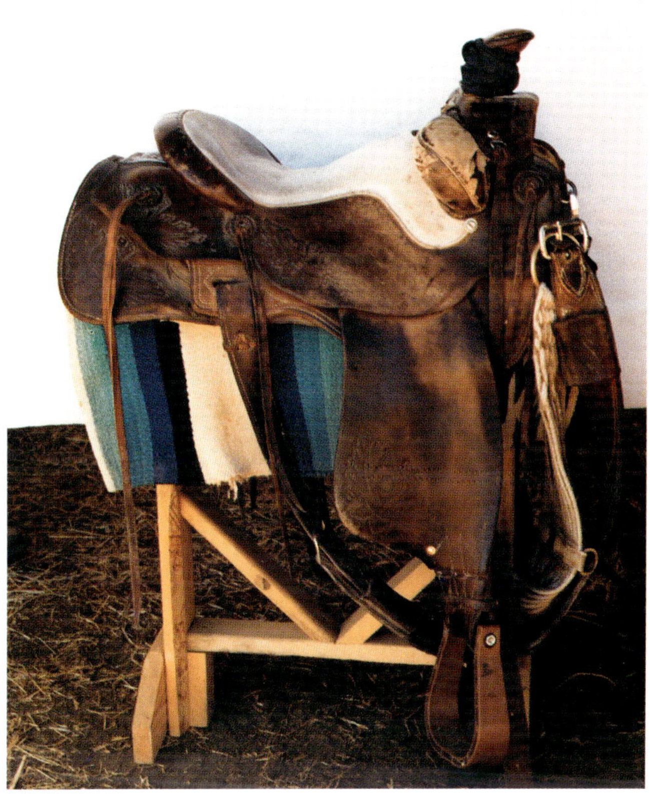

Charlie Baker is the maker of this saddle. Bill Severe made his "pro-roper" tree for it and it has been a real winning combination ever since the completion. The saddle is still in constant use by a full time horse trader and rancher. *Courtesy Bob and Judy Bertsch. $1200 to 1500*

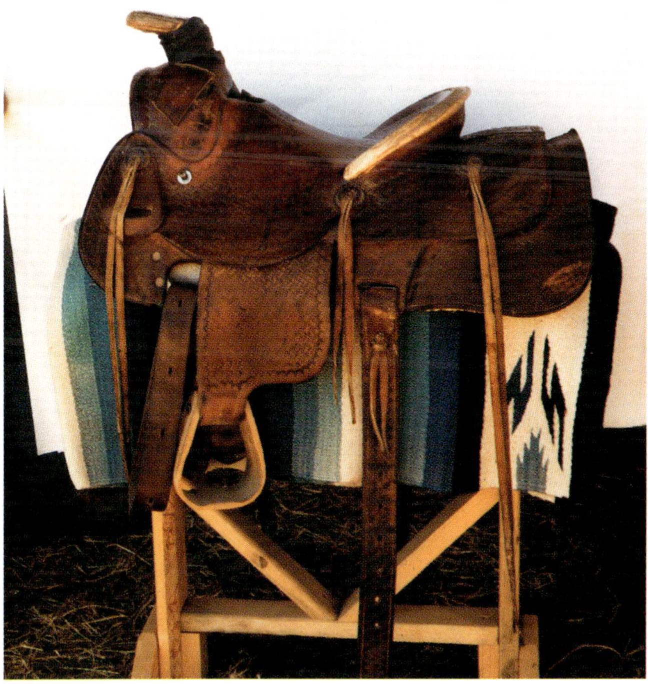

Charlie Baker is the maker, and the saddle has a Wade Roper tree , it was made especially for a young boy being raised on a horse ranch. *Courtesy Bob and Judy Bertsch. $1200 to 1500*

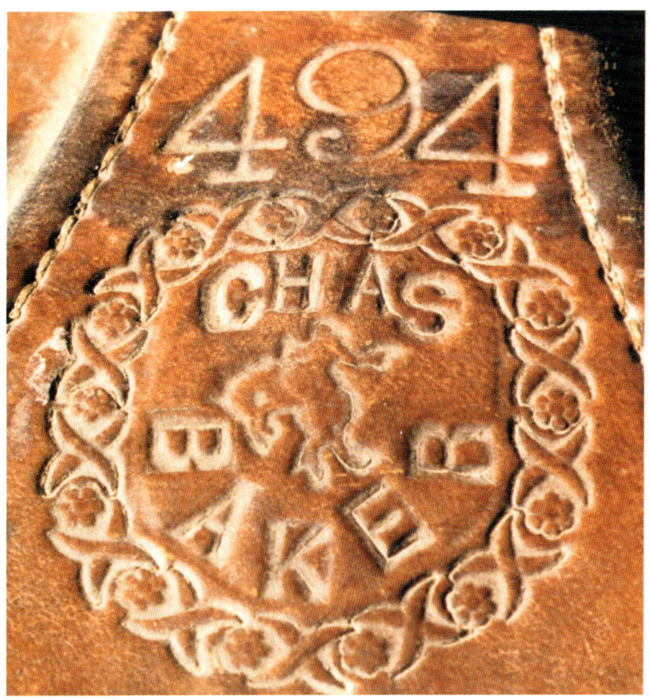

Detail of maker's mark on the child's saddle.

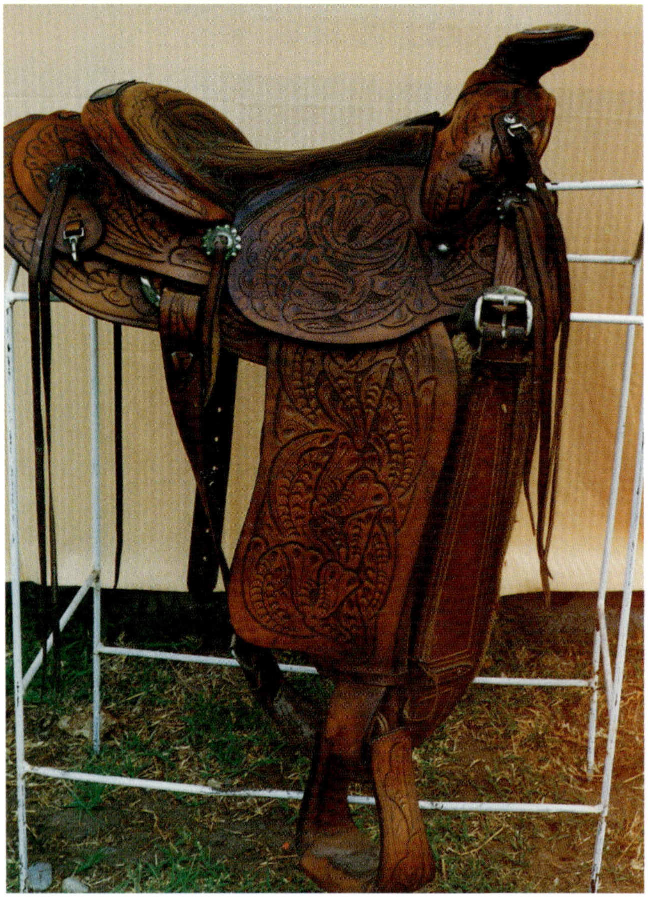

Prison-made in the penitentiary at McCallister, Oklahoma, the saddle is one of the finest using saddles ever made and, best of all, it fits almost any horse. *Overton collection. $1500 to 2000*

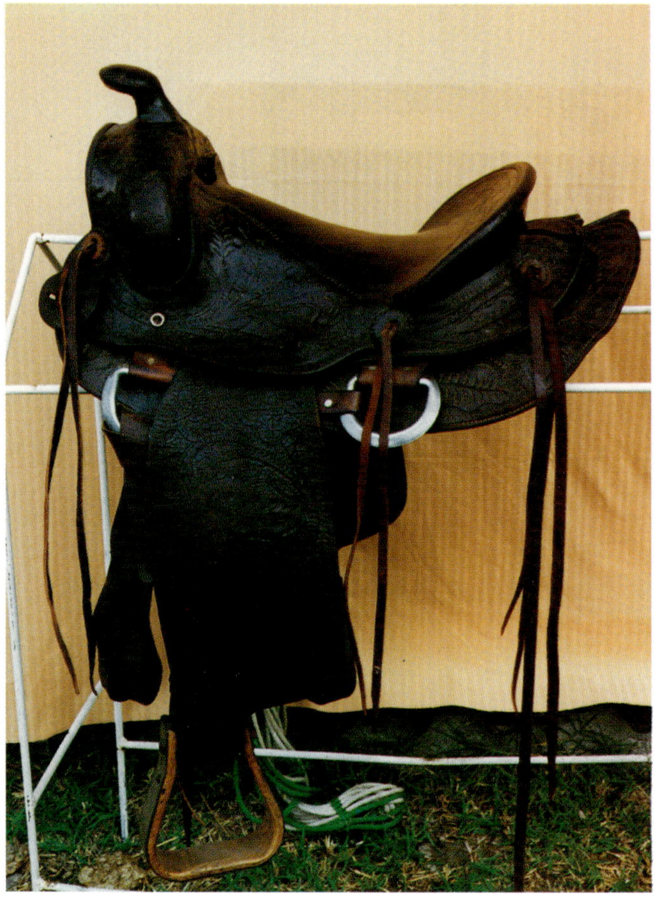

J.C. Higgens saddle, it was originally sold through Sears and Roebuck Company in th 1940s. *Overt collection. $2 to 275*

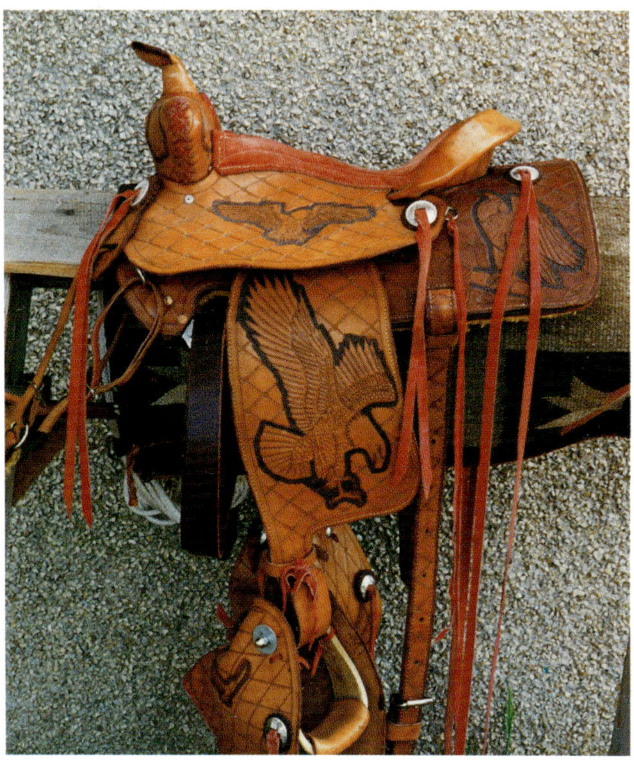

The hand-made saddle is unmarked but made by Bob Christopher with eagle design and a matching breast collar. *Courtesy Gene Christopher. $375 to 425*

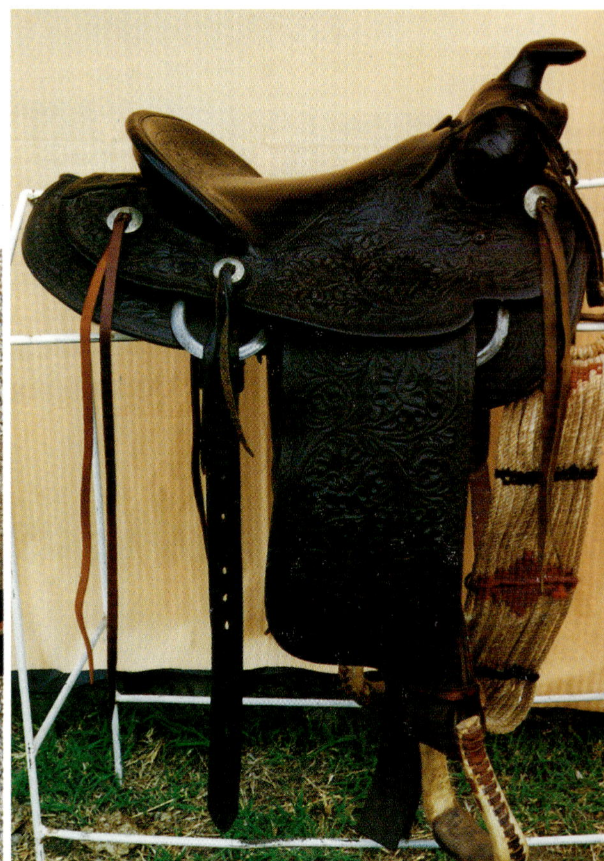

Fred Muehler saddle built on a "lil' wonder" tree, c. 1940s. *Overton collection. $375 to 400*

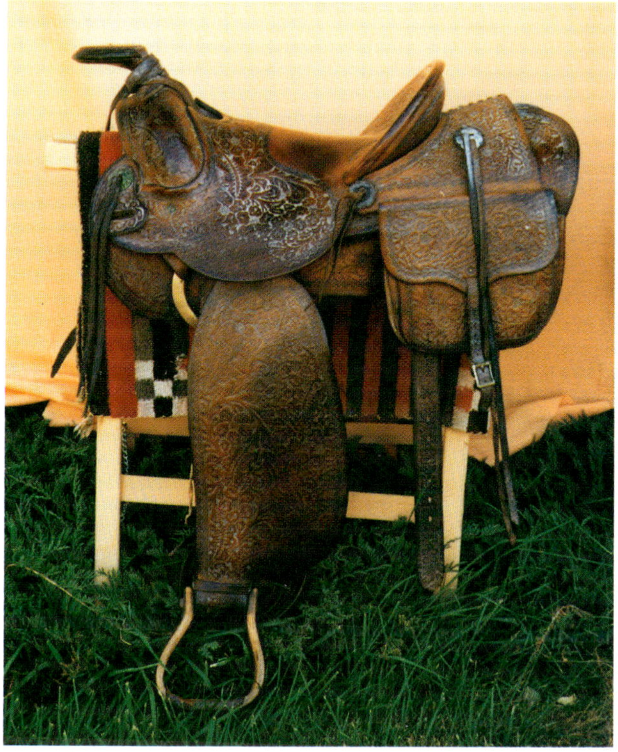

Voss is the maker of this saddle that was custom made in 1943 for George Schiffner. It is a center fire with unusual "airplane aluminum conchos" on it. *Courtesy Schiffner Military Museum, George and Margaret Schiffner. $500 to 700*

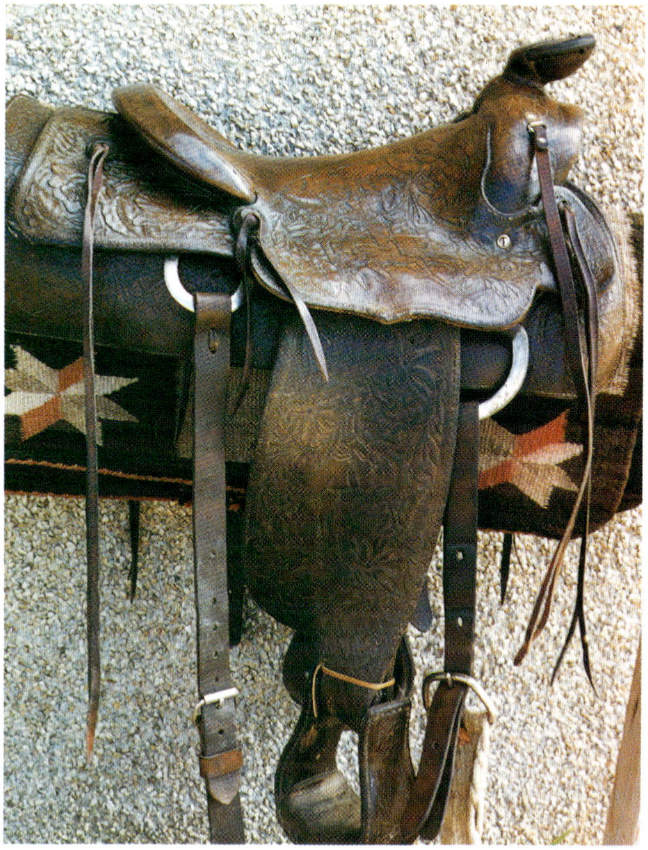

Made in Oakland, California, by Earl Naninga, this has square skirts and wonderful hand carving throughout its design. It is sewn by hand with sinew throughout. Very nice rendition, and very collectible, c.1940s *Courtesy Gene Christopher. $1200 to 1500*

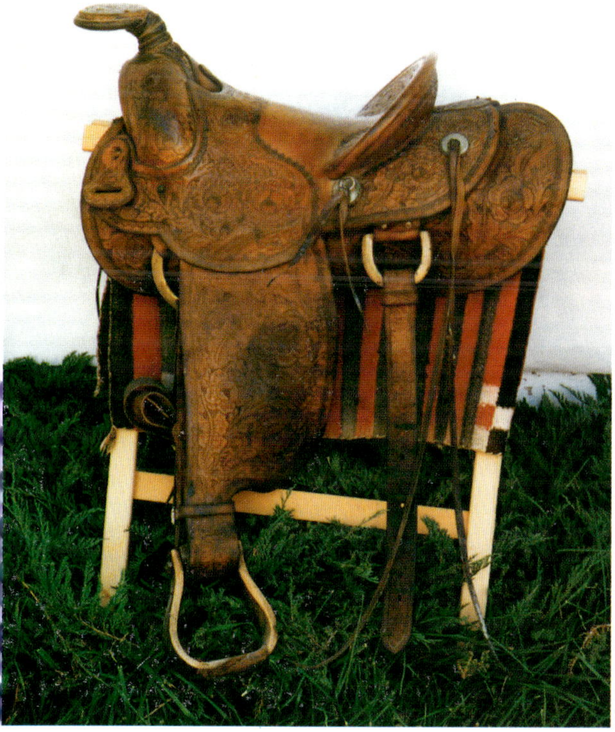

Voss also made this saddle for George E. Schiffner (father and son saddles) both in very nice condition. Made in 1943, this one is a ¾-double rigging. *Courtesy Schiffner Military Museum, George and Margaret Schiffner. $475 to 675*

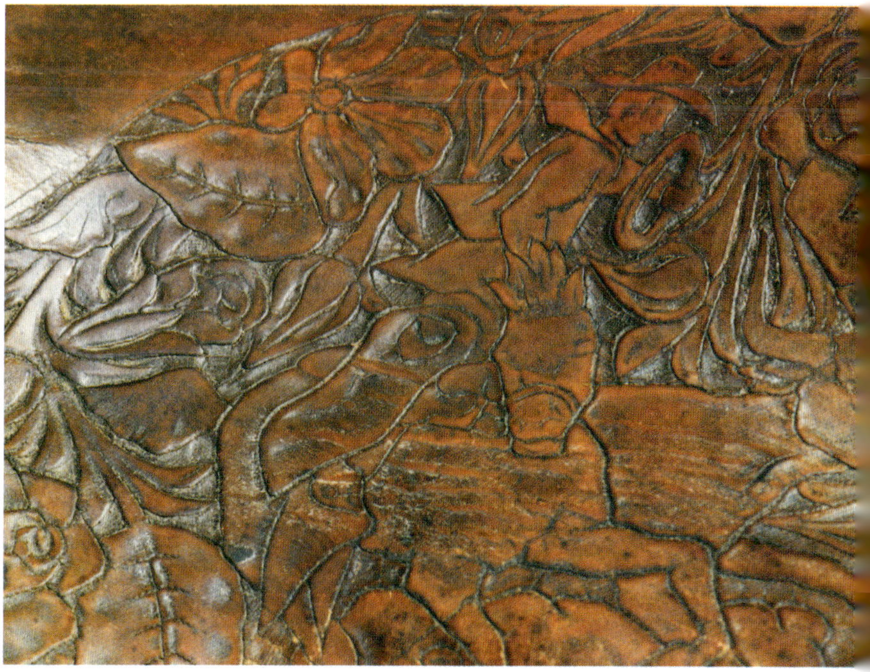

Detail of hand carving on the Naninga saddle showing a horse and rider.

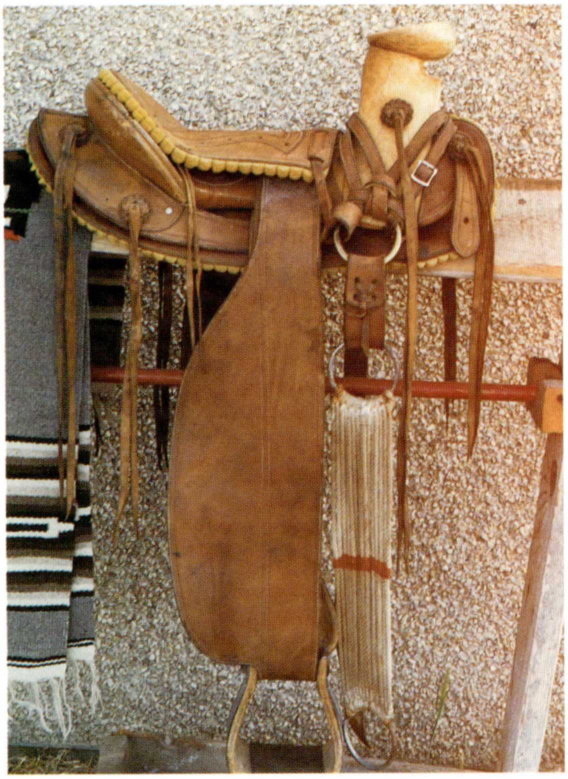

Mexican mule saddle, it is in excellent condition. *Courtesy Gene Christopher. $250 to 500*

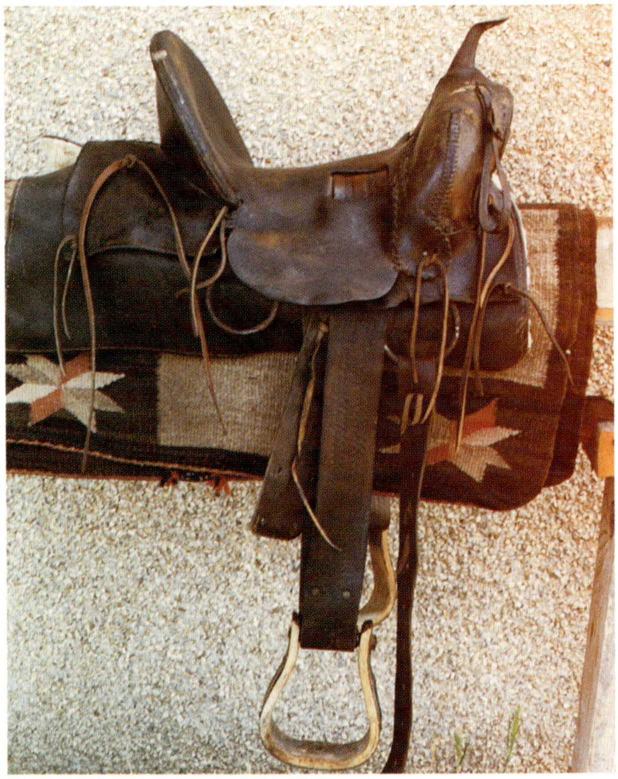

Very old Al Furstnow saddle made with the square skirts and the fender leathers through the seat. The saddle has seen some use but still very collectible. *Courtesy Gene Christopher. $500 to 600*

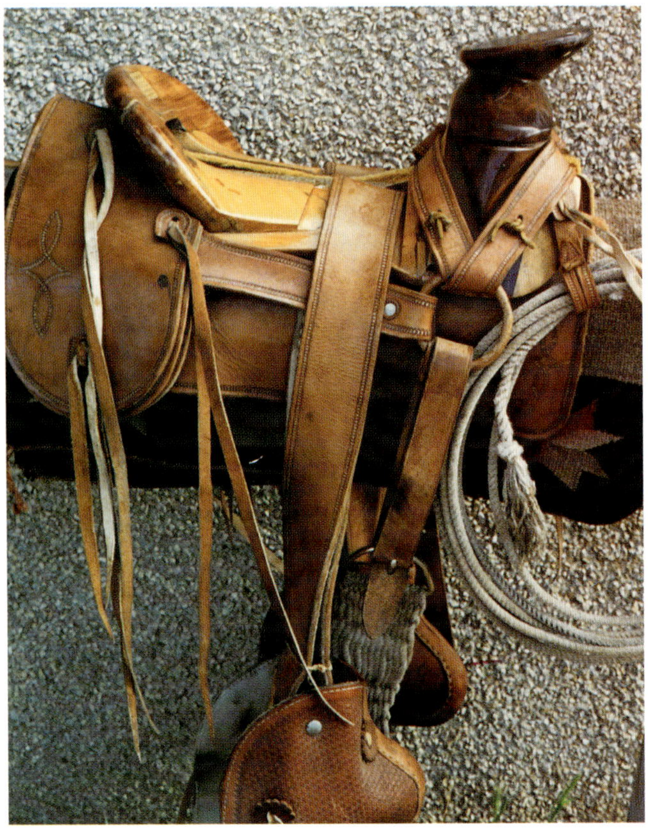

Very nice older Mexican made saddle with tapaderos and clearly marked in the wooden seat who the maker was. *Courtesy Gene Christopher. $300 to 500*

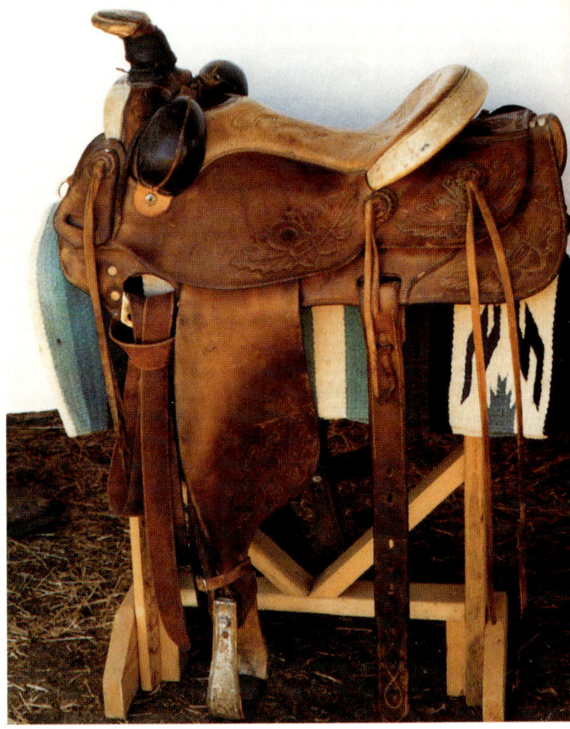

Charlie Baker made this saddle with added bucking rolls and a padded seat with hand-carved acorn pattern throughout. Excellent condition. *Courtesy Bob and Judy Bertsch. $1200 to 1500*

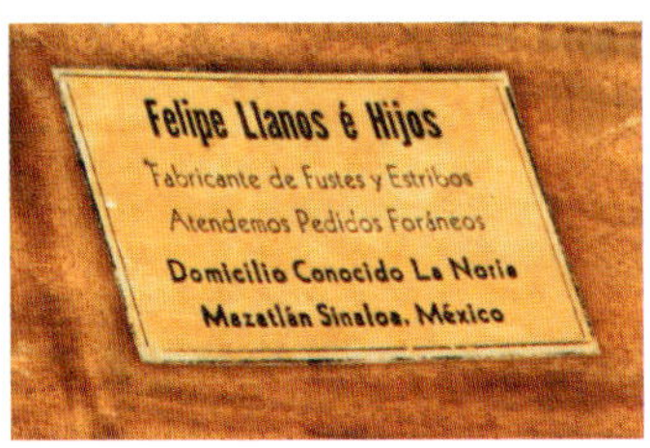

Detail of makers mark on the Mexican saddle.

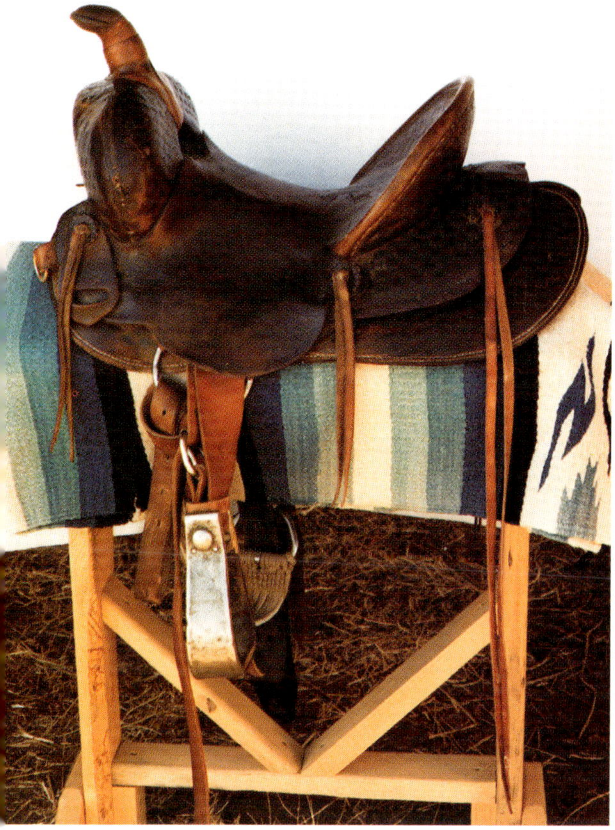

Hamley and Company built the saddle in their store in Pendleton, Oregon, c.1930. *Courtesy Bob and Judy Bertsch. $700 to 800*

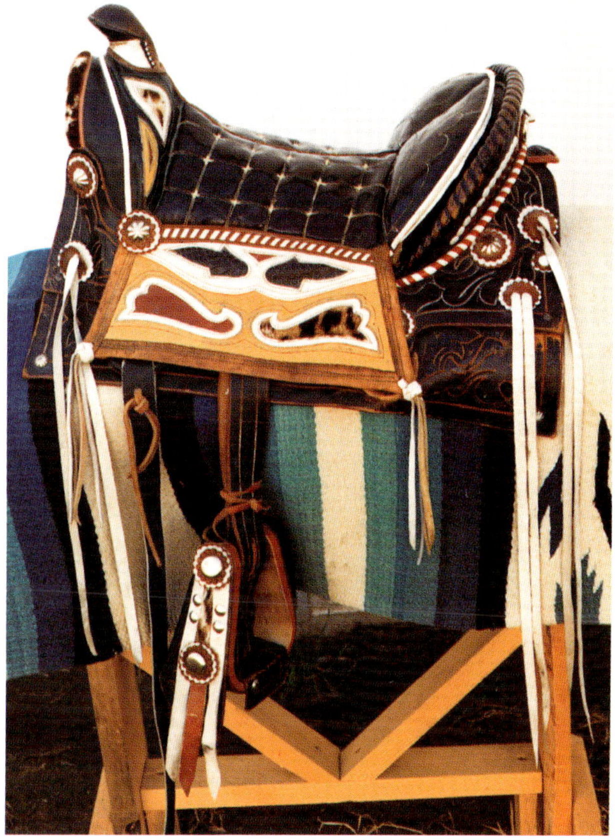

Made in Panama, this is a child's saddle with multiple inlays and overlays of rare animal leather. It sports everything from fur inlays to snakeskins. Quite unique. *Courtesy Bob and Judy Bertsch. $550 to 750*

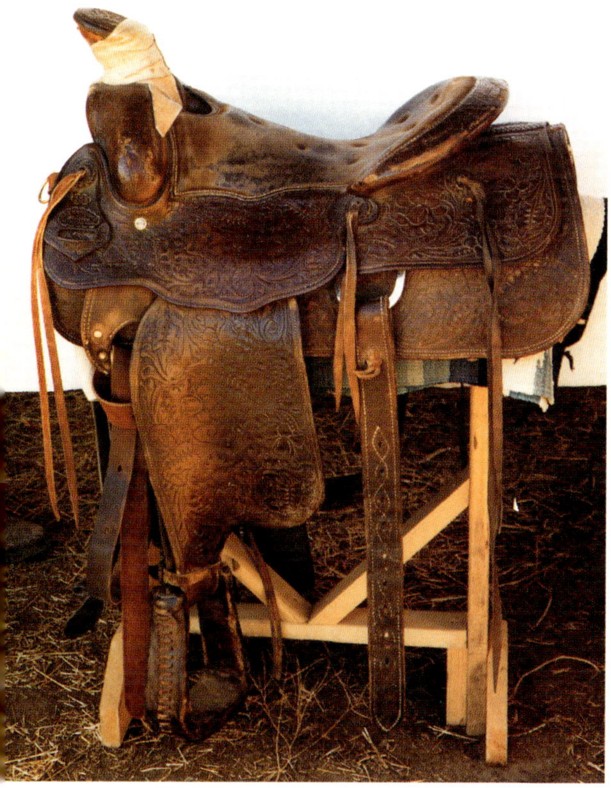

Van Core of Manteca, California, made this full flower tooled and double rigged saddle with a padded seat and covered stirrups. A very nice working saddle. *Courtesy Bob and Judy Bertsch. $2500 to 3500*

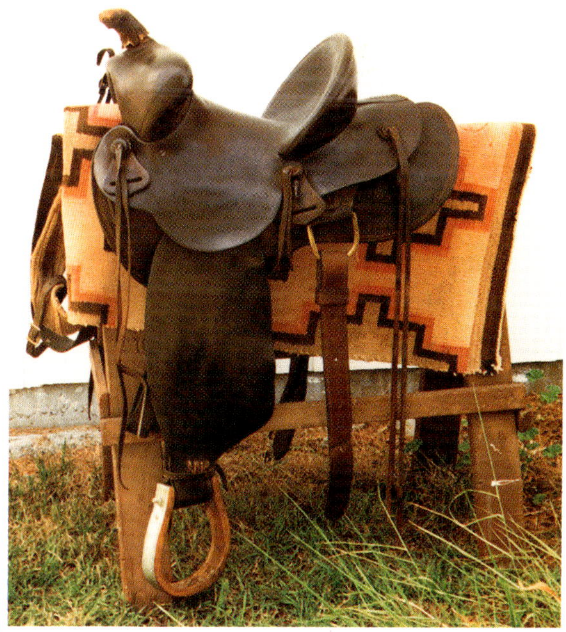

This saddle is a Hamley and Company Gold Medallion, one of the more desirable and collectible of all that Hamley made. It has a form fitter tree and was made in 1915. *Courtesy R.C. and Marvin Bales. $500 to 700*

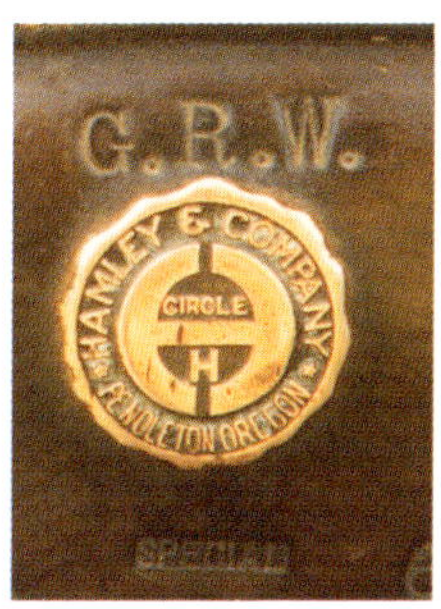

Detail of the Gold Medallion that marked these special saddles from Hamley and Company of Pendleton, Oregon.

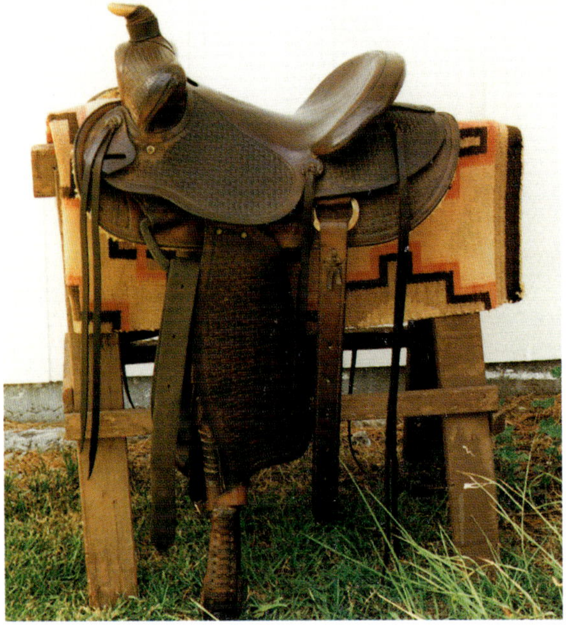

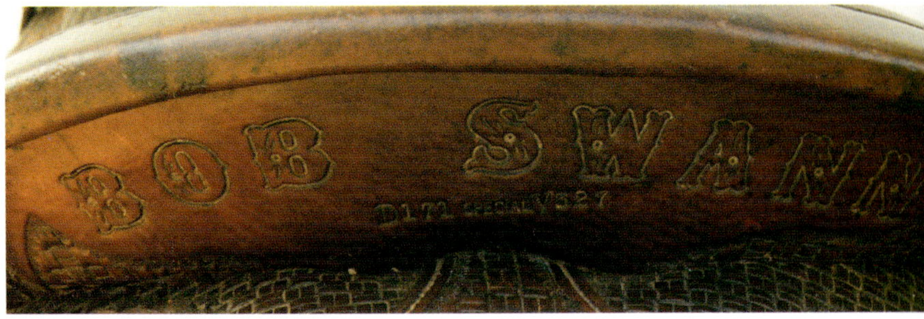

Detail of the Hamley numbering and the initials.

Very nice old Hamley and Company saddle built in the late 1940s. It is basket stamped throughout and was numbered on the back of the cantle and marked with the initials of its original owner. *Courtesy R.C. and Marvin Bales. $1500 to 2000*

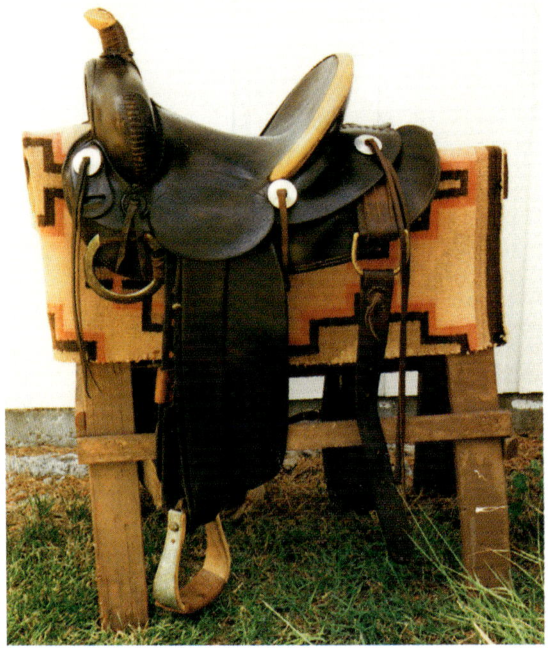

The maker is Victor Ario of Great Falls, Montana. This has a rawhide-bound cantle and is a beautiful early example of a good old "deep-seater." *Courtesy R. C. and Marvin Bales. $700 to 900*

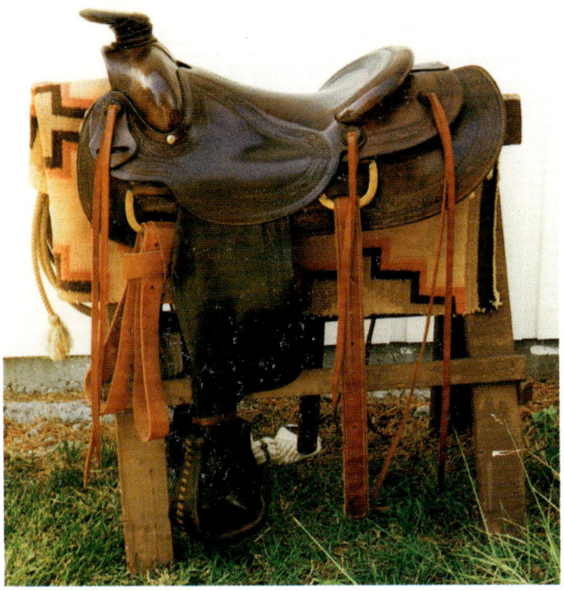

Hamley and Company saddle built on a Crosby Roper tree; it is a very nice saddle that would be considered useable today in just about anything a cowboy wanted to do. *Courtesy R.C. and Marvin Bales. $1000 to 1500*

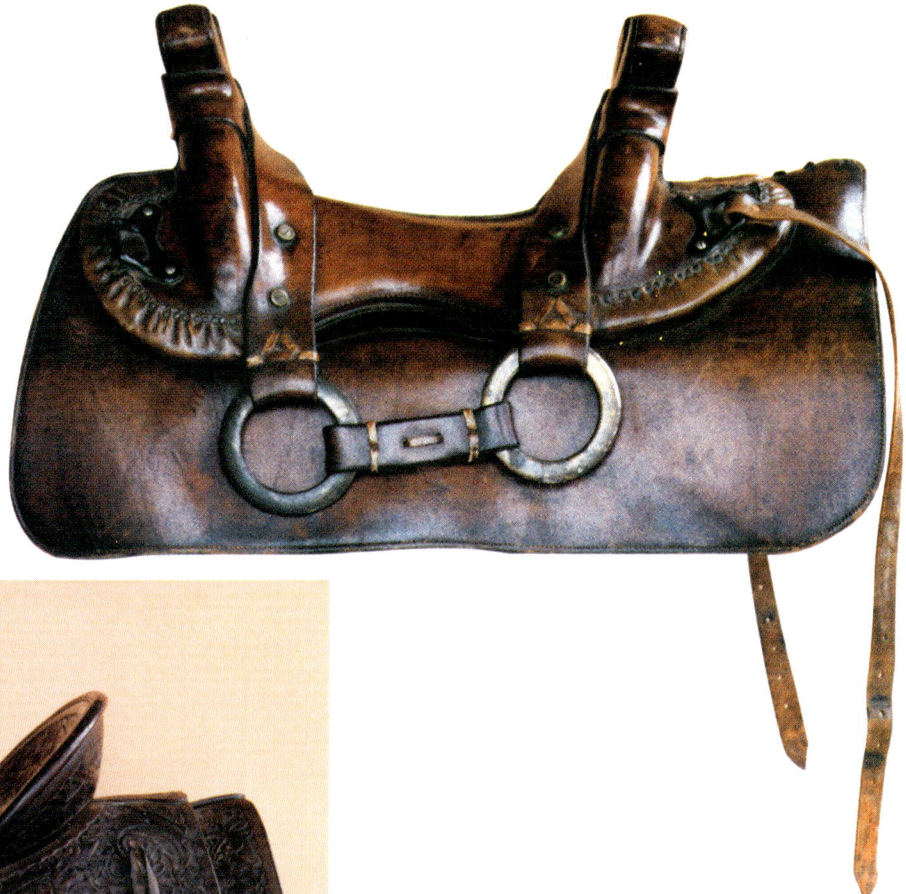

One of two known Hamley and Company pack saddles ever made. The other one is located in the Cowboy Hall of Fame and it was made for President Teddy Roosevelt, c. 1920s-30s *Courtesy Paul and Marlene Snider.* *$3500 to 5000*

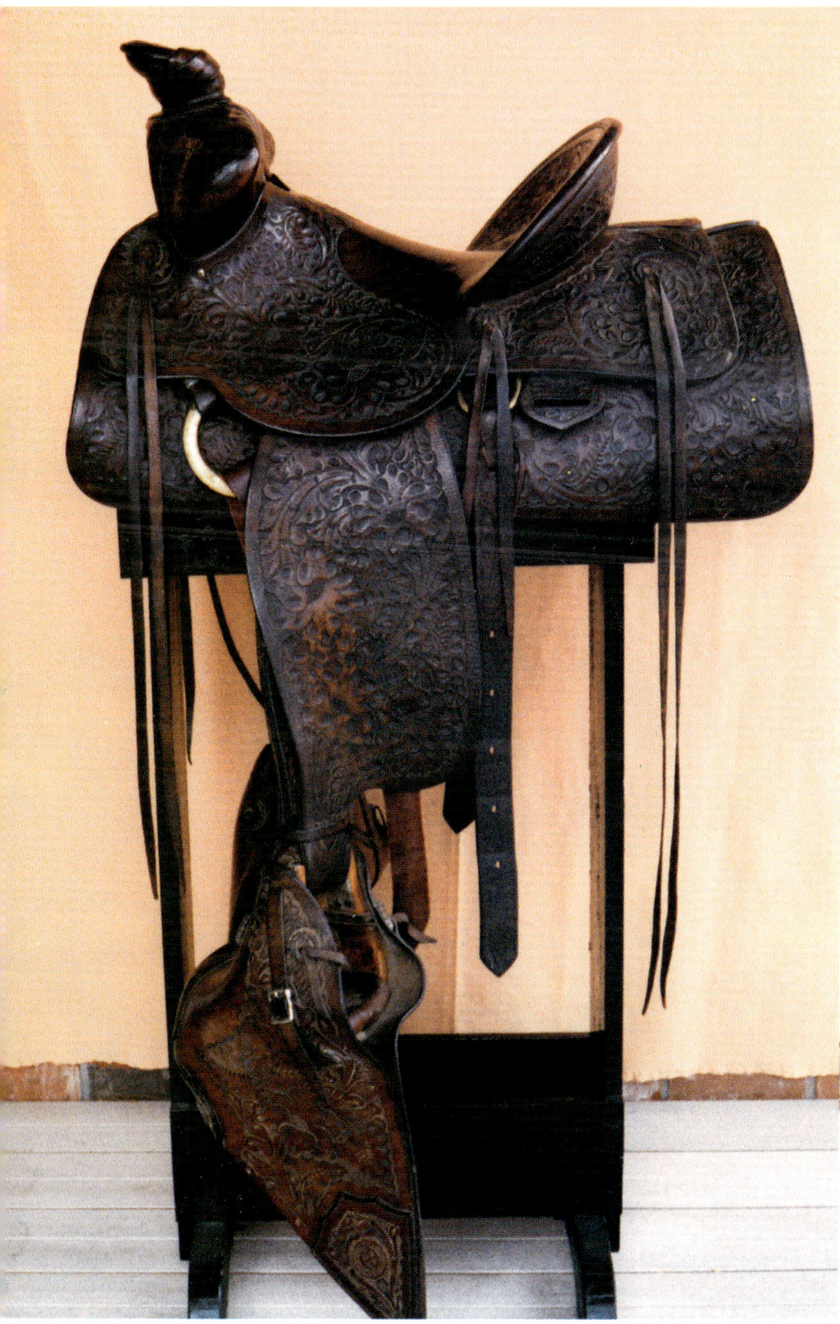

This saddle is an exceptional rendition from Hamley and Company of Pendleton, Oregon, c.1930. It has been kept in fine condition all of these years. Most remarkable is that it bears the maker's mark at the tip of the tapaderos. Beautifully hand carved leather throughout. *Courtesy Paul and Marlene Snider.* *$3500 to 5000*

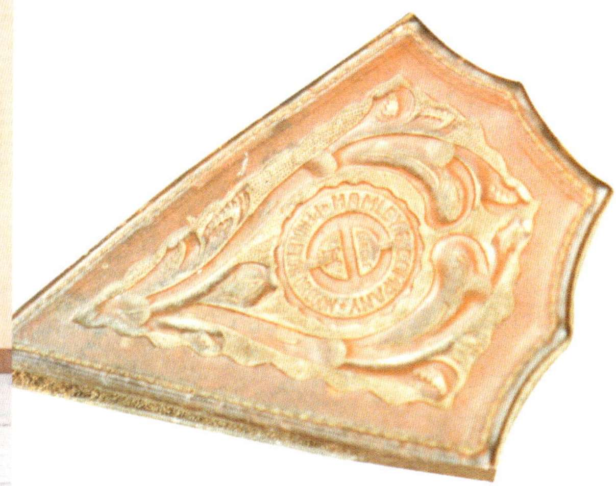

Detail of Hamley mark on the tapadero.

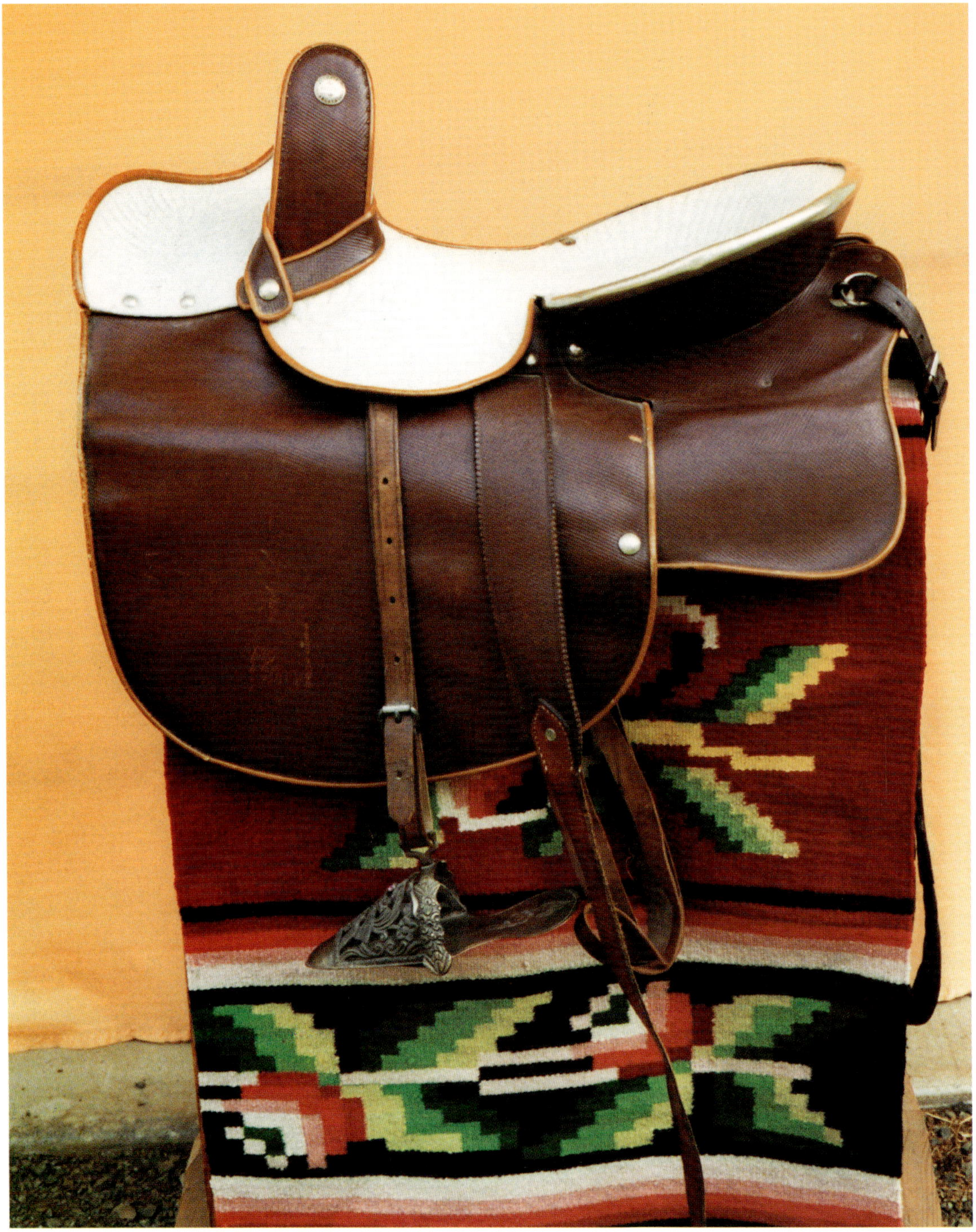

Over one hundred years old, this Peruvian wedding saddle was used by the bride to ride away after the ceremony. The seat is quilted white leather and the small lady' s shoe-shaped stirrup is very fancy bronze. The saddle, of course, is a side-saddle. *Courtesy private collector. $12,000 to 20,000*

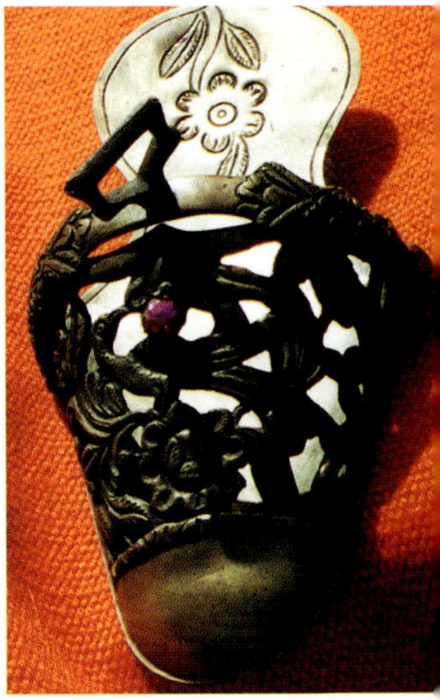

Detail of the lady's stirrup.

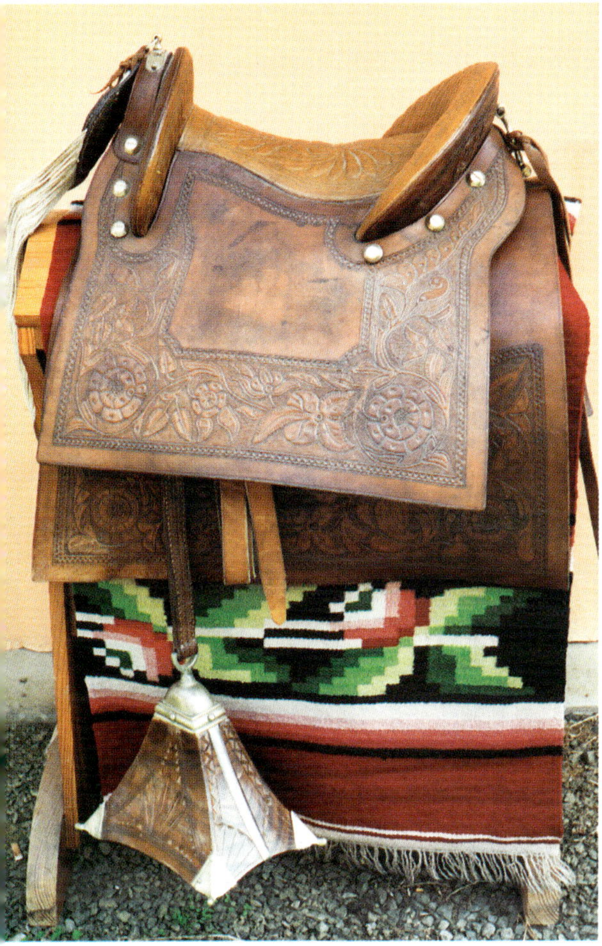

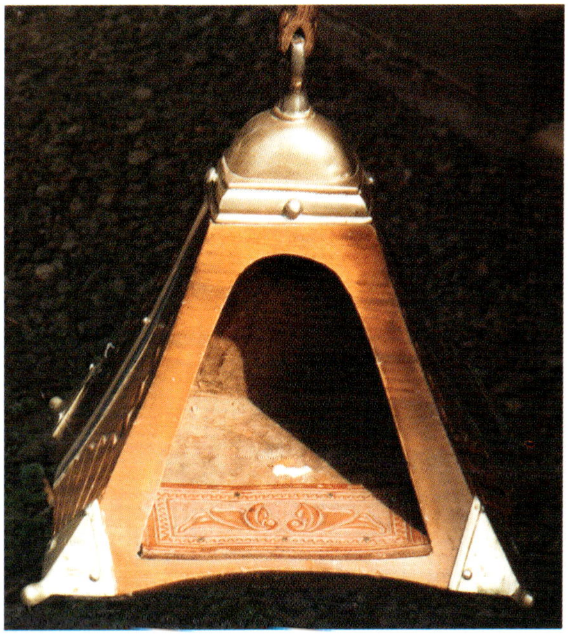

Top left: Peruvian saddle with a leather "corona" underneath, approximately fifty years old. The "bell" stirrups are made of carved wood and silver and are used for many purposes besides stirrups; they serve as weapons, candle holders, and—buried in the sand—they tie horses to the top ring. *Courtesy of a private collector. $2,000*

Top right: Detail of the Peruvian saddle's wooden stirrup. One can easily imagine some of the other uses.

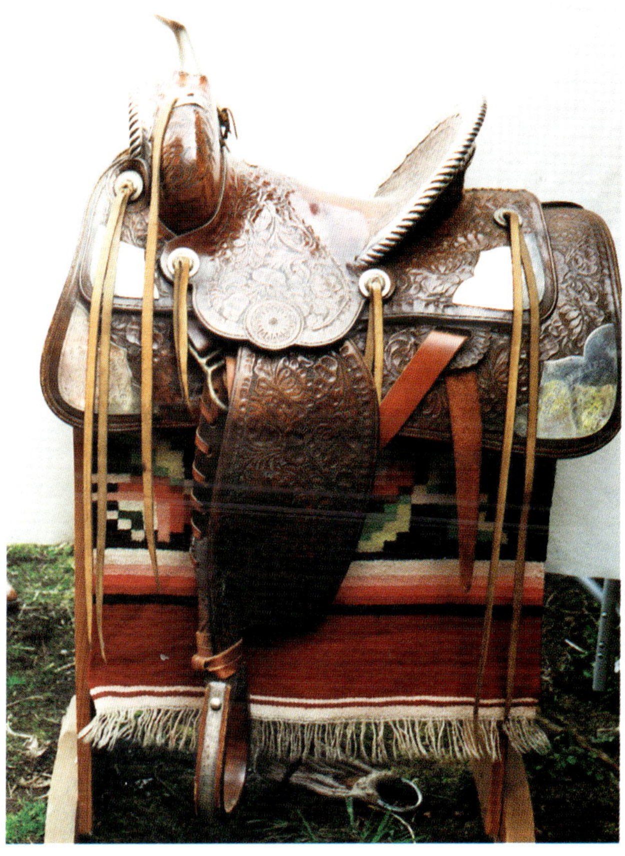

Wonderful old trophy saddle that tells some of its own story. The saddle was won by Jesse Drumheller during the early Frontier Days at Walla Walla, Washington, that was the fore-runner to the Pendleton Round Up. Won in September of 1913, it is a treasure and in pristine condition. *Courtesy private collector. $5,000 to 7,000*

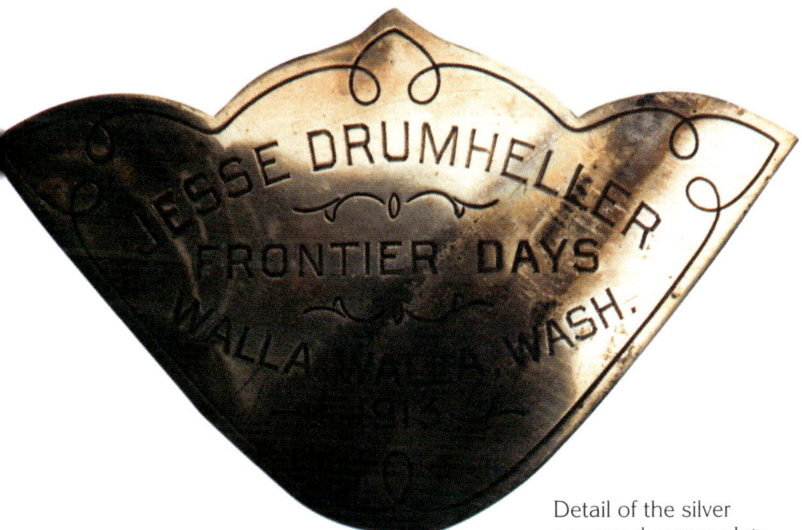

Detail of the silver engraved corner plate.

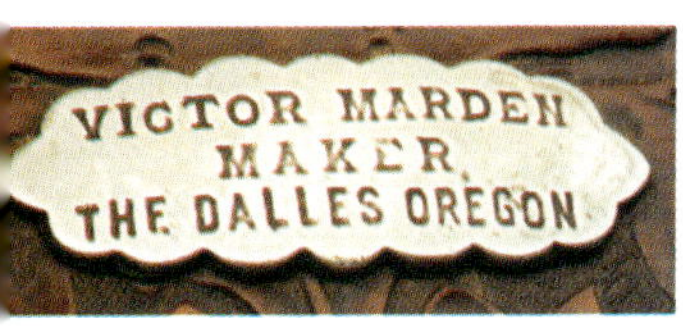

Detail of maker's name on the "Frontier Days" saddle.

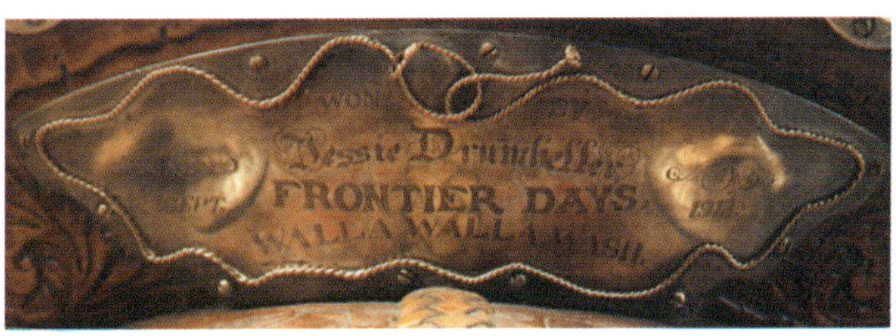

Detail of engraving behind the cantle.

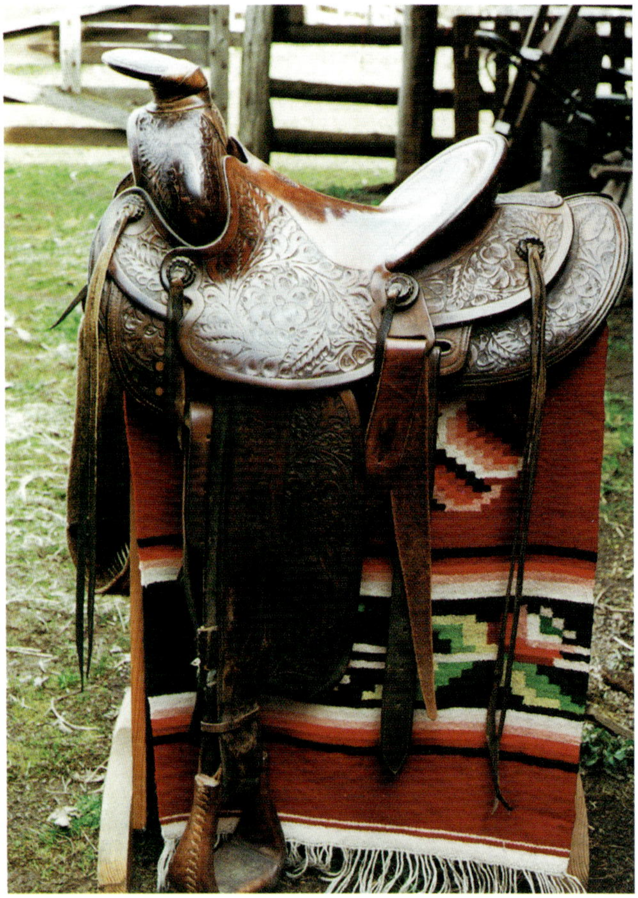

This Hamley and Company "Circle H" saddle has a Roper tree in it and is in pristine condition. *Courtesy private collector. $7,000*

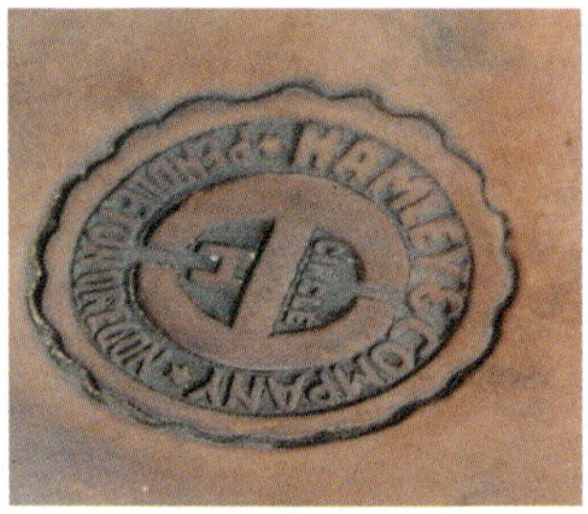

Detail of cartouche showing maker's mark on the Hamley and Company saddle.

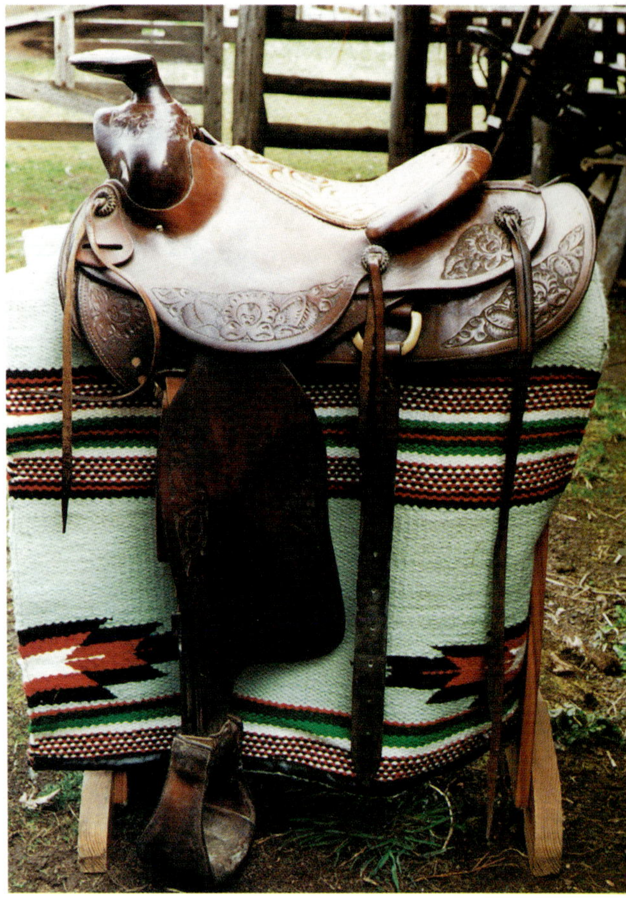

E.V. Horn is the maker of this nice old saddle. It has a Hamley quarter horse tree inside and is approximately fifty years old. *Courtesy private collector. $1500 to 2000*

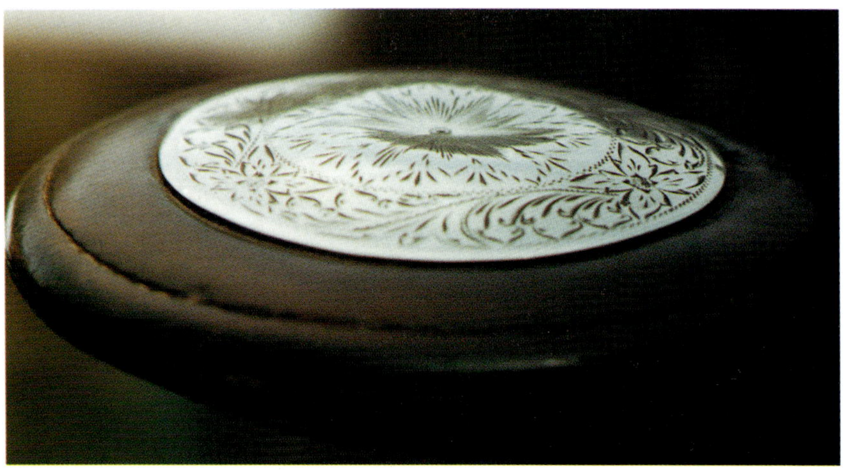

Detail of saddle horn cap on the E.V. Horn saddle.

Chapter Five

Bridles and Breast Collars

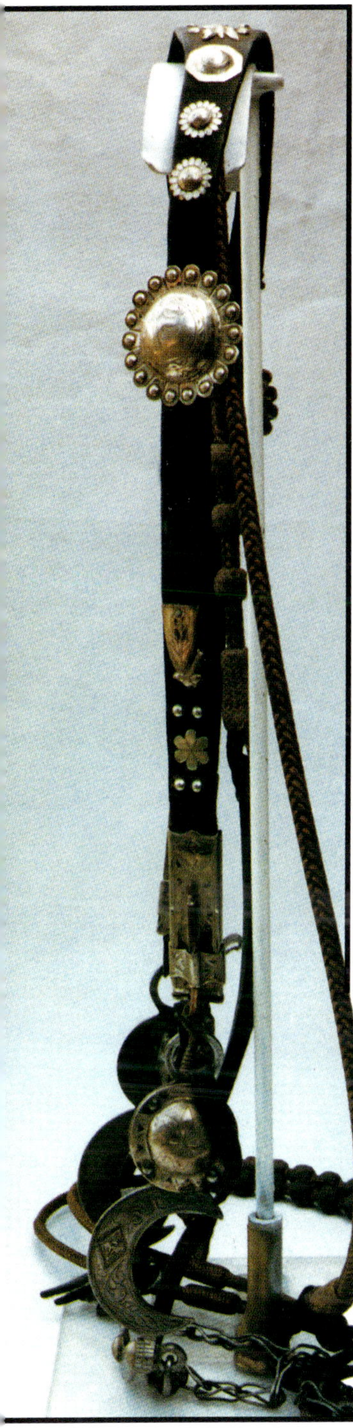

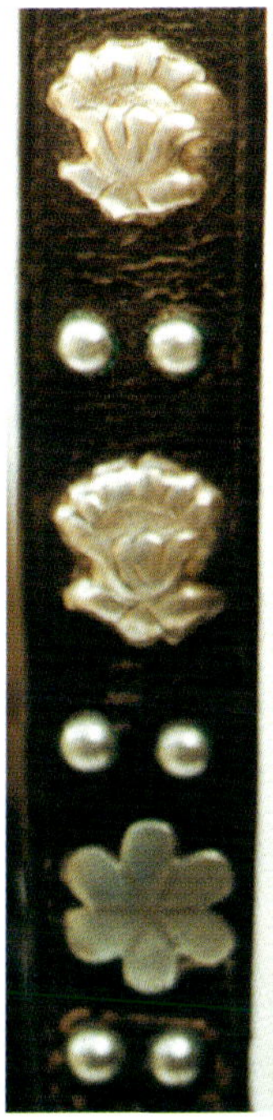

Above: G.S. Garcia made the bit in a Garcia bridle with silver mounted trim. The bit is held into the headstall with two silver "Spanish hooks" and the reins are braided rawhide with knots. Made in 1920, it is a fine old bridle. *Courtesy private collector. $2500 to 3500*

Above center: Detail of silver on the headstall.

"A cowboy's steering wheel"

Bridles

Bridles decorated with "jewelry" have quite a history. The first group to decorate their bridles were nomadic Scythians of the first millennium BC. Excavations of royal burial sites have provided much information on these decorated bridles. Gold was hammered into shapes and precious stones and glass were added before the entire piece was applied to a horse's bridle.

Native American horsemen had the right thinking when it came to simplicity of bridles. They used a single long leather strap that wrapped around the lower jaw of a horse and came up to make a rein on each side, giving them complete control over the horse no matter what the situation. White Americans have called this a "war bridle," simply because it generally was seen being used during early battles and altercations. If they were riding for pleasure or during a normal trek of every-day living, they rode "man to horse," and nothing more. A handful of mane and a strong nudge with a knee or foot was all that was used.

Bridle parts

Horse bridles can be confusing, so here the bridle is broken down to its necessary components. I am sure that if you are already an experienced horse person, all of this seems extraneous to you. If you are a shop-keeper in New York, however and for example, who has never seen a horse except in the busy street traffic, you would perhaps appreciate the information that explains the components making up a bridle.

The ***headstal*** is the part that fits onto the horse's head.
The ***bit*** with an adjustable ***curb strap***
The ***reins*** attach to the bit and come up to the hands of the rider.

If either of the four parts listed above are missing, you do not have a complete ***bridle.*** The parts then need to be described singularly, and separately, but not as a bridle. If even one of the four necessary components are not well matched to the other, the whole thing fails. If even one item is ill fitting to the horse, the entire bridle fails. Therefore, a good bridle must be carefully assembled to fit the horse and the needs of the rider. How it is ultimately put together is really vital to the rider's success with the horse.

Bridles can be simple utilitarian devices or fancy embellished show pieces. Somewhere between these extremes are the standard working bridles used by most cowboys.

The ***Hackamore bridle*** is a different story altogether. It is comprised of a ***bosel,*** usually braided of leather, rawhide, or horse hair, which is nothing more than a nose loop with a large knot at one end. The knot (sometimes woven as a Turk's knot) serves the greatest purpose on the bosel (pronounced bo-zel) because it applies pressure under the horse's jaw when the reins are pulled up. That location on the horse is a most tender place. A horse comes to attention when any pressure is applied here.

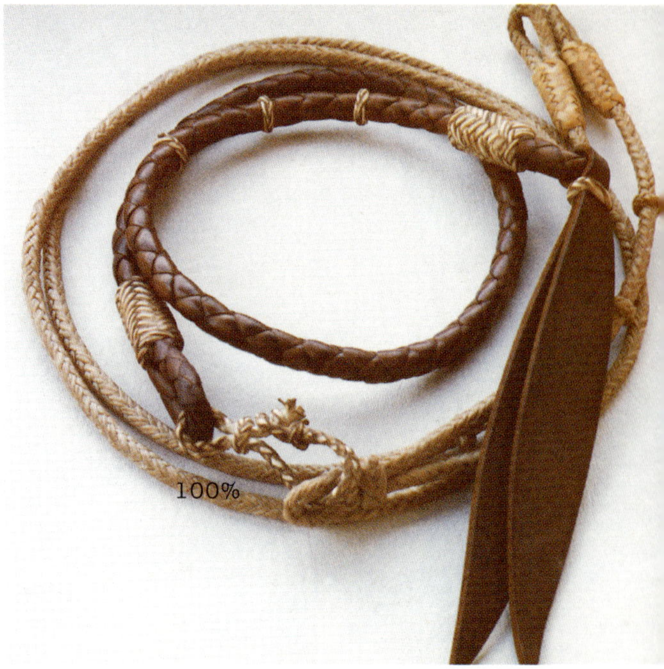

A nice working pair of reins with braided leather and rawhide. They are finished off with a flat leather romal (or popper) at the end. *Overton collection. $65 to 75*

Breast collars and martingales

The breast collar runs straight across the horse's chest, attached at each end to the saddle. Sometimes there is an added strap that runs under the horse's chest.

The martingale, however, is placed over the horses head, like a horse collar with a strap runing under the horse's chest and attaching to the saddle cinch underneath.

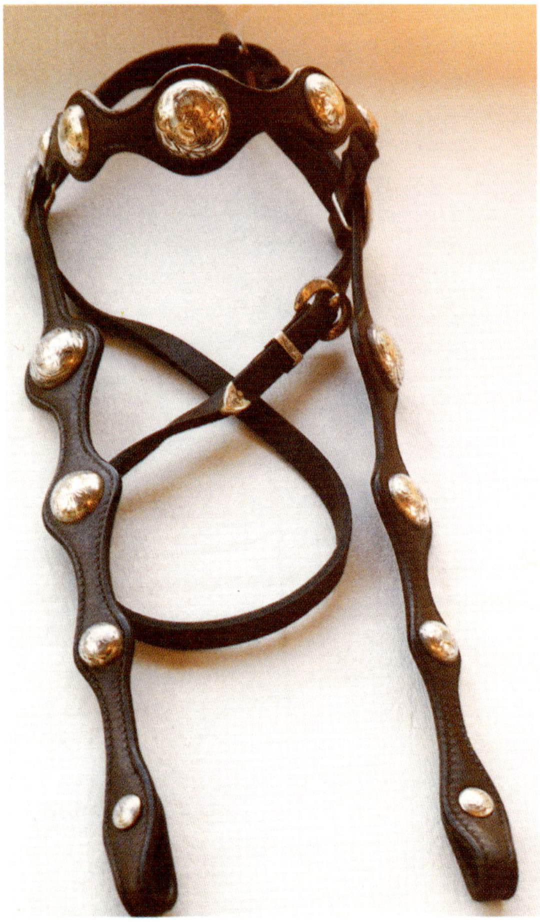

Beautiful sterling silver mounted headstall with small silver buckle set on finished leather. *Overton collection. $300 to 350*

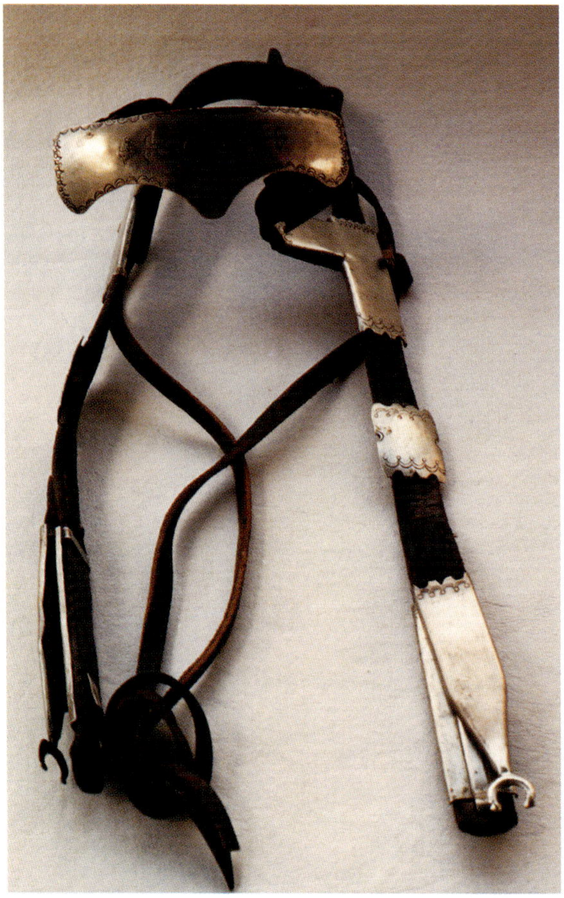

A most unusual and rare headstall most likely made by the Navaho people or Native Americans in the Southwest. Note the small najas hanging at the tips. *Overton collection. value unknown*

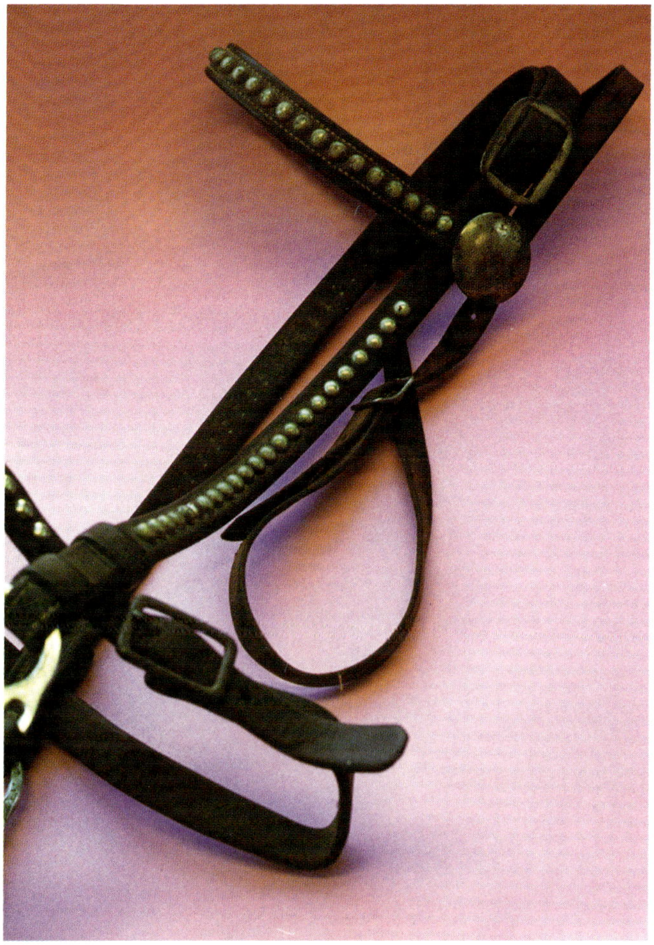

Old nickel silver spotted headstall with a California brow band. *Overton collection. $100 to 125*

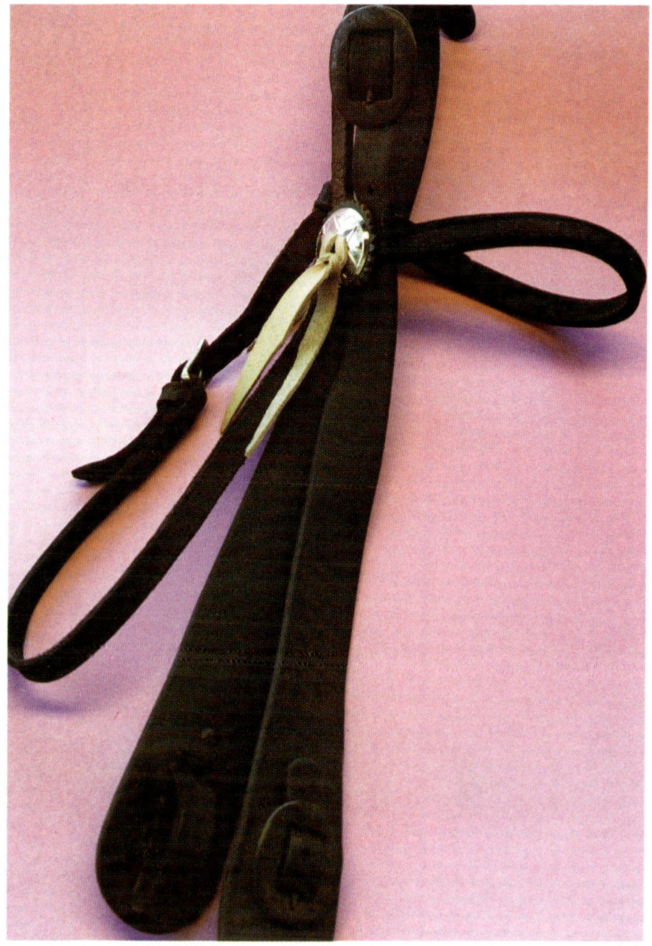

Very old and very plain utilitarian type headstall. *Courtesy R.C and Marvin Bales. $35 to 45*

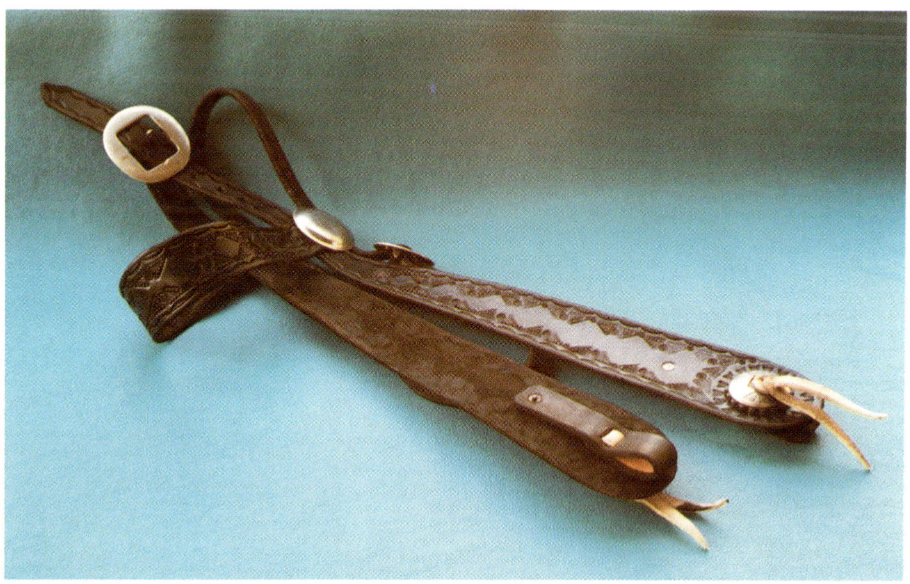

Nice old California style headstall with the broad cheeks and cartwheel buckles, the leather is tooled with designs. *Courtesy R.C. and Marvin Bales. $60 to 70*

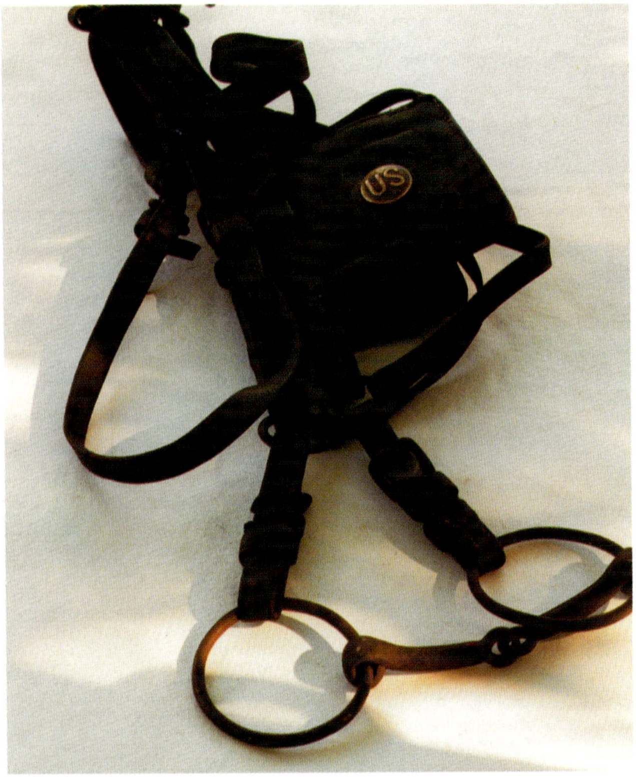

Old U.S. cavalry style work horse headstall with blinders and snaffle bit. *Courtesy R.C. and Marvin Bales. $65 to 75*

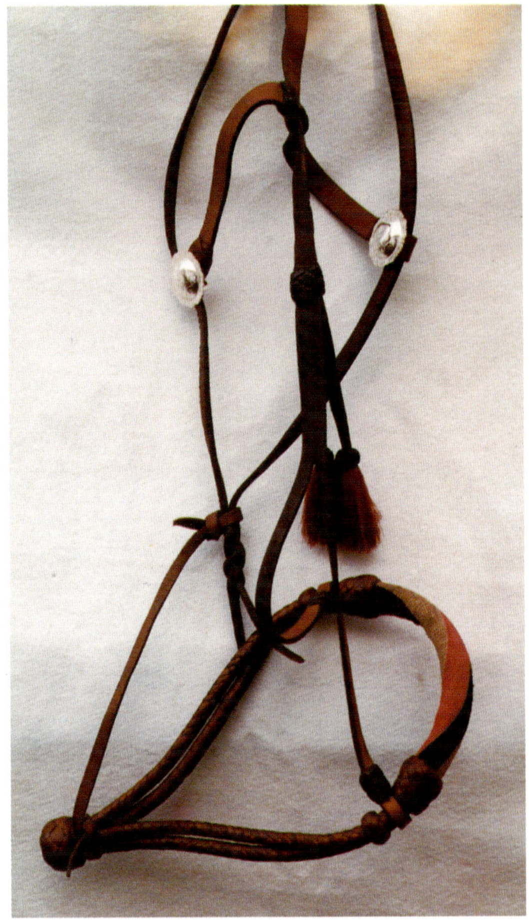

Beautiful old Hackamore with horse hair braiding and silver conchos. The tassels are also horsehair that has been died. Attributed to early Walla Walla prison made. *Courtesy Ron and Sharon Mailloux. $750 to 900*

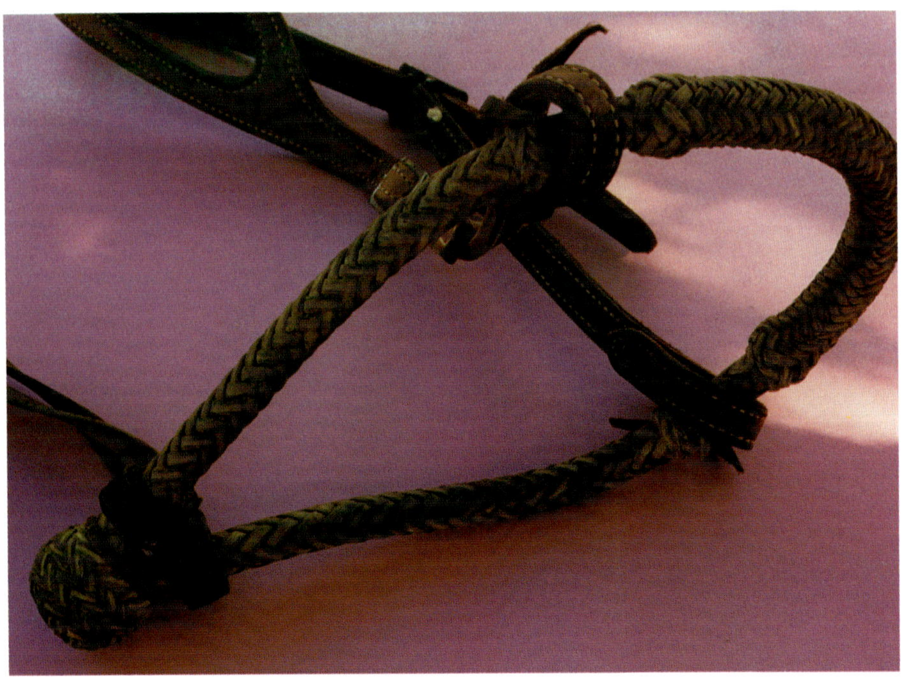

Nice old using type Bosel with large "Turks knot" at bottom. *Courtesy R.C. and Marvin Bales. $75 to 100*

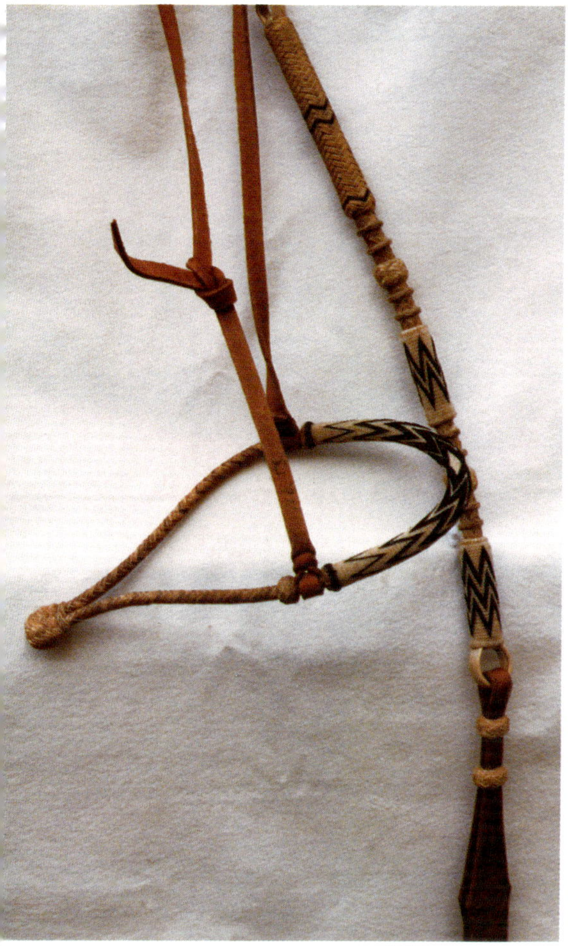

This very ornately braided horsehair Hackamore and reins is part of a matching set with regular bit and reins (the matching half pictured next). The two pieces make up the most attractive, yet still useable, bridles. *Courtesy Ron and Sharon Mailloux. $3000 to 3500 the set of two*

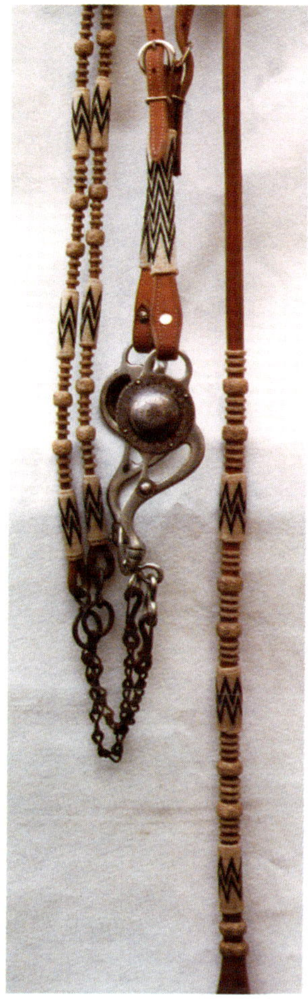

Matching set to the Hackamore, this bridle carries a Visalia "humane" bit within, and is a beautiful piece of braided horsehair; probably the nicest workmanship to be found. *Courtesy Ron and Sharon Mailloux. $3000 to 3500 the set of two.*

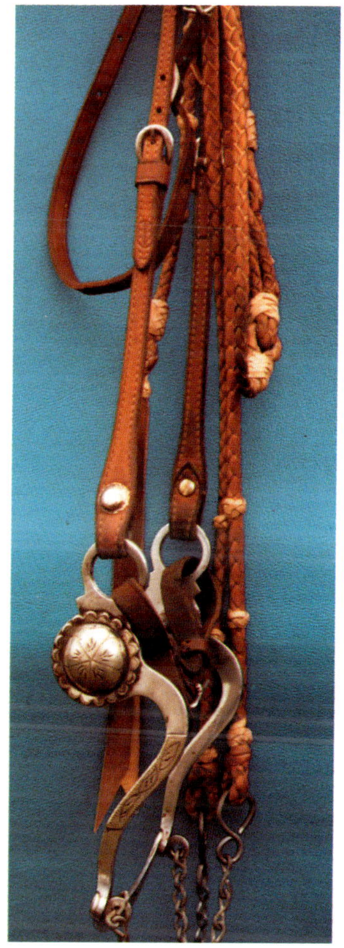

This is a good example of a cowboy's working bridle. With a good leather headstall and braided leather reins, it carries a good Crockett port - mouthed bit with nice rein chains and leather curb strap. *Overton collection. $525 to 700*

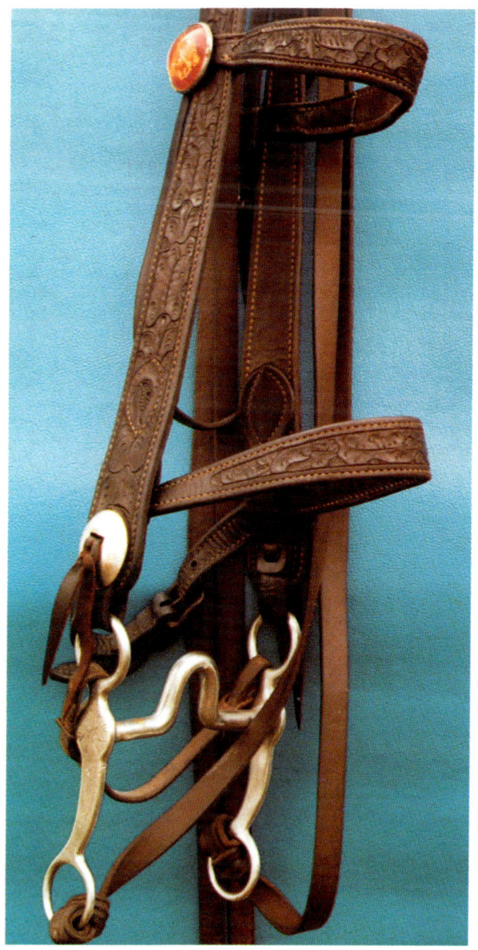

Ellis Horn California style bridle with wide cheeks on the headstall and a nice old Buermann port bit made of nickel silver. Glass horse head rosettes are named and numbered on the back. *Overton collection. $650 to 800*

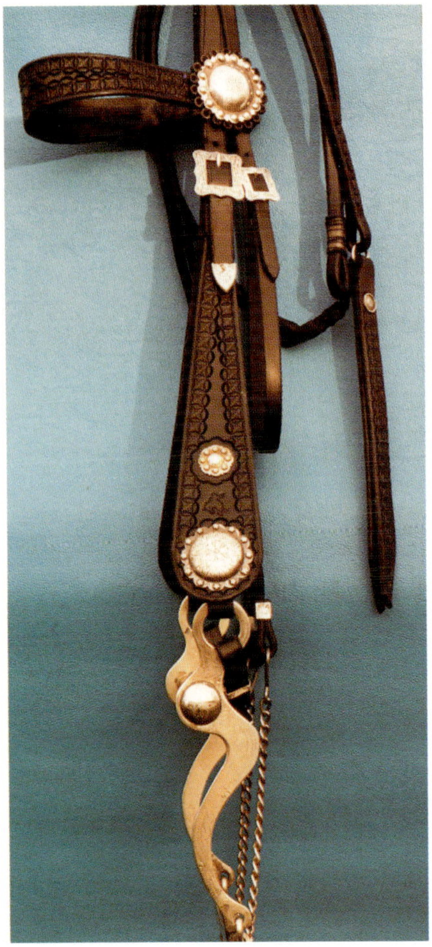

Ricardo bit and beautiful California style wide banded headstall with superior sterling silver conchos and buckles. It is a beautiful bridle, with nice rein chains, leather curb strap and hand-made leather throughout. The romal is decorated with a small sterling concho. *Overton collection. $1200 to 1500*

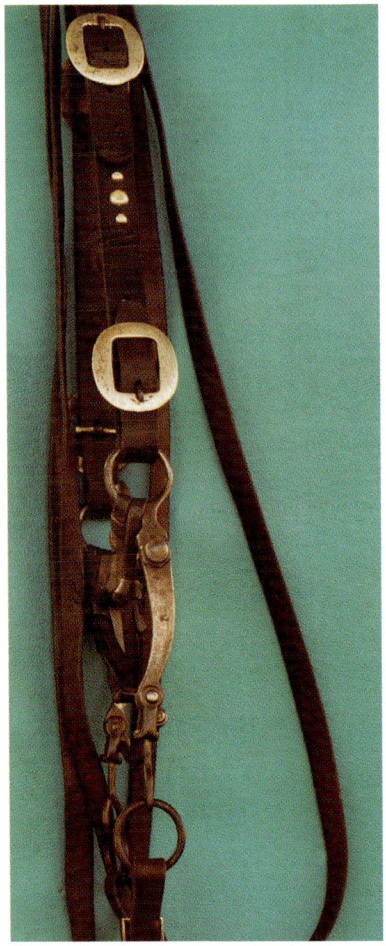

Old North and Judd cartwheel buckles are a part of this bridle, with older Buermann bit. *Courtesy R.C. and Marvin Bales. $250 to 275*

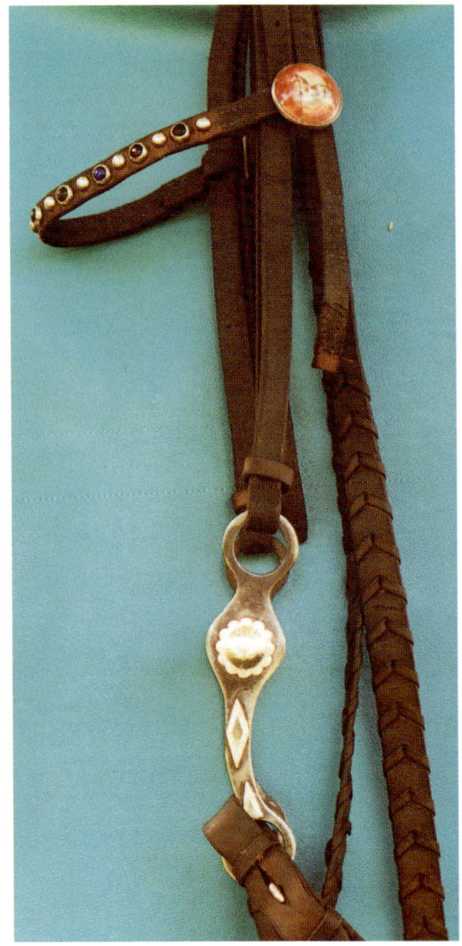

Nice old bridle with glass rosettes and a Crockett bit. *Courtesy R.C. and Marvin Bales. $350 to 400*

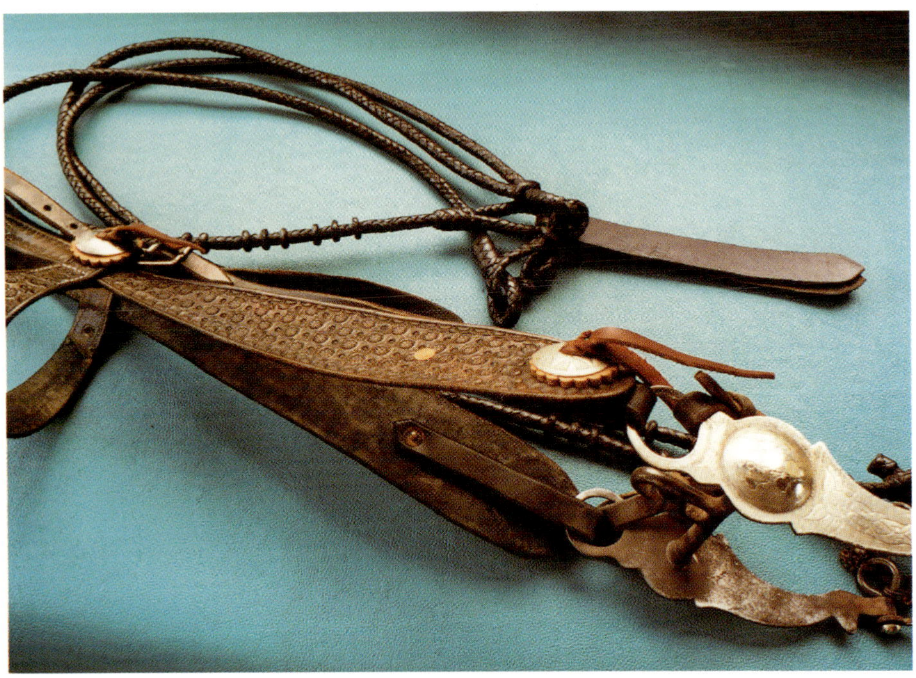

Walla Walla prison-made bit, kangaroo reins, and hand-made headstall with German silver conchos make up this very fine bridle. *Overton collection. $1000 to 1500*

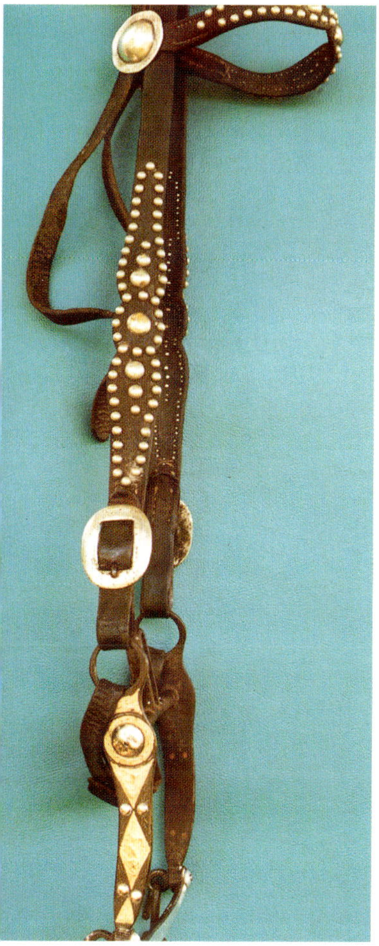

Elegant and flashy, this bridle contains a bit that has Hamley and Company's mark inside it. *Courtesy R.C. and Marvin Bales. $1200 to 1800*

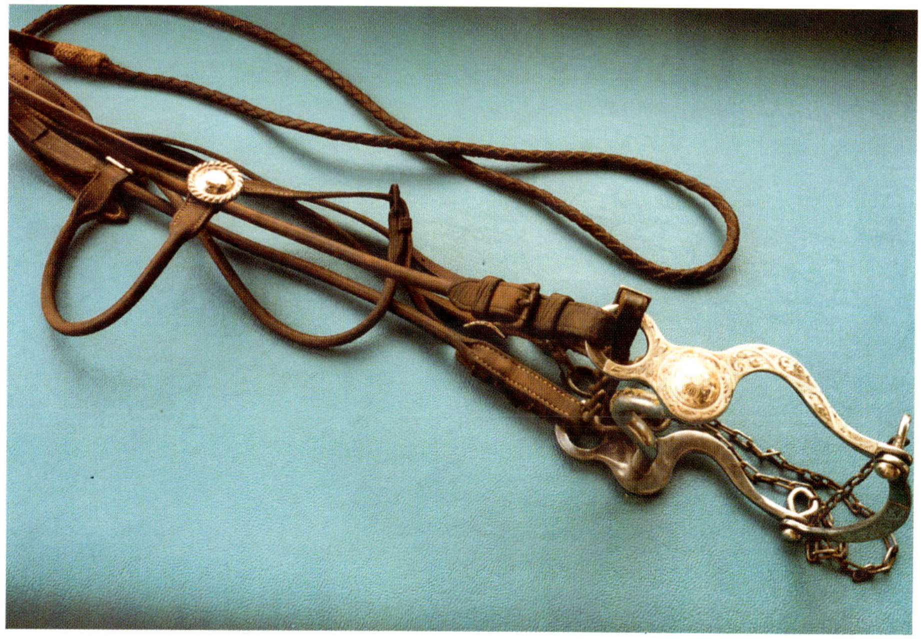

Crockett-Renalde sterling silver mounted bit with a port mouth piece and nice hand-made leather headstall with braided roping rein. *Overton collection. $500 to 600*

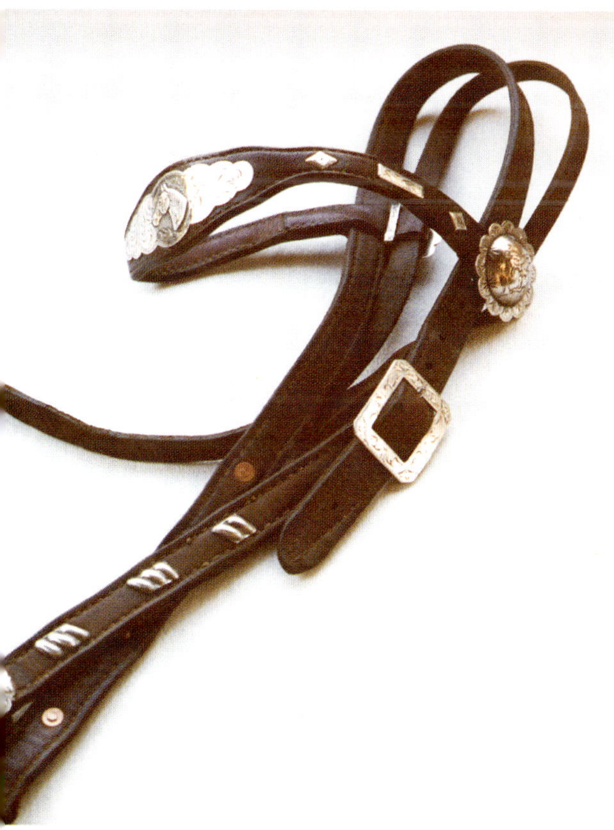

This elegantly adorned headstall was made by Bohlin, the maker to the Hollywood stars. The squared buckle is especially unusual. *Overton collection. $800 to 1000*

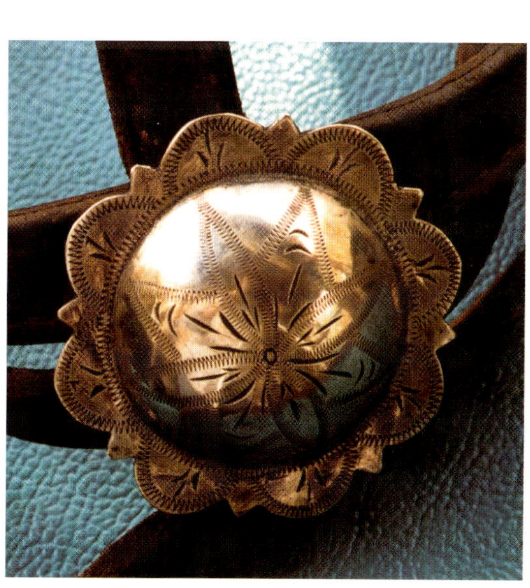

Detail of the large Bohlin concho.

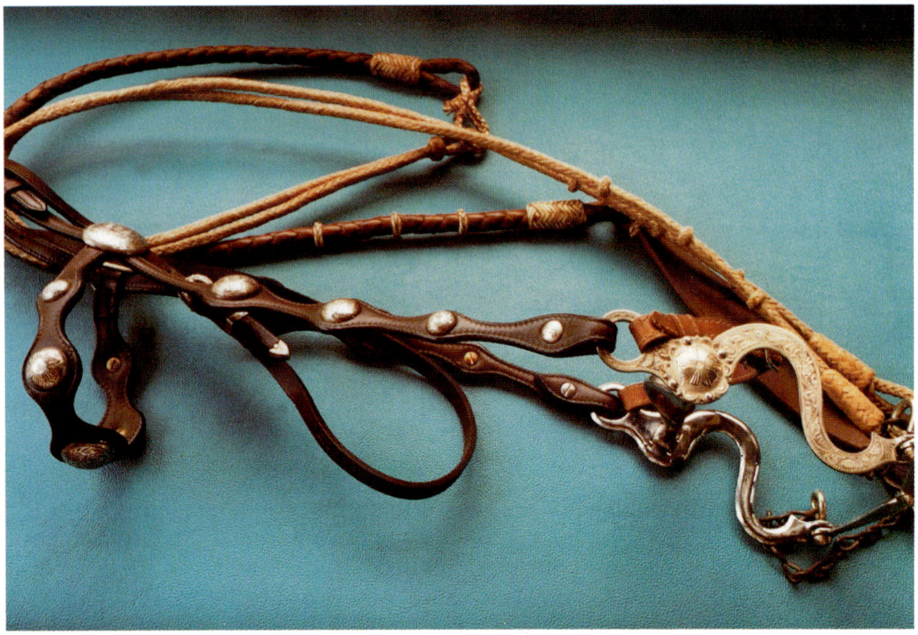

Very beautiful old bridle with a Garcia half breed bit and a Buck Steiner headstall with rawhide braided reins. *Overton collection. $800 to 1500*

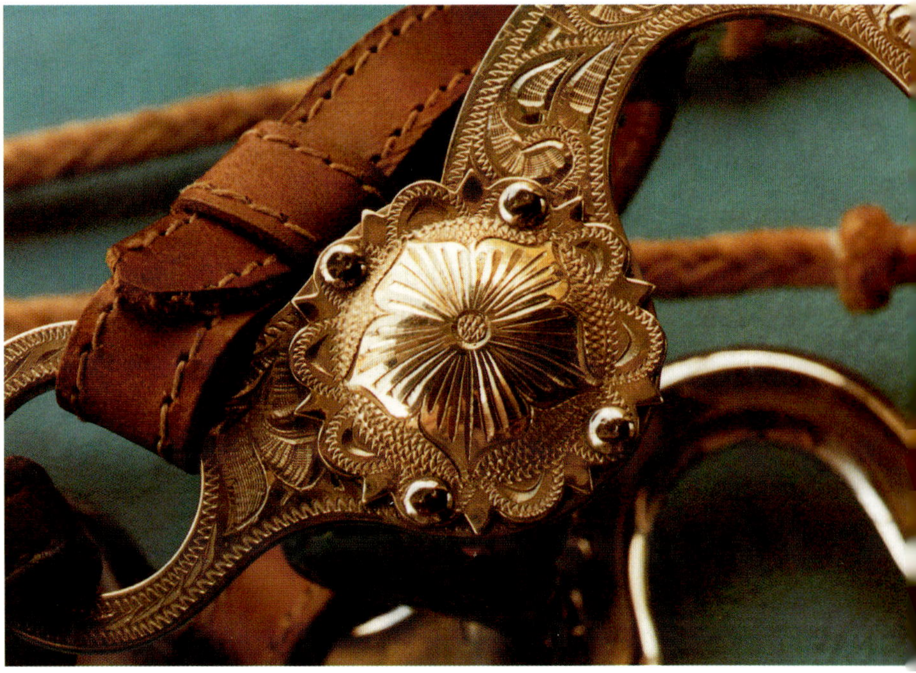

Detail of the silver work on the Garcia bit.

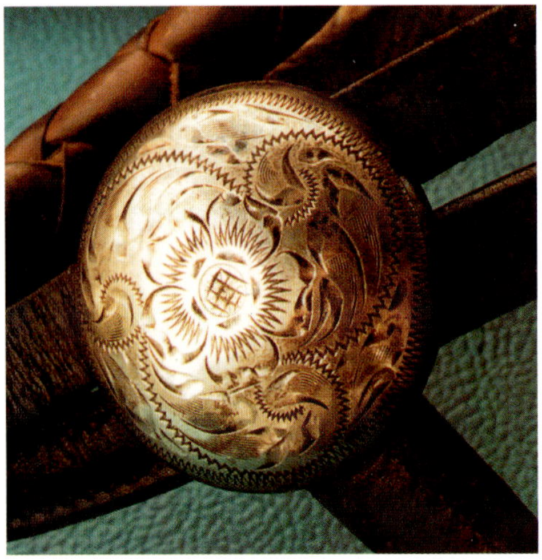

The silver conchos on the old bridle (above) are attributed to Bohlin, who was the cowboy builder for the Hollywood stars in early black and white movies.

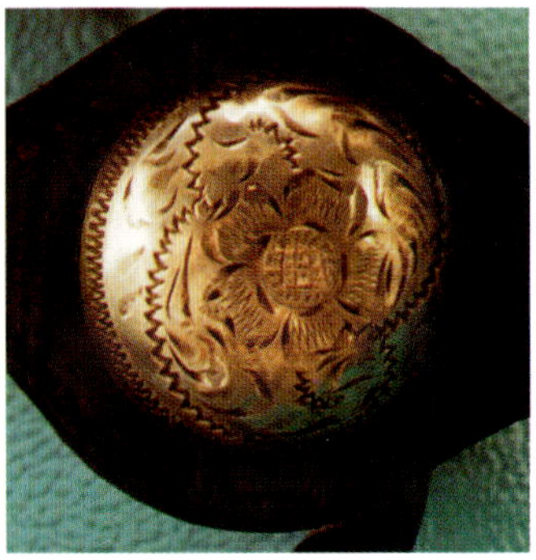

Detail of the very beautiful Bohlin-attributed conchos.

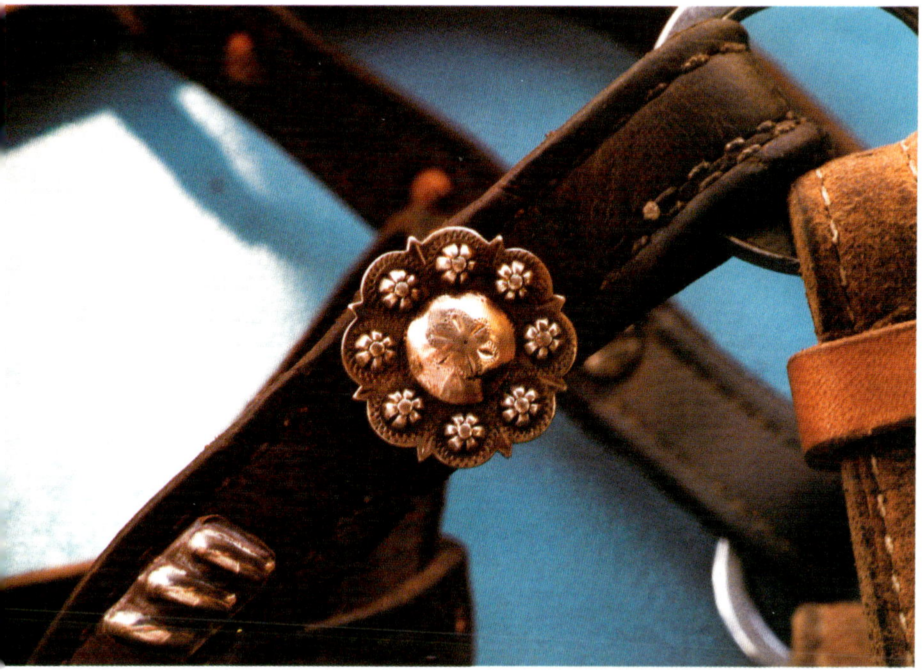

Detail of concho on previous bridle which is attributed to Visalia, and not Bohlin, so has possibly been a contemporary addition. (The concho is not broken, as it appears in the photo....an inexplicable "fluke" of photography that was puzzling until it was rechecked.)

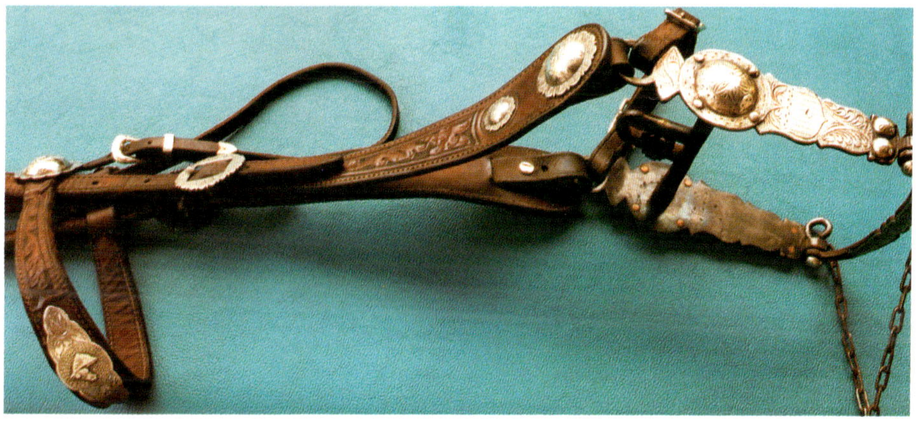

Mike Morales, the famous bit and spur maker, made the patriotic shield bit and Ellis Horn made the leather bridle. Visalia created the silver embellishments. Together they make up a beautiful bridle and one that is useable. *Overton collection. $1800 to 2000*

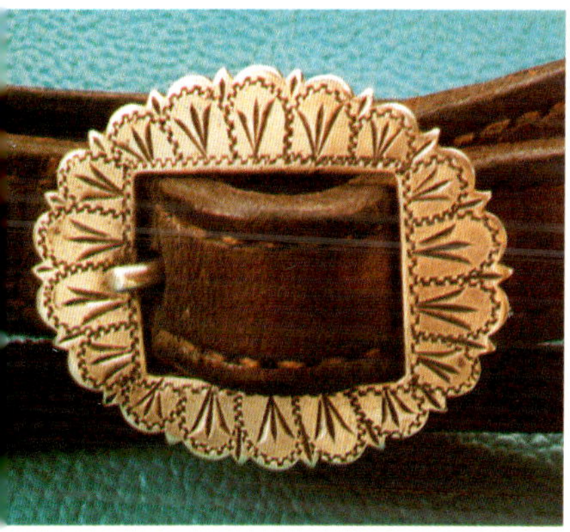

Detail of silver buckle.

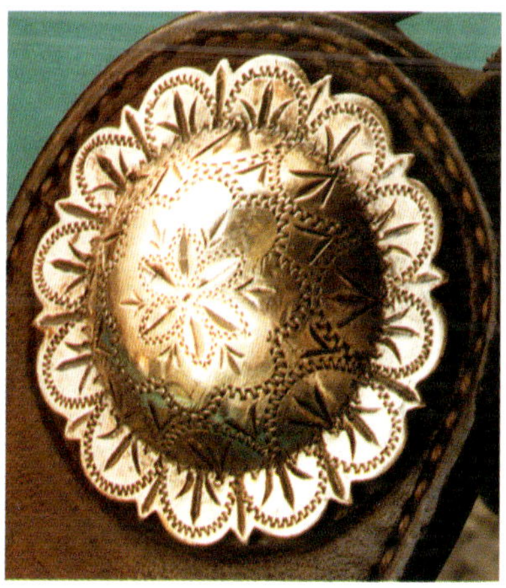

Detail of large concho on the Ellis Horn bridle.

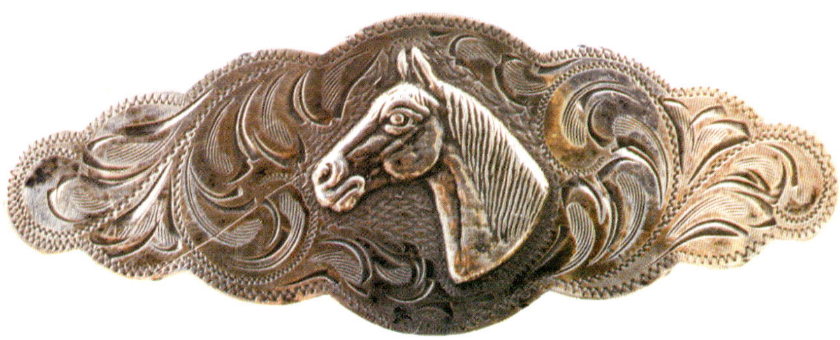

Detail of Visalia brow band decoration.

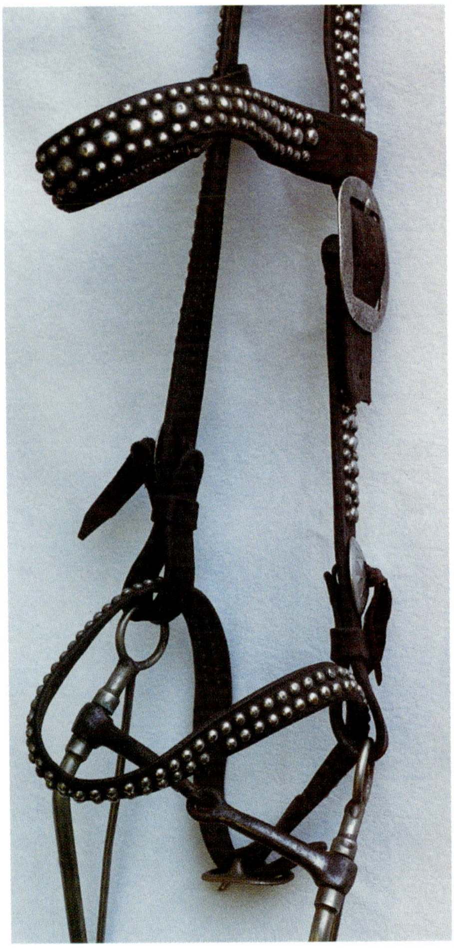

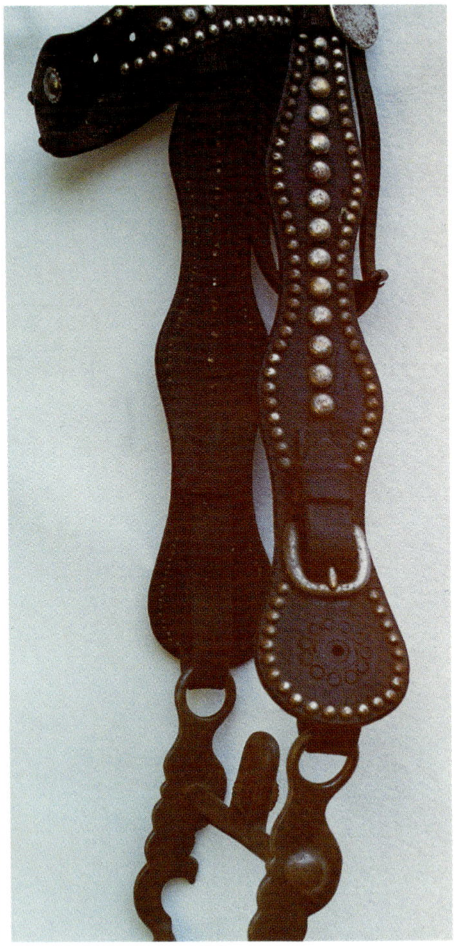

Nice old headstall with nickel studs on a wide cheeked, California style bridle. The bit is an old "single flying bird" bit made by Buermann. *Courtesy private collector. $200*

Long cheeked snaffle bit has been placed in the nice old nickel-studded headstall. *Courtesy private collector. $350*

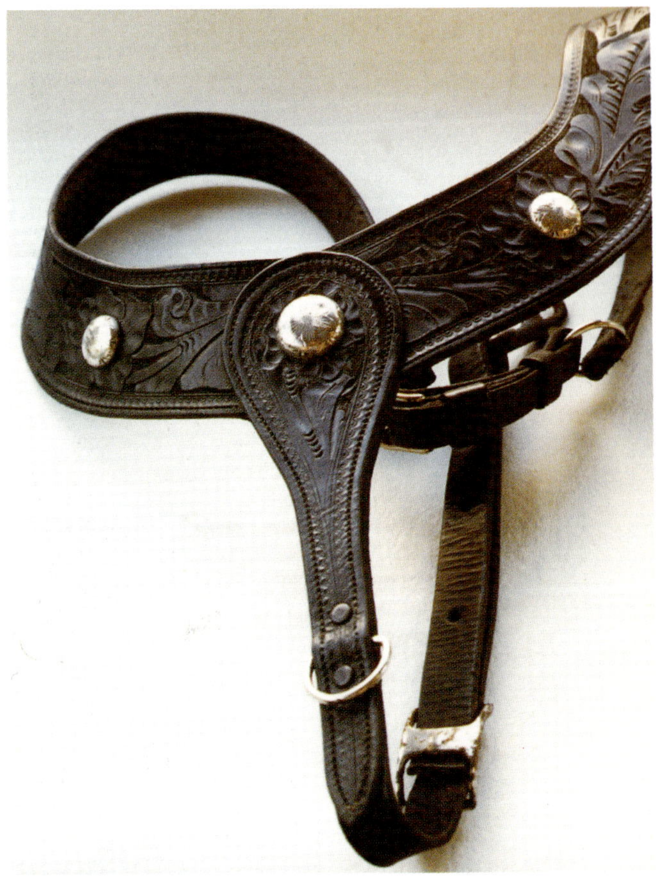

Hand-carved leather martingale made by Bohlin of Hollywood, California. Edward H. Bohlin was the master craftsman for the early Cowboy Kings of the black and white movies. He created silver and leather items with an artistic flair that has never been equaled. *Overton collection. $300 to 350*

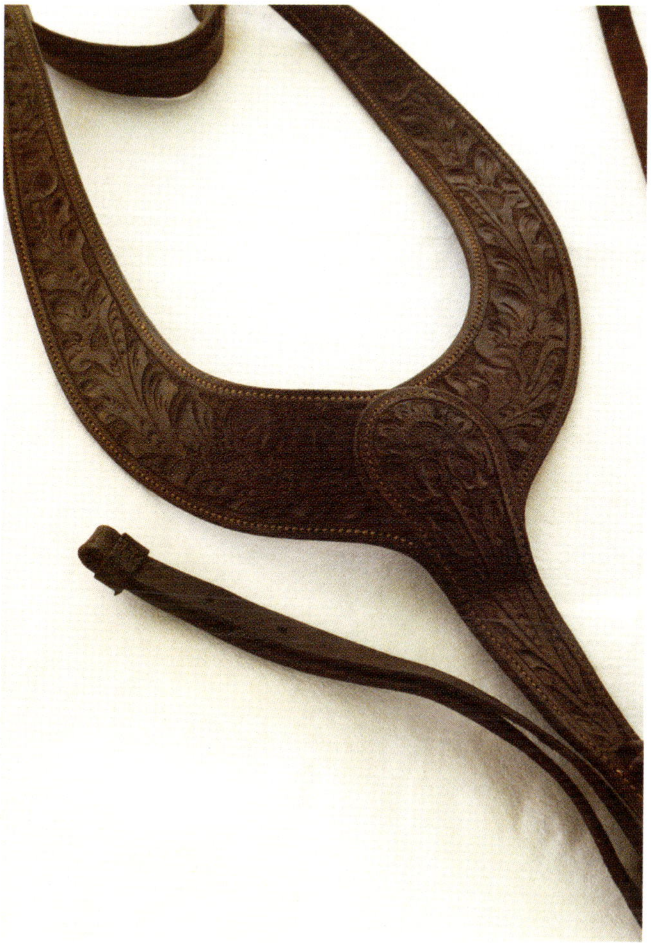

Well carved and put together, this is the standard using type of martingale. *Courtesy R.C. and Marvin Bales. $150 to 250*

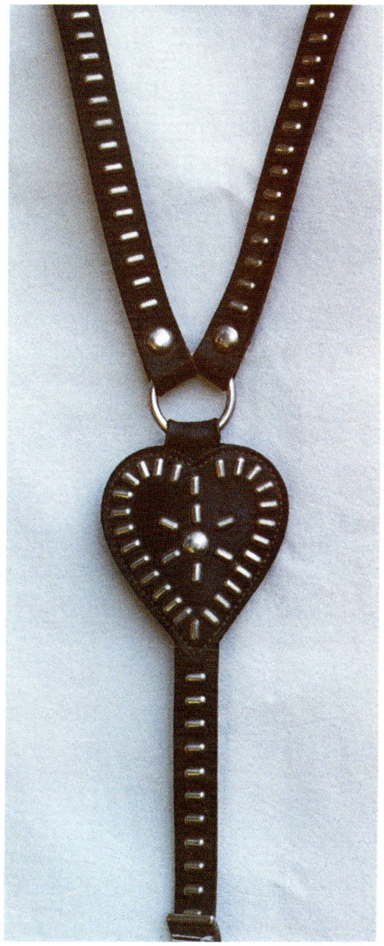

Very old and well studded with nickel silver spots, this is a very attractive old martingale. *Courtesy private collector. $100 to 150*

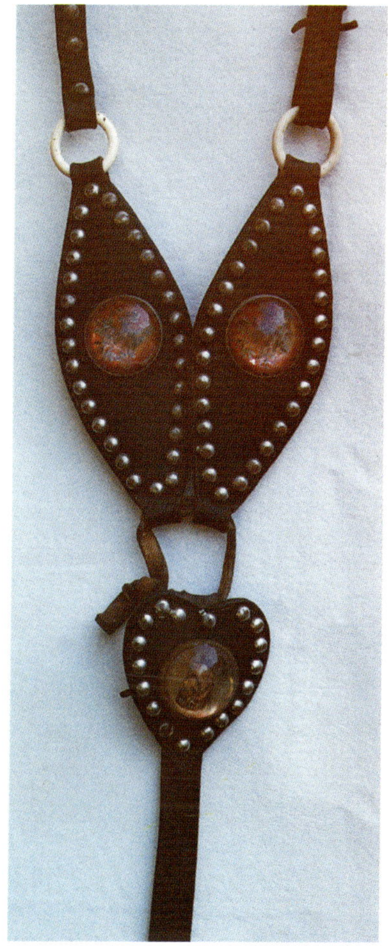

Fine old martingale with three nice glass rosettes and nickel silver spots. *Courtesy private collector. $350*

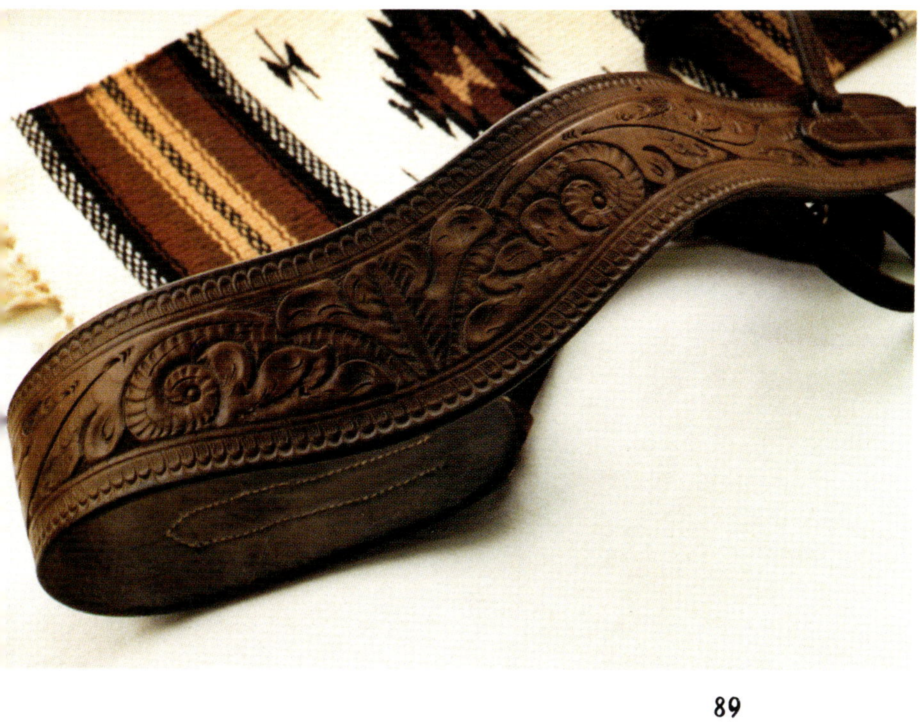

Made by Hamley and Company of Pendleton, Oregon,this is a fully carved leather breast collar. *Overton collection. $150 to 175*

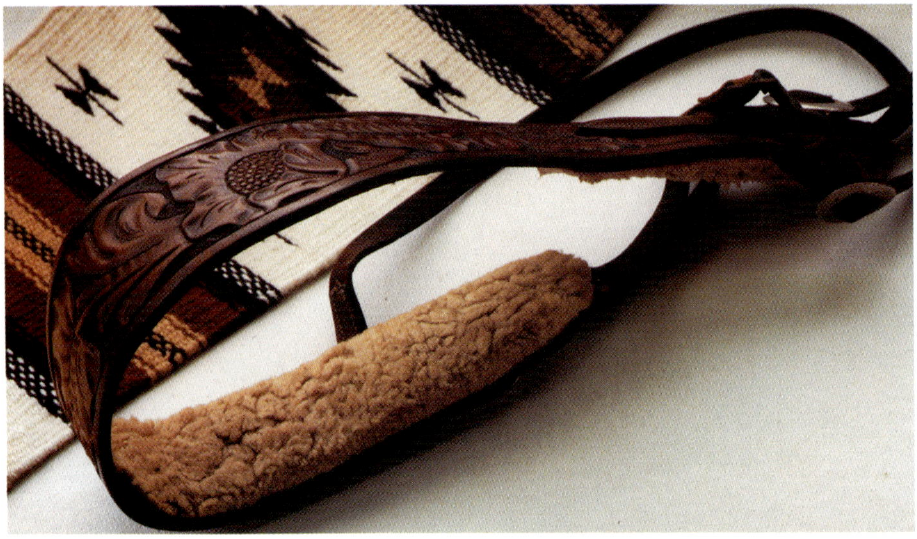

This was made by W.F. Overton, when he was a youngster, as a gift to his father in 1945-46. *Overton collection.* *$155 to 195*

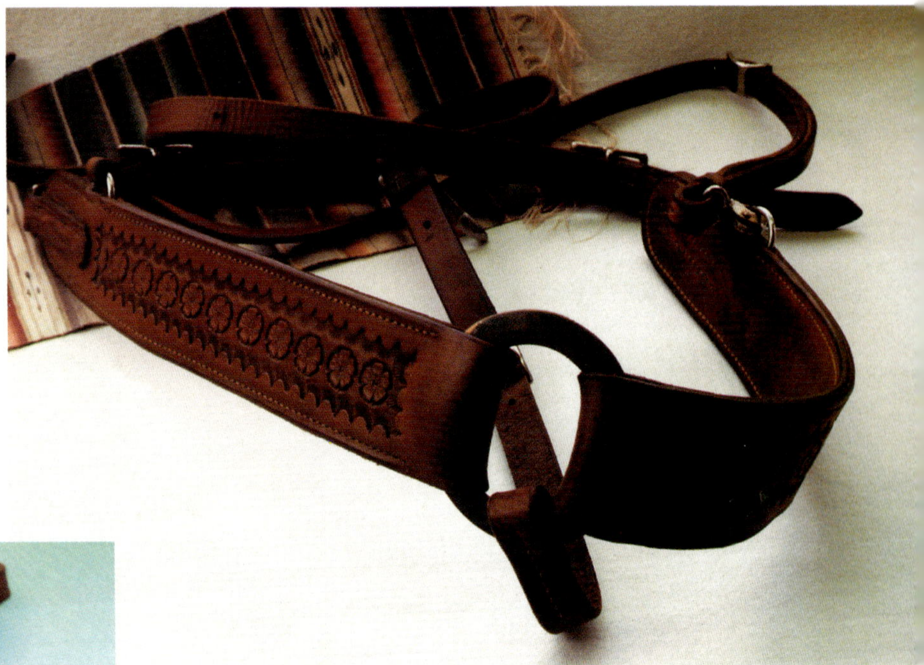

Breast collar that is hand stamped and made by the late great Charlie Baker. *Overton collection.* *$160 to 180*

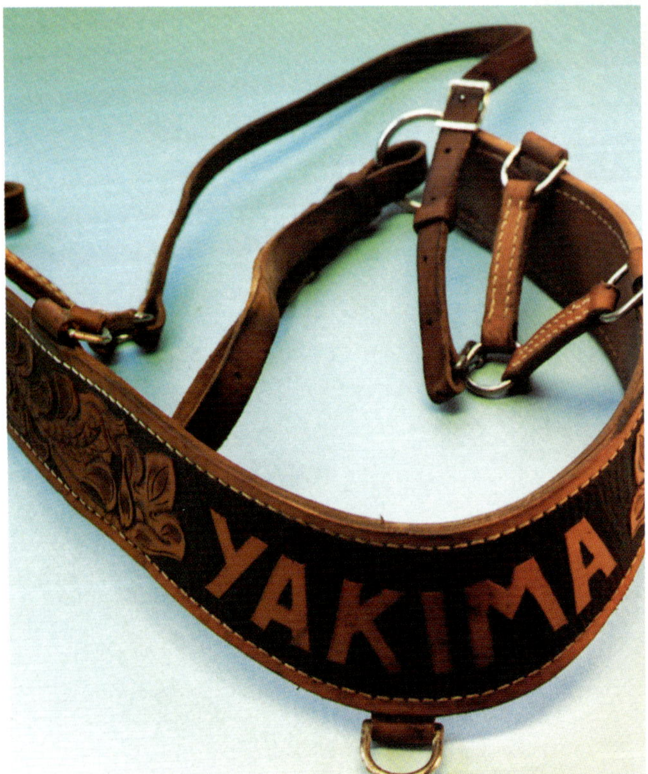

Fairly contemporary, this breast collar was made for one of the Indian princesses at the Toppenish, Washington, Pow-Wow. *Courtesy Wade Brumley. $100 to 125*

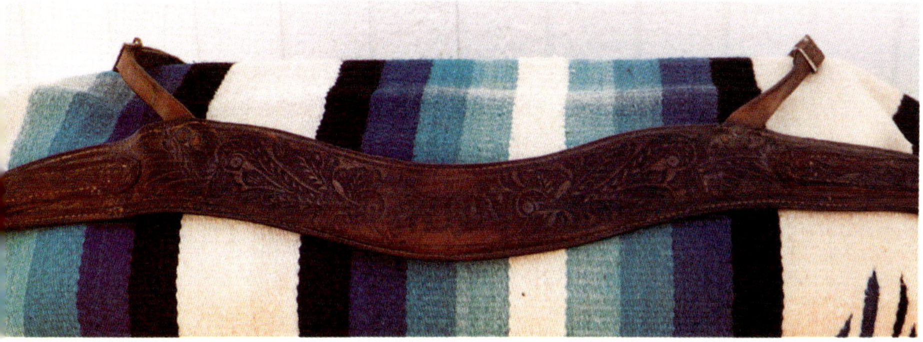

Made for Judy Stirewalt Bertsch by Ray Olsen of Redmond, Oregon, it is a fully carved leather breast collar. *Courtesy Bob and Judy Bertsch. $100 to 125*

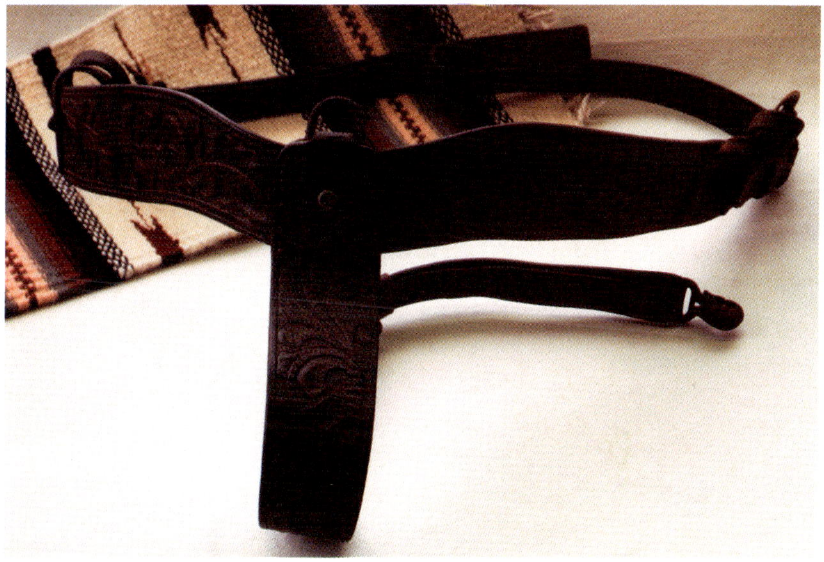

Made by Hamley and Company, Pendleton, Oregon, the breast collar is fully carved leather with a carved leather understrap. *Overton collection. $100 to 125*

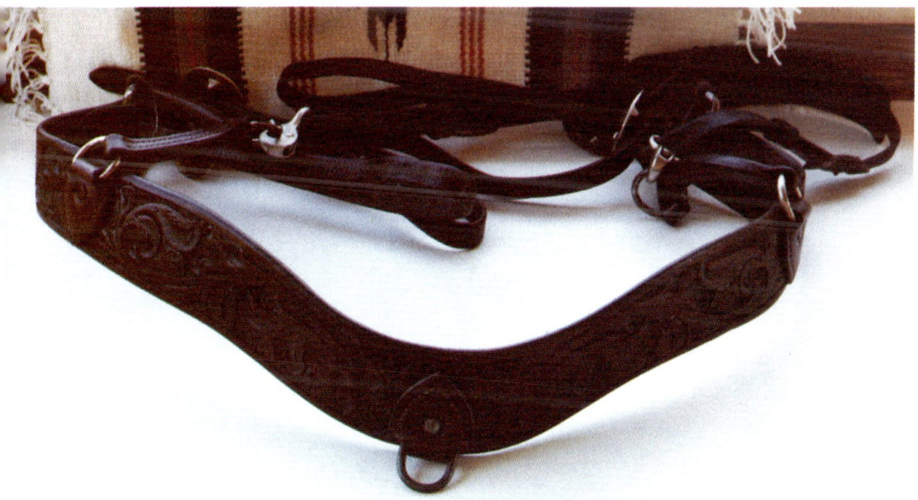

Hamley and Company of Pendleton, Oregon, created this in their saddle shop. It is a very serviceable breast collar (and probably the one I would choose to use if I were to saddle up tomorrow). *Overton collection. $150 to 175*

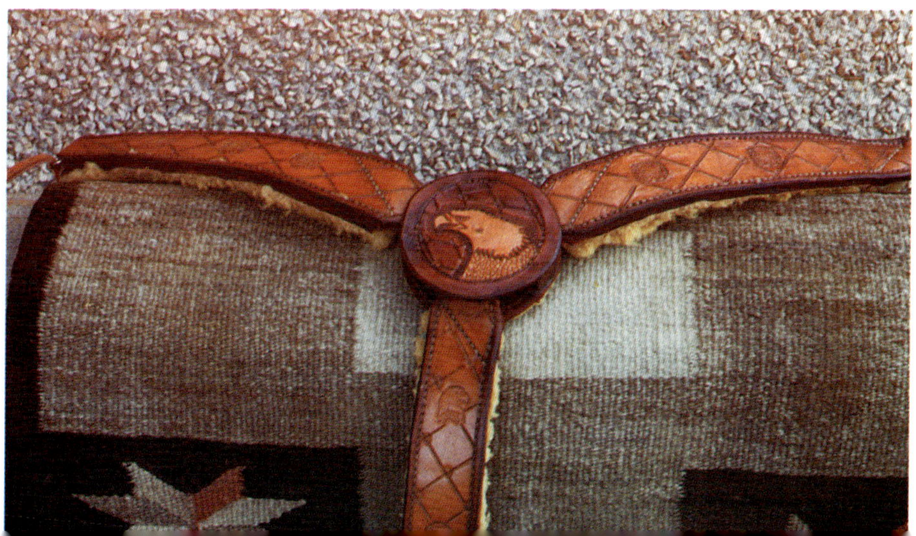

Nicely carved contemporary breast collar with an eagle's head as design. It is part of a set that includes a saddle and matching breast collar. *Courtesy Gene Christopher. $100 to 125*

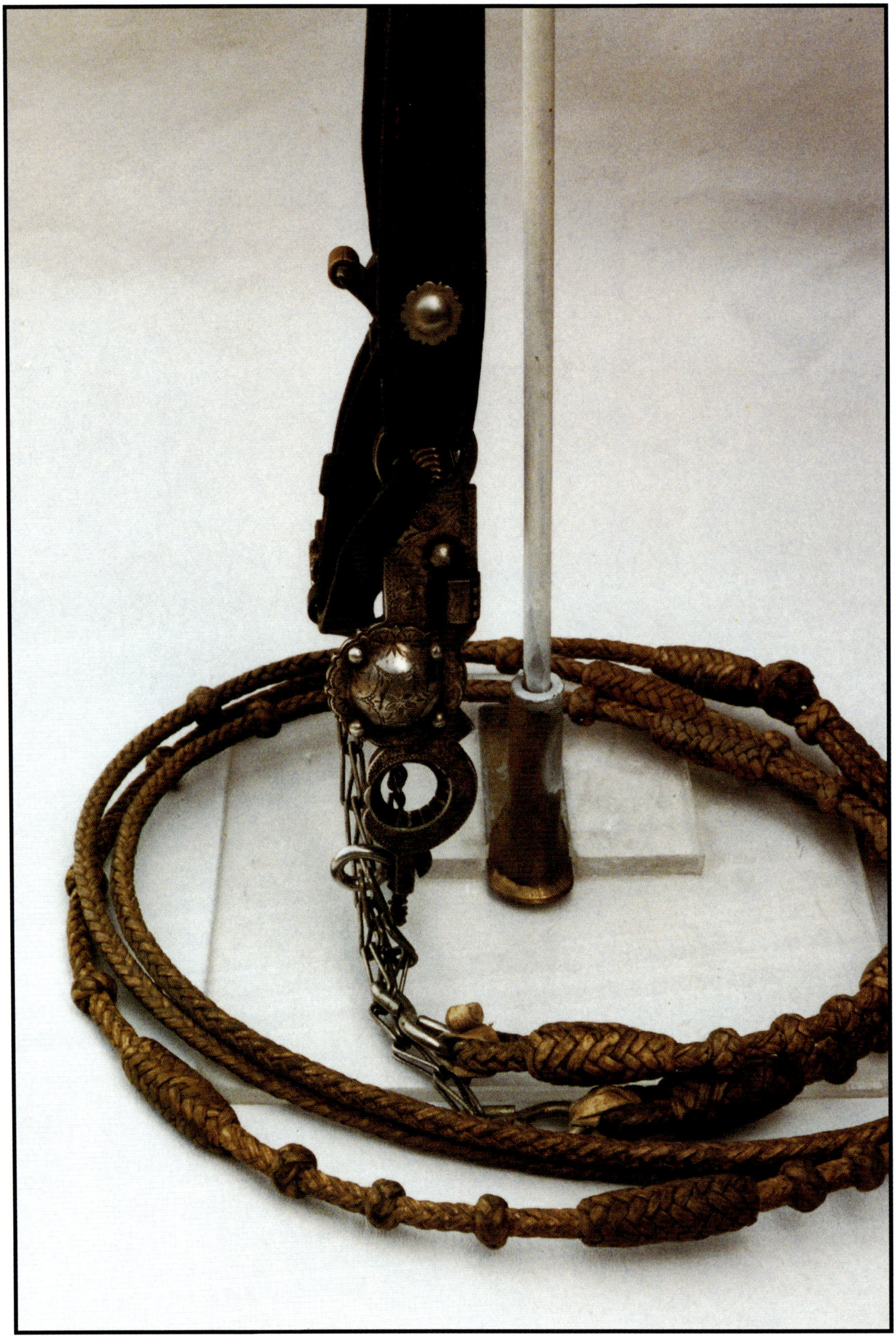

Qualey spade bit in headstall and rawhide braided reins. It is a beautiful bridle made sometime in the early 1950s in the Qualey Bros. Shop in Idaho. *Courtesy private collector. $10,000*

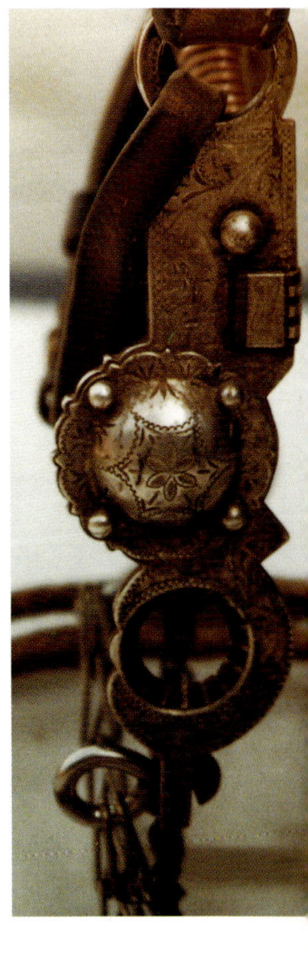

Detail of the very fine Qualey Bros. spade bit.

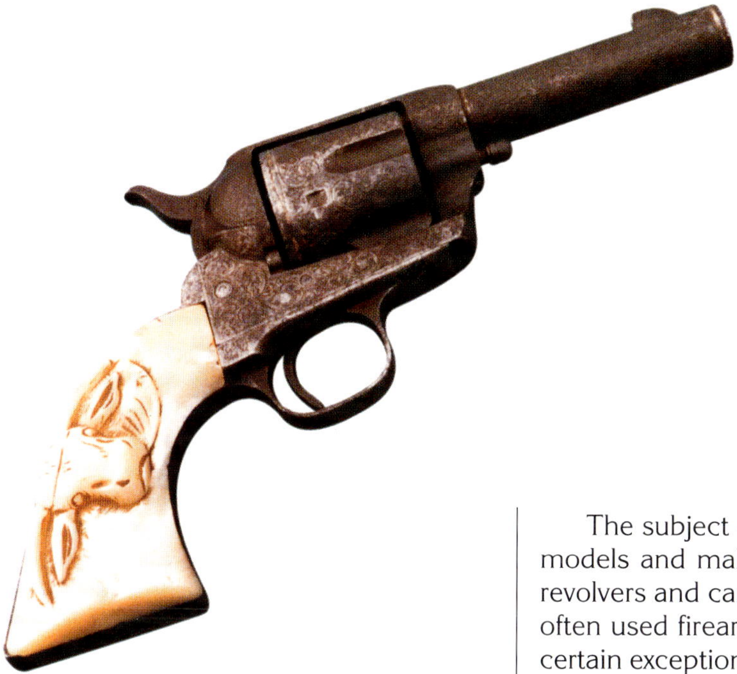

Alvin White is the master engraver who created the art work on this old revolver. It is a .44-40 caliber with a three-and-one-half-inch barrel made without a shell ejector, which makes it an especially rare and fine old piece. *Courtesy Eve Morgan. $3750*

Chapter Six

Firearms

"A cowboy's meat and protection"

The subject of firearms is lengthy and complicated with multiple models and makers. Therefore, information here deals mostly with revolvers and carbines, the two styles that would have been the most often used firearms by a cowboy in the early West, not withstanding certain exceptions of course.

The American Civil War was fought almost entirely with muzzle loading weapons. No other written document portrays the utter chaos and unbridled fear that must have existed on the battlefield with these men and their weapons better than the following:
From a *Report of the Bureau of Ordnance, Navy Department, November 1864, Note "B", page #39*:

> The official report of the examination of the arms collected upon the battlefield of Gettysburg states that of the whole number received (27,574) we found at least 24,000 of these loaded; about one half of these contained two loads each, one fourth from three to ten loads each and the balance one load each.
>
> In many of these guns, from two to six balls have been found with only one charge of powder. In some, the balls have been found at the bottom of the bore with the charge of powder on top of the ball. In some as many as six paper regulation-caliber 58 cartridges have been found, the cartridges having been put in the guns without being torn or broken. Twenty-three loads were found in one Springfield rifle musket, each loaded in regular order. Twenty- two balls and sixty- two buck shot with a corresponding quantity of powder all mixed up together were found in one percussion smooth bore musket.
>
> In many of the smooth-bore guns Model of 1842 rebel make, we have found a wad of loose paper between the powder and ball and another wad of the same kind on top of the ball, the ball having been put in the gun naked. About six thousand of the arms were found loaded with Johnson & Dow' s cartridges, many of these cartridges were about half way down in the barrels of the guns, and in many cases the ball end of the cartridges had been put into the gun first. The cartridges were found mostly in the Enfield rifle-musket.

This sad government document demonstrates the absolute necessity for the invention of better firearms following that terrible war. The need was, most likely, constantly in the minds of inventors and patent holders, and their efforts to create better guns could certainly be understood.

Sam Colt and Oliver Winchester are two names very well known to gun collectors. Added to them are Horace Smith and Daniel B. Wesson, B.Tyler Henry, and Remington Arms. This short list will serve to demonstrate the larger field.

Sam Colt

The following words have been around so long they have almost become trite and cliché: "God did not make all men equal, however Sam Colt did." For a man who lived such a short life (1814-1862), Sam Colt perhaps affected United States history more than any other man with his far-reaching invention and everlasting influence.

Is it any wonder that many people today treasure and pursue old Colt firearms? Somehow they just always seem to come to the top of the wish lists when collectors gather and identify the manufacturers whose weapons they seek.

When the time came to write this chapter on firearms, it was like "coming home," for guns were my first love and cowboy equipment came later. It was a special pleasure for me to see the guns collected by other gun-lovers. Having shot competition in a Target Rifle Team (NRA) as a young woman, I found great pleasure in such competition, and learned a great respect and fondness for all firearms at an early age. My collection is small, but greatly loved. I hope you will enjoy seeing the photographs here from many collections, and somehow come to a realization that, as has been said many times, "Guns don't kill people, people kill people."

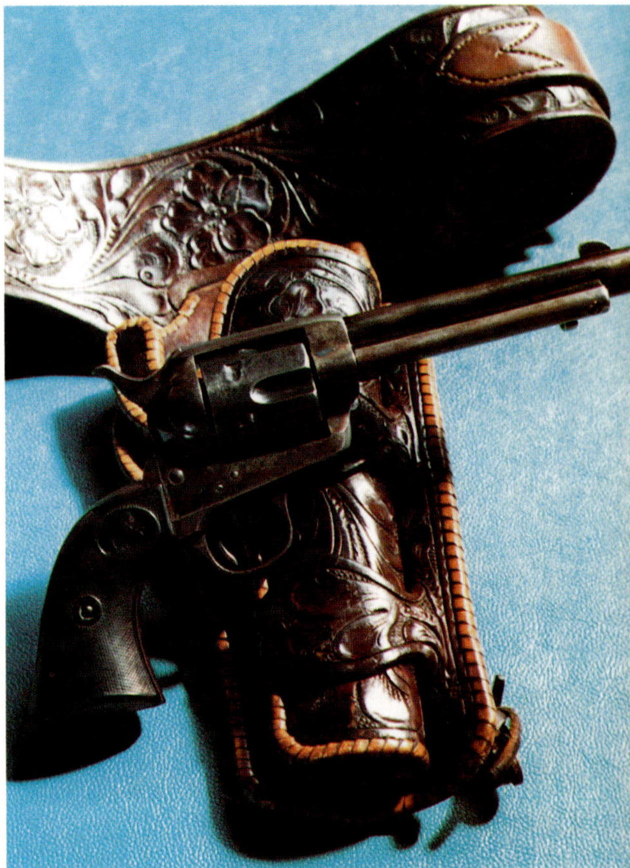

Colt revolver, single action, the gun is a .32 caliber in a beautiful Heiser gun rig; both are in excellent condition and very collectible. *Courtesy Ron and Sharon Mailloux. $4000 to 5000*

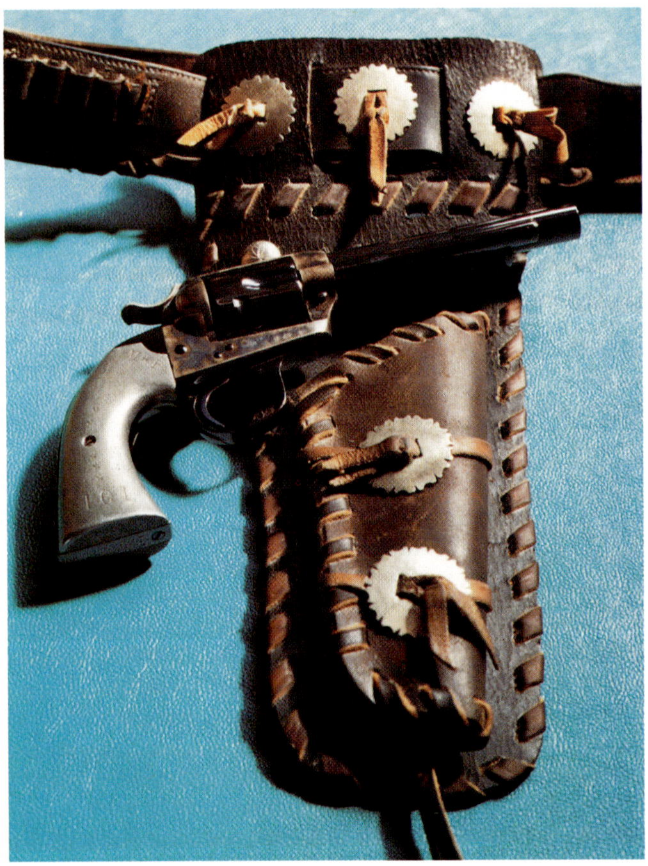

This unique handgun is a Colt Bisley, .38 caliber revolver and bears the mark of the Texas "101" Ranch. It is a treasure from the "101 Wild West Show" which toured the world in the early 1900s under the auspices of Joseph C. Miller. *Courtesy Ron and Sharon Mailloux. $4000 to 5000*

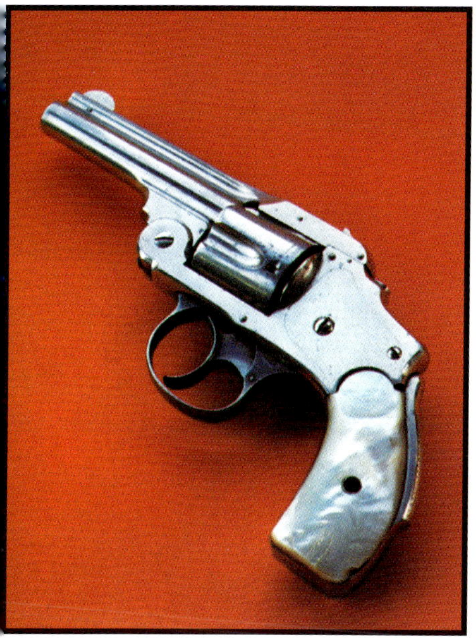

Smith and Wesson, pearl-handled "lemon squeezor," this gun has earned its name from the safety device on the handle. It's last patent date is August 4, 1885. *Private collection. $350 to 450*

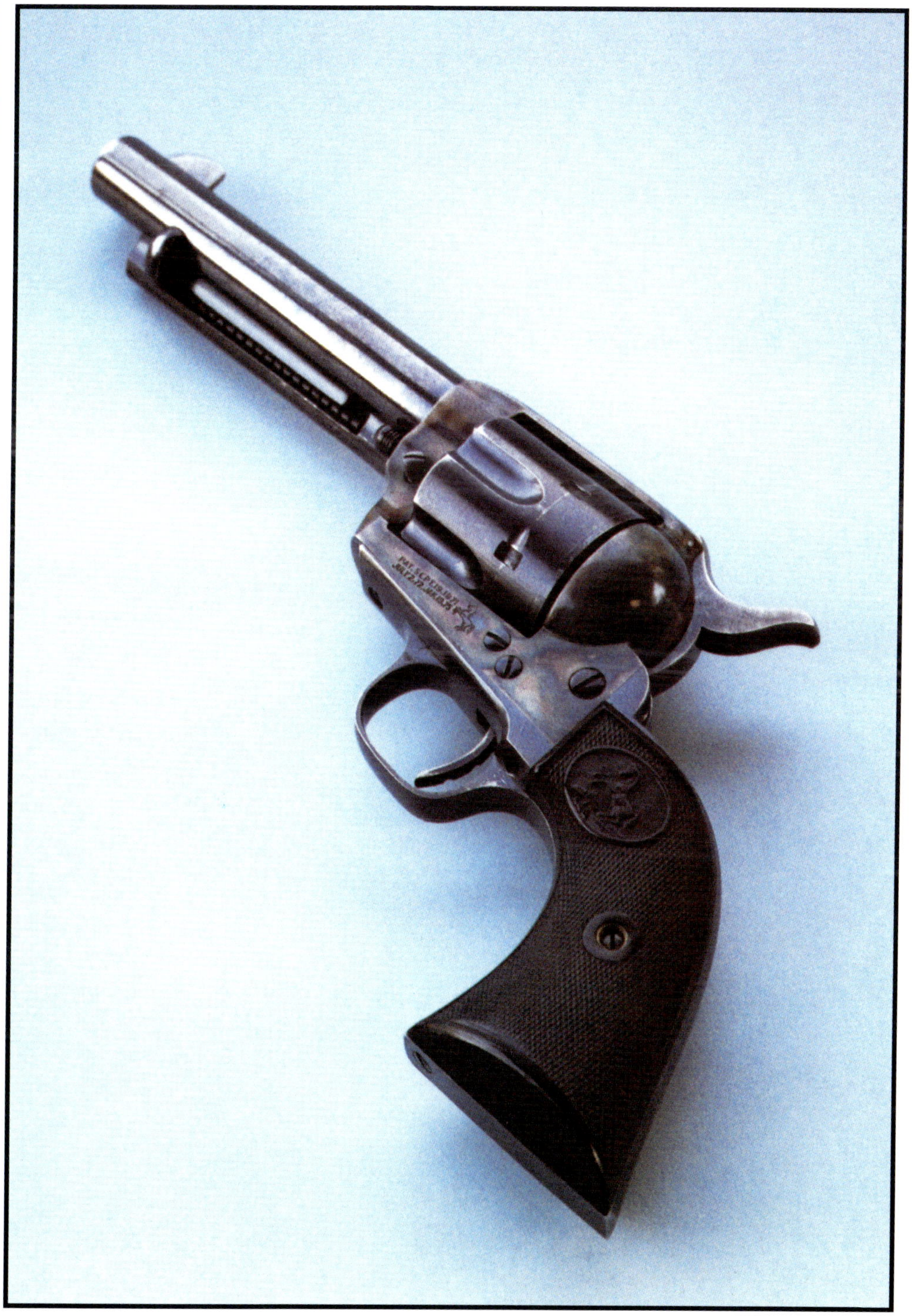

Colt revolver, .45 caliber single action Army style in like-new condition. The gun is one of the popular models currently collected. *Private collection. $6500*

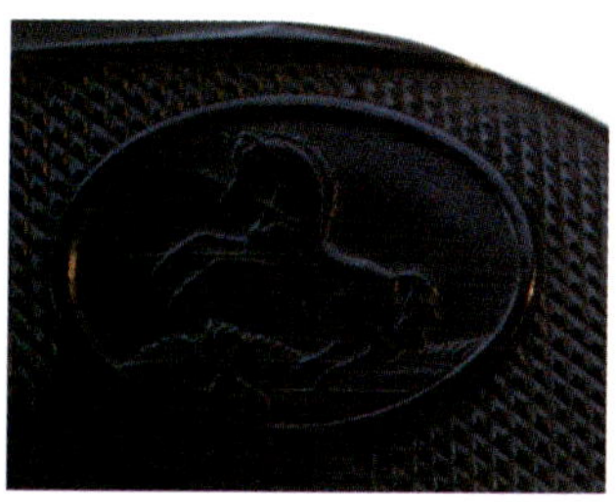

Detail of Colt's famous insignia on the previous pistol.

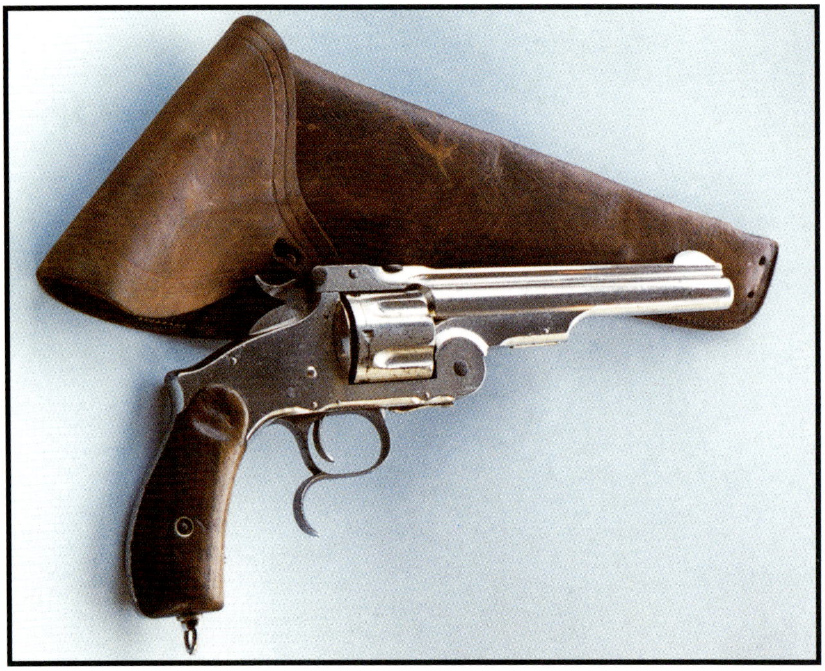

Smith and Wesson .44 caliber #6608 (Russian); the revolver's last patent date is July 25, 1871. This particular one has a custom fitting gun rig marked "Hurd." *Private collection. $1200*

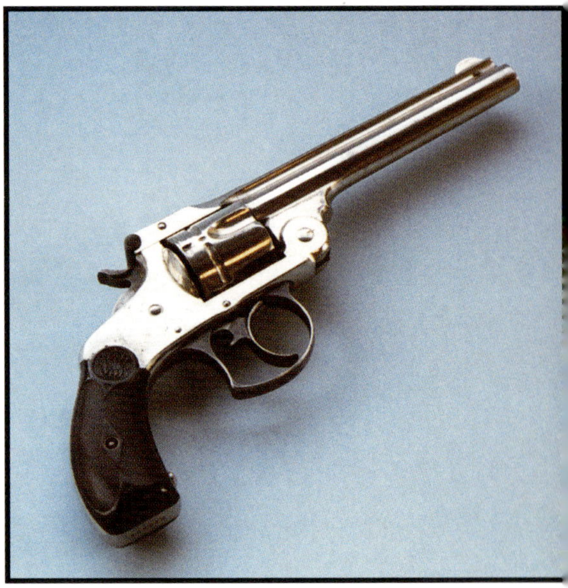

Smith and Wesson revolver, .38 caliber with last patent date of May 1880. *Private collection. $275*

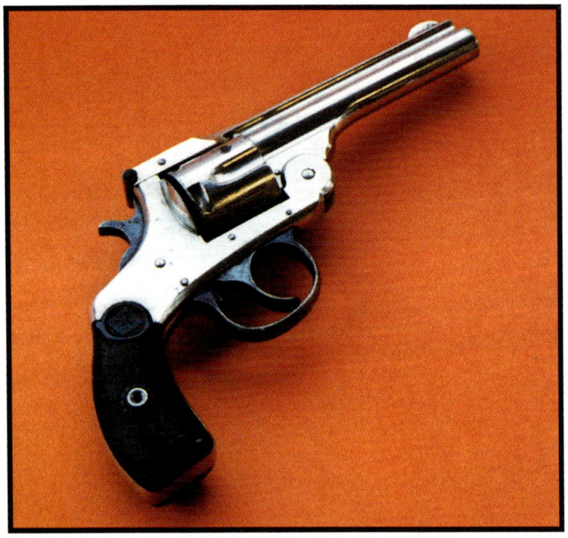

The revolver is a Smith and Wesson .38 caliber with the last patent date of April 1896. *Private collection. $75 to 125*

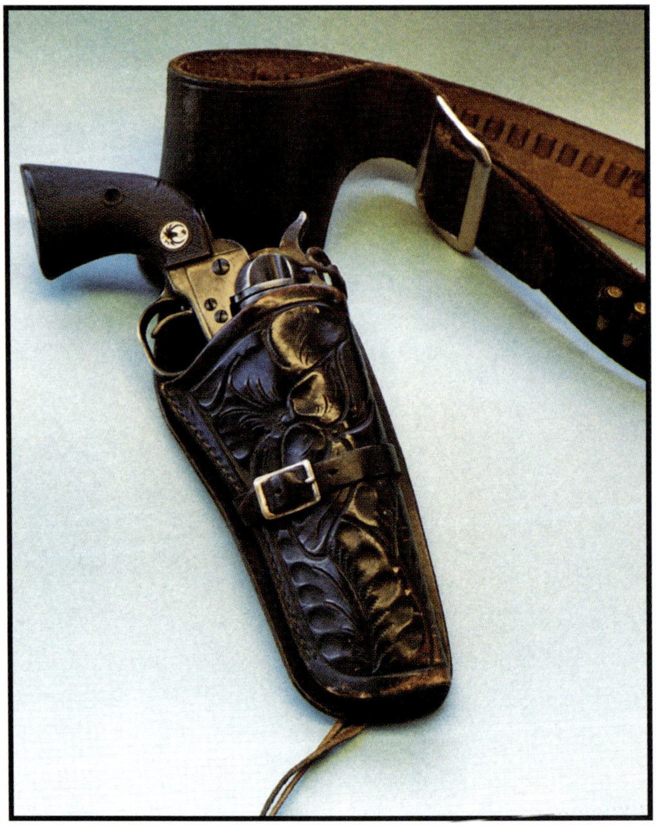

Single six Ruger revolver in a leather gun rig. It is a .22 caliber on a .38 caliber frame. Ruger offered to add a "safety feature" to all owners in the 1970s, and most everyone complied, but this gun has been kept original. *Overton collection. $400 to 500*

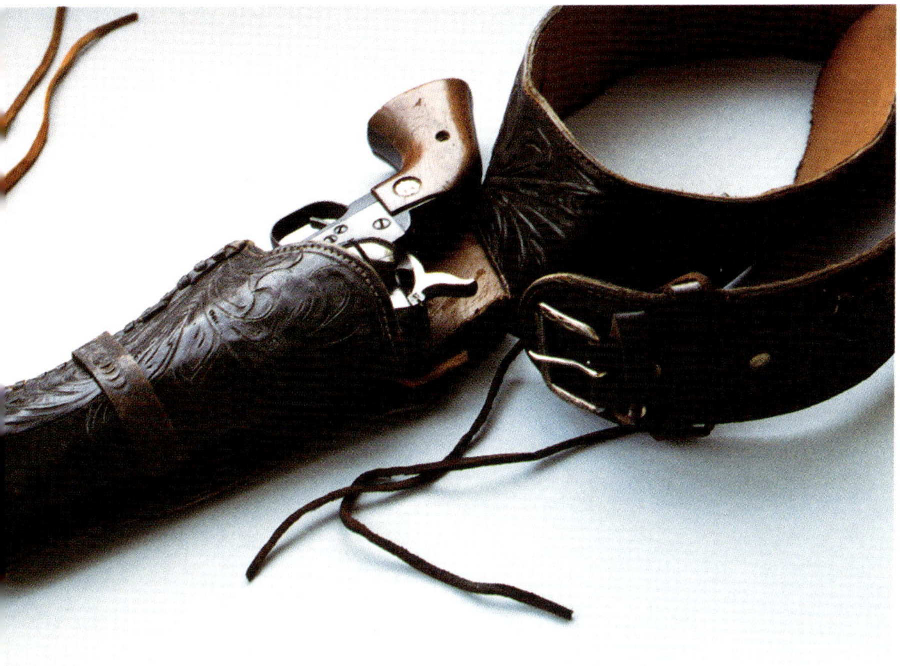

The revolver is a Colt .41 caliber (dubbed Colt "Thunderer")in a tooled leather gun rig. This revolver is considered a rarity in that few are in existence. William Mason designed it for Colt and they were introduced in 1877 with a total of 3000 being produced. *Overton collection. $3500 to 4000*

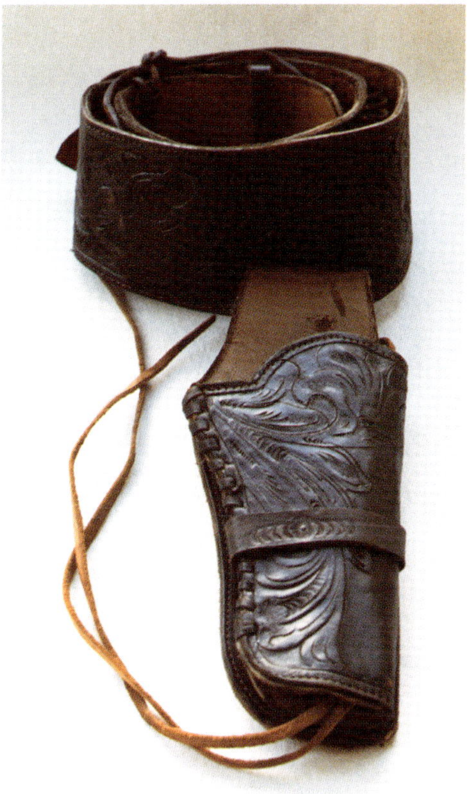

Nice old leather tooled gun rig with belt and lace tie downs. *Overton collection. $60 to 75*

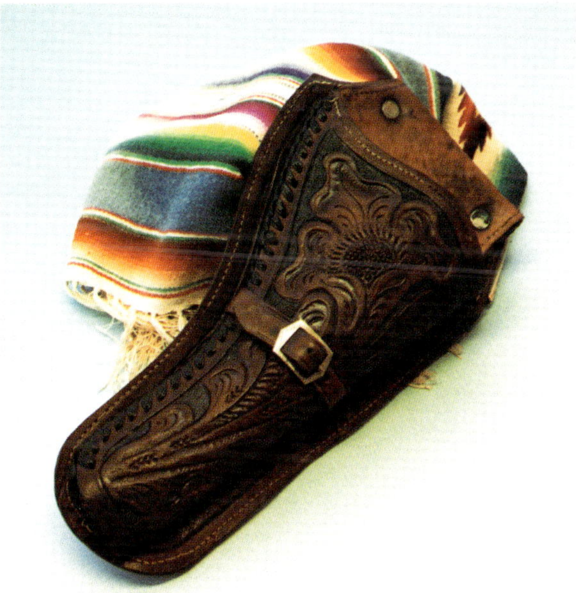

Very nice old hand-tooled gun rig with buckle front. *Courtesy Wade Brumley. $50 to 60*

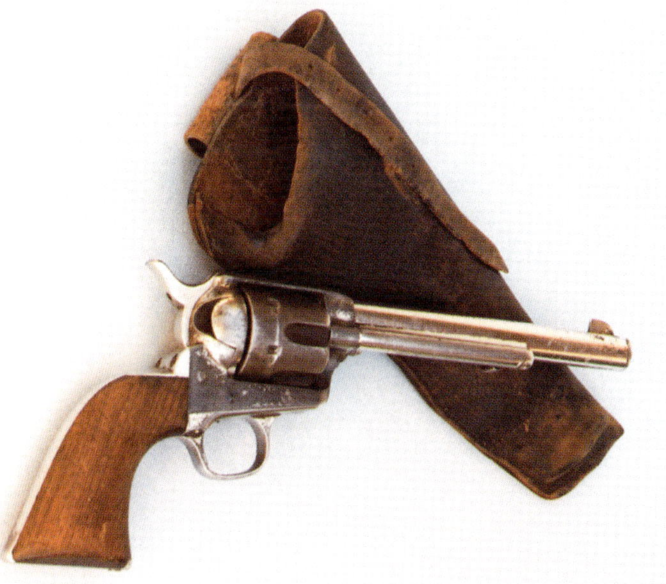

Beautiful Colt Frontier .44-40 caliber with serial #121827 – 1887. The gun has its original leather gun rig. *Courtesy Schiffner Military Museum, George and Margaret Schiffner. $1500 to 2000*

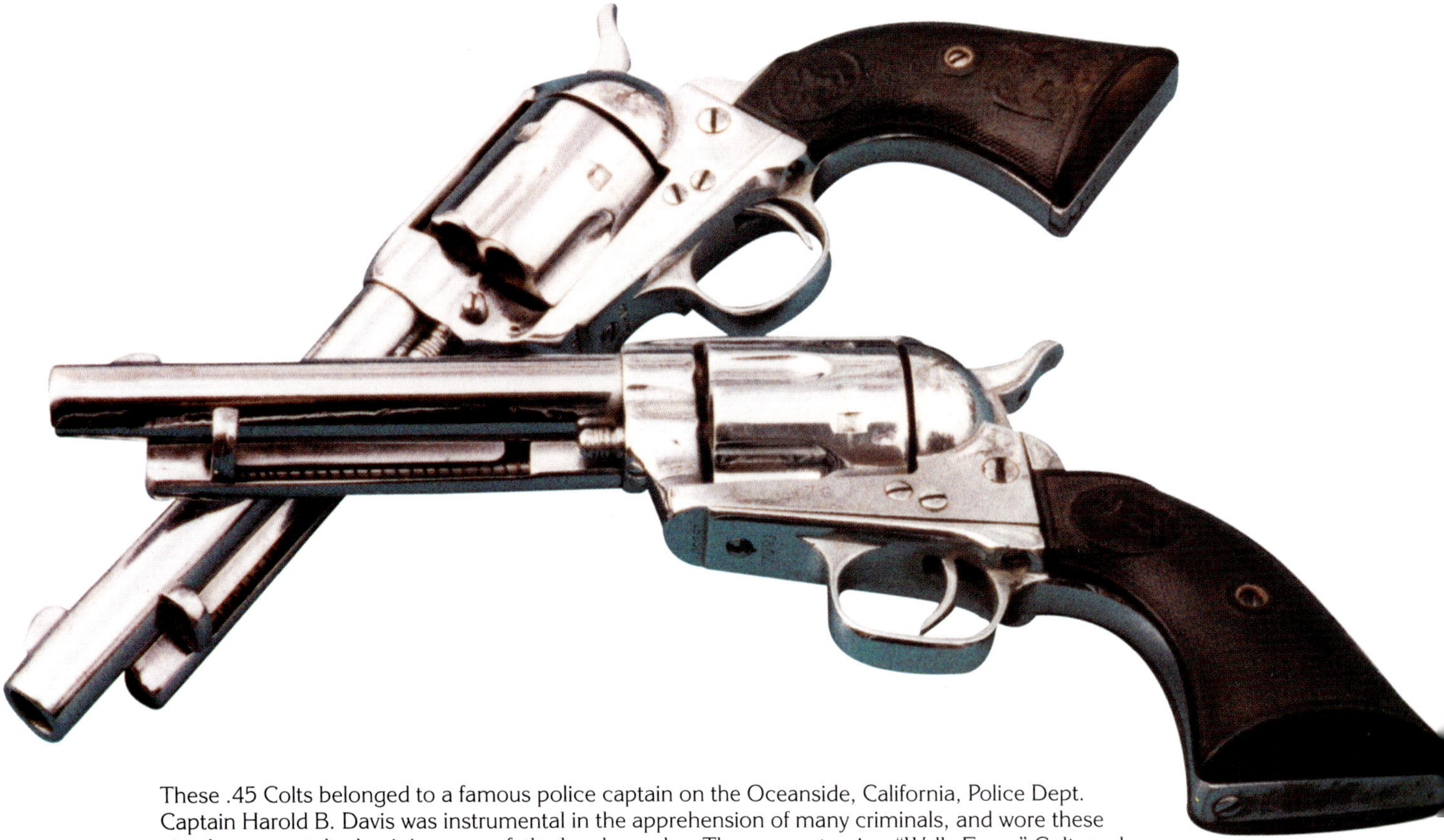

These .45 Colts belonged to a famous police captain on the Oceanside, California, Police Dept. Captain Harold B. Davis was instrumental in the apprehension of many criminals, and wore these pistols as a matched pair in many of the local parades. The one on top is a "Wells Fargo" Colt, and the bottom one is an "Artillery, U.S. Colt." They have excellent written provenance in the form of newspaper articles and photos. *Courtesy Eve Morgan. $6000 pair plus gun rig*

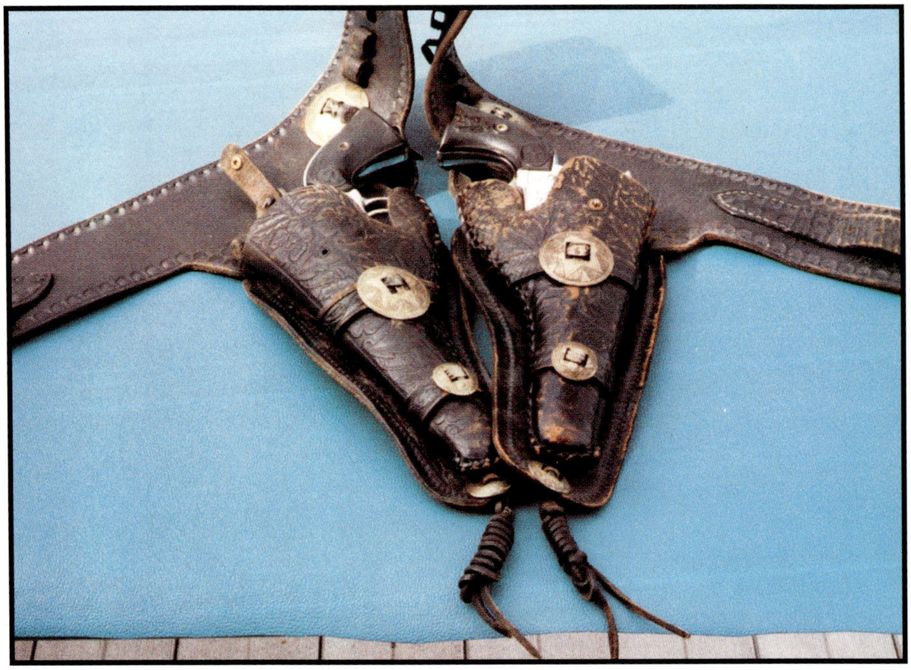

The gun rig for the matching Colts shows some of the wear suffered in the line of duty by Captain Davis.

Captain Harold B. Davis.

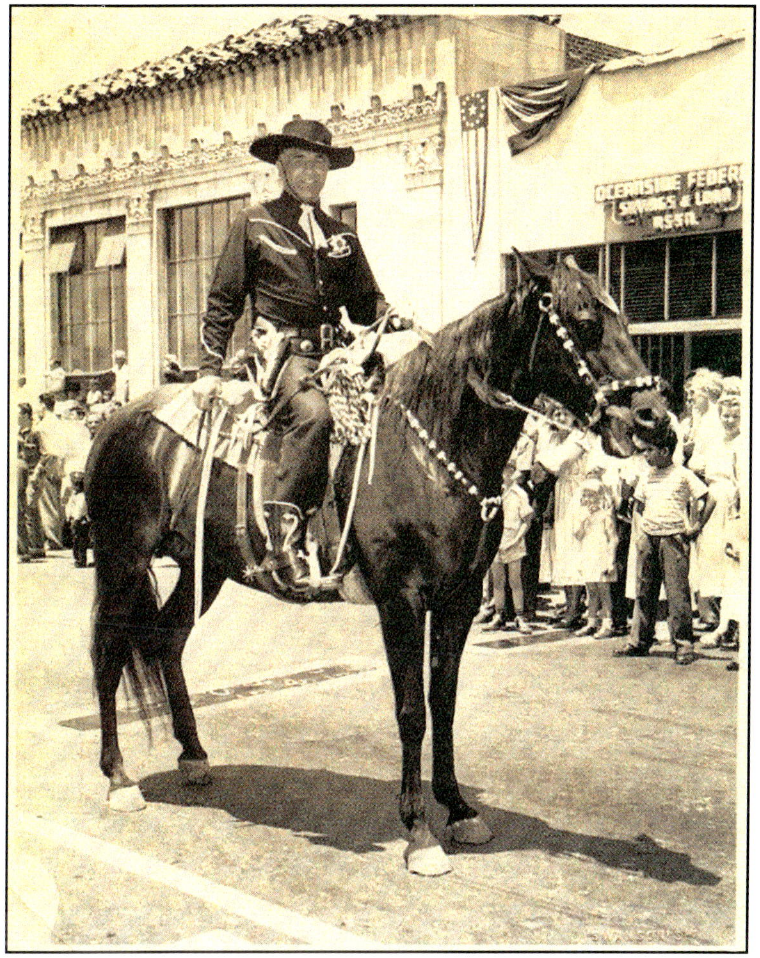

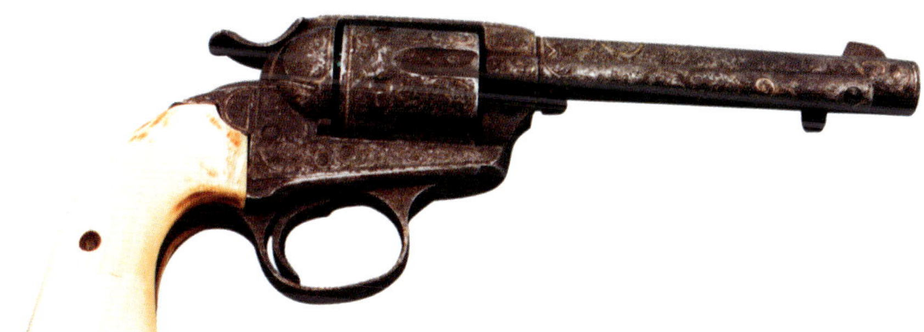

Colt Bisley, which is longer in barrel length than the previous single action shorter barrel but is also engraved by same master engraver. Both handguns had been in a fire in Montana years ago. *Courtesy Eve Morgan.* *$3750*

Fine old Colt Dragoon, 2nd Model, only 8000 to 11000 were made. This particular one is a "fluke" because its serial number #6297 is too low for a 2nd Model. The reason for this gun having such a low number is a mystery, but it makes it very rare indeed. All 2nd Models have a square trigger guard and rectangular cylinder stops. This Colt's patent stamp is "US 1849-50." *Courtesy Eve Morgan. $6000*

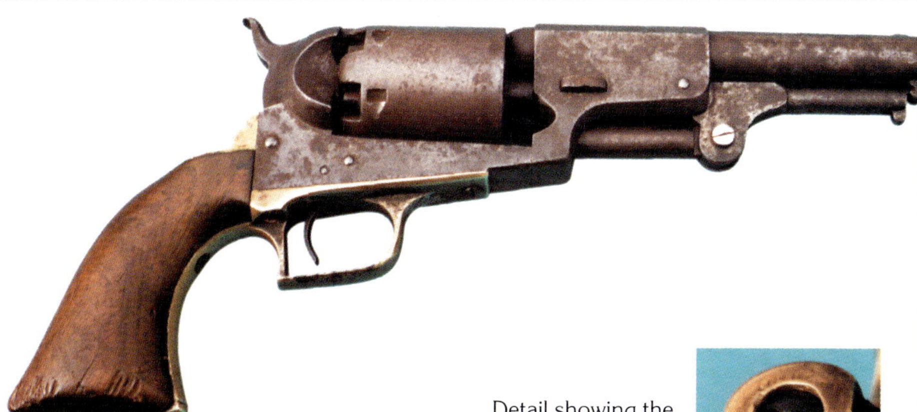

Detail showing the unusual low number on the Colt Dragoon.

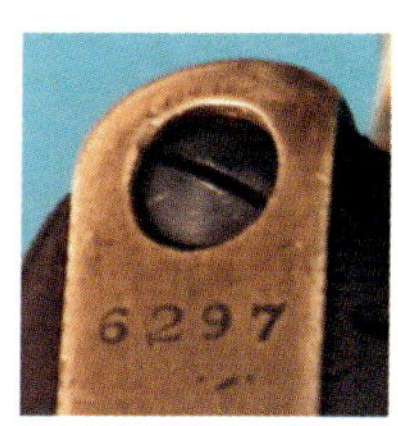

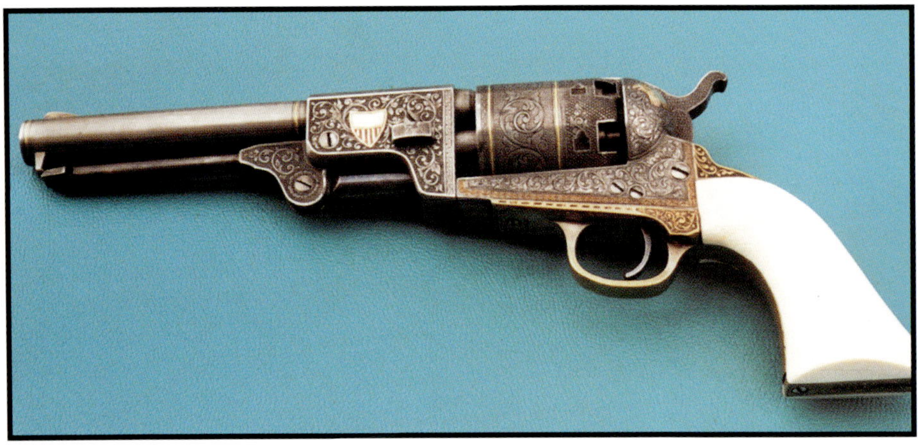

Replica of a Colt Dragoon made by Colt in the 1960s and engraved by Captain W.A. Thorton. *Courtesy Eve Morgan. $3000 to 3500*

Detail of engraving on the replica Colt Dragoon.

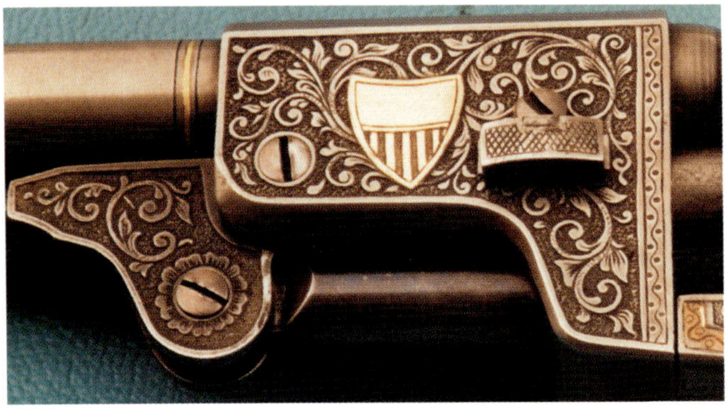

Detail of patriotic shield and various engraving on the replica Colt Dragoon.

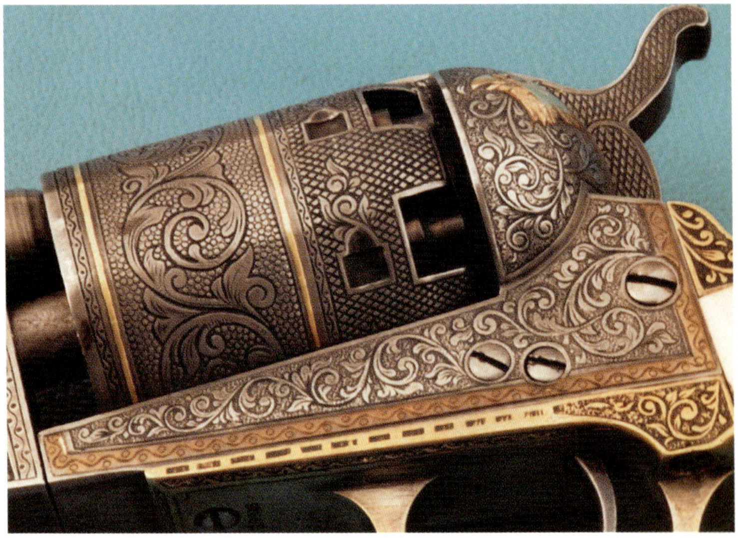

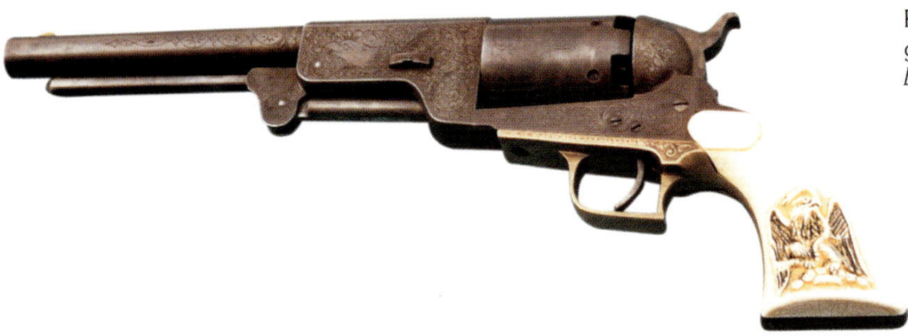

Replica of the Walker Colt .44 with genuine ivory grips carved with an eagle and snake. *Courtesy Eve Morgan. $3000 to 3500*

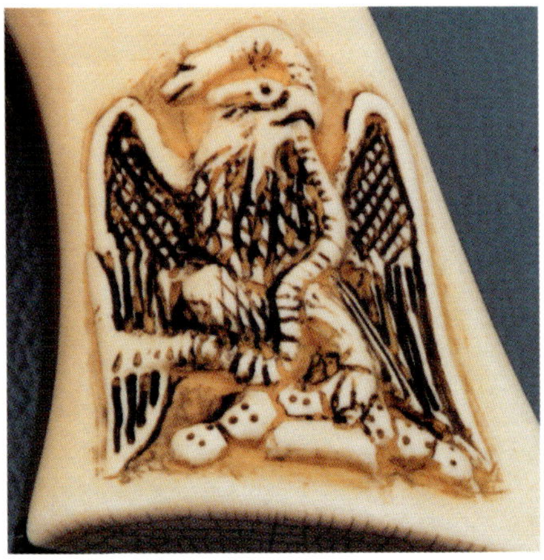

Detail of ivory grips on the Walker Colt replica.

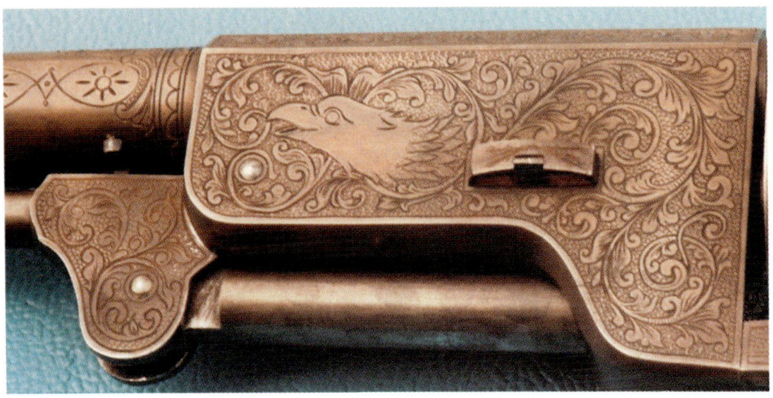

Detail of engraving on the Walker Colt replica.

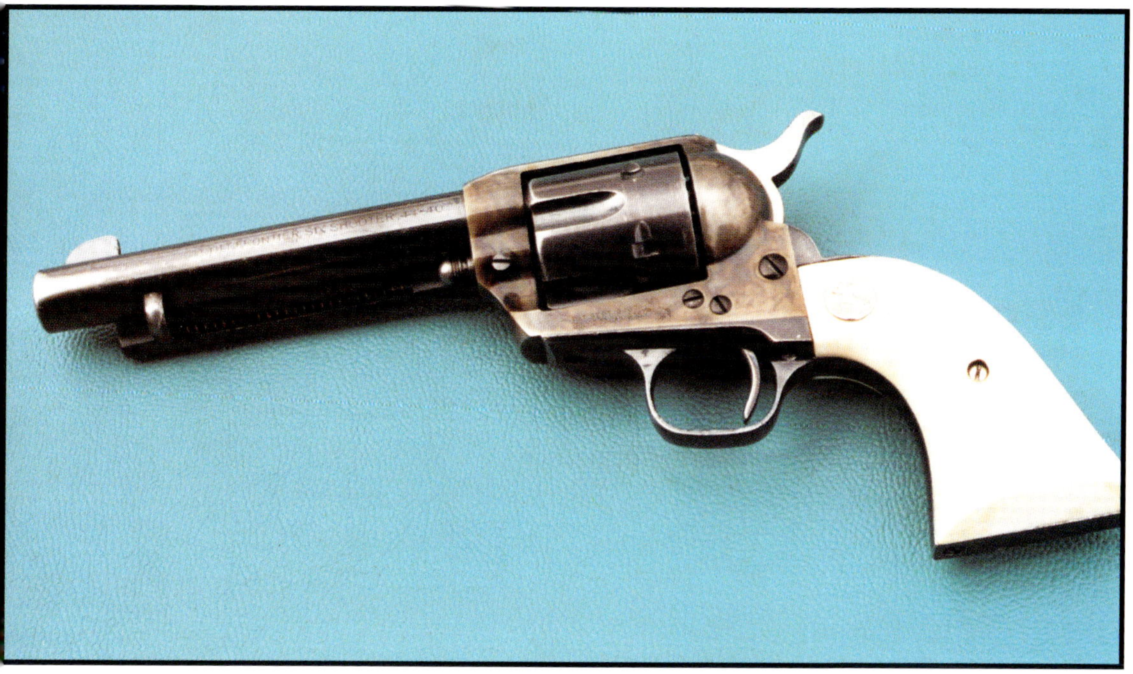

This hand gun was carried by "Little Joe" on the television show "Bonanza" and comes with a very good written provenance to prove it. It was also owned at one time by the country singer Hank Williams, Jr. It is a .44-40 Colt Frontier six shooter with genuine ivory grips. *Courtesy Eve Morgan. $6000 to 7000*

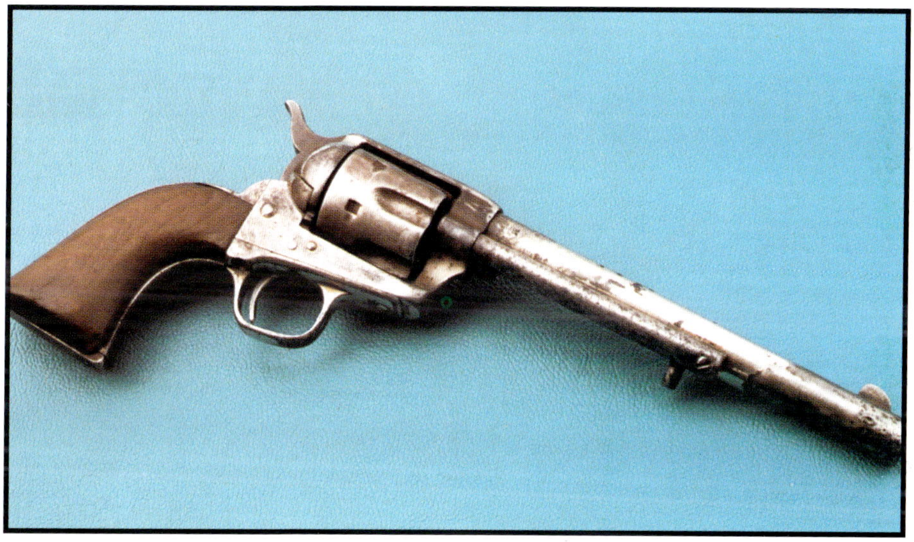

This Colt pistol at one time, many years ago, found its way into the Mexican government, most likely during the revolution headed by Benito Pablo Juarez because it has the "RM" with a "Gorro Frijio" sunburst stamped into it. It bears its US serial number #13321 *Courtesy Eve Morga. Priceles.*

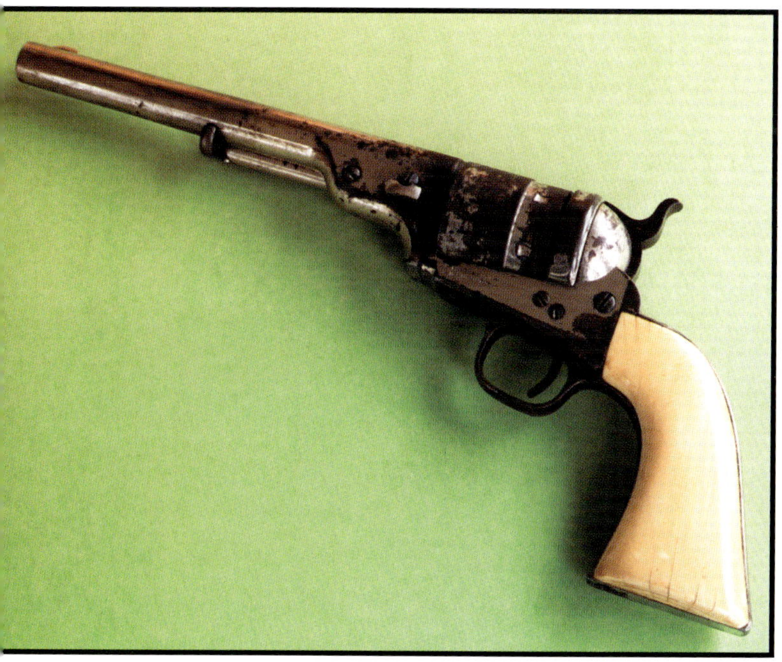

.44 caliber Colt, Richard Mason Conversion with genuine ivory grips. There were only about 1800 to 2200 made. *Courtesy Eve Morgan. $3500*

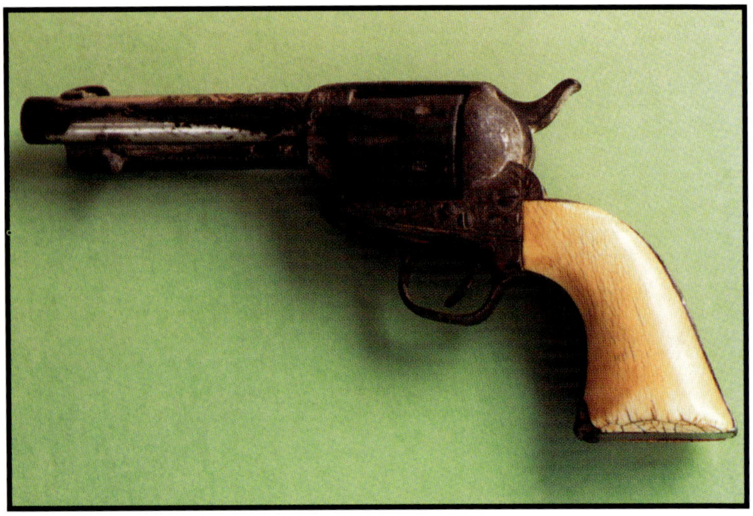

This old Colt Peacemaker .44 was found in 1999 in a tree and, once released from its mysterious hiding place, was found to be still in good working condition. It has original ivory grips and was engraved by "Harley Ingrams, NY" *Courtesy Eve Morgan. $3000*

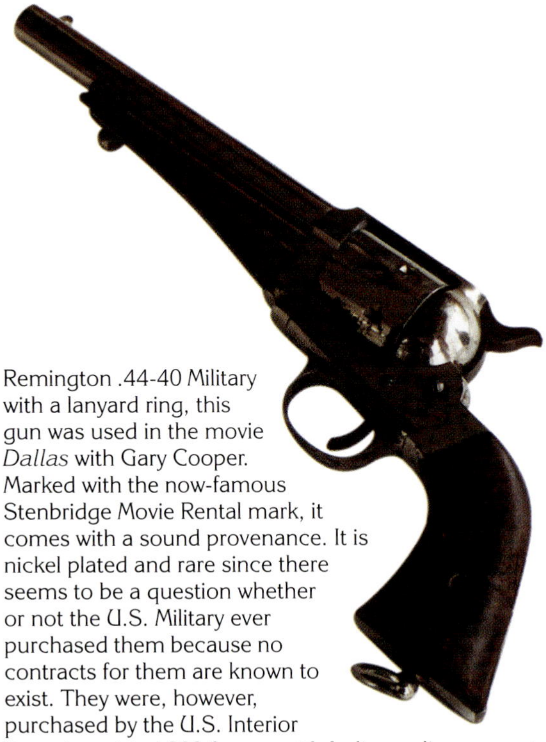

Remington .44-40 Military with a lanyard ring, this gun was used in the movie *Dallas* with Gary Cooper. Marked with the now-famous Stenbridge Movie Rental mark, it comes with a sound provenance. It is nickel plated and rare since there seems to be a question whether or not the U.S. Military ever purchased them because no contracts for them are known to exist. They were, however, purchased by the U.S. Interior Department in 1883 for use with Indian police on western reservations. *Courtesy Jack Snider. $2,000*

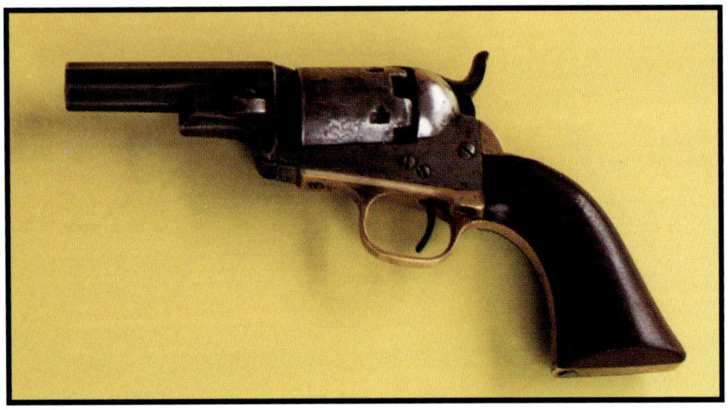

Colt five shot hand gun with a three-inch barrel with no loading lever, c.1850s. This model was given to Wells Fargo employees and Pony Express riders for personal protection. It is a very rare gun. *Courtesy Eve Morgan. $1500*

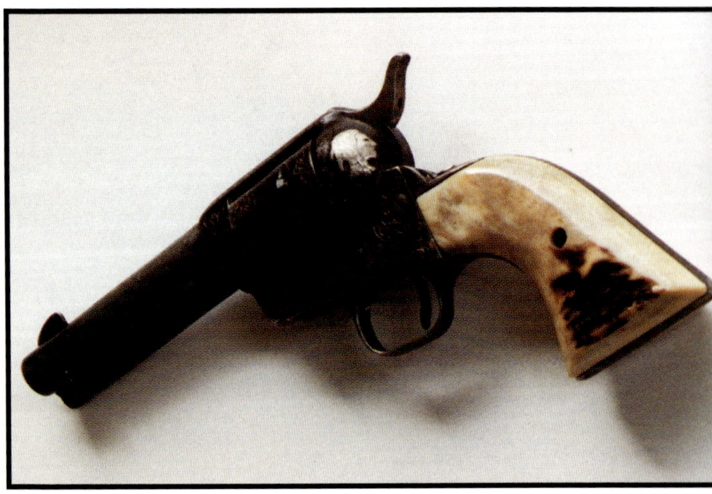

Colt single action Army .45 caliber with stag horn grips and a silver Indian head overlay on one side and a silver spur on the other side. The pistol also bears excellent engraving throughout. *Courtesy Paul and Marlene Snider. $900 to 1200*

Detail showing tiny silver spur.

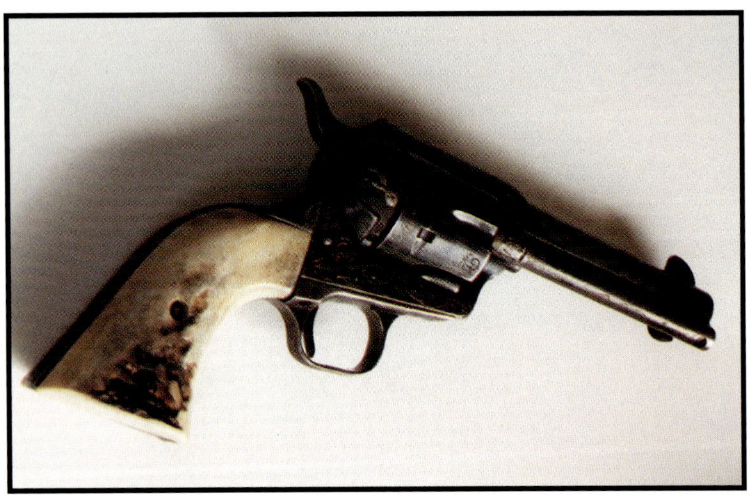

Opposite Page:

This pair of Colts had been ordered to sell to the Mexican market by Wolf and Clark Pawn Shop in Ft. Worth, Texas years ago. They were engraved right on sight at the pawn shop with a bull on one grip and a snake and eagle on the other. They are .45 caliber. *Courtesy Eve Morgan. $10,000 the pair*

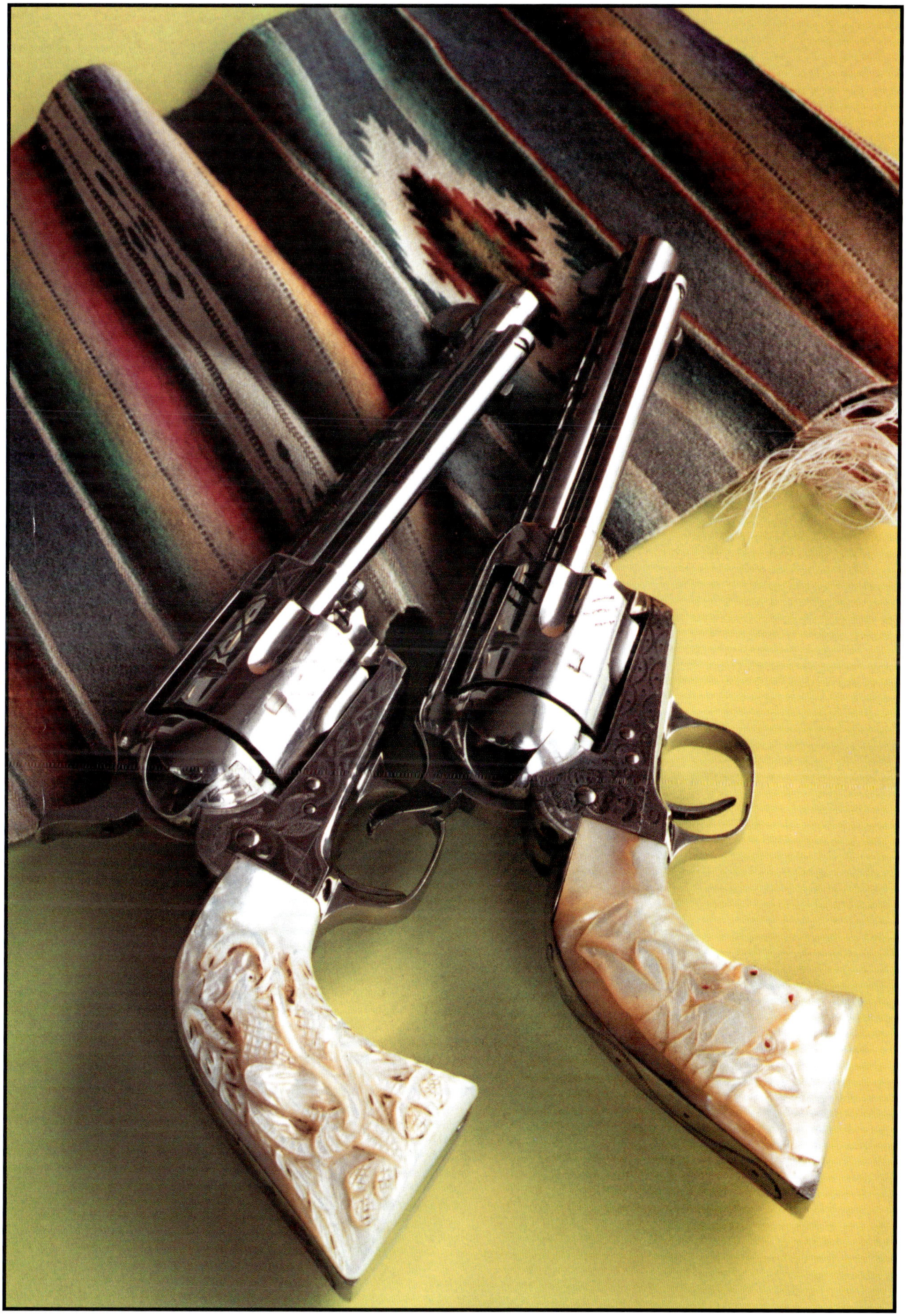

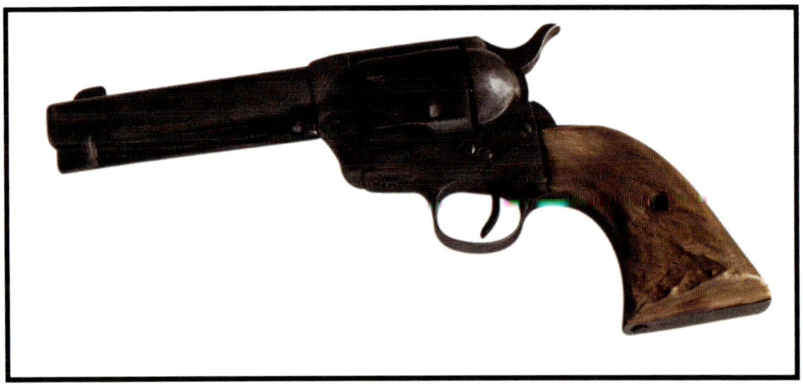

Bisley model Colt .45 with wooden grips, c.1906. Classic in every way, it is definitely a "Cowboy's Gun." *Courtesy Paul and Marlene Snider. $1800 to 2000*

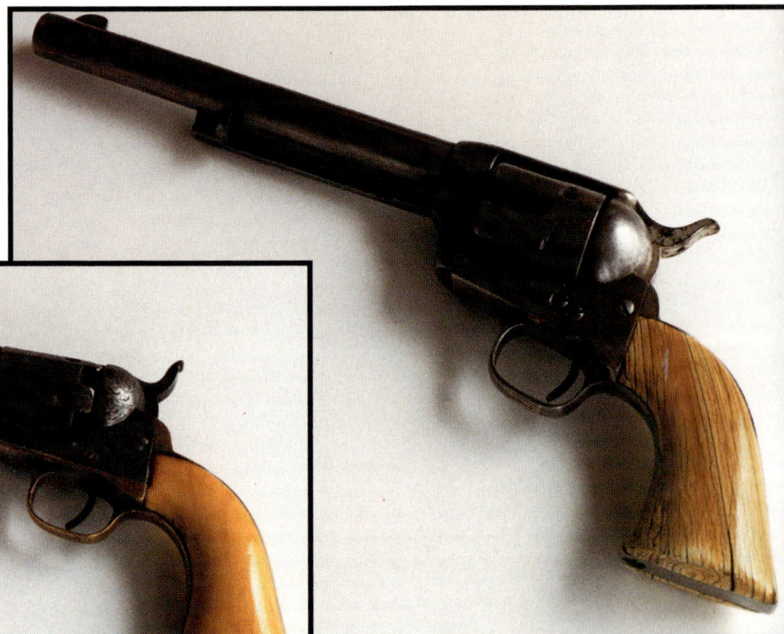

Colt .45 with bone grips and a long barrel, this gun is typical of early frontier use. *Courtesy Paul and Marlene Snider. $600 to 750*

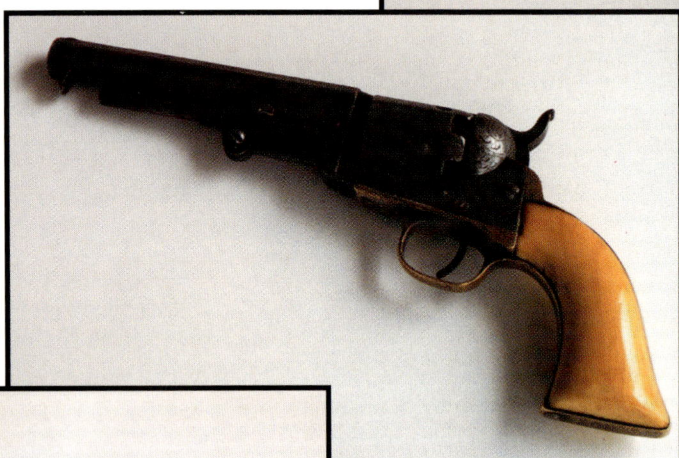

Factory engraved and with elephant ivory grips, this Colt .31 caliber pocket gun is from 1849. Gustov Jones was the Master Engraver for Colt at the time. *Courtesy Paul and Marlene Snider. $2500 to 3500*

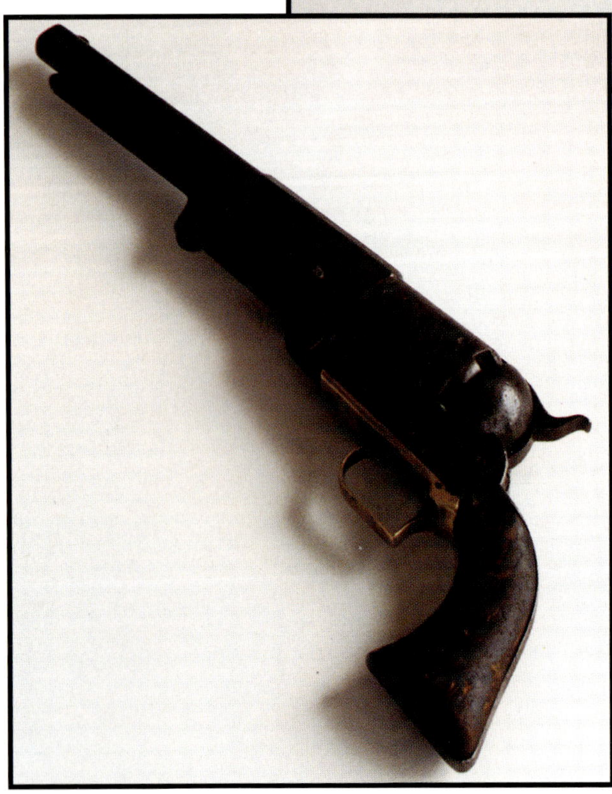

Walker Colt, Texas c.1900, it is a replica and very nicely rendered with wooden grips. *Courtesy Paul and Marlene Snider. $5000 to 7000*

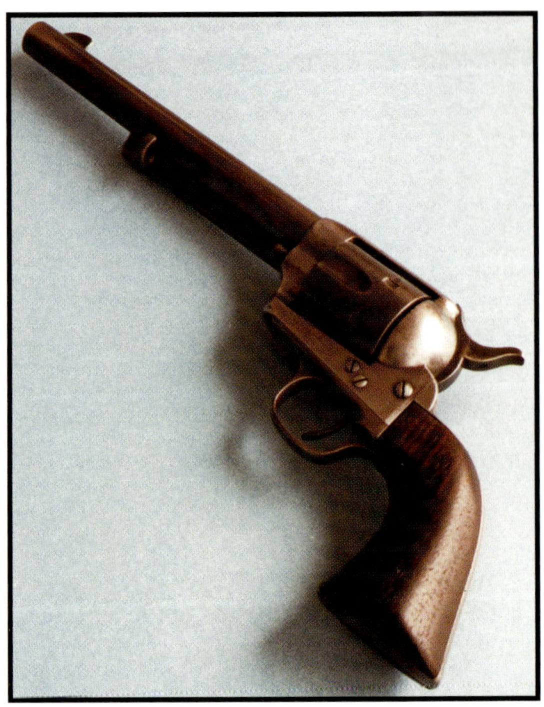

Colt Frontier six shooter, .44-40 caliber, c.1892 –94 model. *Courtesy Paul and Marlene Snider. $3000*

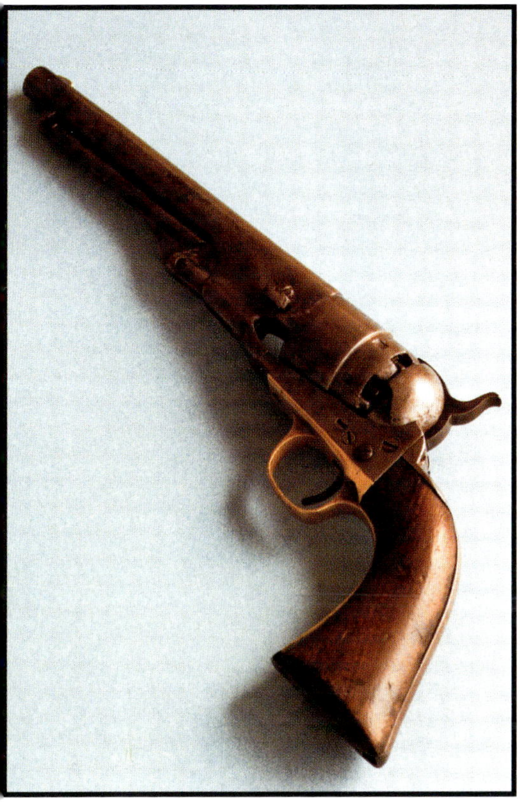

Army Colt .44 caliber gun in excellent condition and rare today, c.1863-64. *Courtesy Paul and Marlene Snider. $1200 to 1500*

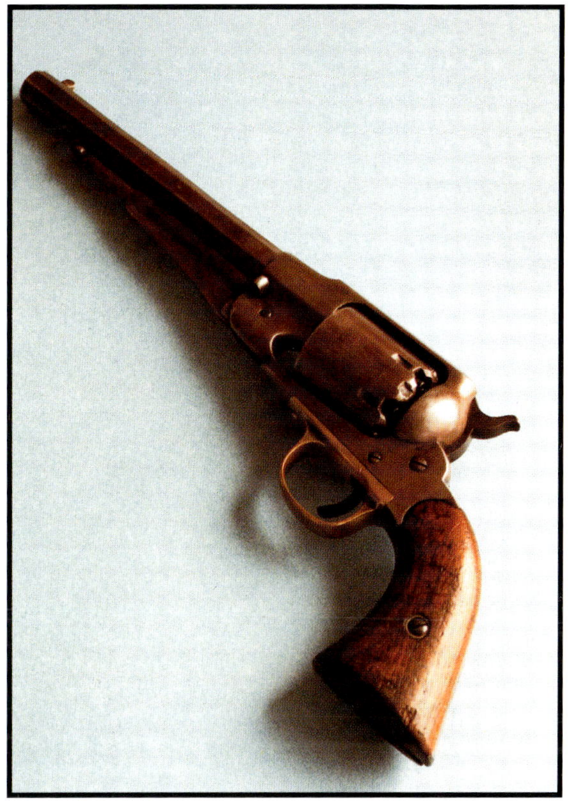

Remington Capp and Ball used in the Civil War, this is a .44 caliber. It is considered a "movie gun" because the "S" stamped on it is the mark for the Stenbridge Movie Rentals company. *Courtesy Paul and Marlene Snider. $800 to 900*

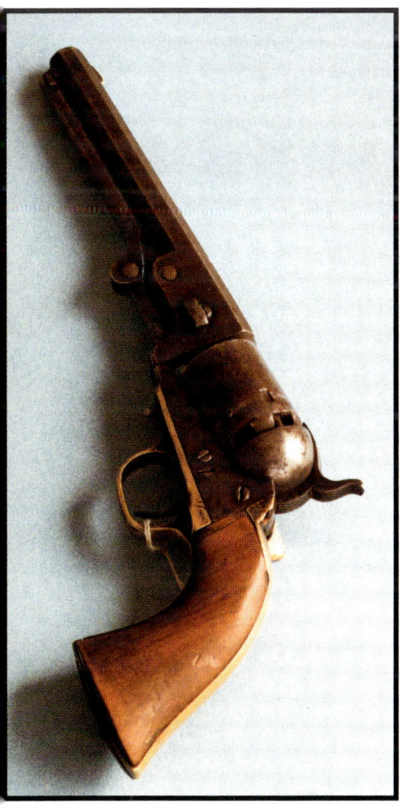

This is a .36 caliber, 1851 Navy Colt with wooden grips. This particular gun has mis-matched numbers and replaced pieces. *Courtesy Paul and Marlene Snider. $700 to 800*

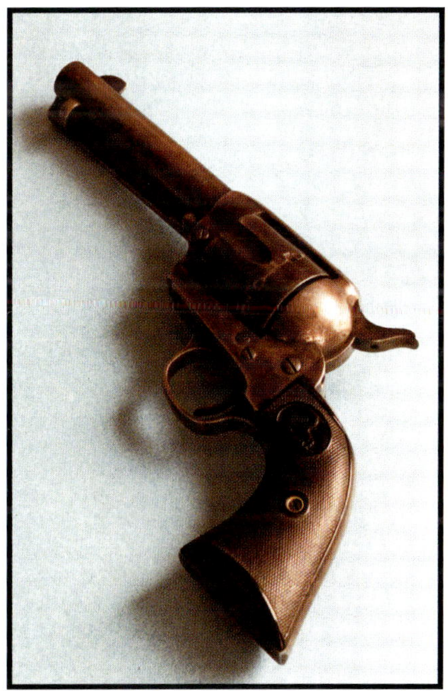

.41 caliber Colt single action with black rubber grips and is typical of cowboy equipment, c.1898 to 1900. *Courtesy Paul and Marlene Snider. $1500 to 1700*

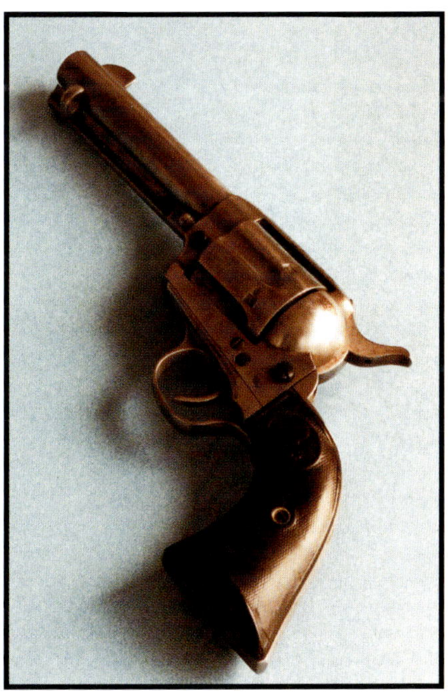

This hand gun would be a typical "cowboy' s gun" and representative of what was widely used in the West. It is single action with black rubber type grips and the Colt logo with a horse on the grips. *Courtesy Paul and Marlene Snider. $1000 to 1200*

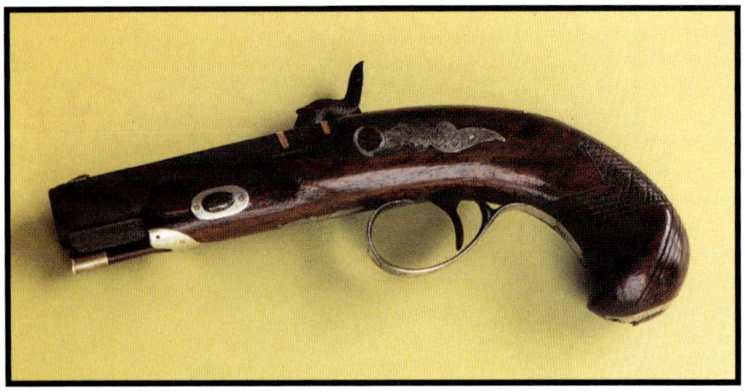

Genuine Philadelphia Derringer, one like this was used to kill President Lincoln. It has gold bands on top with silver inlays and rare cap box and cleaning rod in the grip bottom. .48 caliber Cap and Ball, it has a very rare address on top of the barrel: "Mfg. For Hyde and Goodache, Athens, N. O." *Courtesy Eve Morgan. $2500*

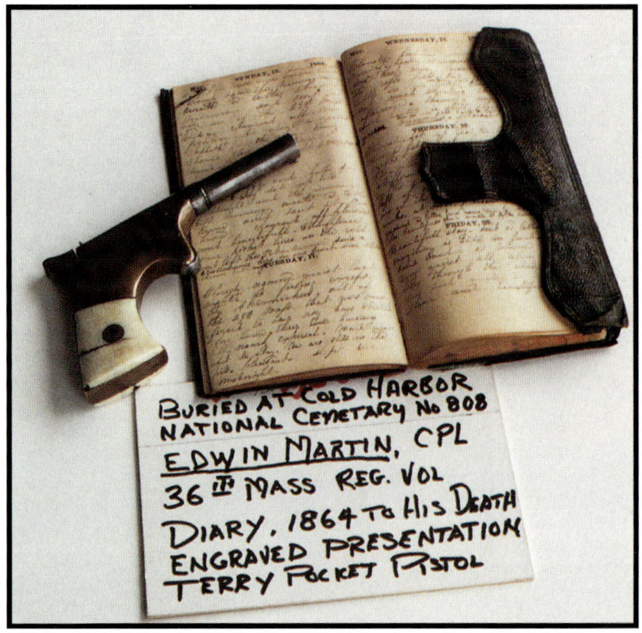

This rare Derringer with owner's name engraved is a .22 caliber short, with ivory grips. It comes with a diary kept during the Civil War and a provenance. *Courtesy Eve Morgan. $4000*

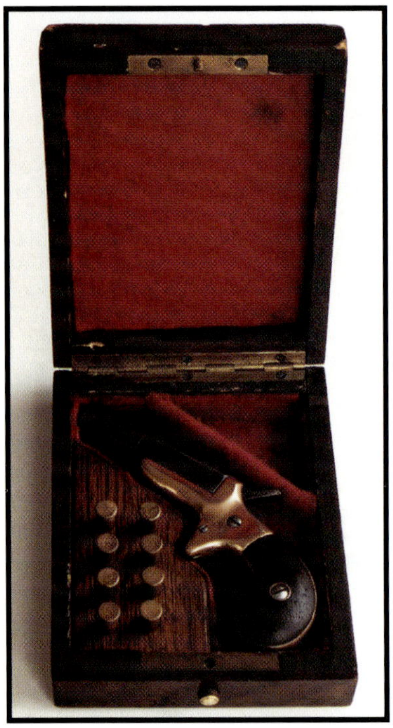

This tiny gun has the distinction of being the smallest working Derringer. It is a .22 caliber lady's gun in a case with "E. Allen and Co. makers" written on it and serial number 349. *Courtesy Eve Morgan. $450 to 600*

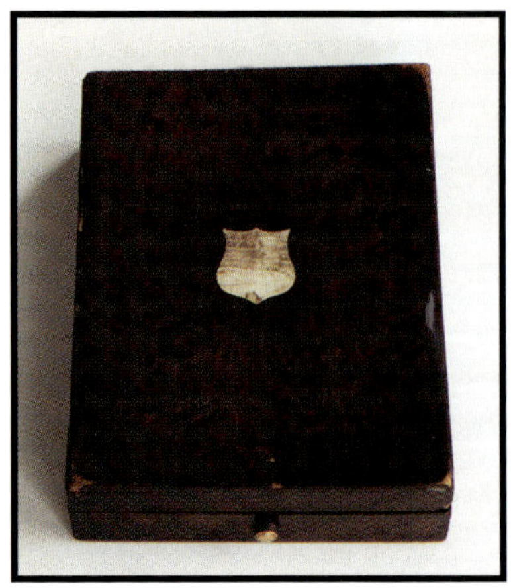

The case of the tiny Derringer showing the silver crest on top.

Detail showing the tiny Derringer out of its case.

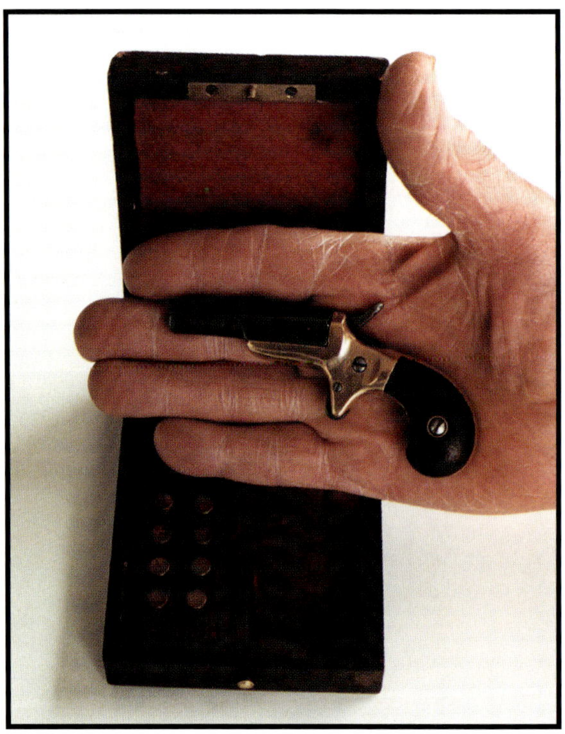

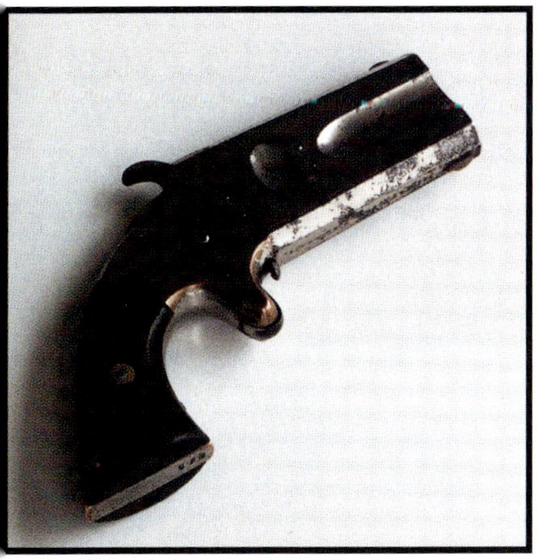

Double "Swivel Derringer" .41 caliber, rare since only about 800 were made by American Arms of Boston, Massachusetts. This ones' serial number is 875. *Courtesy Eve Morgan. $1200*

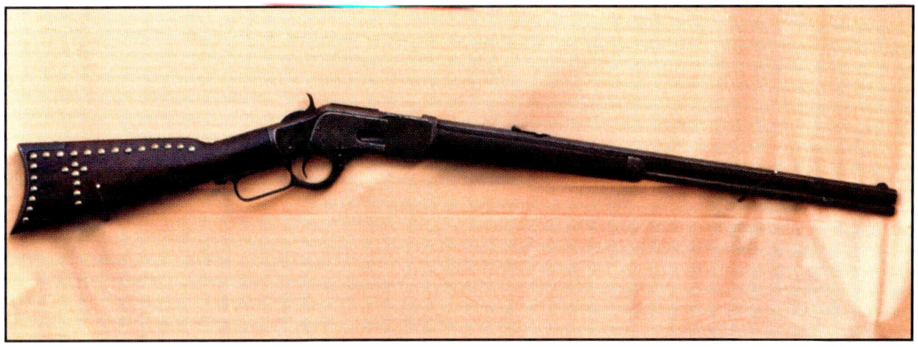

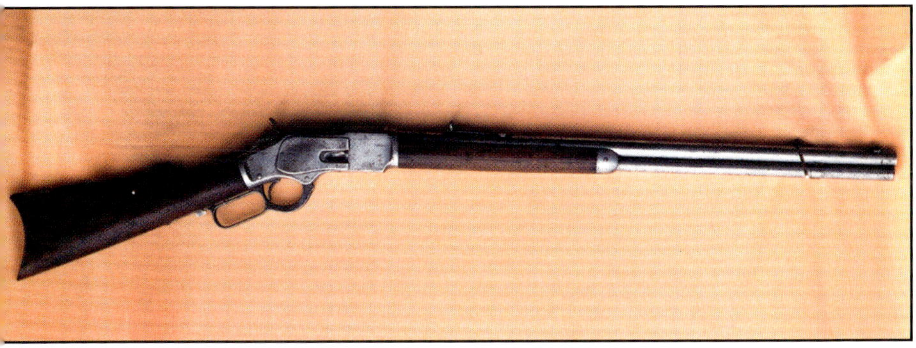

.32 caliber Winchester carbine, model 1873 Indian Gun. *Courtesy private collector. $1050*

Model 1873 Winchester .38 caliber carbine. *Courtesy private collector. $785 to 900*

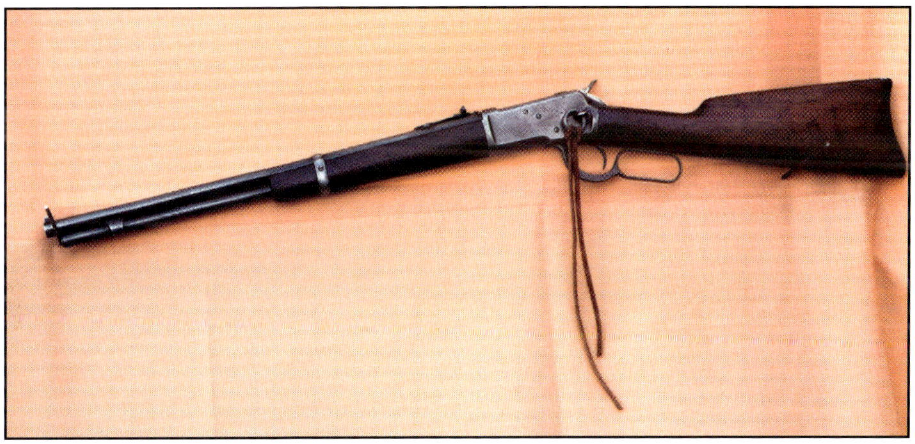

Model 1884 Winchester carbine, .25-20 caliber. *Overton collection. $900 to 1200*

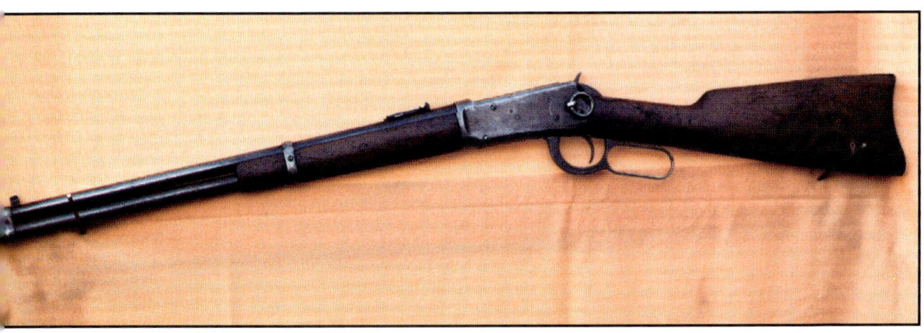

Winchester carbine of .30 caliber with a saddle ring and is considered Cavalry Issue. *Overton collection. $1000 to 1200*

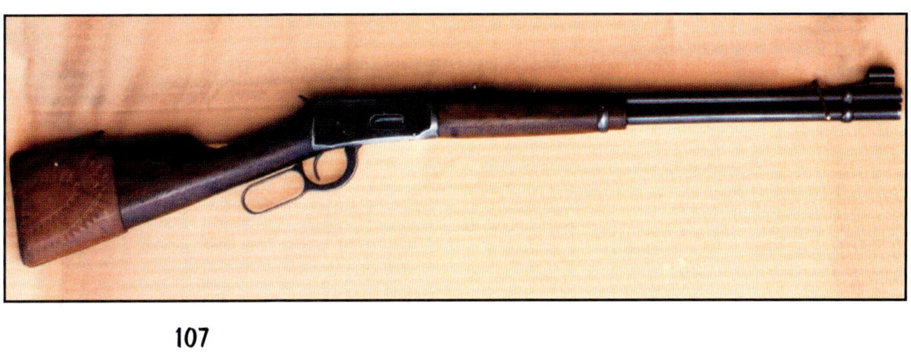

A Winchester carbine is considered a good saddle gun and this one is a .30-.30 caliber with a hand-tooled leather stock protector. In recent years these are used as a big game hunting gun. *Overton collection. $600 to 800*

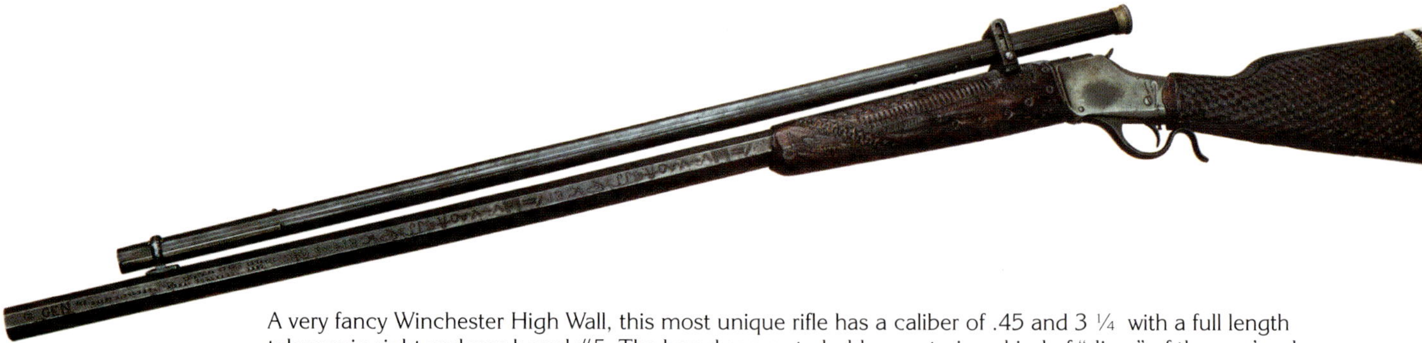

A very fancy Winchester High Wall, this most unique rifle has a caliber of .45 and 3 ¼ with a full length telescopic sight and rare barrel #5. The barrel seems to hold a mysterious kind of "diary" of the gun's whereabouts: "Palisades, Colorado 1914," "Hillsboro, New Mexico, 1917," and "Los Angeles, California, 1921." The long barrel is also covered with strange Indian symbols and the butt of the rifle has Cheyenne Indian beadwork covering the stock. It also bears the engraving "General Harry K. Bogert, Thompsons Utah 1890 1894" and is covered in hand-tooled leather. It takes a very husky man to lift this gun. *Courtesy Eve Morgan. Priceless.*

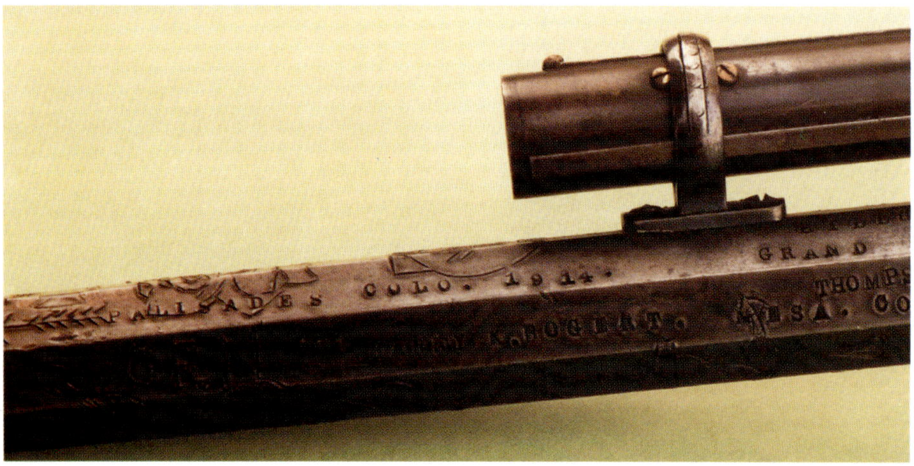

Detail of the symbols and "diary."

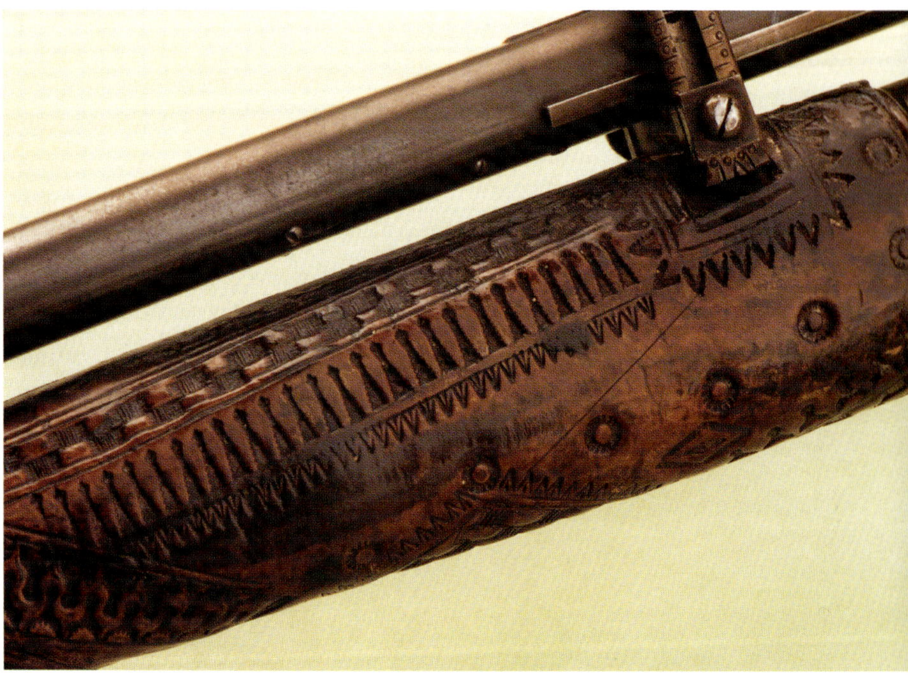

Detail of the hand-carved leather covering the gun.

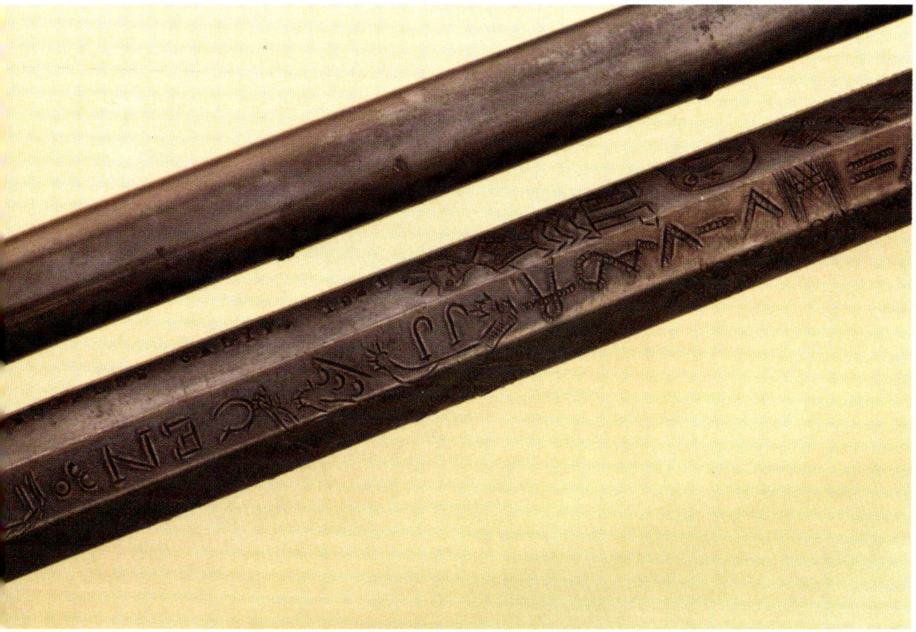

Detail of symbols on the barrel.

Detail of action and leverage setting on the scope. A similar gun was used in the movie *Quigley Down Under*.

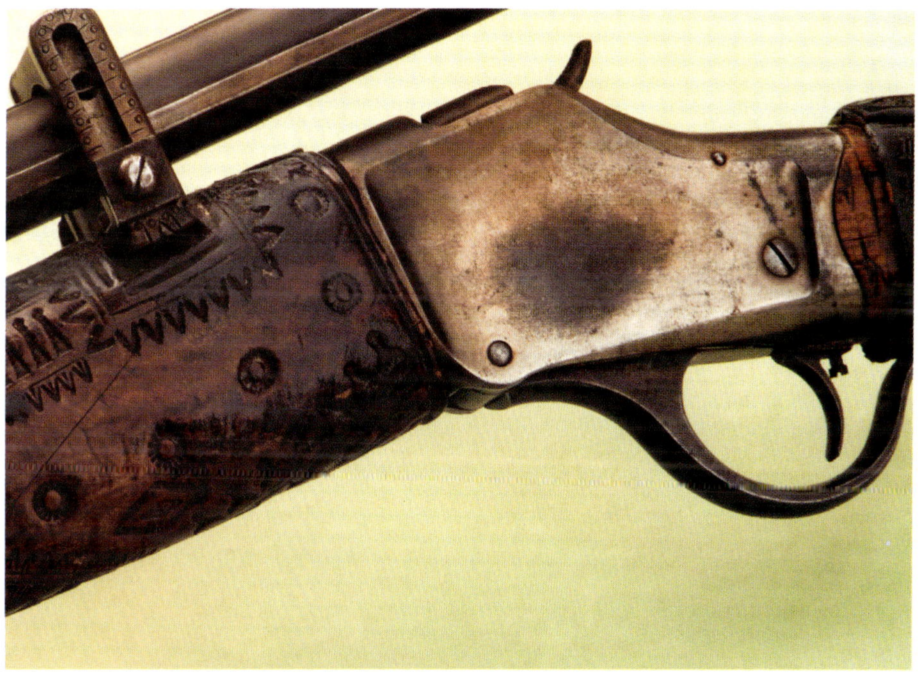

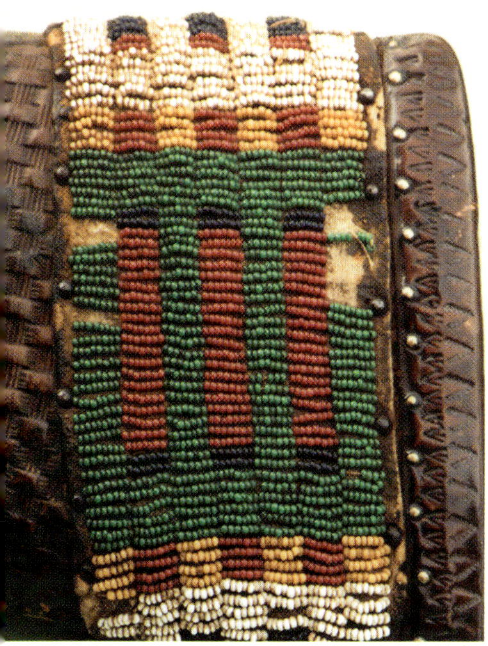

Detail of beadwork on the rifle's stock.

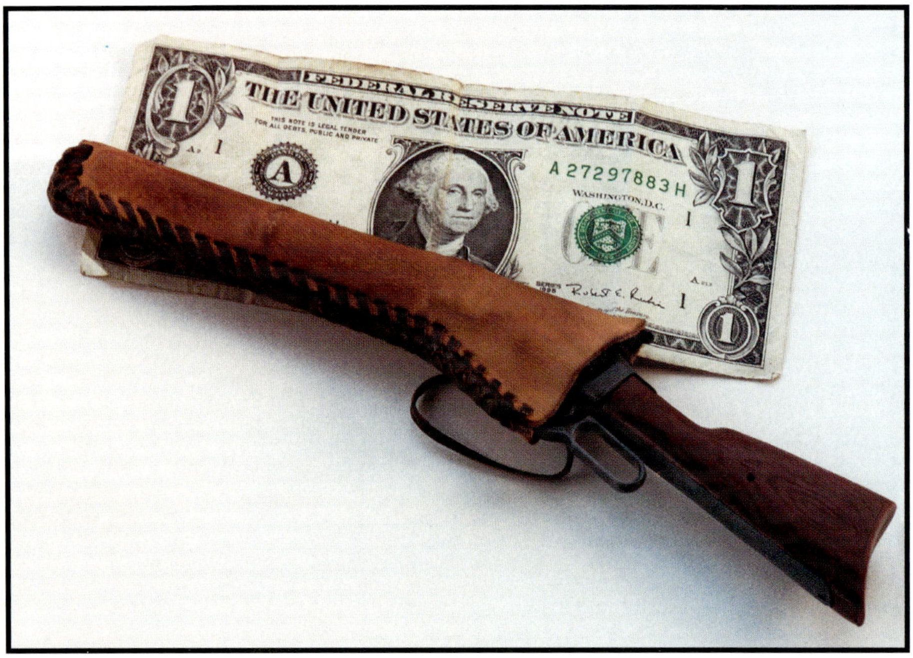

Miniature carbine in a leather scabbard; trigger and lever are actual moving parts. *Overton collection. $25 to 35*

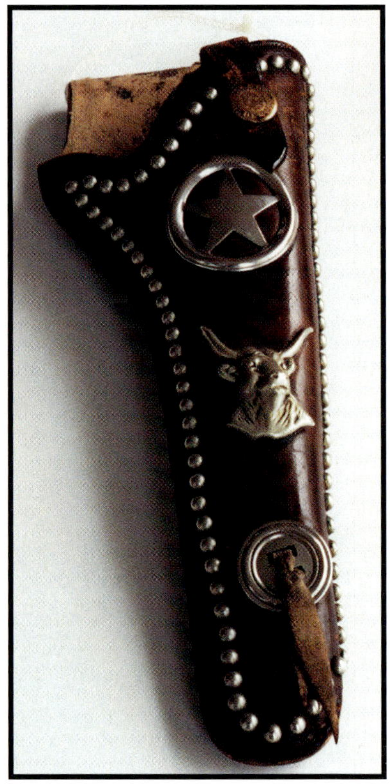

Fancy steer-head holster with star, conchos and studs. It is most unusua c.1920. *Courtesy Ev Morgan. $1500*

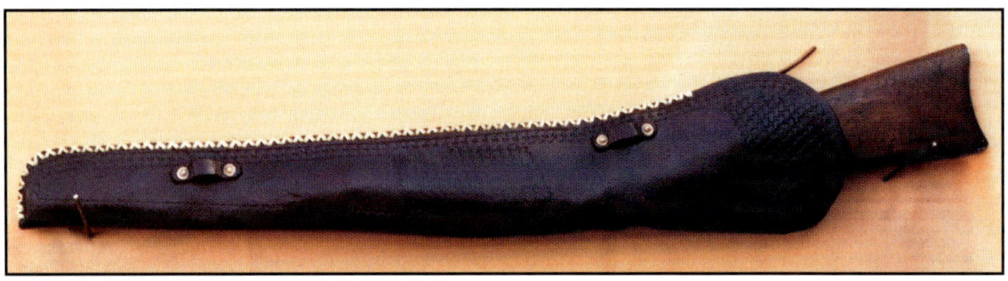

Hand-made scabbard marked "Boise Leather Co." 1910. *Overton collection. $300*

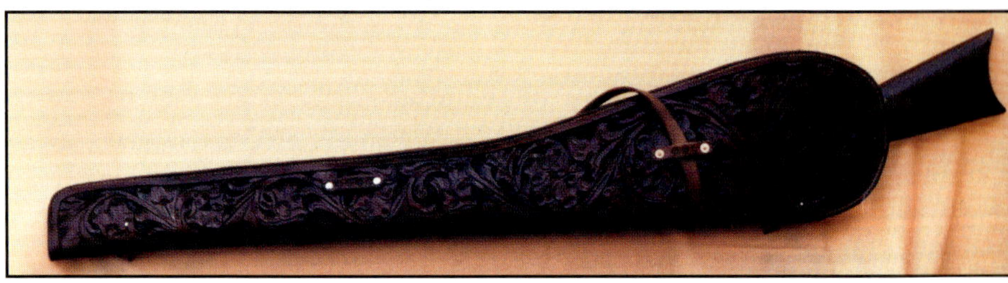

Beautiful hand-carved scabbard attributed to Edward Bolin, and shown in his catalogue. He was the "maker to the stars" in Hollywood, California. *Overton collection. $300 to 400*

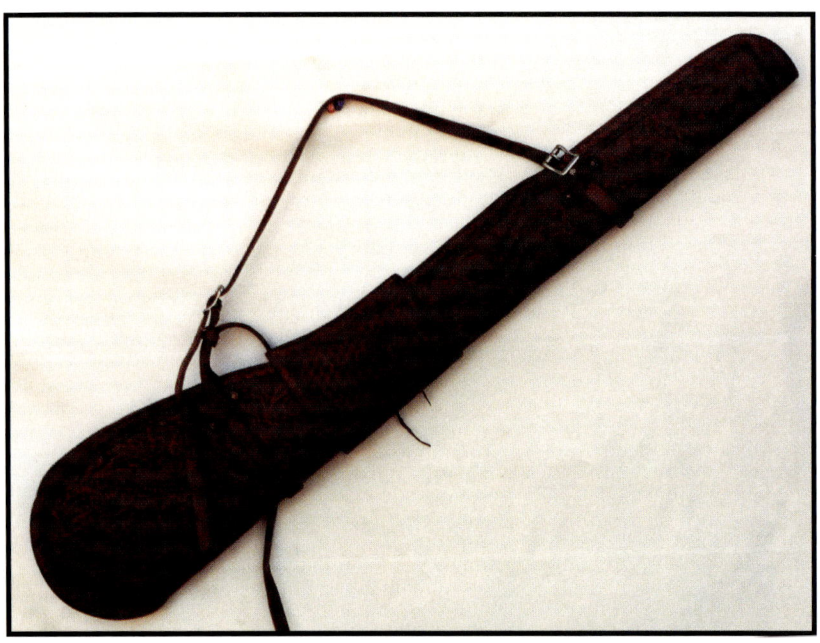

Hand-carved leather scabbard made by Voss in 1943 for George G. Schiffner. *Courtesy Schiffner Military Museum, George and Margaret Schiffner. $150 to 250*

Chapter Seven

Law Enforcement

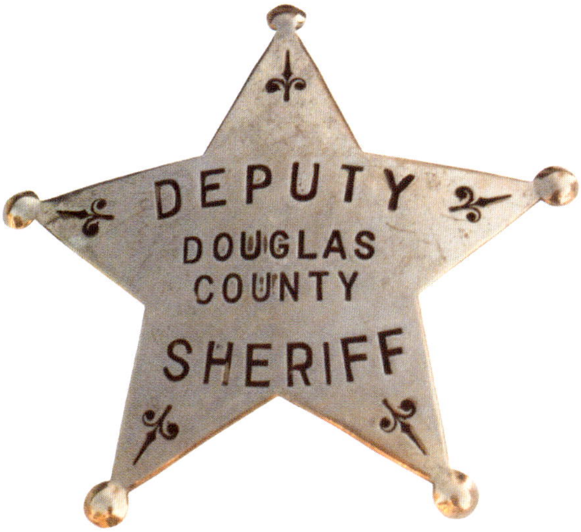

Douglas County, Washington, Sheriff badge with ornate designs. *Courtesy Schiffner Military Museum, George and Margaret Schiffner. $120 to 125*

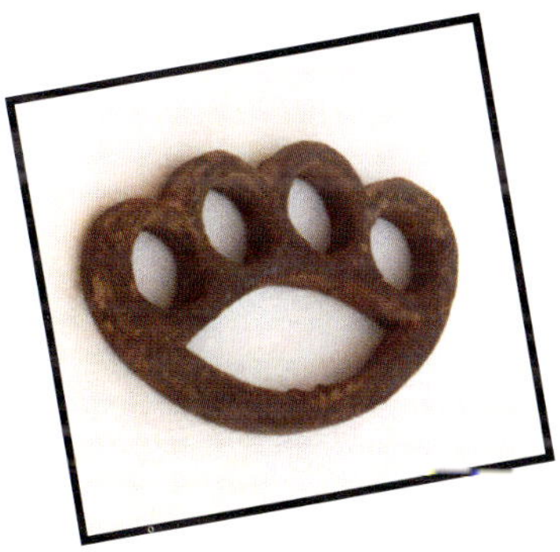

Heavy iron knuckles were considered proper when a lawman had to initiate their use. *Courtesy Schiffner Military Museum, George and Margaret Schiffner. $20 to 50*

"The toughest kind of cowboy"

There is a special attraction that emanates from items that a lawman owned. In the 1880s in the United States, the line between lawman and lawbreaker was sometimes a very thin one, and often indistinguishable. Wyatt Earp, for example, had been charged with horse stealing back in Oklahoma before he became a policeman in Wichita, Kansas; Assistant Marshall in Dodge City; and Deputy Sheriff in Arizona. Many professional gunfighters who fought for the law led double lives and often worked under pseudonyms.

Oftentimes a cowhand gave up his career of trail hand or cow puncher to join a somewhat cleaner, if not deadlier, trade. One of those trades was that of law enforcement. In the early West, the job of lawman frequently was wide open, with very few references required. A man's best reference was the way he handled his guns and just exactly how much "iron" he had in his "craw."

One very small, almost unobtrusive, item separated the lawman from the townspeople and law breakers; that was the silver badge he wore. Everything hung on that small piece of silver. With it pinned to his chest, he had the right to shoot or hang a man. The magic that badge radiated, once pinned to a man, brought with it many deep emotions aimed at the man who wore it. Some held the badge in highest regard, with respect and honor; others saw it as a challenge to out-draw him. The pay was low and generally the living quarters provided, if at all, were poor, to say the least. Yet, every day, the lawman of the early West pinned on the badge and went out to do his job in towns that were wild, at their very best. It is no wonder that collecting those badges today has become such a fascinating hobby; it is a link with the men who first wore them.

In 1880 one young attorney wrote that his town of Tombstone, Arizona, had "two dance halls, a dozen gambling places, and more than twenty saloons." "Still...." he wrote, "there is hope, for I know of two Bibles in town." It was only natural that towns like that would need a few good lawmen!

Justice was swift and sometimes a little on the uncivilized side. There are many accounts of various ways a judge's sentence was carried out. Stories of men having been lashed to windmill blades and left to hang there turning upside down in the wind abound. Ranches housing outlaws and horse thieves were sometimes set on fire in the middle of the night while the lawbreakers slept. There are accounts of warning posters being hung throughout a town with drawings of coffins on them in order to frighten or drive away would-be thieves and rustlers.

Many rigged "gallows" are spoken of and pictured in early drawings. If all else failed, a simple lasso rope and a nearby tree often sufficed.

The story of the "Oregon boot"

When Oregon was but a young territory, the places of incarceration were nothing more than a pole stockade with sharpened poles buried into the ground with the pointed tips up. Prisoners would often scale these poles and escape in spite of the sharpened poles. So that prisoners could not scale the poles, Oregonians had the local blacksmith fashion a very heavy, usually 18 to 20 pound, shackle which was fastened with a huge key to one of the prisoner's ankles. This was the first Oregon boot. In order to walk, the prisoner would take one step with his free foot and drag the other one up. There was no way he could possibly climb the poles. It stands to reason now, that those "boots" are very rare.

Other items used in law enforcement helped to give the lawman an edge when it came to fighting outlaws. Leg irons and handcuffs were great innovations. With them he could restrain one man even while dealing with another. Many of these old items are very rare and hard to find today, especially the leg irons. I hold a special interest and place in my heart for the men who protect us while we sleep. One of my sons holds a law enforcement position today. And here in a free society, can't we all see how fortunate we are to still have men who are tough enough and willing to lay their life on the line every day so that we can live in an ordered society instead of chaos?

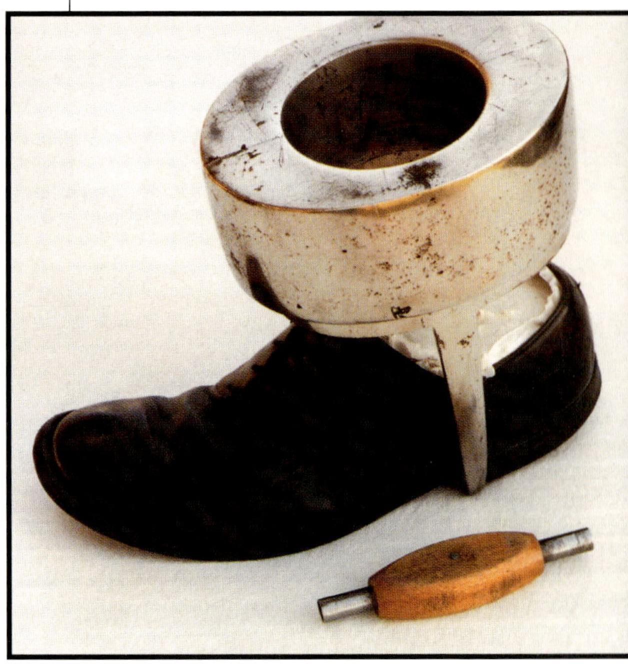

"The Oregon Boot" displayed with the "key" and a contemporary shoe showing the way it was attached to the foot. Marked "Gardener Shackle, July 3, 1866," last known use was in 1962. *Courtesy Schiffner Military Museum, George and Margaret Schiffner. $400 to 500*

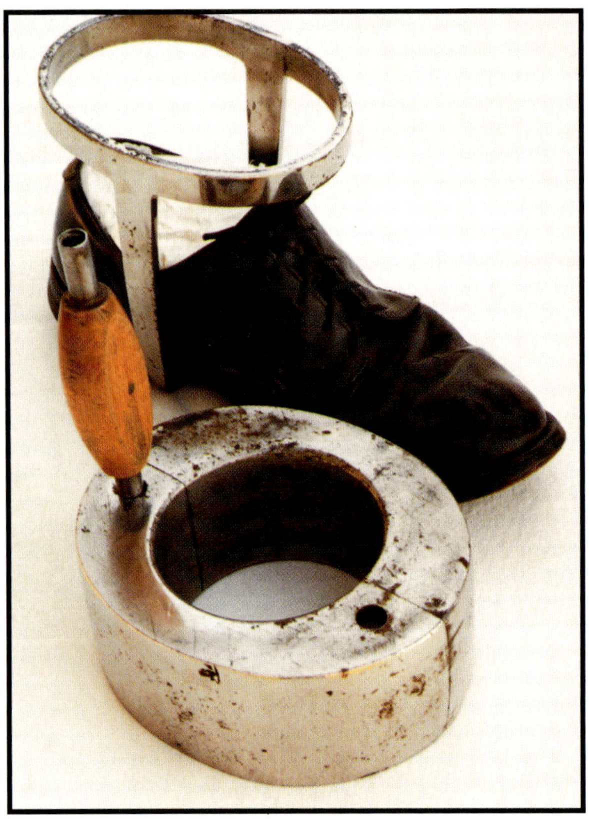

Separated, the Oregon Boot is shown in its pieces. It was perhaps cruel, but very effective to deter escapes. *Courtesy Schiffner Military Museum, George and Margaret Schiffner. $400 to 500*

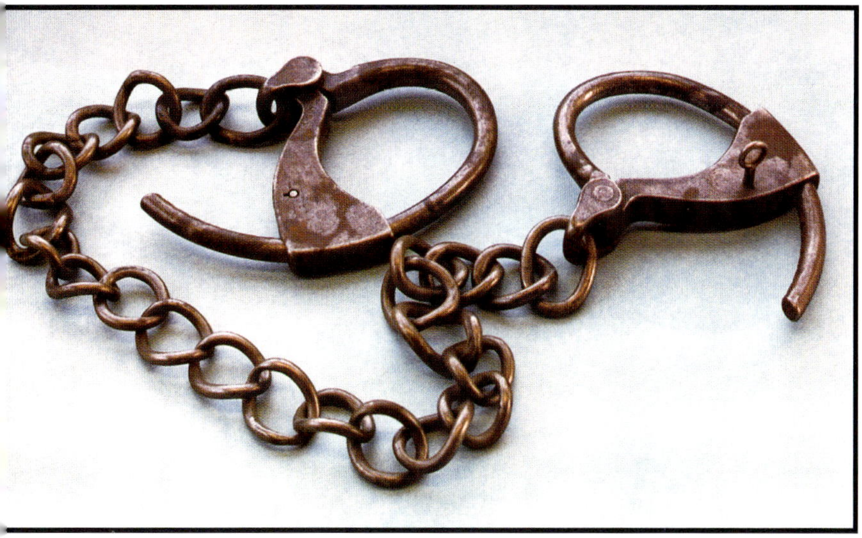

Locking adjustable leg irons marked with the Walla Walla, Washington State Prison's mark. *Courtesy private collector. $175 to 200*

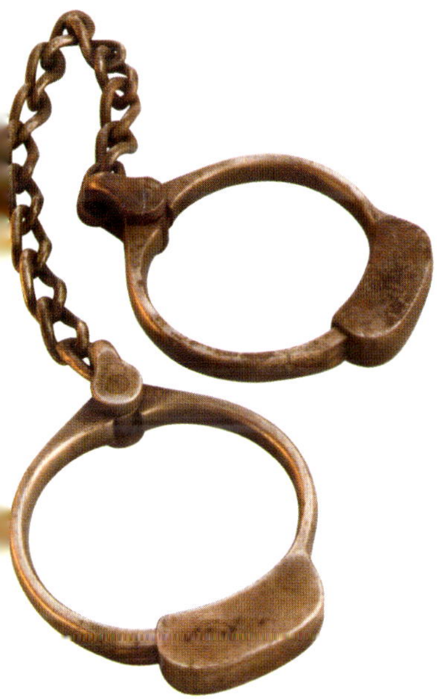

nkle shackles were used in the late 880s, as a general rule. *Courtesy chiffner Military Museum, George nd Margaret Schiffner. $150 to 175*

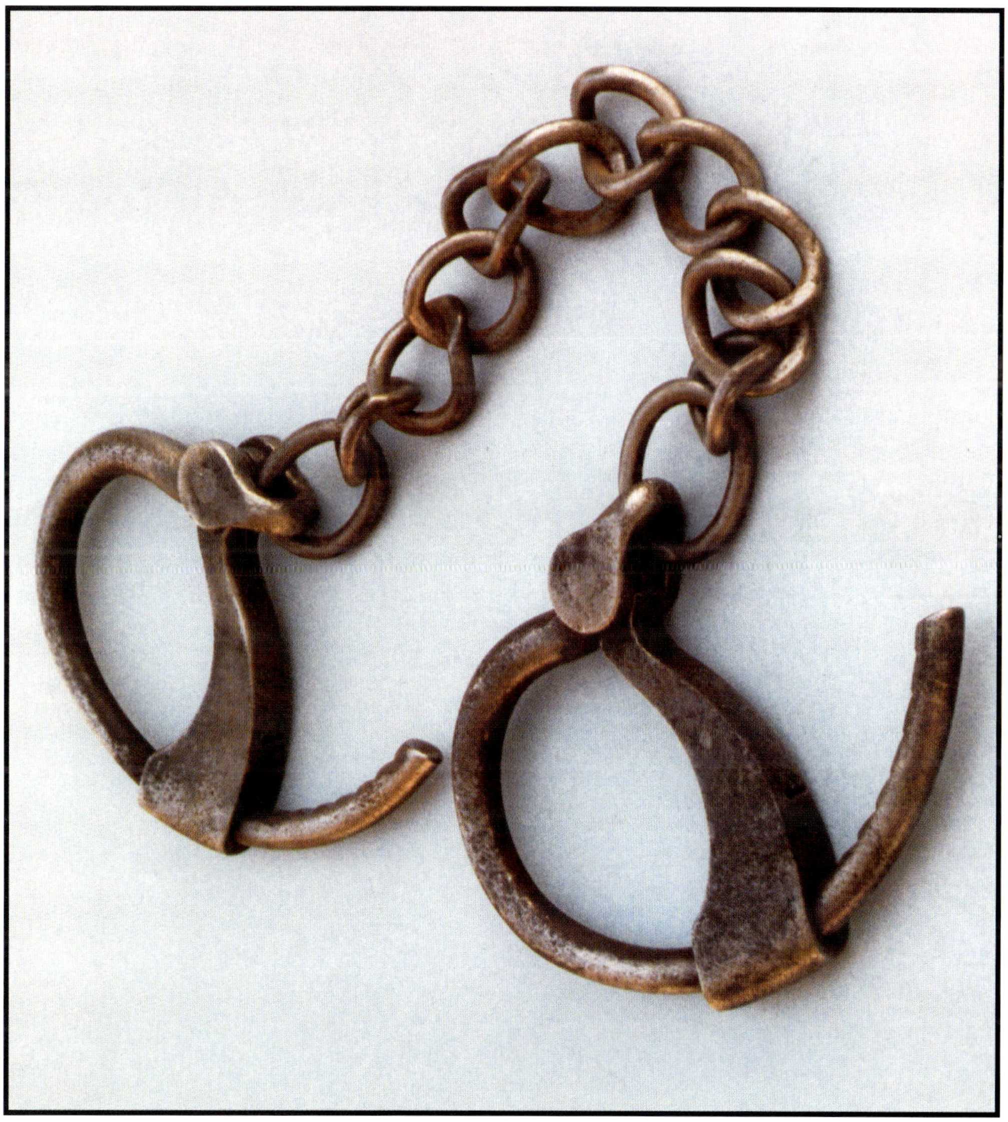

Locking leg irons in excellent condition; most were patented in the late 1880s. *Courtesy Schiffner Military Museum, George and Margaret Schiffner. $175 to 200*

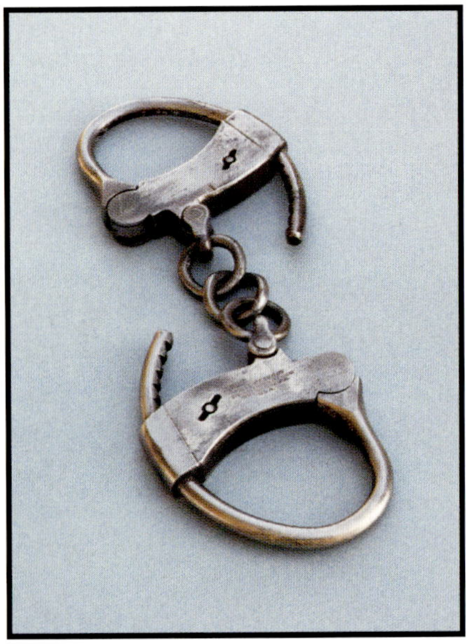

The Mattatuck Mfg. Co. of Waterbury, Connecticut, made this pair of handcuffs around the 1920s to 1930s. *Courtesy Schiffner Military Museum, George and Margaret Schiffner. $80 to 95*

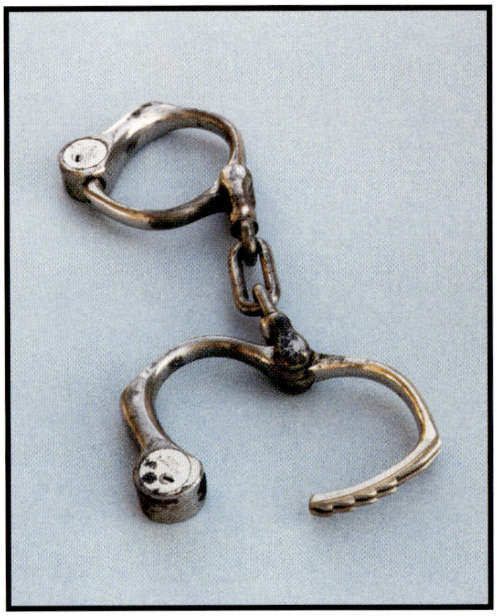

Handcuffs are patented May 2, 1899. *Courtesy Schiffner Military Museum, George and Margaret Schiffner. $100 to 125*

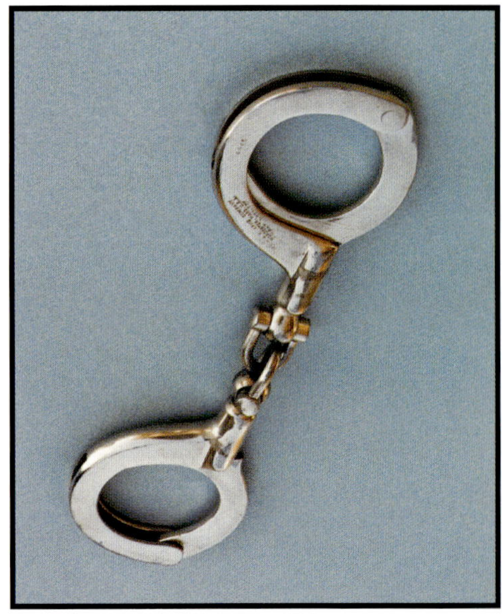

H&R Arms Company, Worchester, Mass. U.S.A *Courtesy Schiffner Military Museum, George and Margaret Schiffner. $100 to 125*

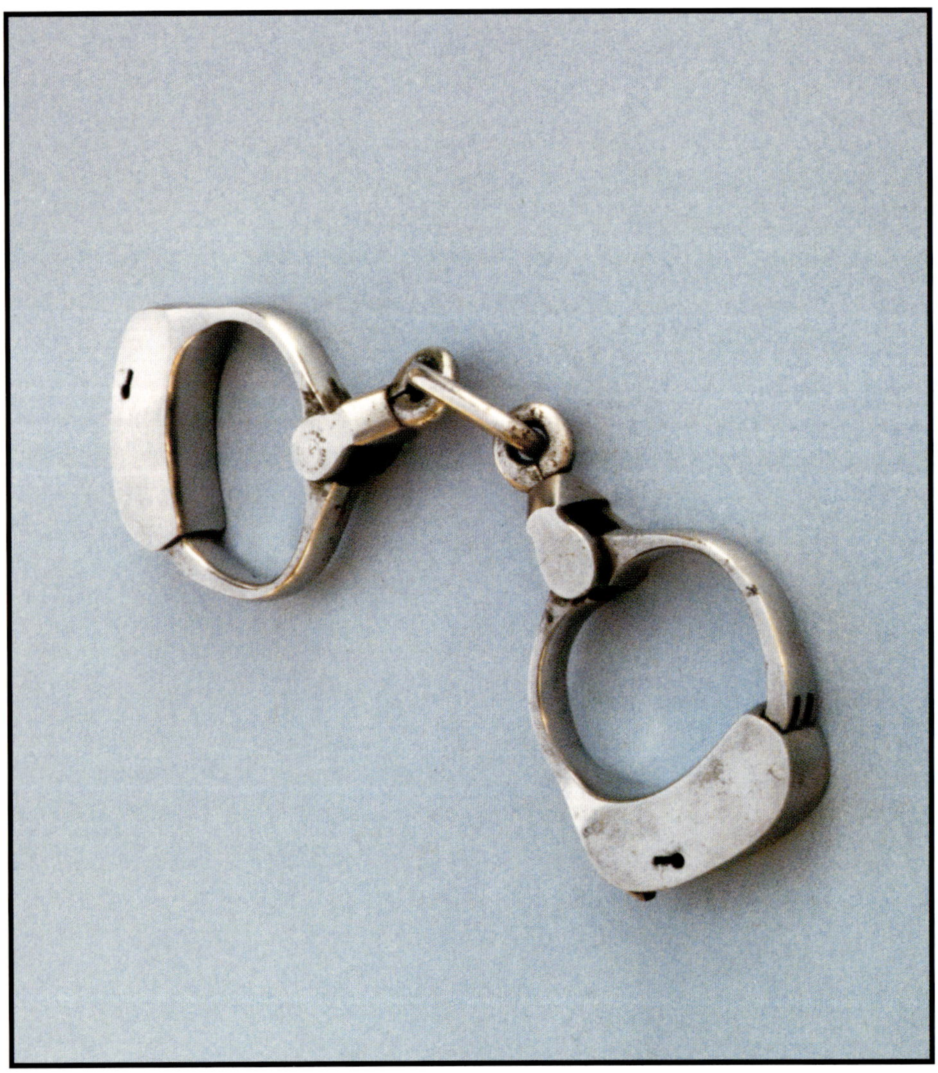

The handcuffs are marked with the "T" mark, and were patented Nov. 28, 1882. *Courtesy Schiffner Military Museum, George and Margaret Schiffner. $90 to 120*

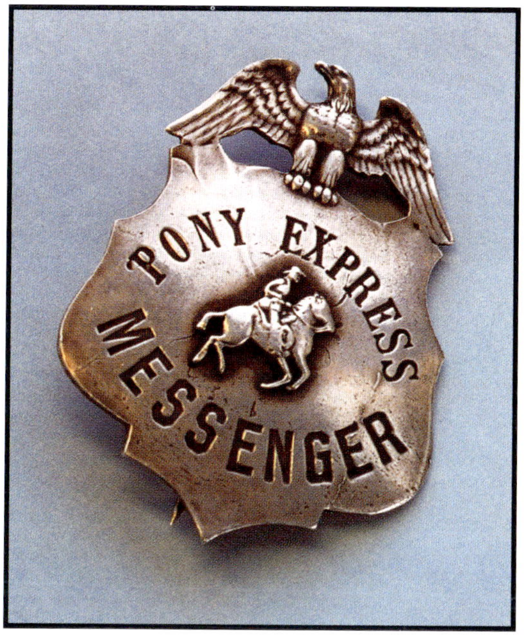

Old Pony Express badge with a simple pin back. *Courtesy private collector. $300 to 325*

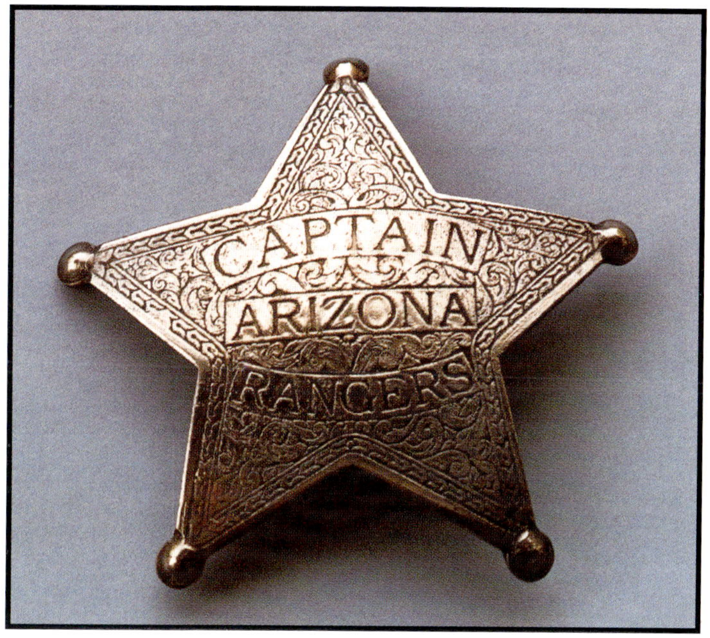

Arizona Ranger badge in good condition; if authentic, it warrants the value placed. *Overton collection. $300 to 325*

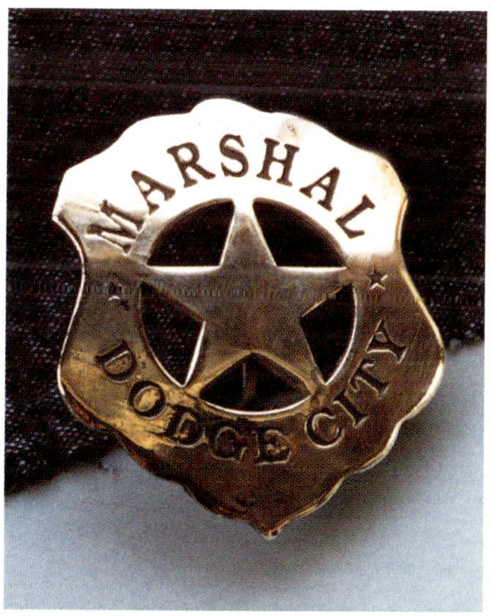

Dodge City did employ both a marshal and deputy marshals; if the badge is authentic, it warrants the value placed. *Overton collection. $250 to 300*

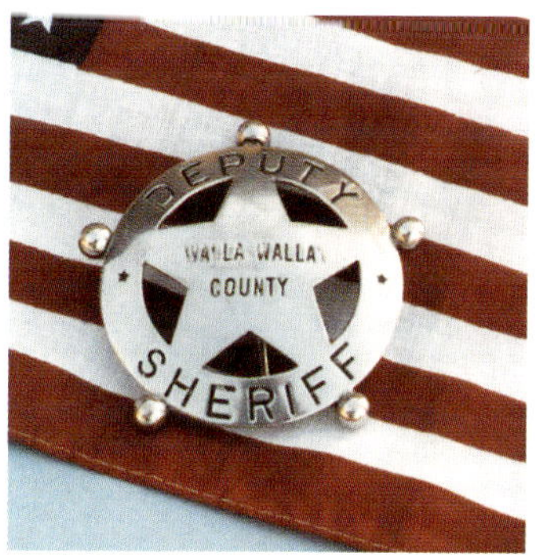

This badge dates before 1889 when Washington State was still a Territory. *Courtesy Schiffner Military Museum, George and Margaret Schiffner. $200 to 225*

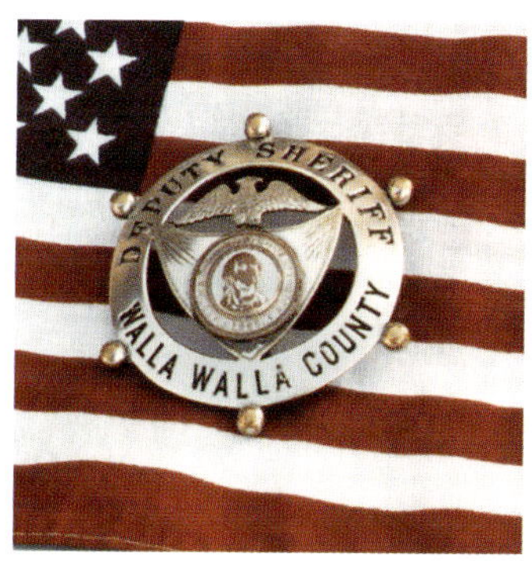

Deputy Sheriff badge used after Washington State attained statehood in 1889; it has the proud seal of the state on it. *Courtesy Schiffner Military Museum, George and Margaret Schiffner. $160 to 175*

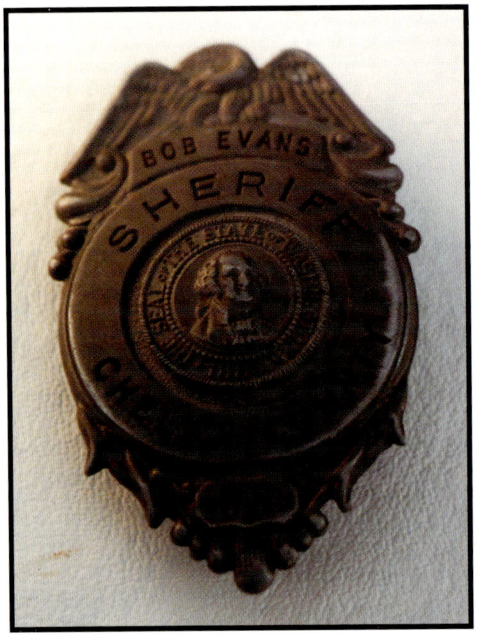

During World War II there was a shortage of various metals; this badge reflects the shortages in that it is made of pewter. *Courtesy Schiffner Military Museum, George and Margaret Schiffner. $100 to 125*

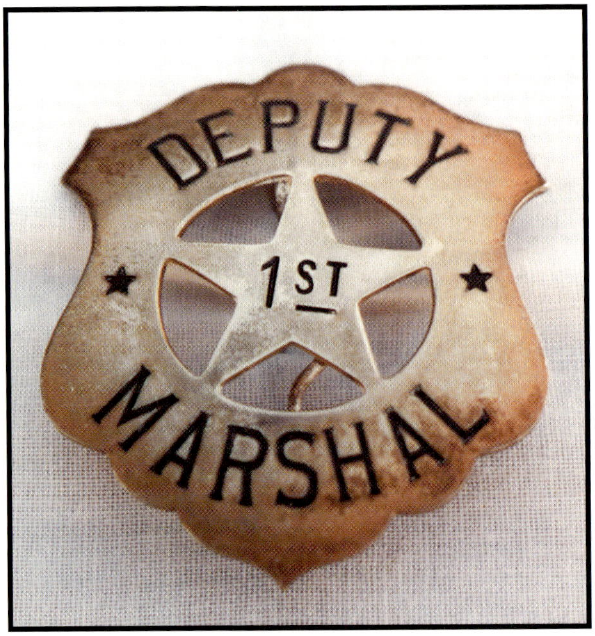

Washington State "Deputy 1st Marshal" badge. *Courtesy Schiffner Military Museum, George and Margaret Schiffner. $40 to 50*

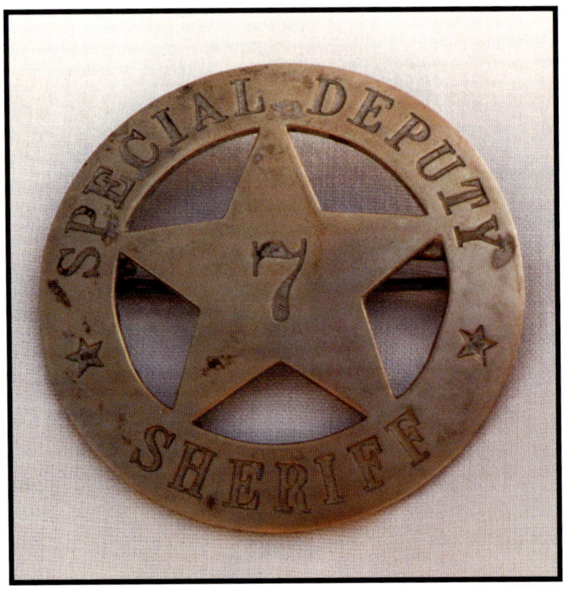

His number was "7" and he served as Special Deputy Sheriff, but we know not who he was. *Courtesy Schiffner Military Museum, George and Margaret Schiffner. $150 to 175*

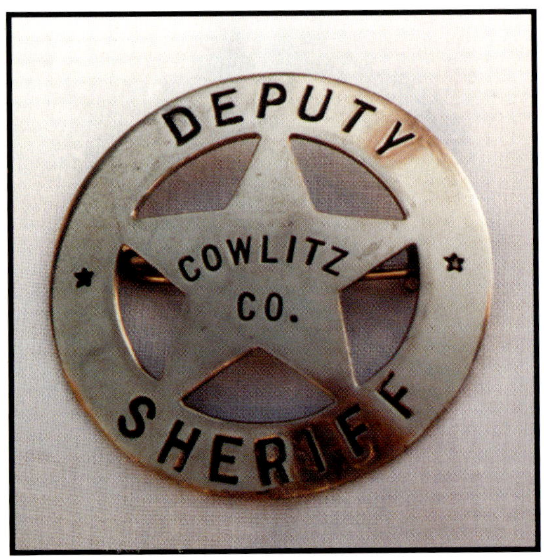

Cowlitz County Deputy Sheriff badge; it is an old one. One way to determine the age of a badge is to look at the way it is pinned at the back. If it has a straight simple pin, it may be old; locking pins were not used in the 1800s. *Courtesy Schiffner Military Museum, George and Margaret Schiffner. $125 to 150*

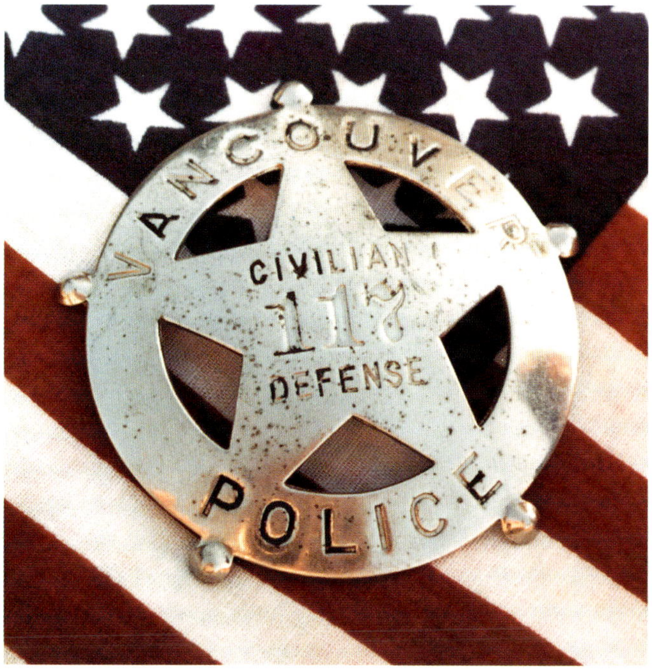

Vancouver, Washington, "Civilian Defense # 117" badge. *Courtesy Schiffner Military Museum, George and Margaret Schiffner. $60 to 70*

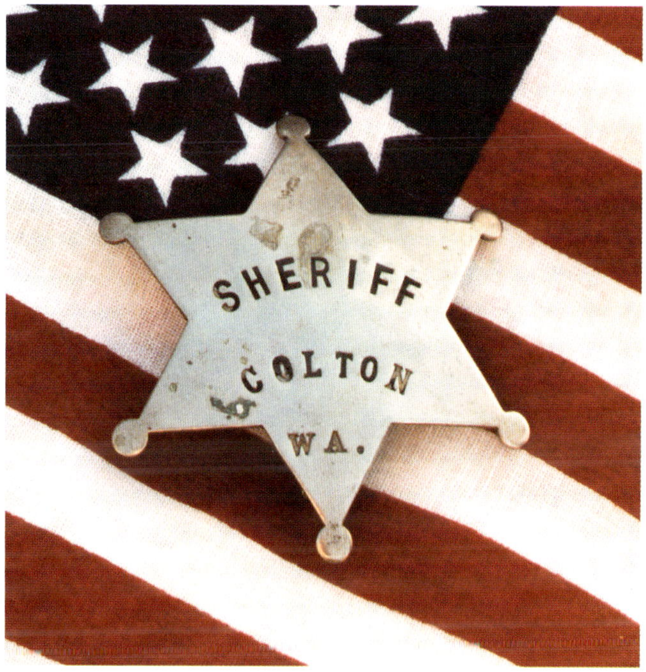

Old sheriff's badge from Colton, Washingaton. *Courtesy Schiffner Military Museum, George and Margaret Schiffner. $125 to 150*

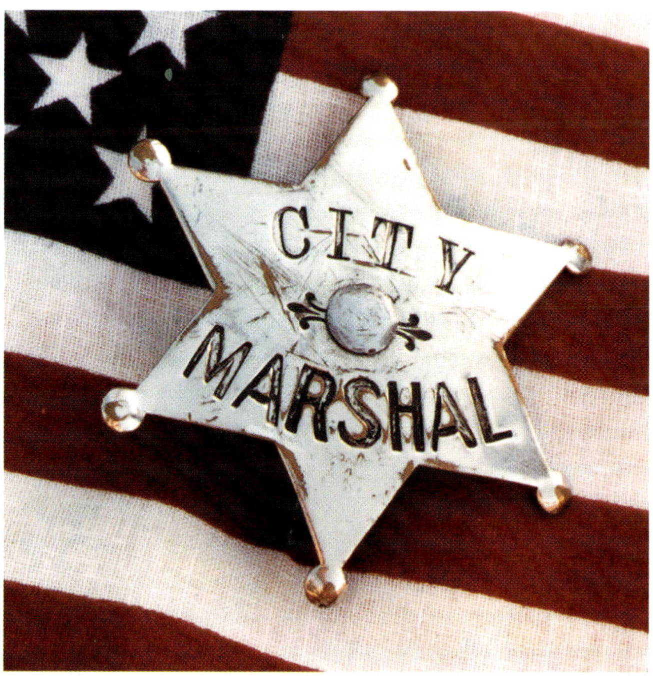

"City Marshal" badge for an unknown city. *Courtesy Schiffner Military Museum, George and Margaret Schiffner. $75 to 120*

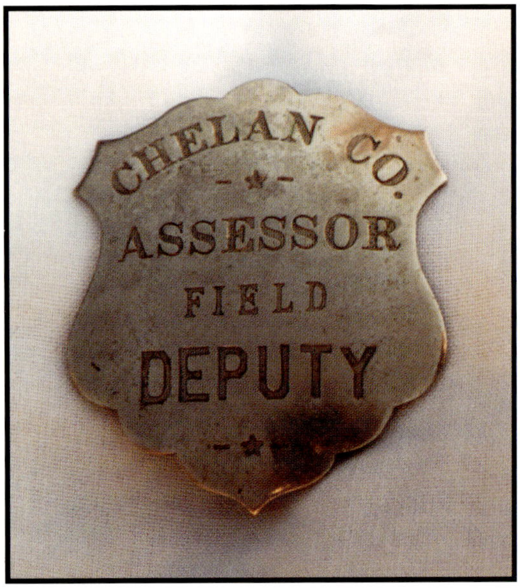

A badge for a tax or land assessor, this is unusual. *Courtesy Schiffner Military Museum, George and Margaret Schiffner. $60 to 80*

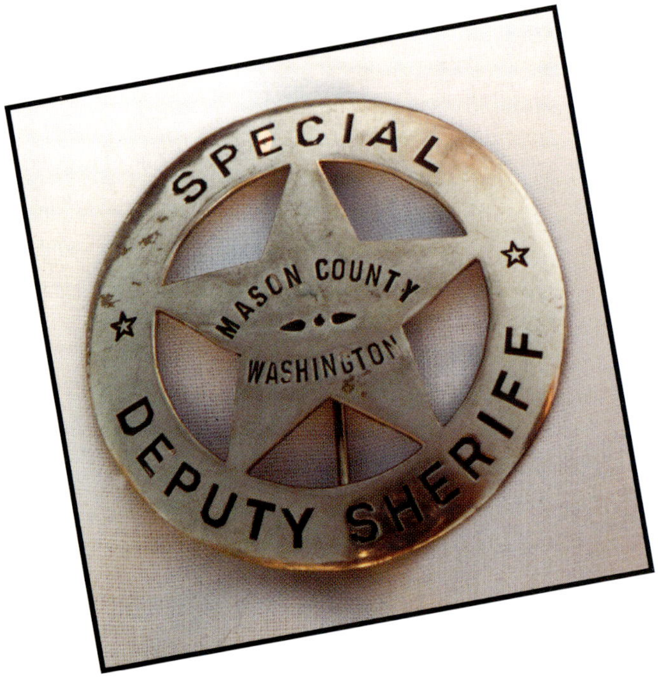

Wouldn't it be interesting to know what the "special" meant and for what field of law enforcement it served? *Courtesy Schiffner Military Museum, George and Margaret Schiffner. $75 to 100*

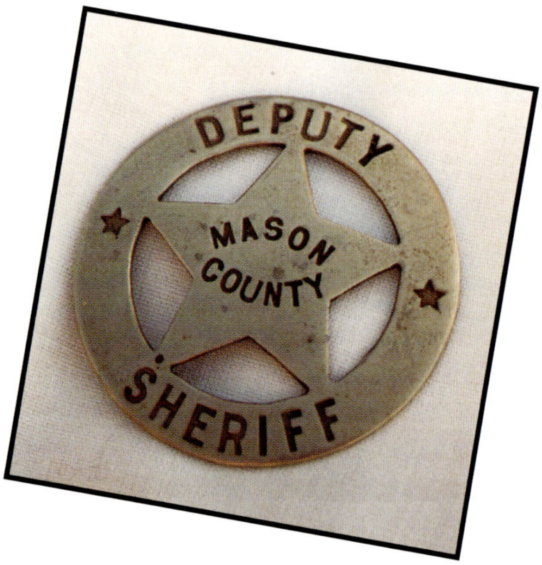

A Deputy Sheriff badge was a little smaller and less impressive. *Courtesy Schiffner Military Museum, George and Margaret Schiffner. $50 to 75*

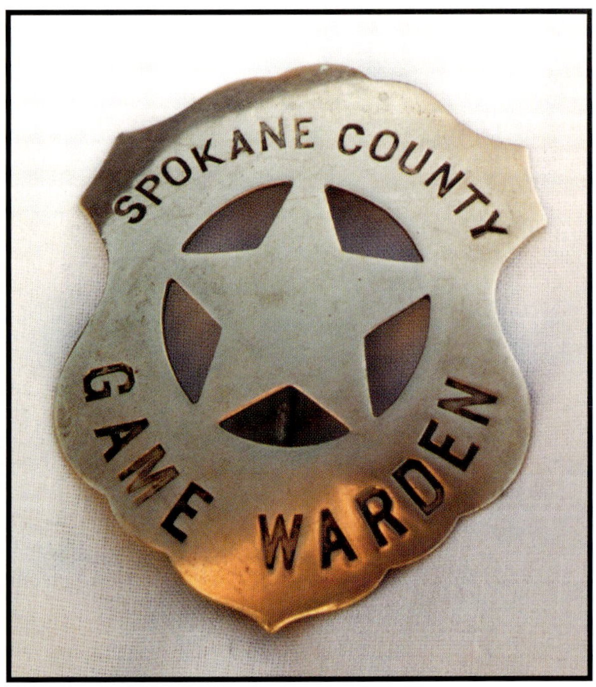

Game wardens in the West were at just as much risk for their lives as other law enforcement personnel and they were always identified with badges. *Courtesy Schiffner Military Museum, George and Margaret Schiffner. $75 to 100*

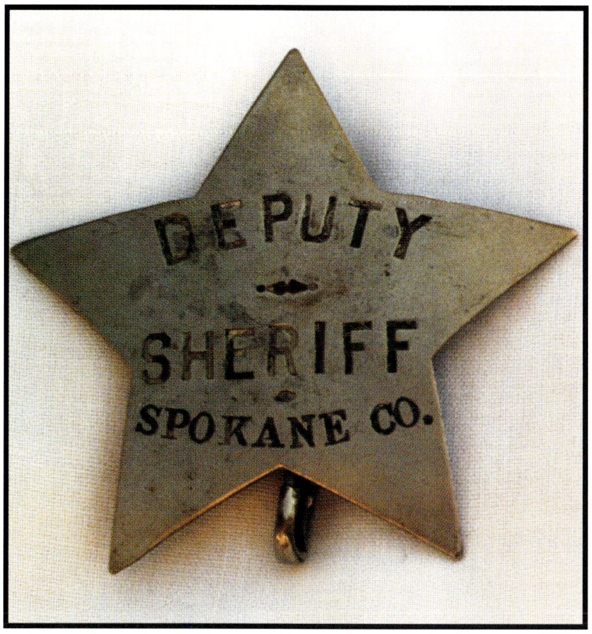

A nice old Deputy Sheriff badge. *Courtesy Schiffner Military Museum. $70 to 90*

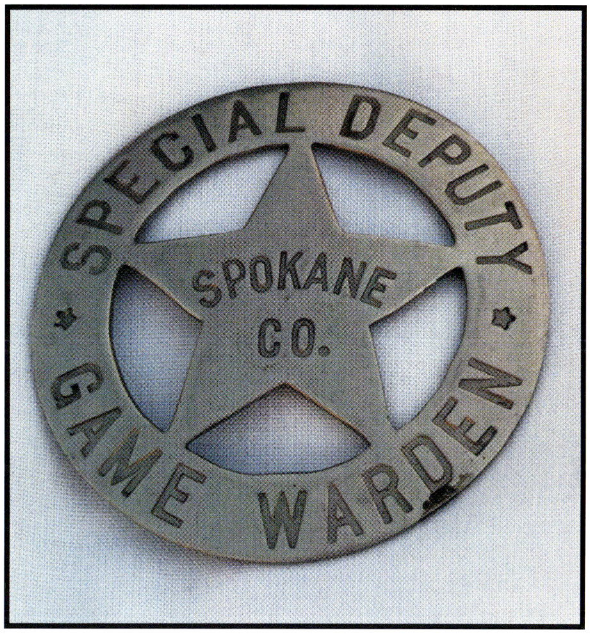

Another interesting job, and not without its perils and risks. *Courtesy Schiffner Military Museum, George and Margaret Schiffner. $55 to 70*

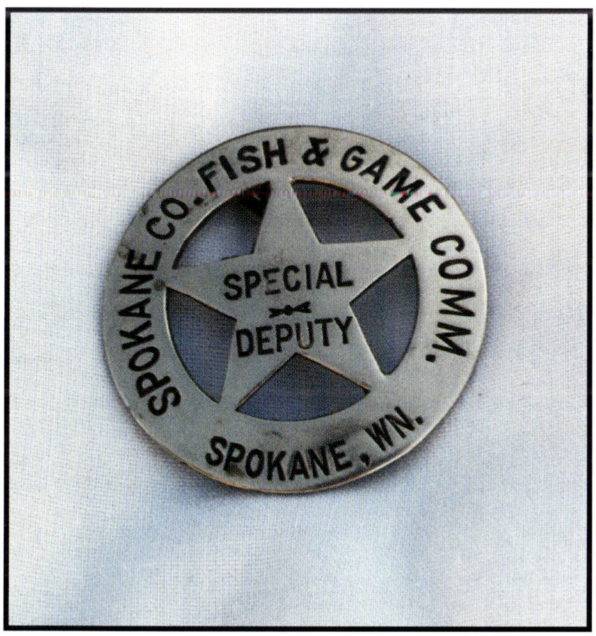

The Fish and Game Commission issued badge to its Special Deputies. *Courtesy Schiffner Military Museum, George and Margaret Schiffner. $50 to 75*

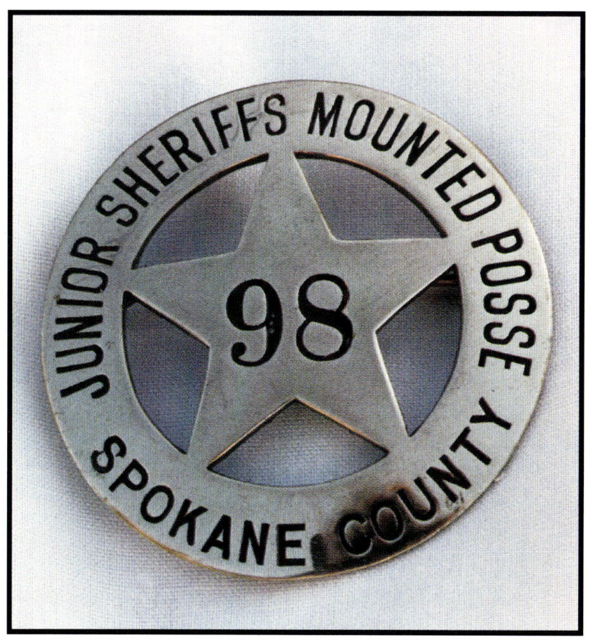

Mounted posse groups of law enforcement personnel are still used in the U. S. West for man-hunts in steep areas where it is difficult to take a motorized vehicle. *Courtesy Schiffner Military Museum, George and Margaret Schiffner. $60 to 80*

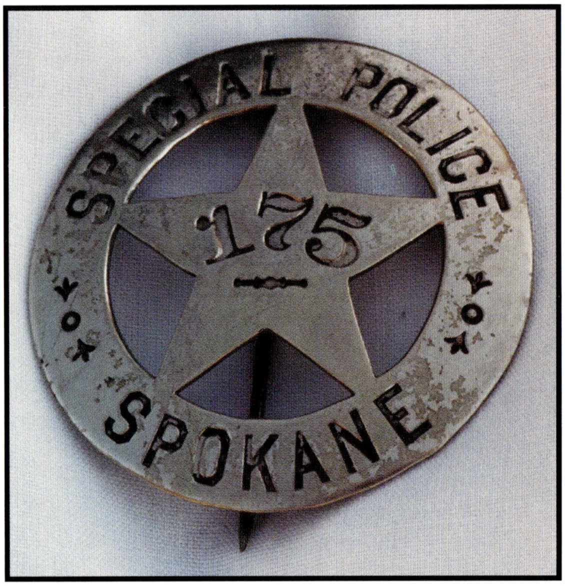

Nice old badge with decorative cuts; one wonders what the Special Police did? *Courtesy Schiffner Military Museum, George and Margaret Schiffner. $75 to 100*

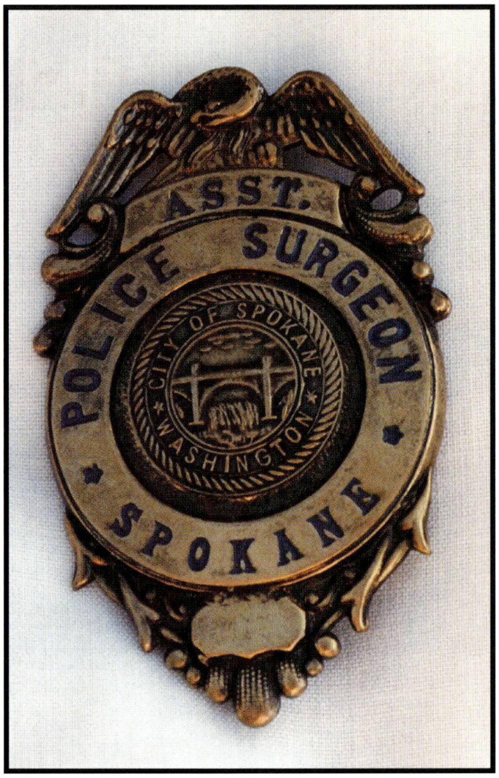

Nice brass badge depicting the famous old bridge in Spokane, Washington. *Courtesy Schiffner Military Museum, George and Margaret Schiffner. $100 to 125*

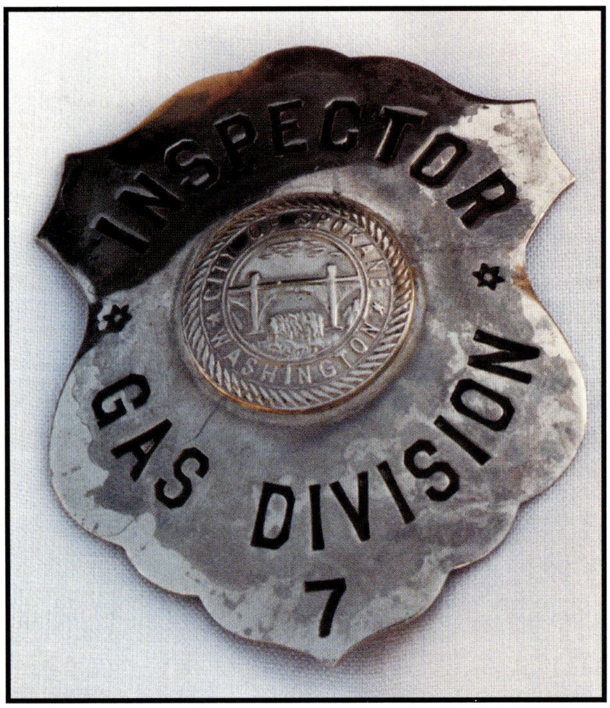

One can only imagine what this area of law enforcement entailed. *Courtesy Schiffner Military Museum, George and Margaret Schiffner. $75 to 100*

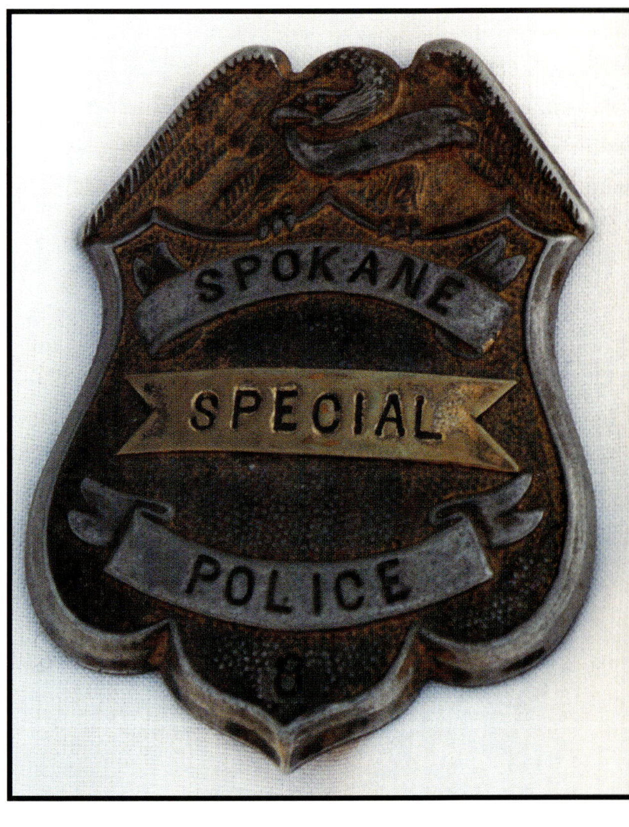

Pot metal badge probably used during the 1940s. *Courtesy Schiffner Military Museum, George and Margaret Schiffner. $80 to 125*

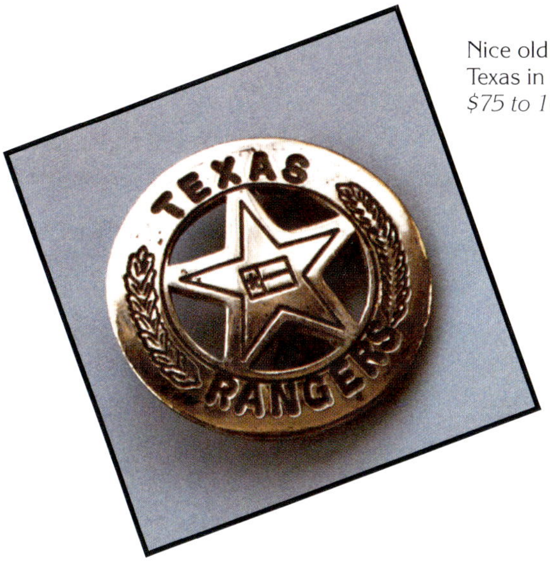

Nice old Texas Ranger badge with the flag of Texas in the center of a star. *Overton collection. $75 to 100*

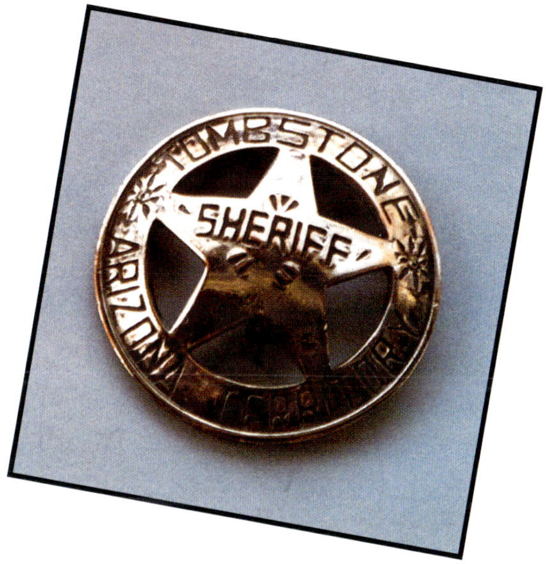

Tombstone Sheriff badge; it may be coAntemporary, yet has definite indications of being original. *Overton collection. $75 to 100*

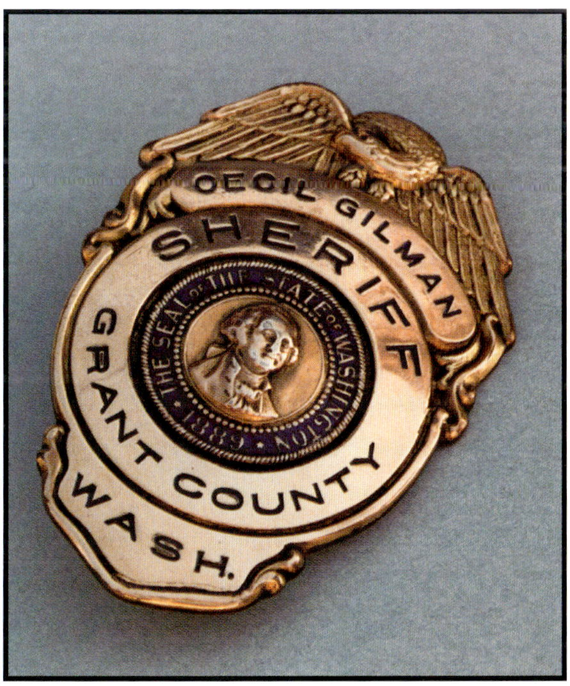

This most elaborate and expensive badge is gold with a bronze backing and, in the center, the seal of the State of Washington, 1889. *Courtesy Schiffner Military Museum, George and Margaret Schiffner. $500 to 550*

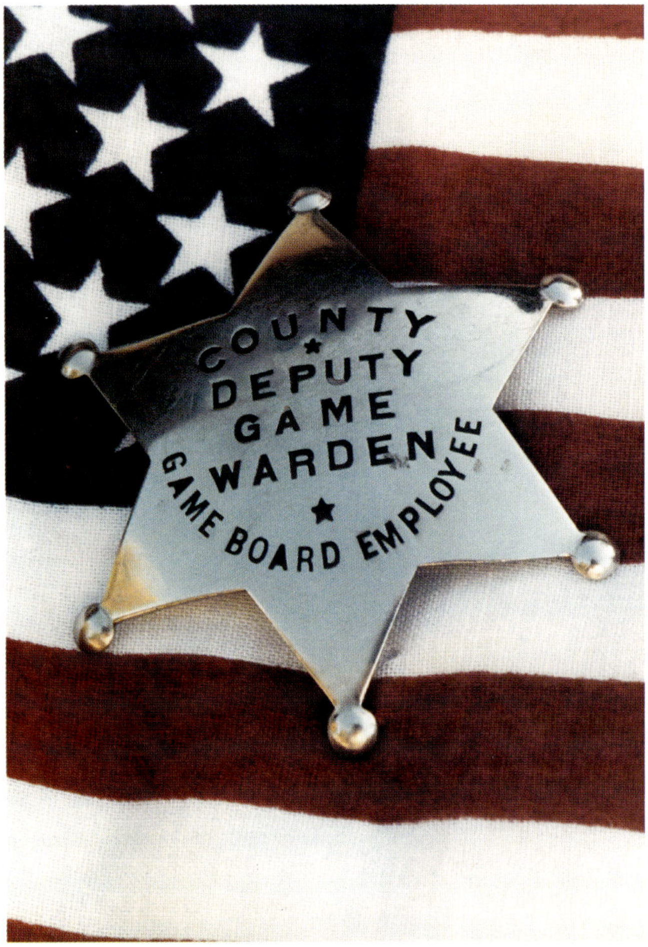

Game Board Employee badge with traditional star shape. *Courtesy Schiffner Military Museum, George and Margaret Schiffner. $60 to 75*

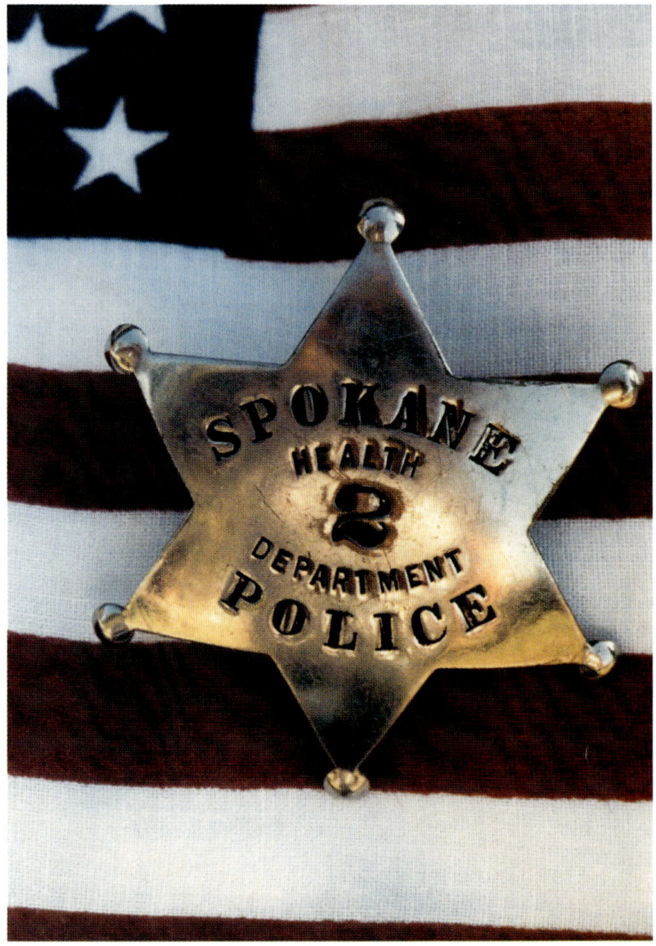

Health Department Police, a rather unusual law enforcement badge and an original one. *Courtesy Schiffner Military Museum, George and Margaret Schiffner. $75 to 100*

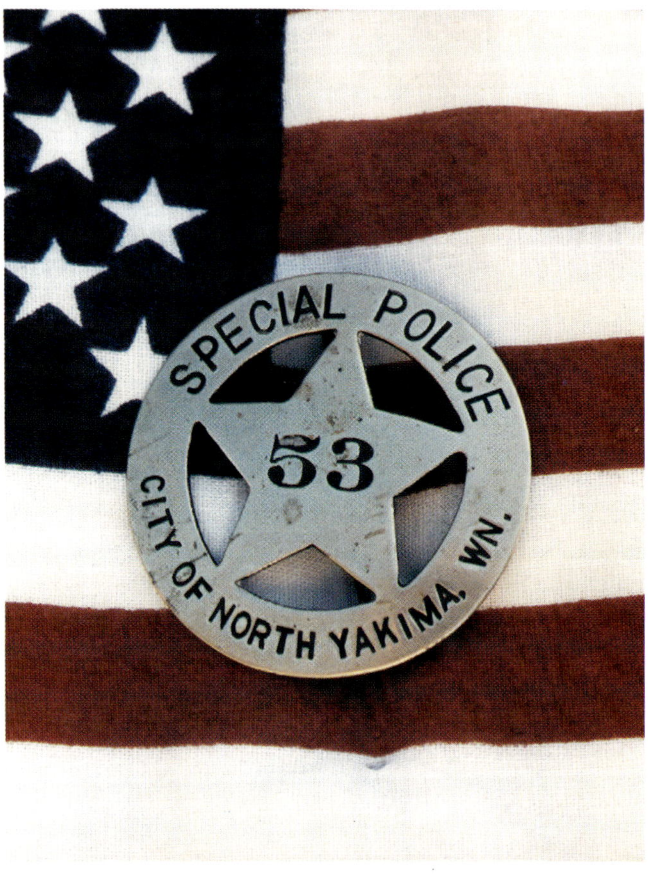

It has been a very long time since there was a City of North Yakima, Washington, so the badge is quite old. *Courtesy Schiffner Military Museum, George and Margaret Schiffner. $75 to 100*

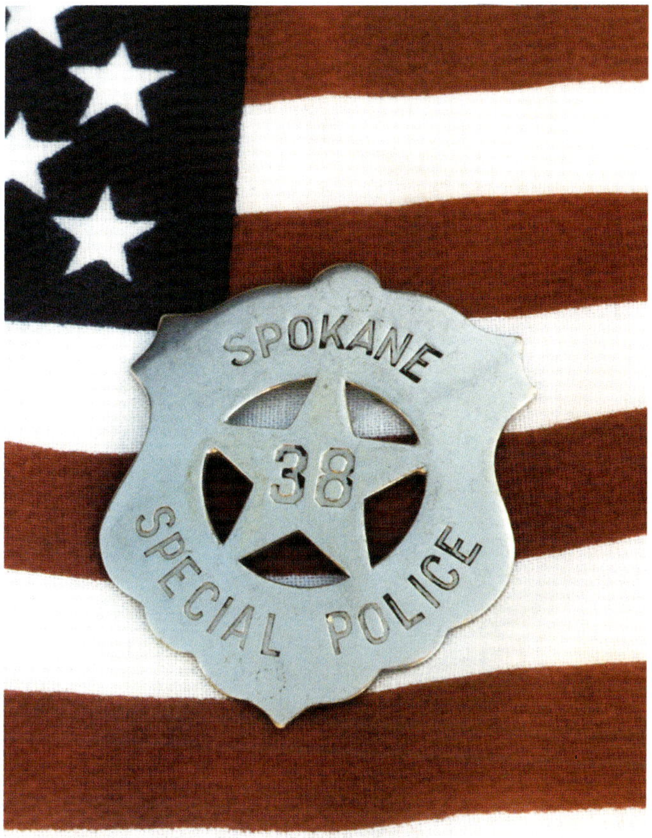

Nice old badge from the city of Spokane, Washington. *Courtesy Schiffner Military Museum. $75 to 100*

Very decorative star badge, c. 1909 to 1910. *Courtesy Schiffner Military Museum, George and Margaret Schiffner. $325 to 375*

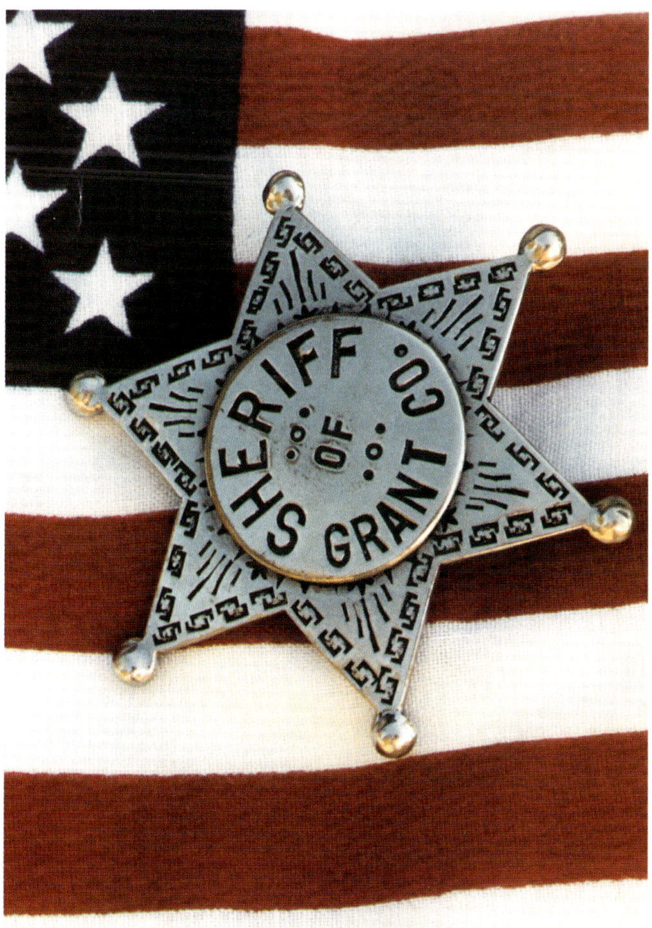

Deputy Sheriff badge in a circle star. *Courtesy Schiffner Military Museum, George and Margaret Schiffner. $75 to 100*

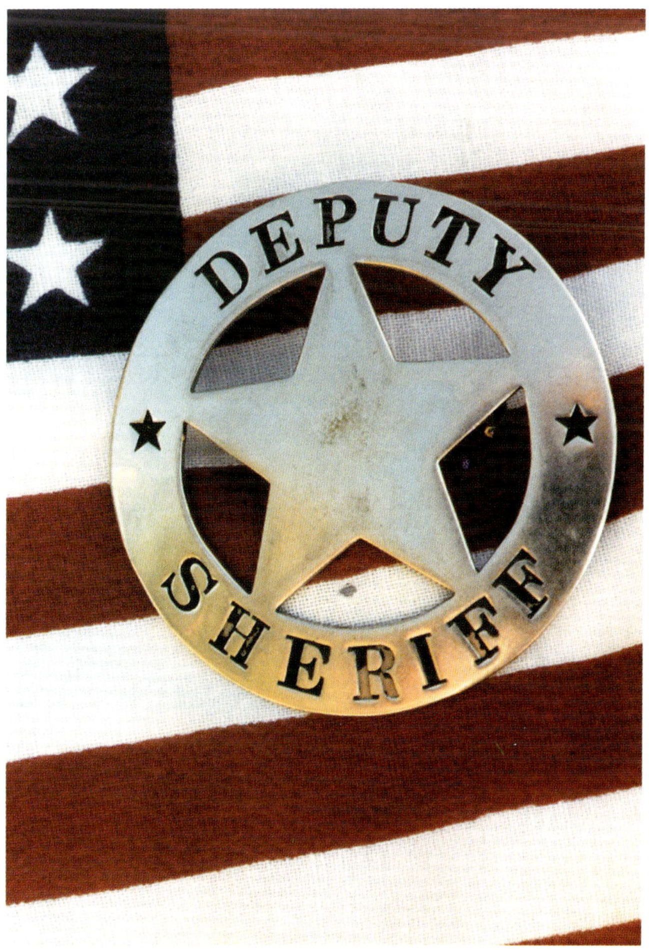

Chapter Eight

Bunkhouse Items

"A few cowboy helpers"

Items in this section are fairly representative of various effects a cowboy or a rancher might come in contact with during the course of his lifetime.

The Will Rogers trick rope featured here has a very solid provenance that stays with the rope to authenticate that it is genuine. The white leather dye has faded very slightly; other than that the smooth leather rope is in excellent condition. It is not what one could call "standard" for cowboy equipment, as it was created to show off a trick roper's skill, not to hold a 1200 pound steer.

The braided quirts and whip were fairly standard, except for the fancy hair-braided ones.

The strange looking barbed wire was one of the earliest styles invented. Barbed wire has a fascinating history of its own that is worth researching.

Since cowboys generally kept some kind of personal bag or box where special small items were placed and saved, one of those is included along with other things of specific interest to their lives..

A fancy Bible would not have been a common one for a traveling cowhand to carry, but would have been rather seen on a marble-topped table, perhaps, in a well-to-do rancher's parlor. A working cowboy' s Bible would have been very small and plain.

Every cowboy owned and carried some form of knife. Pocket knives had so many uses to the working cowboy that it would be impossible to list them all. One that has been overlooked or forgotten in today' s world, however, is their use as a good castration tool which, on the range, instantly turned a bull into a steer.

The popular habit of carrying a pocket knife today is practical as well as a strong carry over from the working cowboys of yesteryear. They are just too handy and useful to be without.

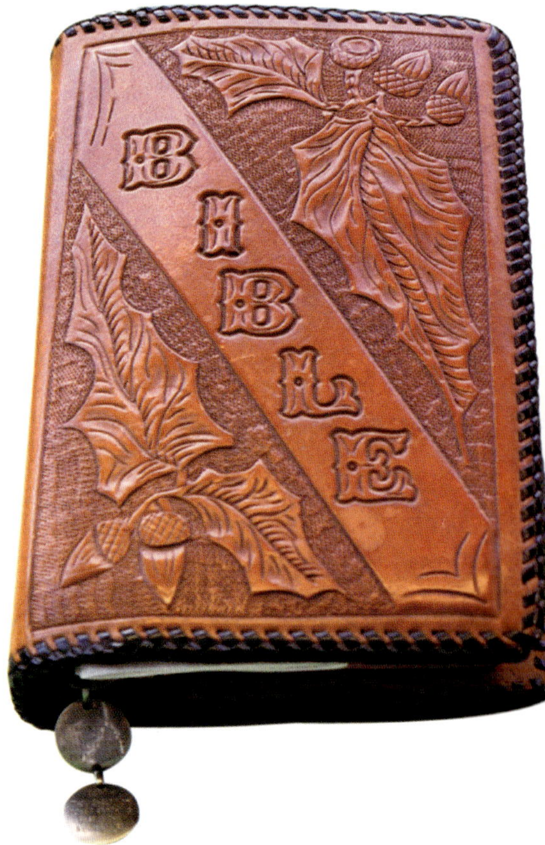

Beautiful carved leather Bible cover hand-tooled with oak leaves and acorns and completely hand-laced. *Overton collection. $50 to 60*

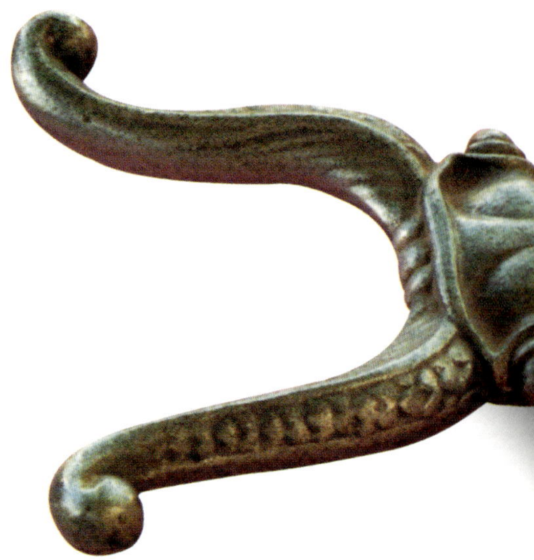

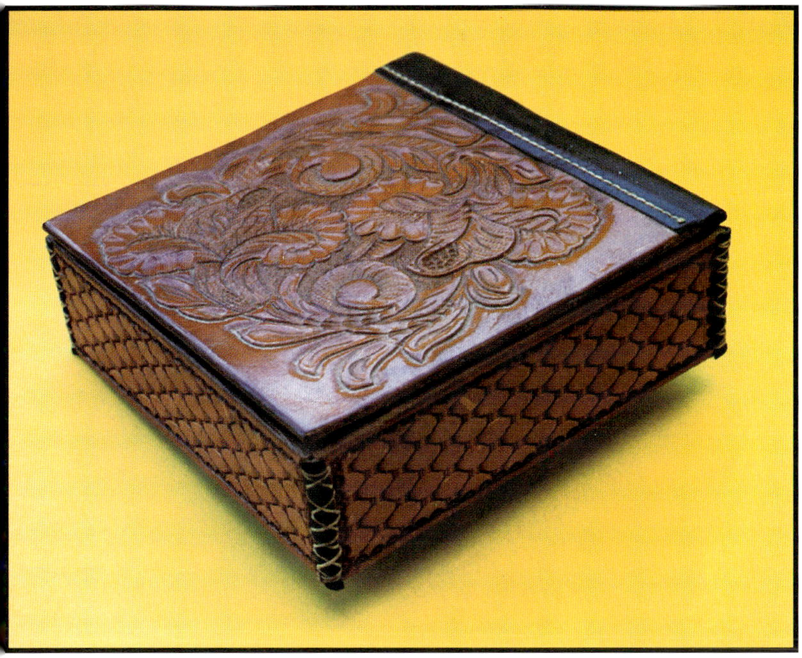

The leather box is sewn and assembled completely by hand, and would have been used as a dresser-top accessory. The carving in the leather is *par excellence. Overton collection. $65 to 75*

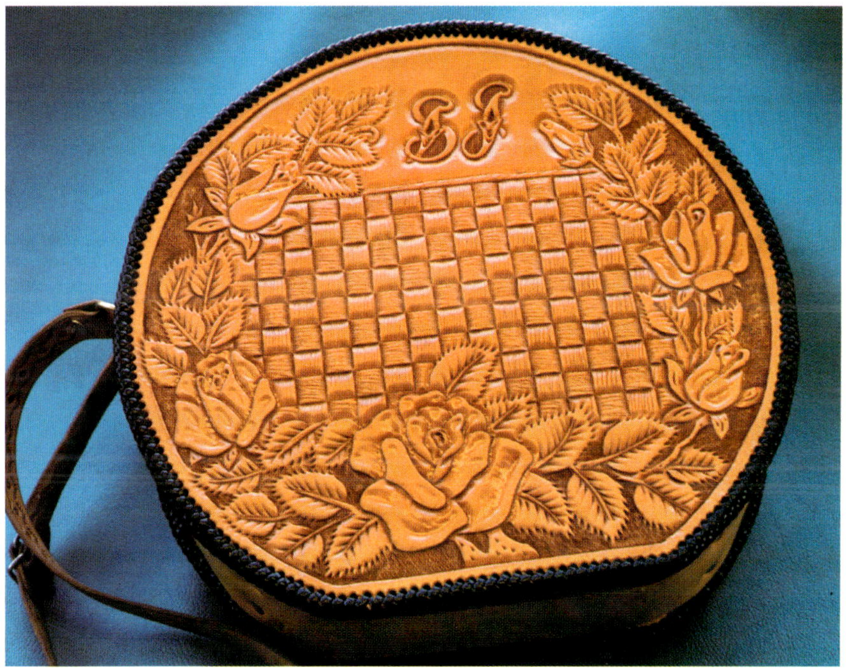

Contemporary elegantly carved leather bag with roses and initials made by a lady saddle maker, Ethel Patterson. *Courtesy Pat and Ethel Patterson. $250 to 350*

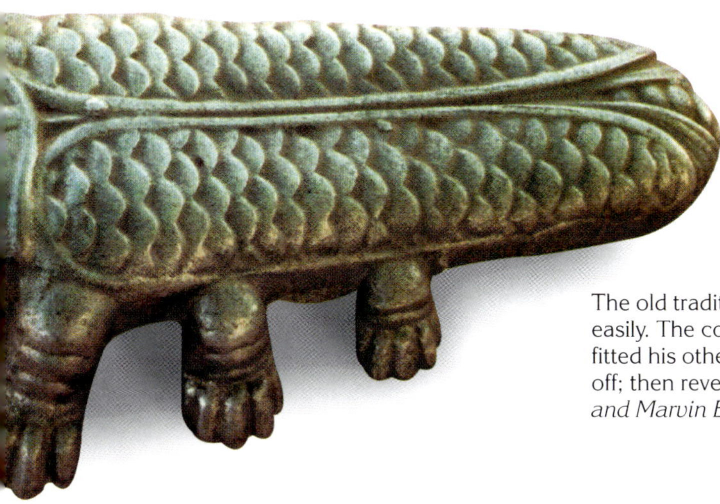

The old traditional "beetle bug" boot jack, used for taking boots off easily. The cowboy stepped on the back of the bug with one foot, fitted his other boot heel into the bug's antennae, and pulled the boot off; then reversed the procedure for the other boot. *Courtesy R.C. and Marvin Bales. $25 to 45*

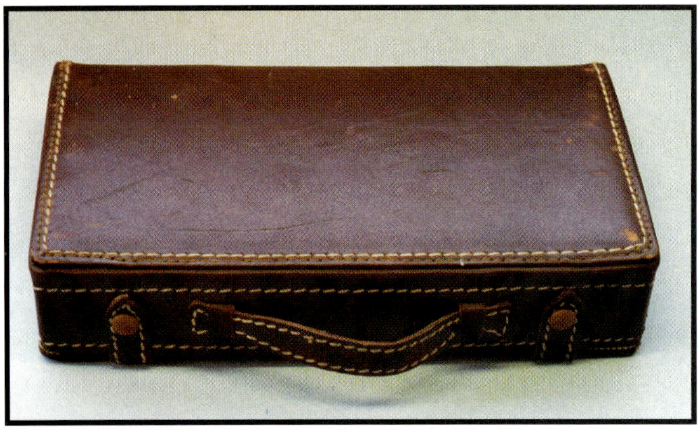

Smooth leather bag containing a man's toiletries, c. 1940s. *Overton collection. $35 to 45*

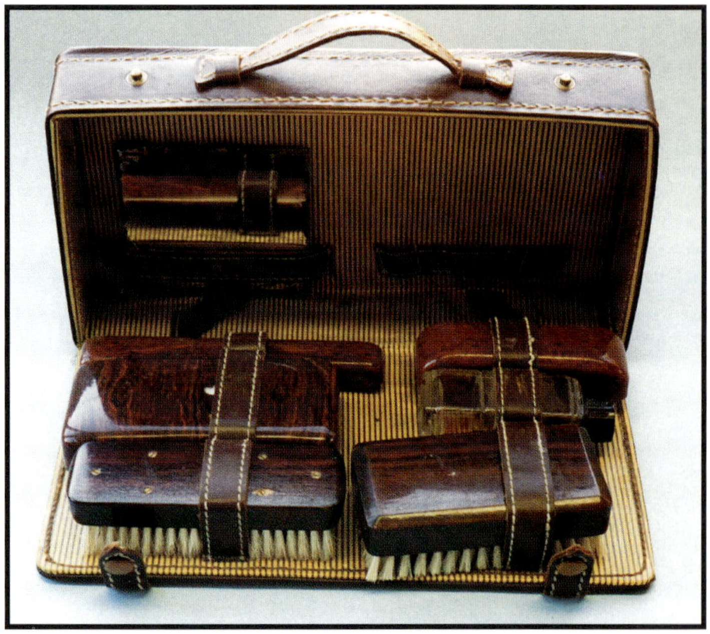

Inside the man's toiletry bag.

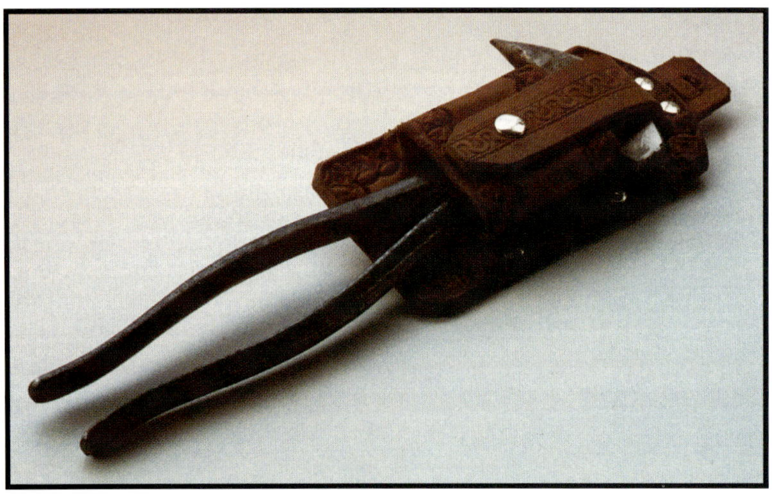

One of the best tools a cowboy carried was his fence pliers in a leather holder. They were quite an innovation that followed the invention of barbed wire, c. late1860s. *Overton collection. $25 to 45*

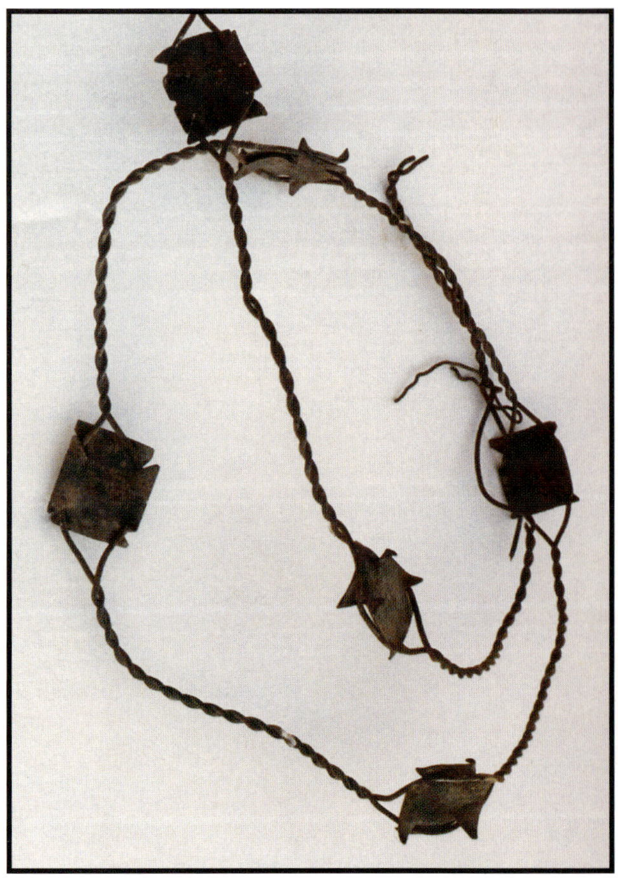

Unique piece of early barbed wire. Barbed wire was patented in the 1860s and this particular kind was made not long after that. *Courtesy Schiffner Military Museum, George and Margaret Schiffner. $25 to 35*

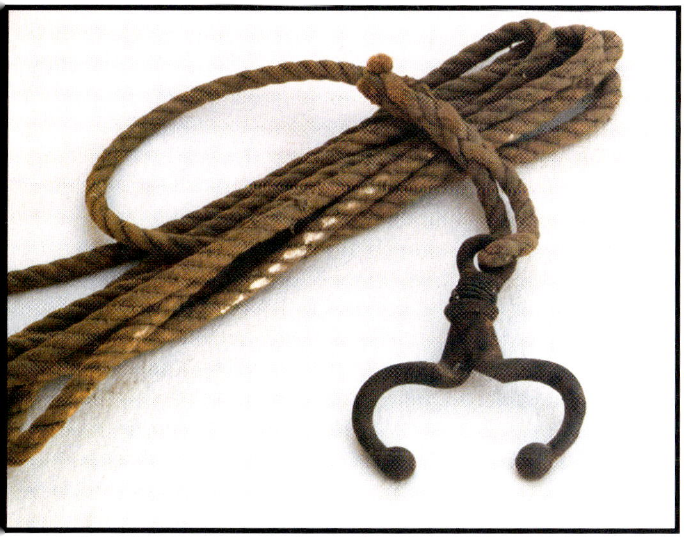

Bull ring for leading the bull around by his nose; it was quite effective. *Courtesy Schiffner Military Museum, George and Margaret Schiffner. $25 to 35*

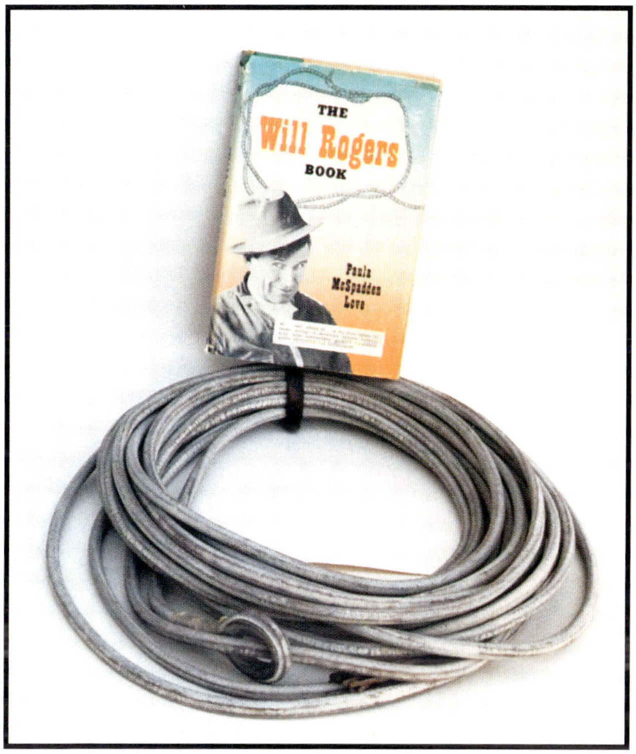

Will Rogers' trick roping rope, accompanied by a solid provenance and therefore is genuine, also in great condition. The early applied white leather dye has faded somewhat with age, but otherwise is pristine. *Courtesy Ron and Sharon Mailloux. $1200 to 1500*

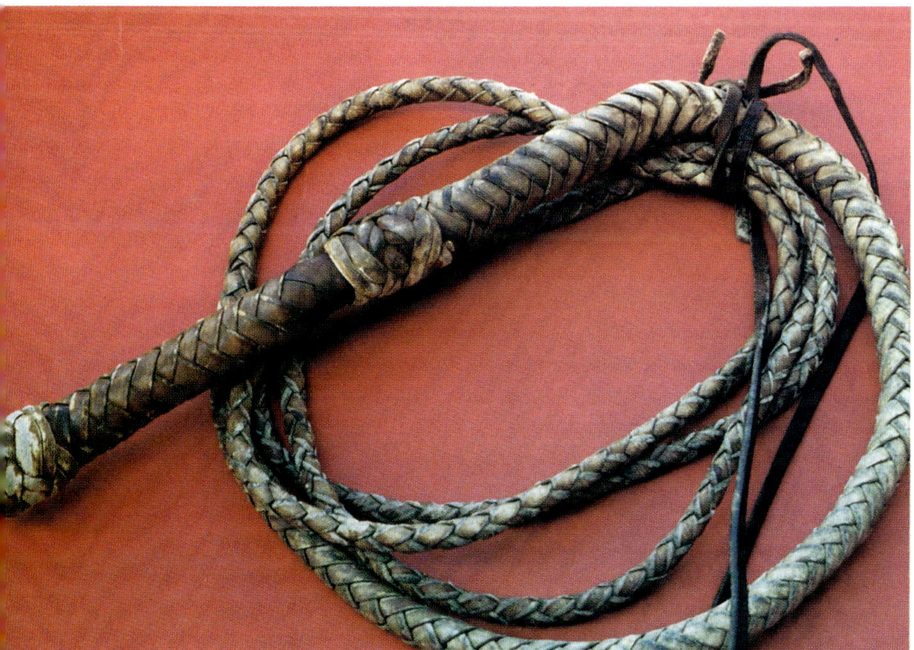

Rawhide braided bull whip, sometimes still an effective tool when training a horse. *Courtesy Gene Christopher. $60 to 75*

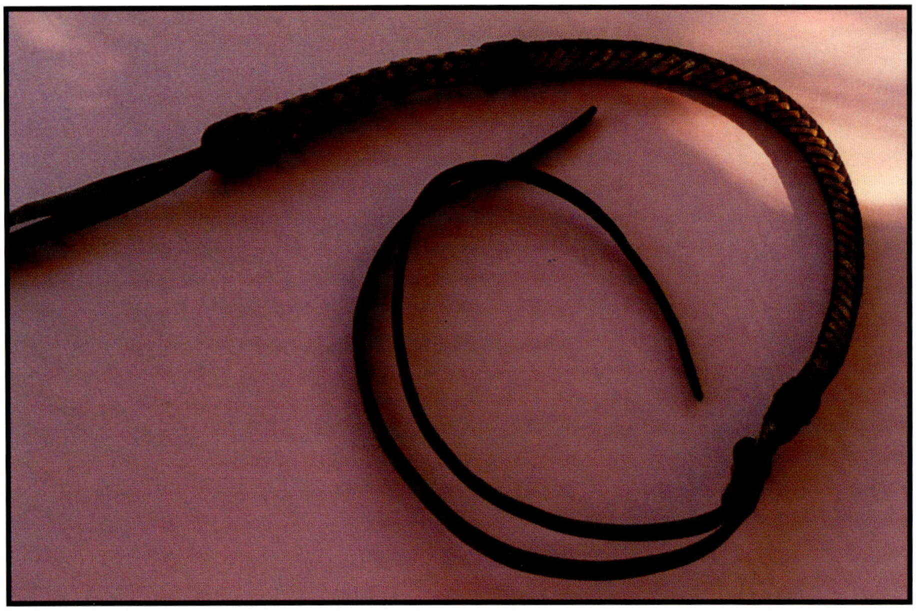

Braided quirt in excellent condition. *Courtesy R.C. and Marvin Bales. $75 to 85*

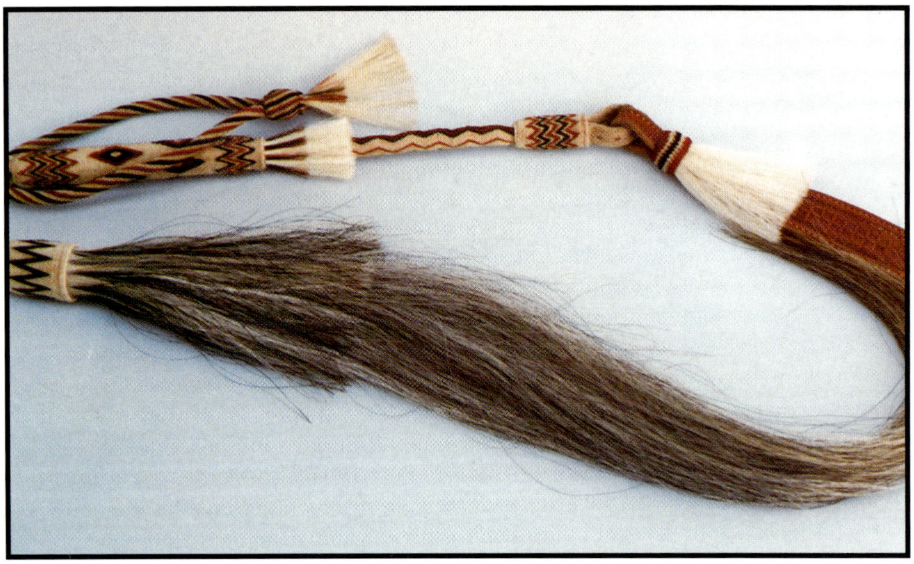

Two quirts, one is a horsehair "shoofly" style while the other is horse hair braided with an attached leather pommel. Both are beautiful works of art. *Courtesy Ron and Sharon Mailloux. Quirt: $800 Shoofly: $400*

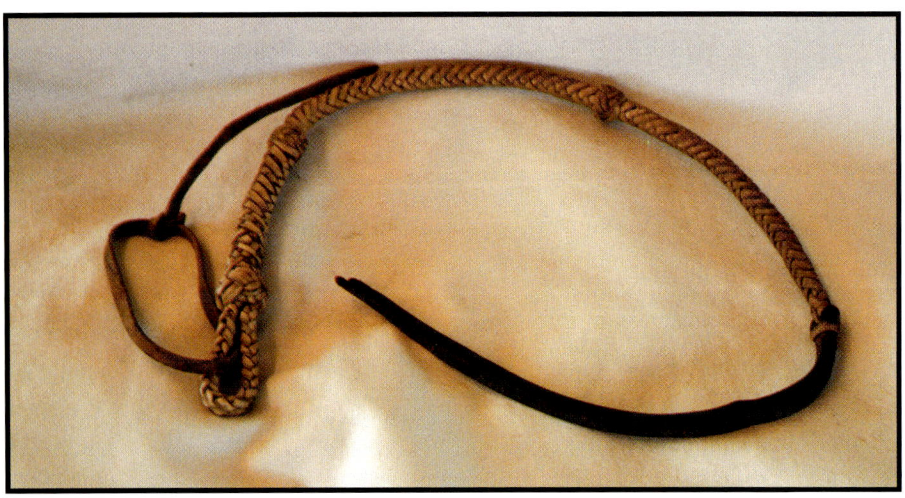

Rawhide braided quirt with a leather tip, still a very useful item. *Courtesy Bob and Judy Bertsch. $40 to 50*

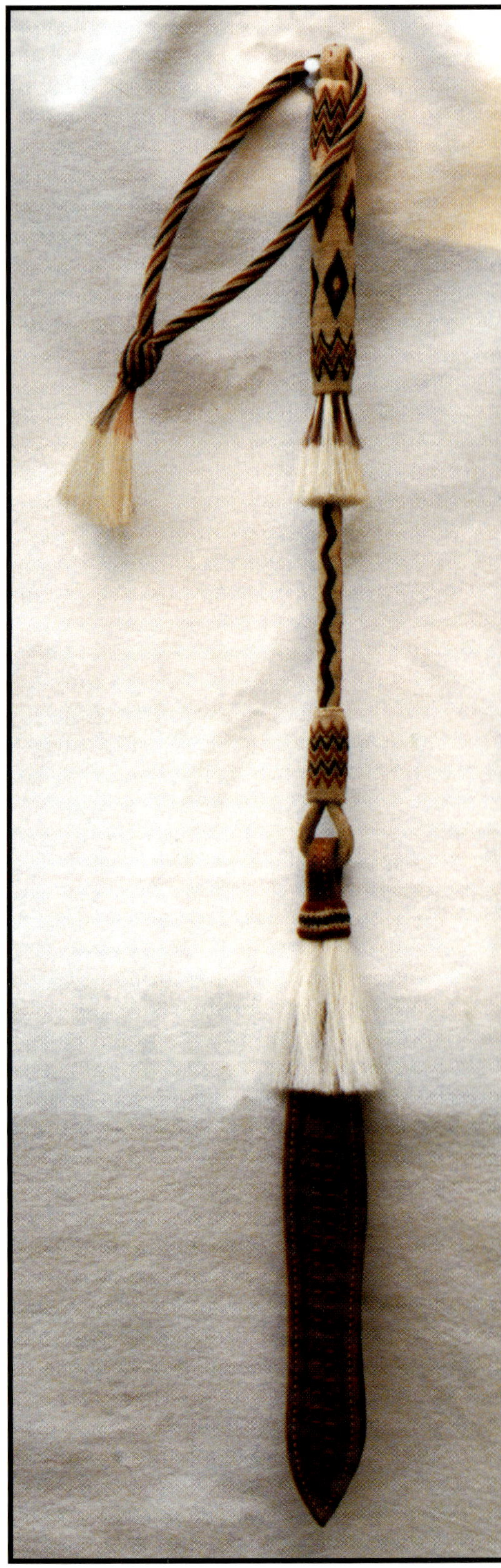

Beautifully detailed with superior hair braiding, this quirt is unique. Sometimes a fine piece like this takes a very long time to complete, but once finished it is a work of art like no other. *Courtesy Ron and Sharon Mailloux. $750 to 800*

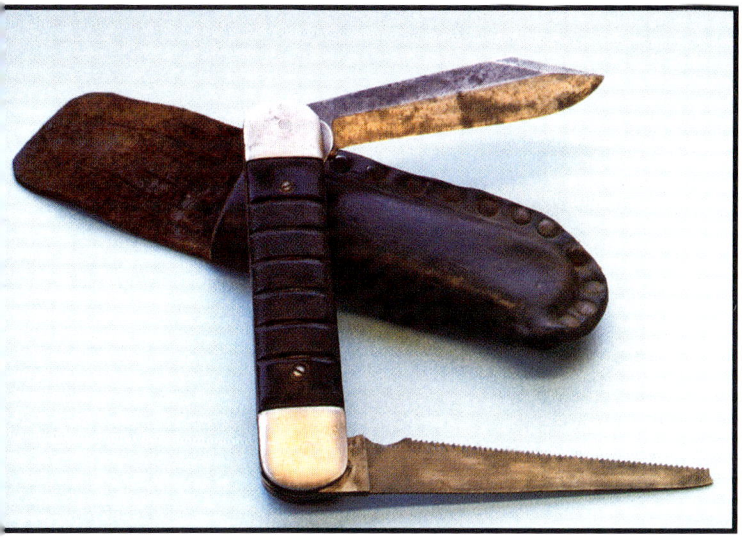

A cowboy would have carried a pocket knife with a regular blade and a utility blade. The old leather case is probably original to the knife. *Courtesy Wade Brumley. $55 to 75*

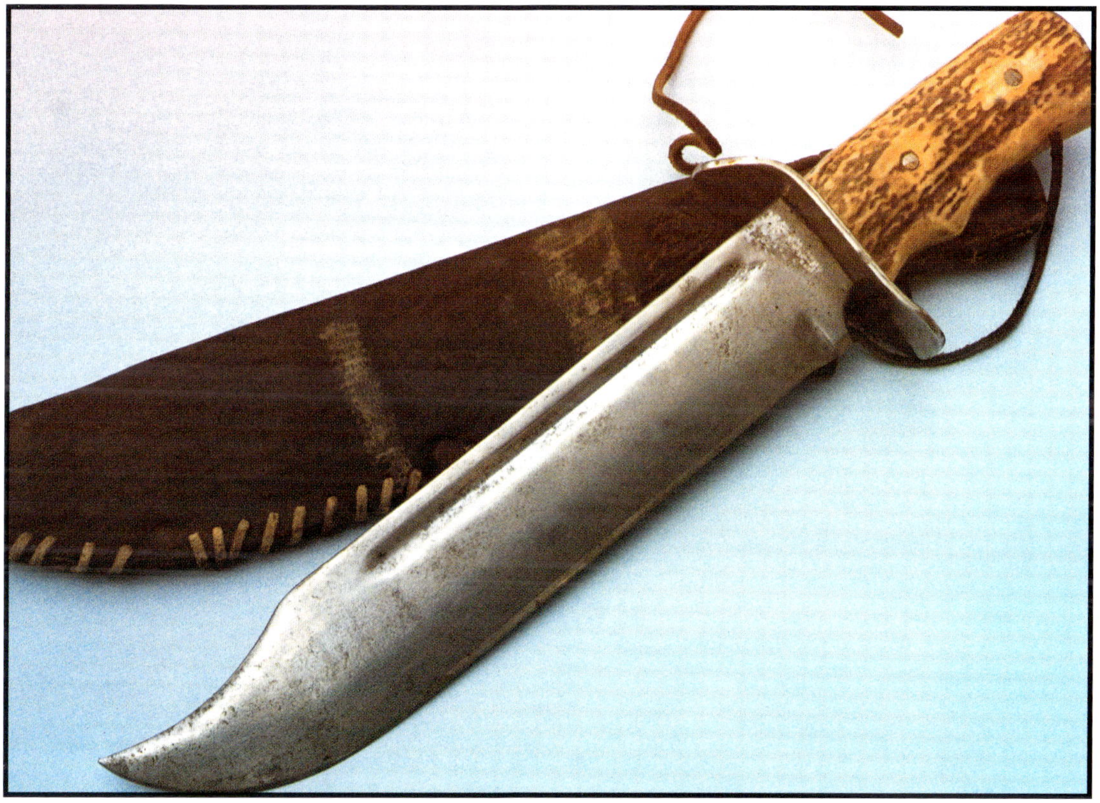

A full sized, original, old Bowie knife— named for Jim Bowie who became famouse at the Texas Alamo. This one has a horn handle and a hand-laced case. *Courtesy Gene Christopher. $325 to 400*

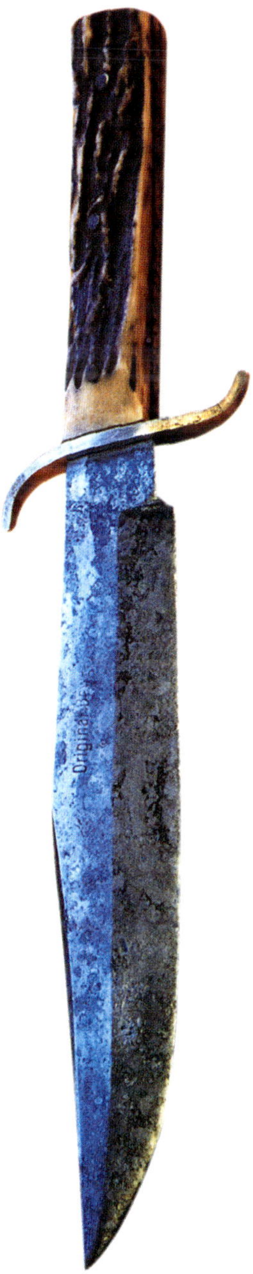

Long bladed with a horn handle, this type of knife was used for many things, but often as a meat-cleaning or hunting knife. *Courtesy Wade Brumley. $150 to 200*

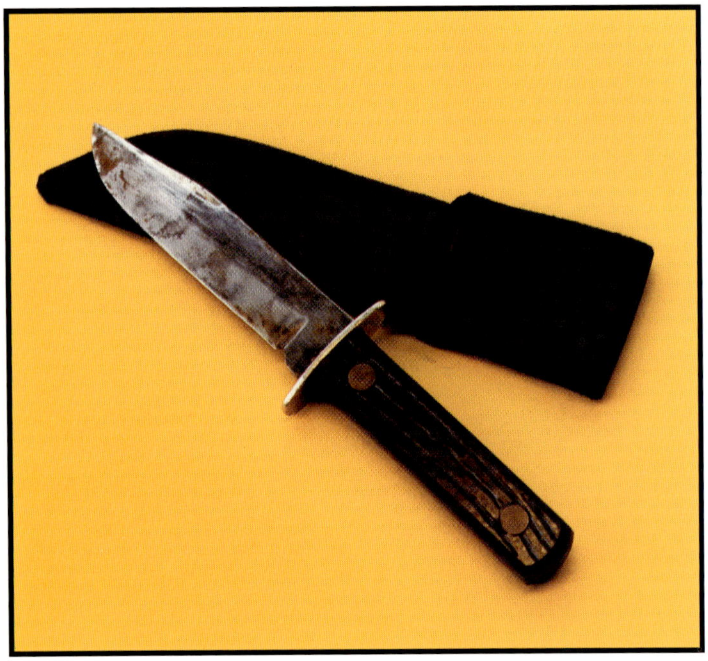

A good old hunting knife with a leather sheath. *Overton collection. $45 to 55*

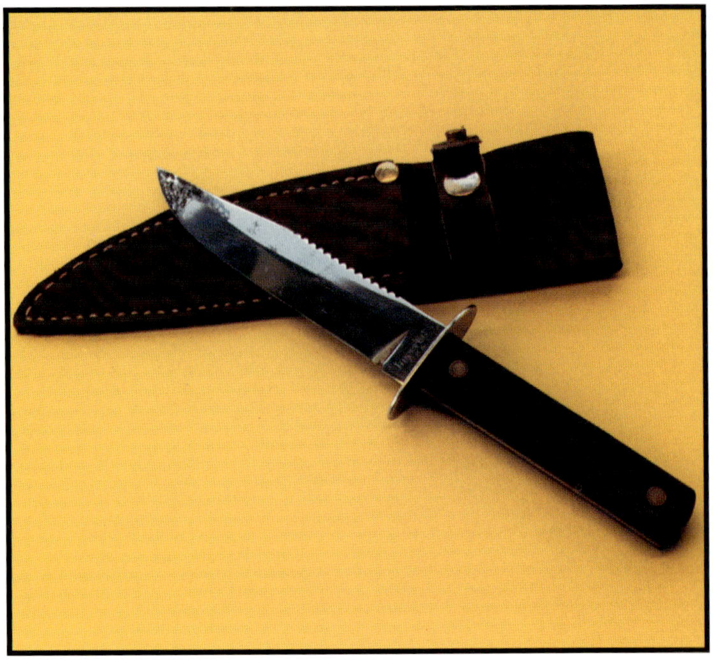

Hunting knife with a serrated edge on top of the blade and a hand-made leather sheath. *Overton collection. $35 to 45*

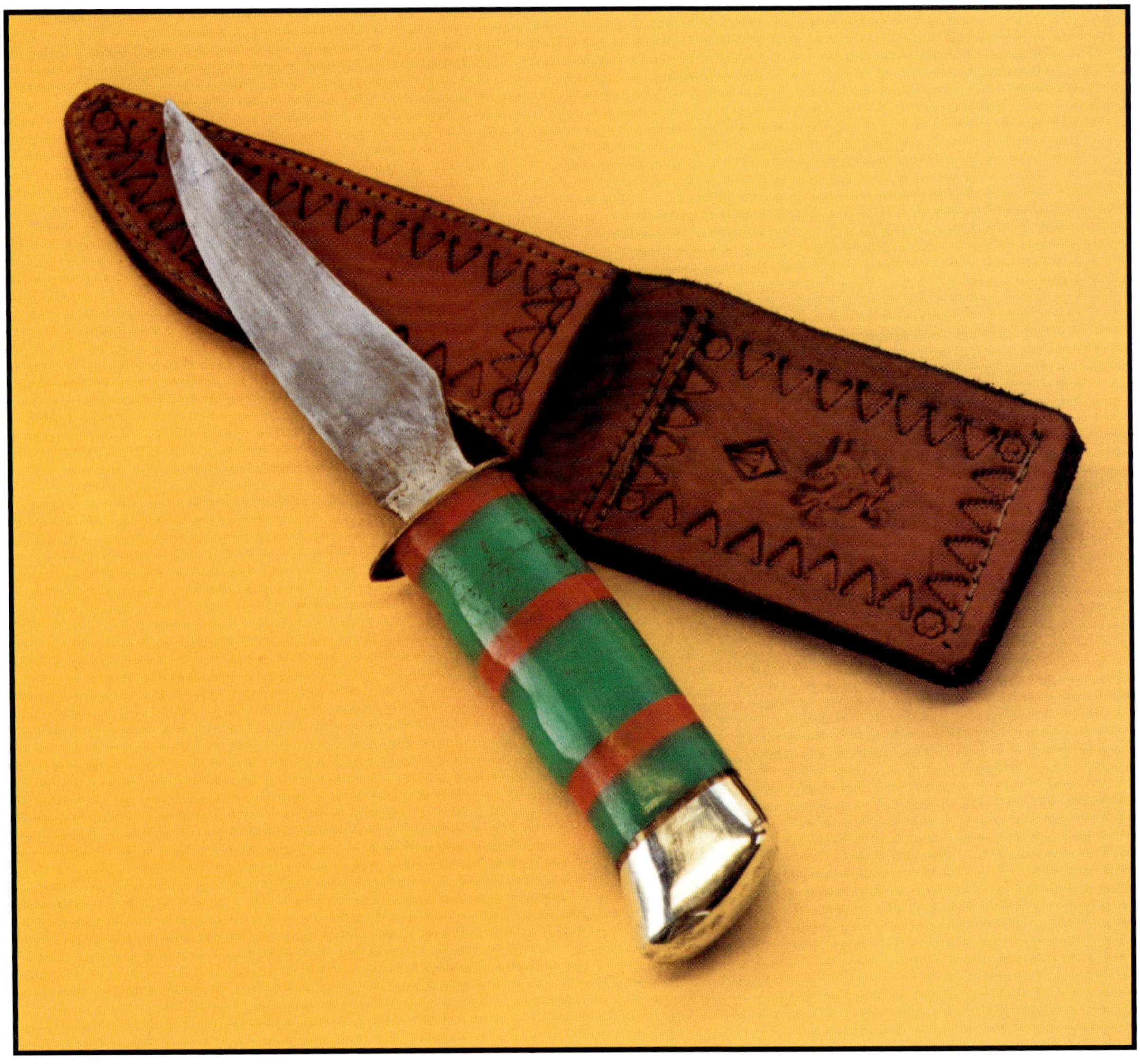

Very attractive hunting knife with decorative handle and hand-made sheath. *Overton collection. $35 to 45*

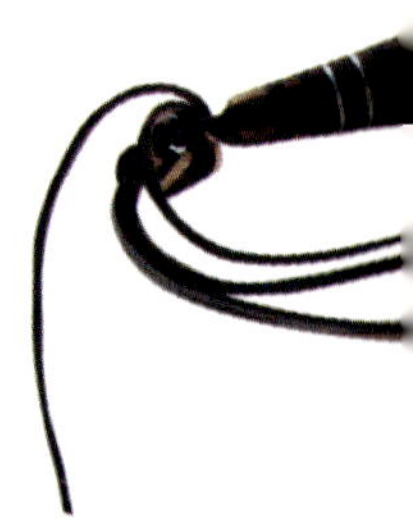

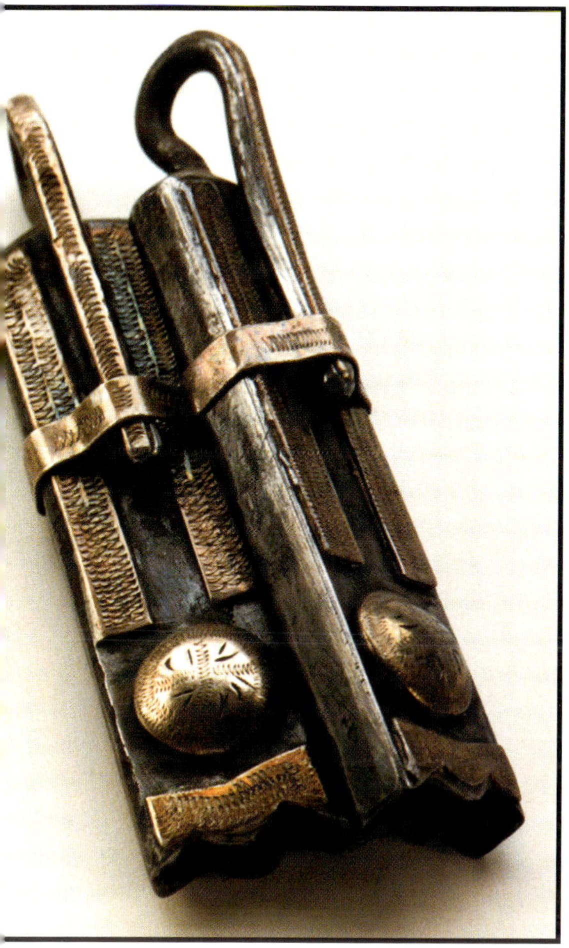

A pair of hand-made "Spanish hooks." It takes a knowledgeable cowboy to know how they were used. They attached to the headstall leather, and the hooks attached to the bit; it made a quick change for a different bit possible. *Overton collection. $ 65 to 75*

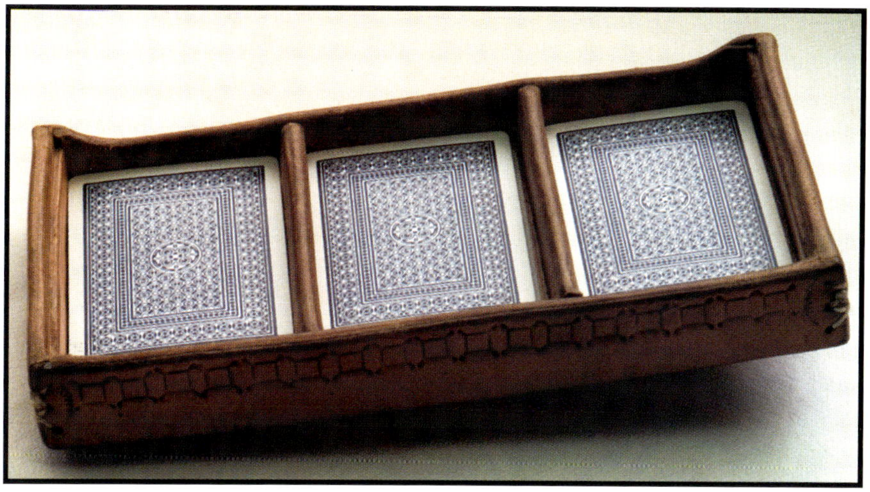

One of the most popular pastimes for a cowboy was playing cards. This card holder is hand-made from heavy leather with a stamped design on the edges. *Overton collection. $20 to 30*

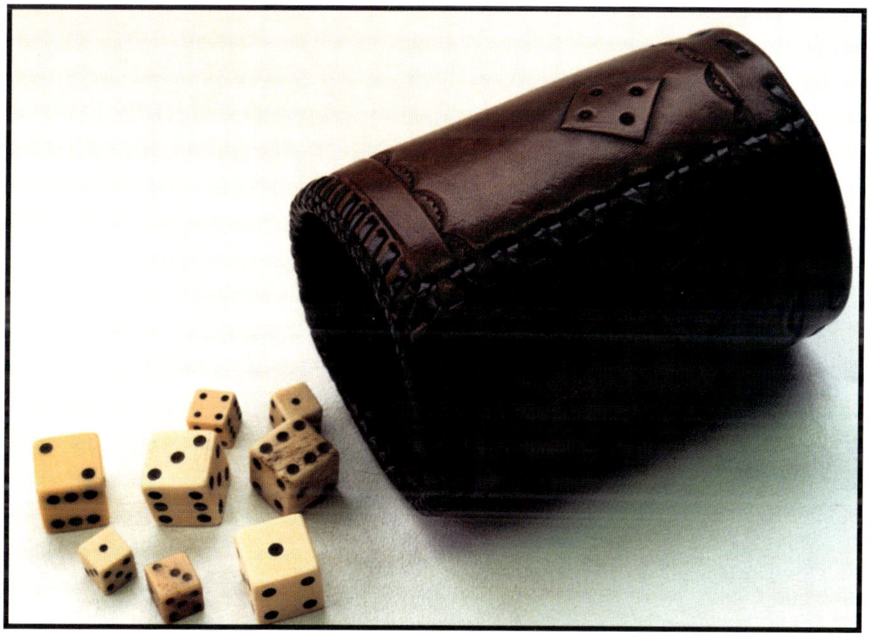

Dice was another popular pastime for a cowboy; early dice were like these, made from real ivory. The dice cup is hand-made from heavy leather and hand-laced. *Overton collection. $25 to 45*

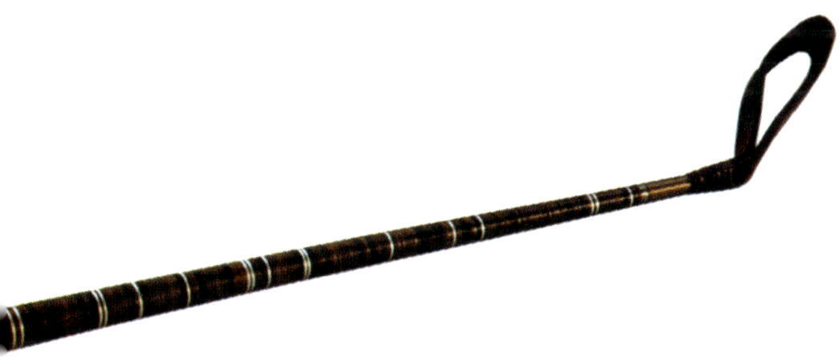

This riding crop is believed to have been made in a prison, possibly c. 1940s. It is a most unusual piece with inlays the length of the handle. *Overton collection. $175 to 200*

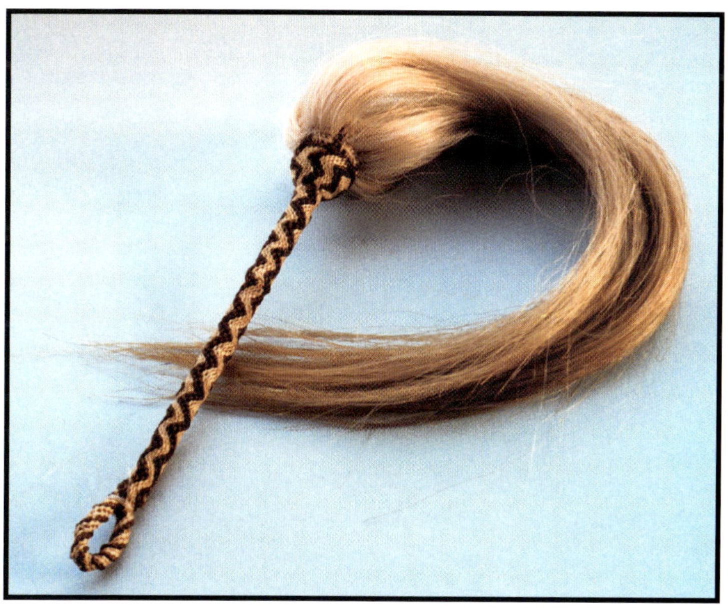

A hand-made "shoo-fly" of unusual construction in woven hemp and containing almost a full horsehair tail; possibly made by American Indians. *Overton collection. $100 to 125*

Chapter Nine

Cowboy Accessories

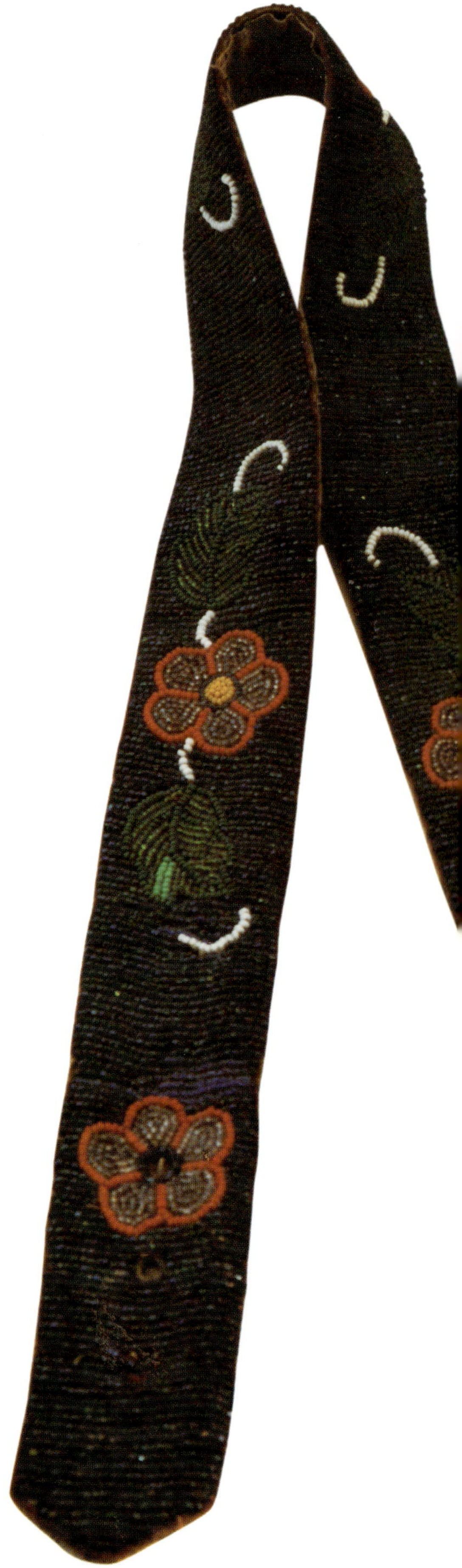

"It all counts to a cowboy"

Belts, buckles and cuffs, they all played important roles in the everyday life of a cowboy. In the nineteenth century, most of these items were somewhat on the plain side and more utilitarian than what came along a little bit later. Like many other innovations, these items were soon to become a part of the cowboy's own personality and so, of course, they became personalized to fit the man who chose them or embellished them.

Belts

Belts, for instance, were generally so plain that they were often cut out of a chunk of cured or tanned leather with his own pocket knife, and holes drilled in it with the knife tip. A good leather belt would last him many years though, and as leather has a way of conforming to the wearer or user, it became so comfortable and shaped to his waist that he became reluctant to exchange it for a new one anyway. Not all cowboys wore belts. There were two distinct kinds of belts that were often an absolute necessity: the belt that held his chaps on, and the belt that carried his holster or gun rig and cartridges. Because these were worn often, they made a cowboy's waist kind of bulky to have too many belts and buckles around it, and the belt that was often forgone was the one that might have been worn in his Levis. Even though Levi Strauss and Company had patented the riveted pockets by 1873, they still had not attached the belt loops that are so familiar today. If extra support was needed back then, it was found in the form of a good pair of suspenders, often called "galluses."

Buckles

Buckles were another matter, and the investment of a good buckle for his sometimes-worn dress belt would often require a week's wages, if it was a good silver one. Most often worn or used as a dress-up, Saturday-night-on-the-town kind of item, these buckles were usually of the type we term "ranger" buckles, or the old standard square open ones. They were the earliest to be used and made up by the silversmiths, or "smithys." Ranger buckles are of the traditional buckle shape with a matching keeper and tip. Today most buckles that are worn in the West are of the "trophy" type. Trophy buckles are generally oval or square and quite large, with various insignias pictured and sometimes the date and place where the buckle was won in a rodeo event; hence the term "trophy" buckle.

Cuffs

Cuffs were very useful items to the cowboy. They saved his shirtsleeves and often saved his wrists from bad rope burns and other hazards. Cuffs were generally made to either lace or snap onto the cowboy's wrist. Most were plain to begin with, but soon caught on as an extra flashy addition to his outfit. Nickel silver spots were added as decorations. Cuffs have become popular to collect.

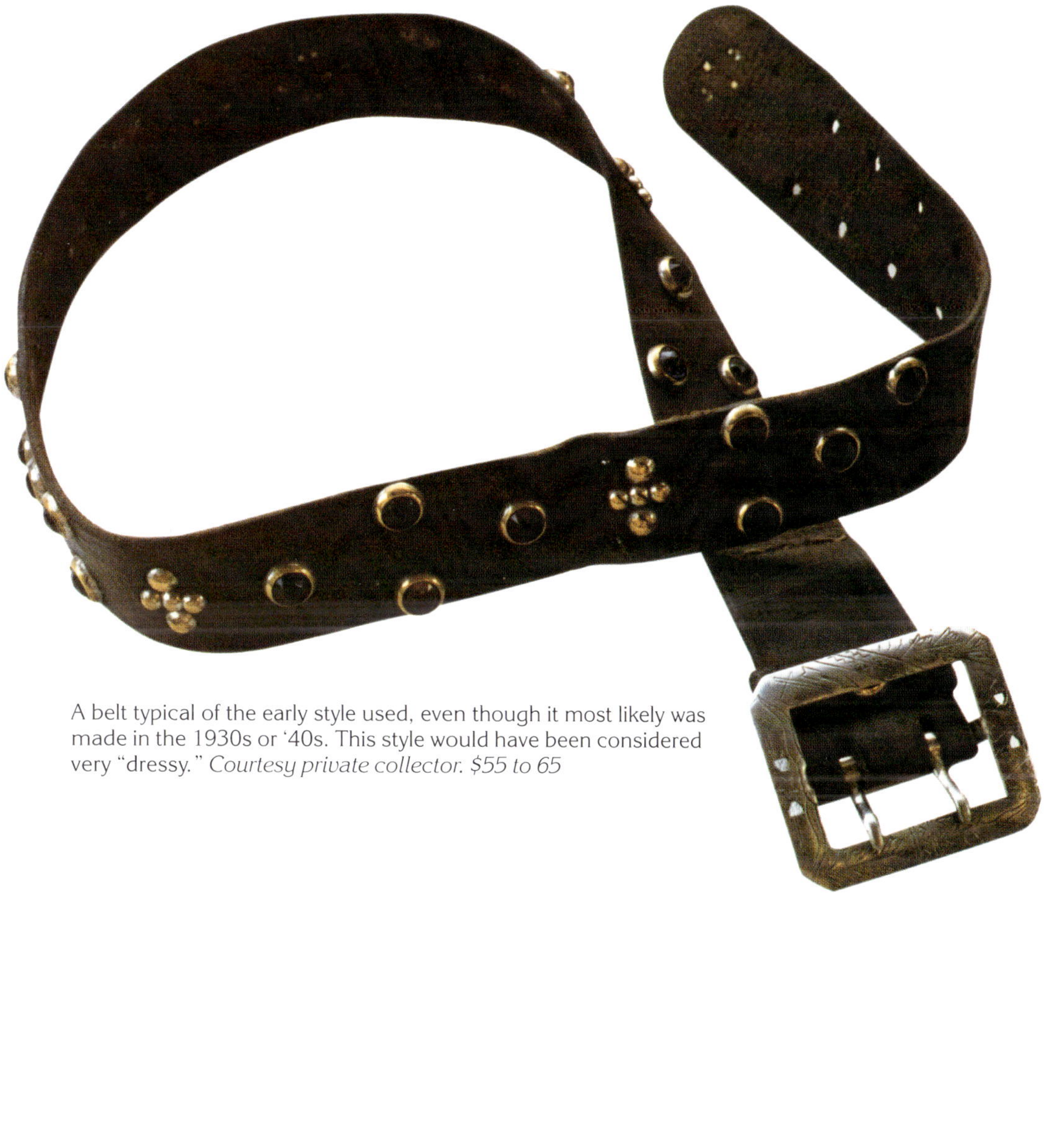

A belt typical of the early style used, even though it most likely was made in the 1930s or '40s. This style would have been considered very "dressy." *Courtesy private collector. $55 to 65*

Opposite Page:

The belt is solid beadwork on a simple calico lining with the traditional buckle. It was probably created by a talented Native American. *Courtesy private collector. $100 to 150*

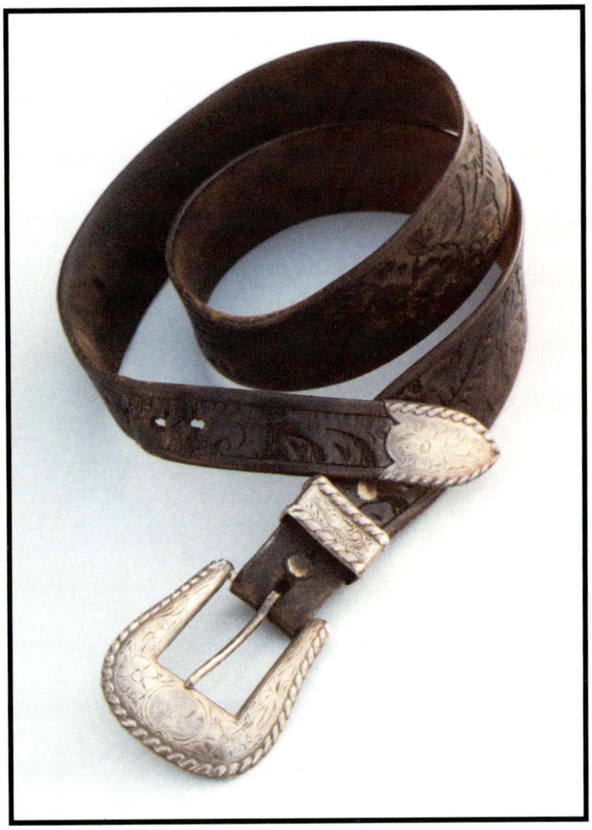

A well-used, hand-carved leather belt with a very nice silver ranger buckle with keeper and tip. *Courtesy Schiffner Military Museum, George and Margaret Schiffner. $80 to 100*

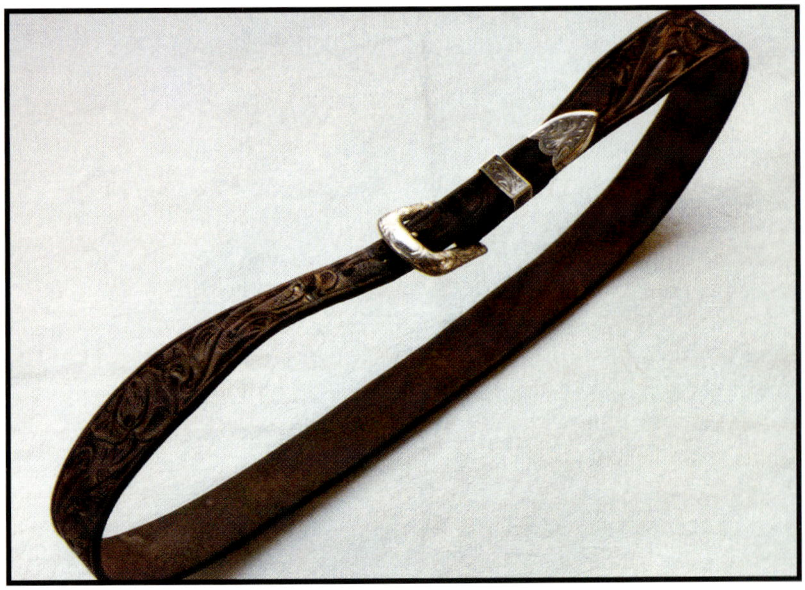

Hand carved leather belt with a nice silver ranger set. *Courtesy private collector. $35 to 55*

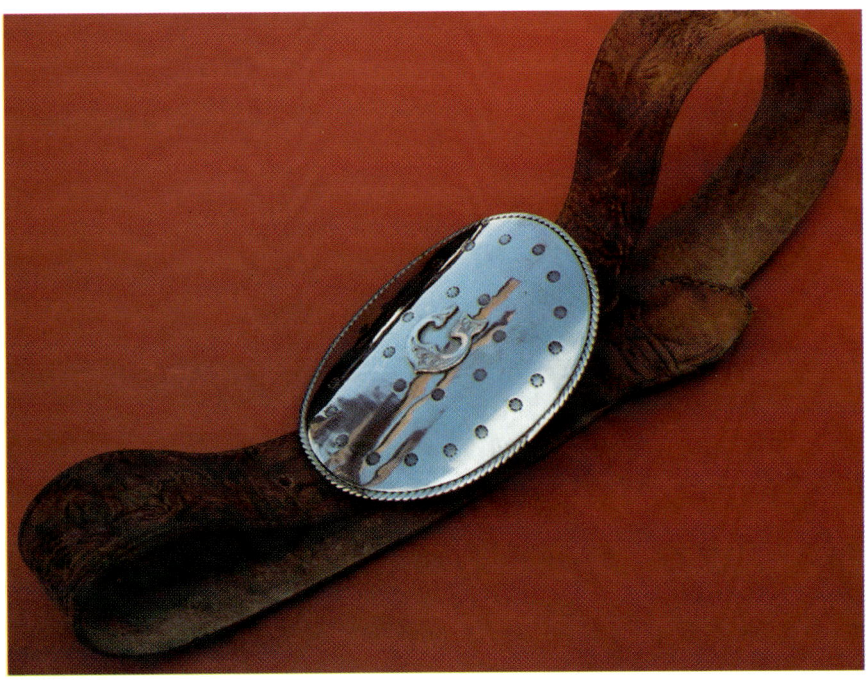

Contemporary belt and hand-made trophy style buckle created by Bob Christopher. *Courtesy Gene Christopher $100 to 200*

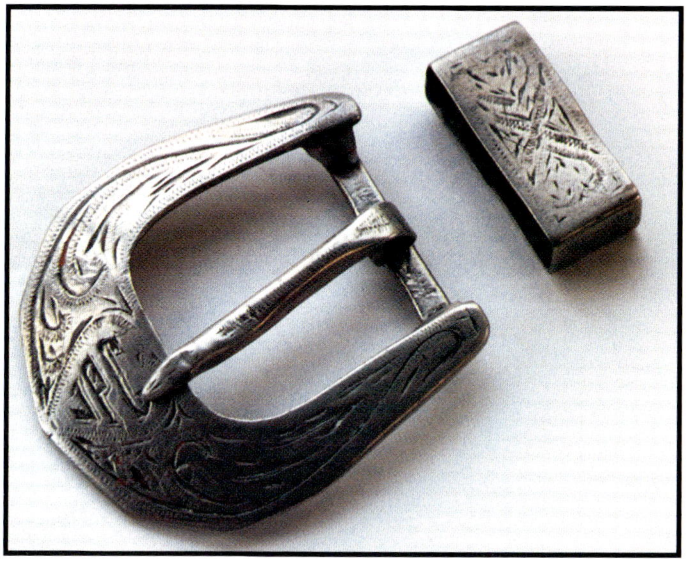

Lovely old ranger buckle bearing the engraved initials "JPG." *Courtesy private collector. $25 to 55*

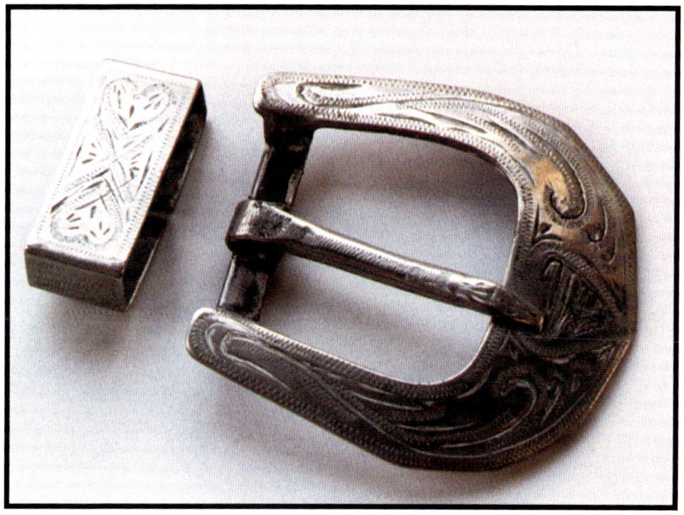

This is the lady's version of the previous buckle set; they were probably made as "Mr. And Mrs. sets." The initials on this are "FMG." *Courtesy private collector. $25 to 55*

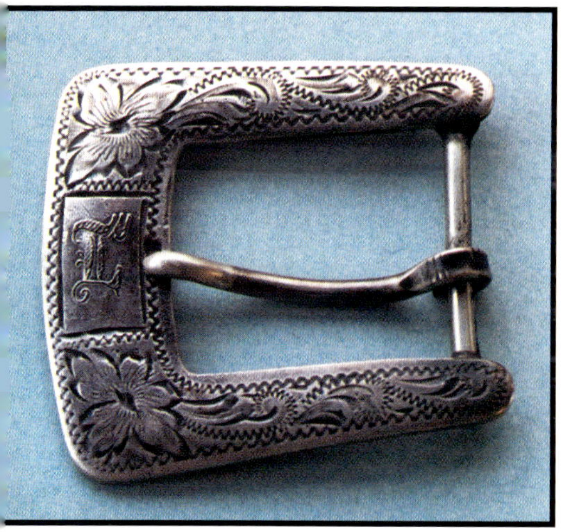

Older silver engraved buckle with initial "L." *Courtesy private collector.* *$65 to 75*

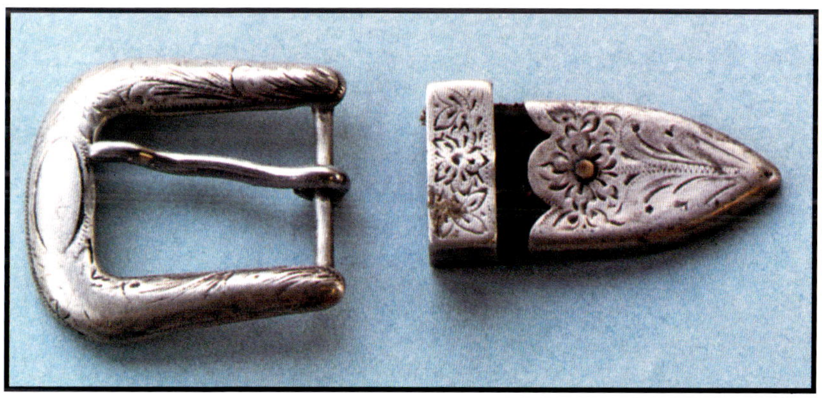

Nice old silver ranger buckle set with engraving. *Courtesy private collector. $60 to 65*

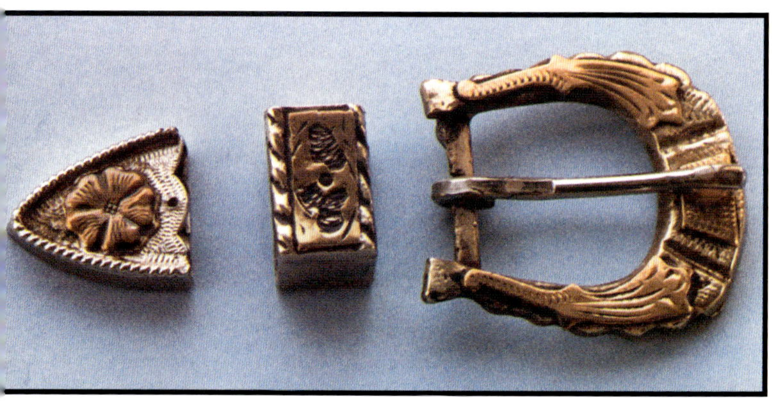

Very ornamental silver ranger buckle set with gold overlays. *Overton collection.* *$55 to 65*

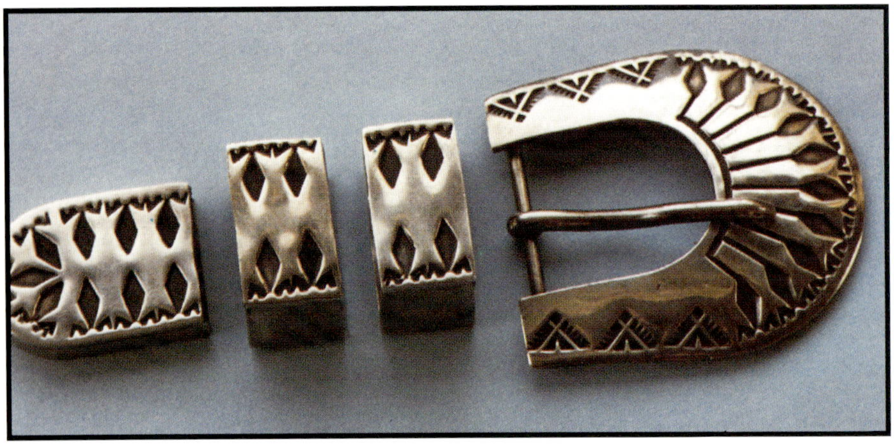

This Ranger buckle set has a "Southwestern style" in silver with stamping throughout. *Overton collection. $45 to 55*

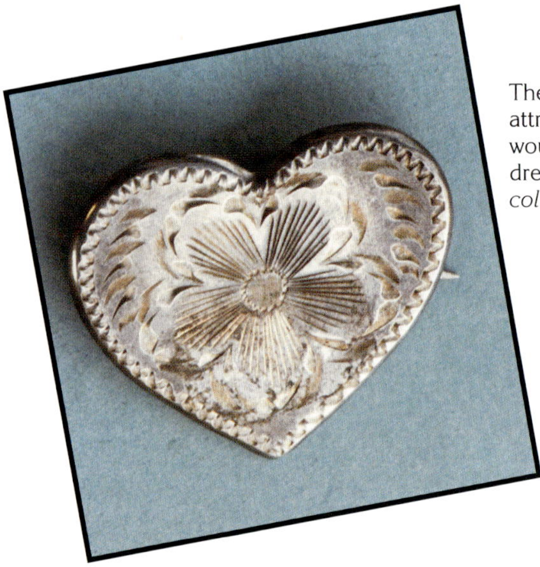

The engraved heart is a very attractive pin, not a buckle, that would be worn on a vest or a dress. *Courtesy private collector. $28 to 48*

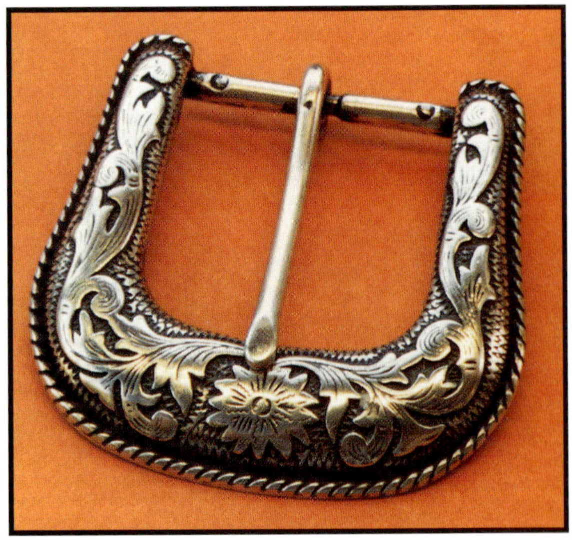

This is a beautiful ranger buckle that at one time certainly had a matching keeper and belt tip. *Courtesy Wade Brumley. $25 to 45*

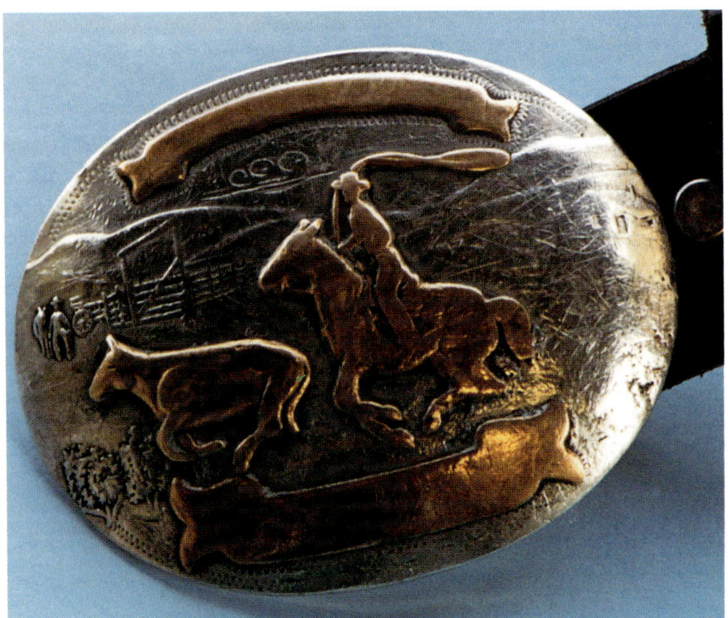

This old trophy buckle commemorates a calf roping event, but the names and dates have worn off completely leaving only a mystery. *Courtesy private collector. $50 to 75*

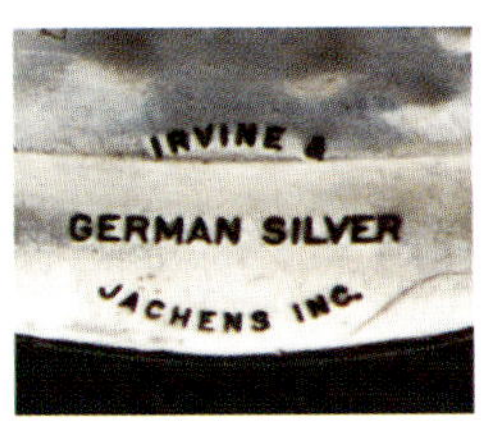

The back of the trophy buckle. Buckle backs often tell us many things about the buckle, such as name of maker, location, and date.

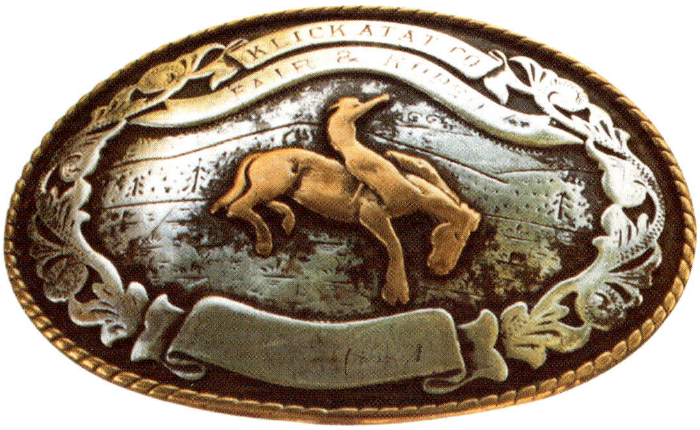

A genuine trophy buckle of silver and gold won at a bareback riding event at a Klickitat County Fair and Rodeo in the state of Washington. The date and name is worn off. *Courtesy R.C. and Marvin Bales. $375 to 400*

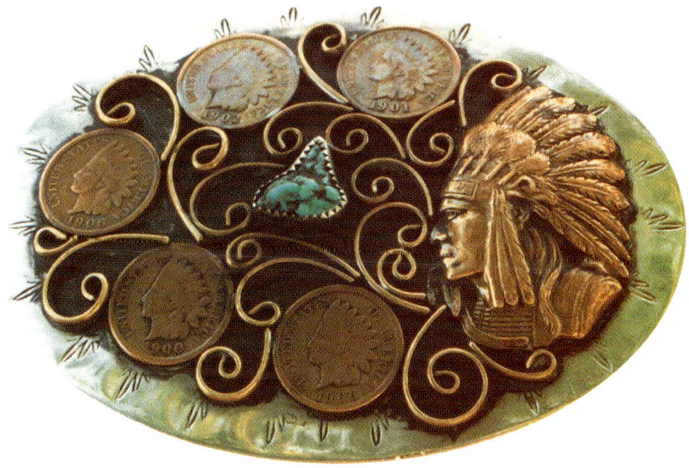

An Indian-head trophy buckle with five Indian-head pennies and a small turquoise stone in the center. *Courtesy Wade Brumley. $45 to 75*

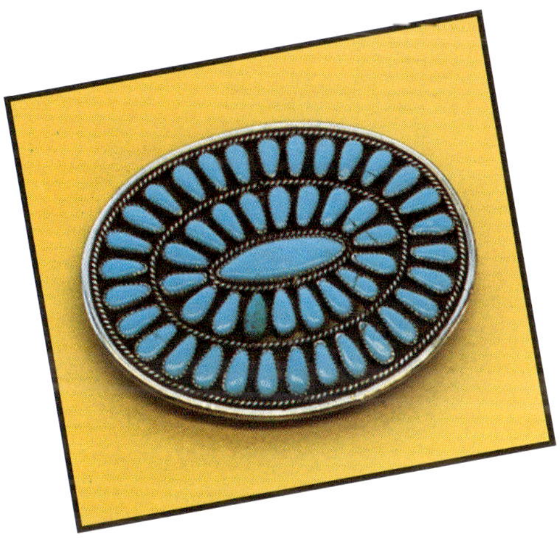

Large turquoise-mounted trophy buckle. *Overton collection. $150 to 200*

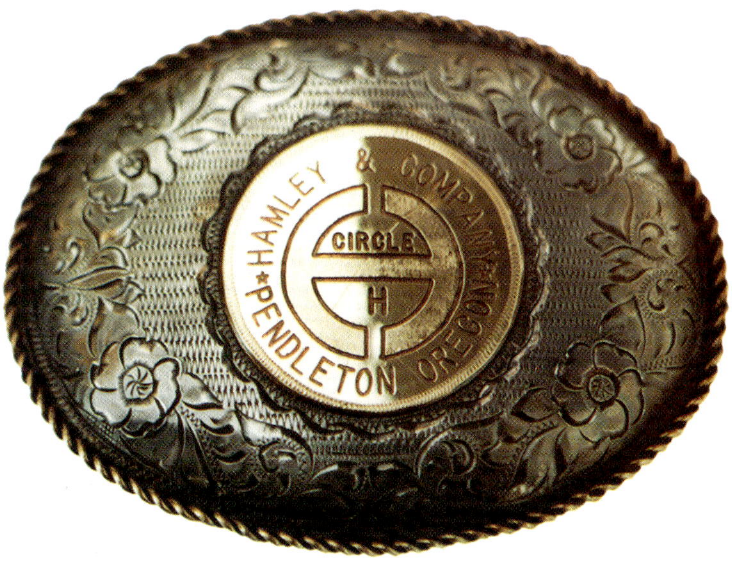

Probably the epitome of all trophy style buckles, this Hamley and Company buckle has silver flowers engraved around it and Hamley's gold medallion in the center. Hamley and Company is no longer in business, but had been a great saddle and cowboy supply store since 1885 in Pendleton, Oregon. *Courtesy Ron and Sharon Mallioux. $375 to 400*

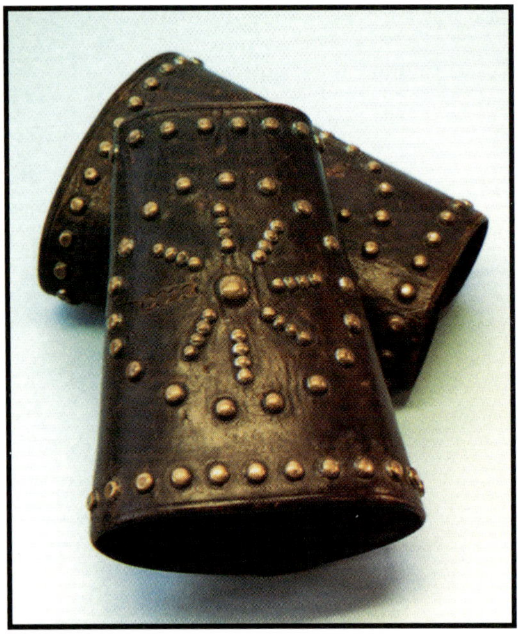

A nice pair of old cuffs with the decorative spots on them. *Courtesy Wade Brumley. $200 to 250*

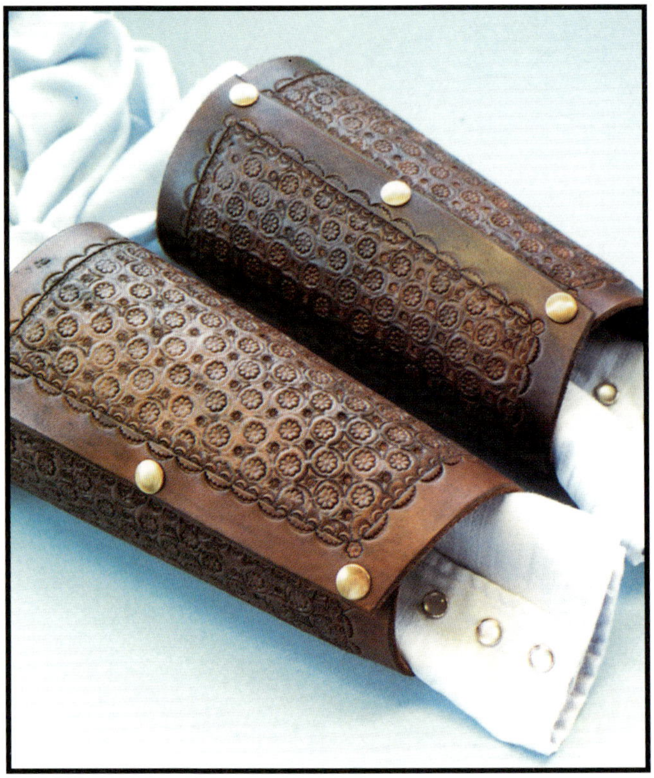

A large set of cuffs that would probably have fit a big-armed man; they are nicely stamped leather and fasten onto the wrists with snaps. *Overton collection. $100 to 150*

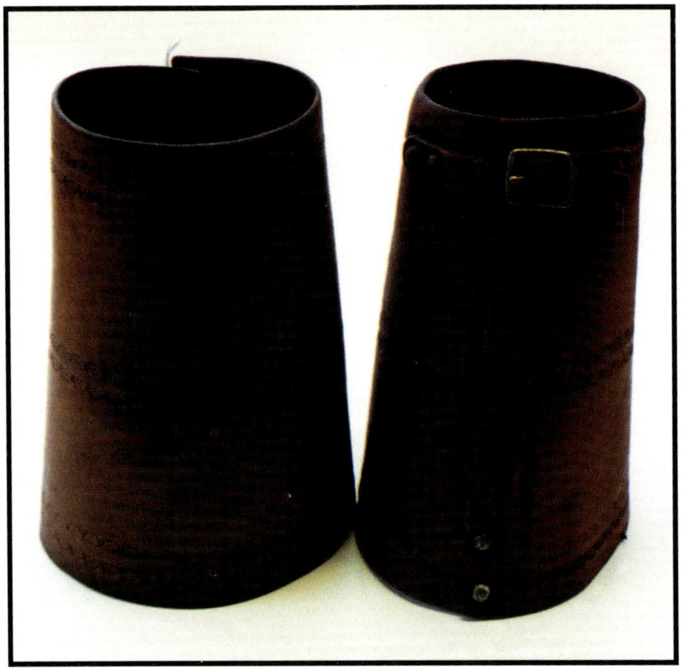

This pair of cuffs have a stamped leather design and attach with both a buckle and snaps. *Courtesy private collector. $275*

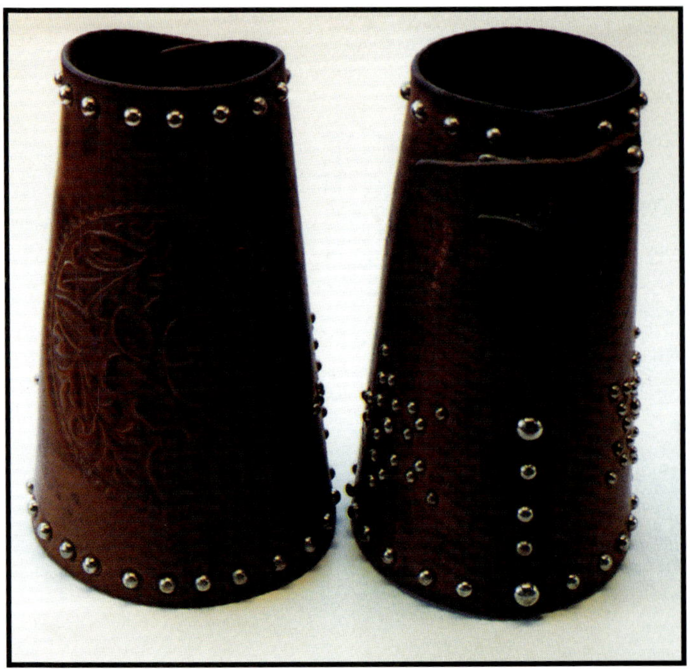

These very attractive cuffs fasten with both a buckle and two snaps. They have a star, tiny designed spots, and a flower carved in the leather. *Courtesy private collector. $285*

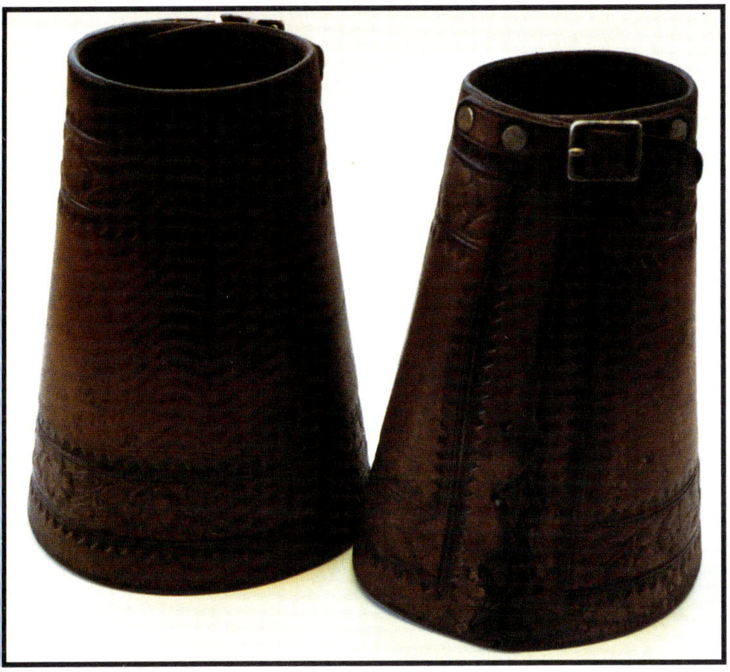

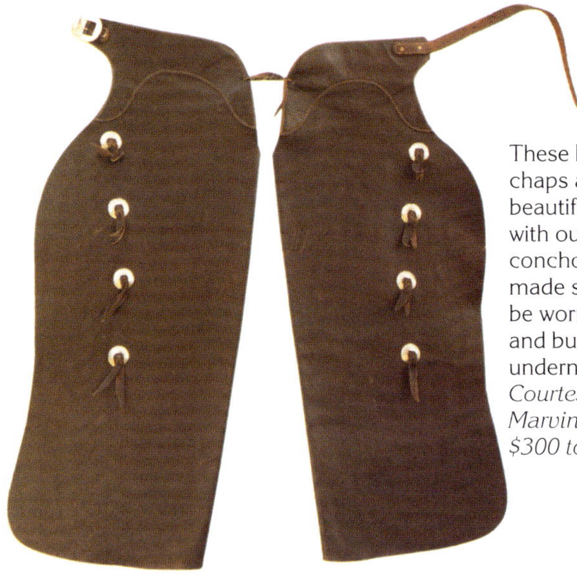

These Ferguson chaps are in beautiful condition with outside tie-conchos and were made so they could be worn with a belt and buckle underneath. *Courtesy R.C. and Marvin Bales. $300 to 400*

With a flower border stamped on them, these cuffs are both buckled and laced on. They are in very nice condition. *Courtesy private collector. $285*

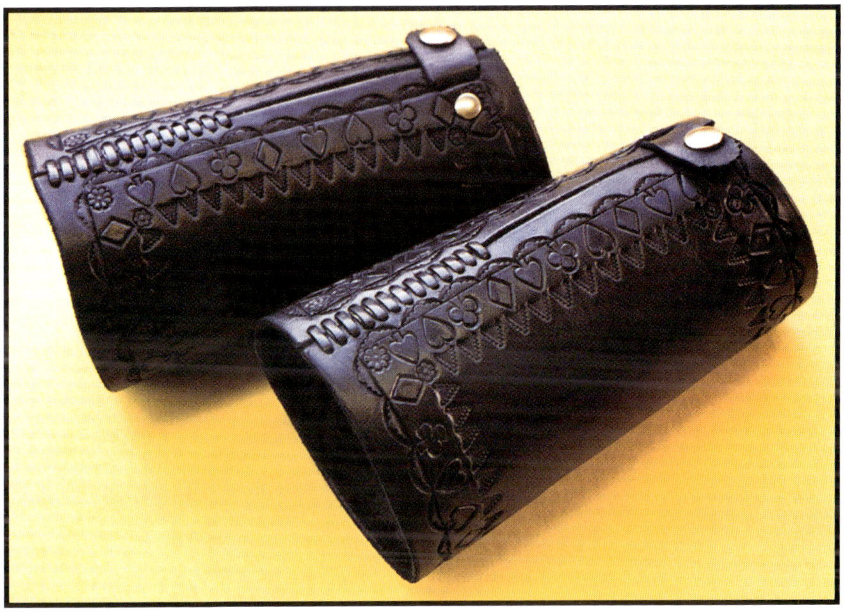

These attractive cuffs with a "card suit" design have a large snap and lacing. *Overton collection. $150 to 200*

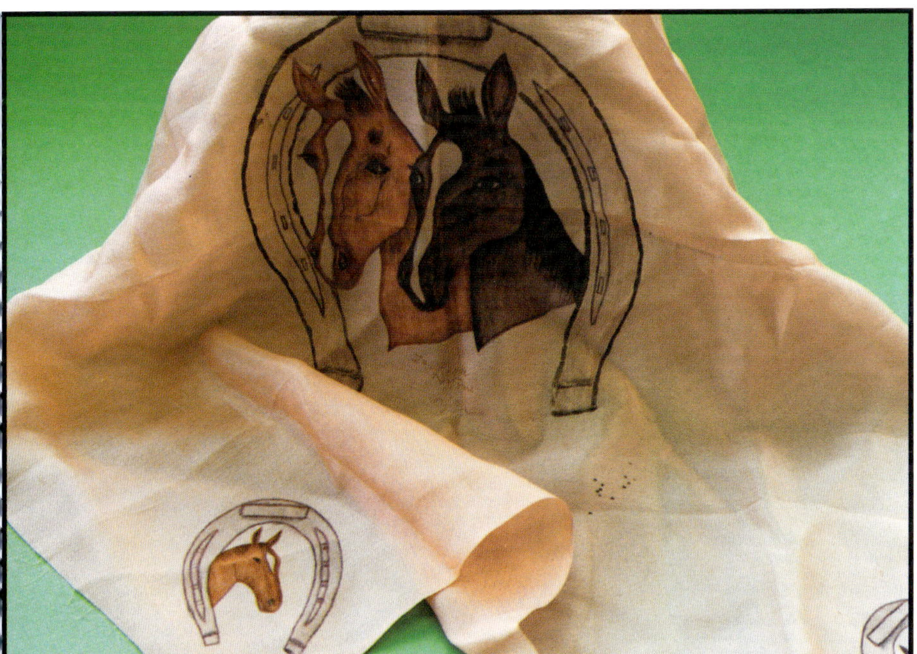

Neckerchiefs were often called "wild rags" in cowboy terminology. This silk one was made in the Boise (Idaho) State Penitentiary in the late 1930s, during the great Depression, by a man who had been caught stealing two chickens to feed his family. After hiding them in a deep snow bank, he was reported as the thief, convicted, and sent to the state prison. After some time there, his wife and two children (one a tiny baby) pled with the warden and obtained the man' s release. The author was the tiny baby. *Overton collection. $100 to priceless*

Chapter Ten

Boots and Bolos

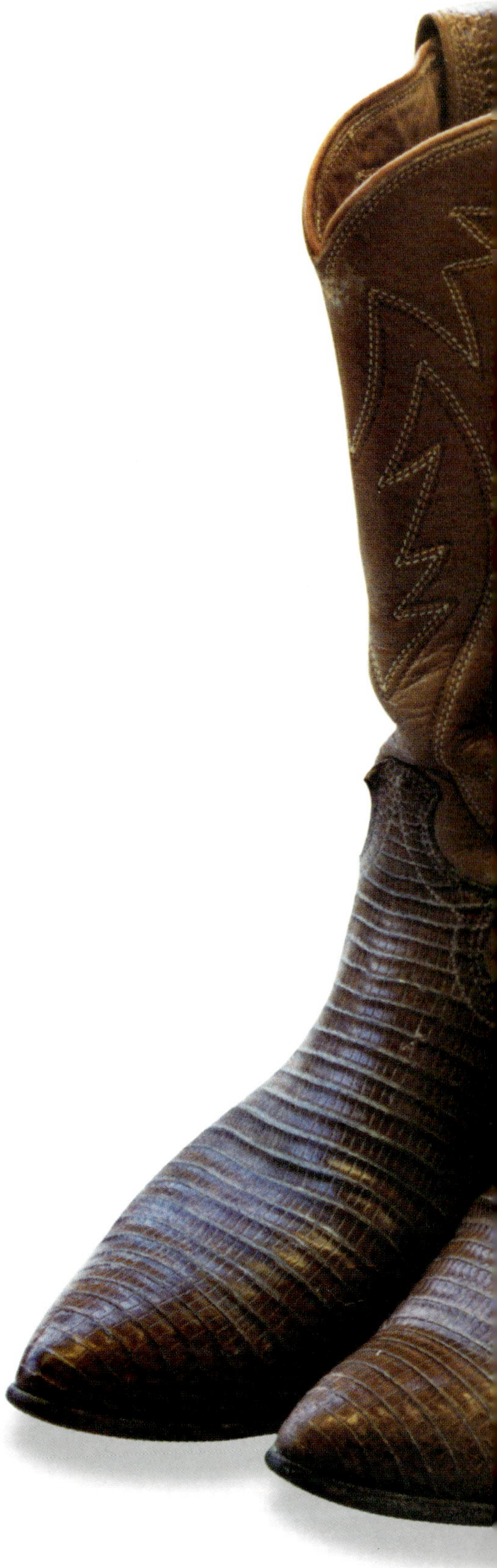

"Cowboy Saturday night"

We are back to an old "Harvey Overton proverb" in this section, for we can still understand what he meant when he said, "Look at a man' s head, then at his feet, and you'll know what's in between!" That "proverb" probably also held true when looking at a man's necktie (Bolo), then at his belt buckle, and finally his boots, and you pretty well had him sized up.

A "cowboy tuxedo" today consists of his best pair of jeans, a good shirt with a Bolo tie, his best pair of boots, and a jacket. There are still places (in the West) where this is considered acceptable attire when "Black Tie" is mandatory for functions. Never doubt the effect that the combination has on people, regardless of locale. The following story may illustrate the concept.

It was summer when William and I decided to take a train to North Carolina to see our newest grandchild recently born at the Camp Lejune military base. We had a travel agency arrange everything and one of our overnight stops was to be in Washington, D.C. Needless to say, William dressed in his best jeans, western shirt, Bolo, boots, and hat. When we arrived at our hotel in downtown D.C. near Embassy Row, we had no way of knowing what a stir we might make. Everyone snapped to, and we were immediately treated like royalty. When we got into the room and were finally alone, I asked him, "What in the world do you think's going on?" He replied that he was "kinda' dumbfounded" also. We dismissed it, and did a little unpacking and then decided to take the elevator down to the restaurant. We seemed to spark the same amount of interest there. Finally, one person asked if William was perhaps a Congressman from Texas. We said, "No," and had a good chuckle over it. When we paid the bill, the young worker there brought him his hat from the coat and hat rack. He asked William if he could, "maybe just try it on?" William told him, "Sure, help yourself." The hat got passed around for quite some time there in that posh eatery, as first one, then another, tried it on. And I guess the moral to the story is: *There's just something about a good black Stetson, folks.*

Old Cowboys

He still wears his old felt hat, but the boots are out of style. Old horse-wrecks and all his heartaches, he still has his cowboy smile.

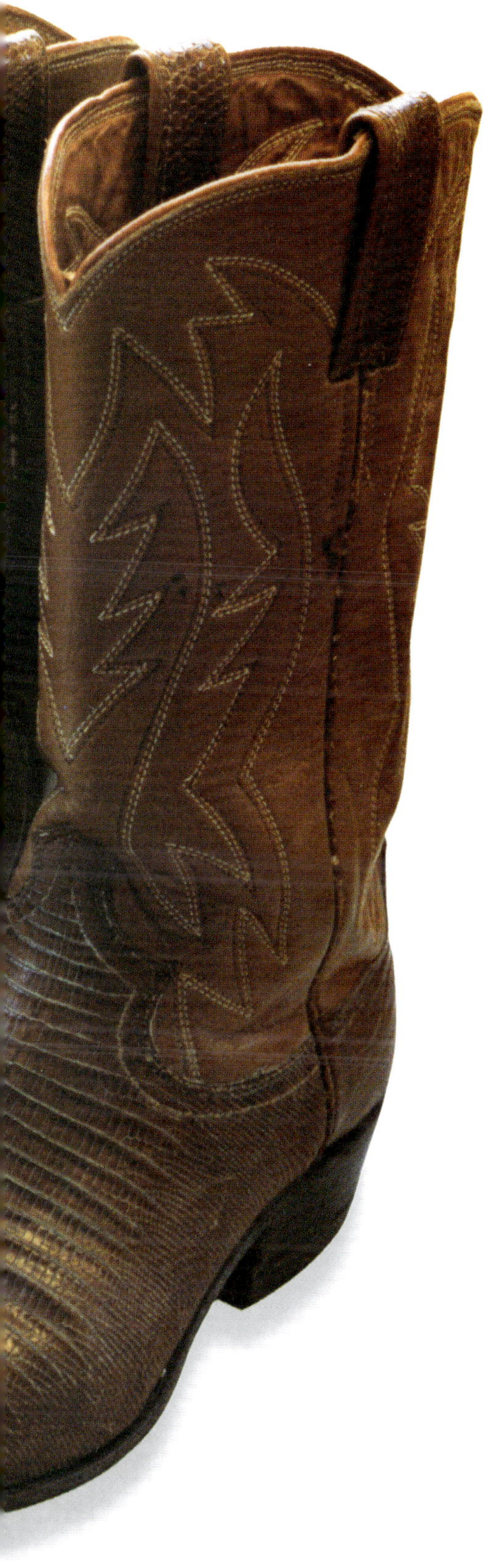

Armadillo skin made a very tough and attractive boot for the cowboy and cowgirl. The marking on these reads, "Justin 1879 Fort Worth, Texas." The boots are not that old; the date indicates the founding of the company that is still building boots today. *Courtesy Pat and Ethel Patterson. $300 to 500*

He hung his saddle in the barn, sold his horse to some old trader. Gave his spurs to one grandson, then went to bed and almost stayed there.

Heres to all the old cowboys around, and the day they last hit the ground. They've made all of their rides, in the great arena of life.

Boots

It is not only the well dressed cowboy who makes heads turn, but also the well dressed cowgirls. Another little story:

I wanted to add some very fancy boots to this book, so I let that fact be known around "the old Cow Sale circle of friends." One day a lady friend of mine, who competed in the rodeos many times as a young woman and who probably knows more about horse gear than many men do, came to see me. Now this is a lady who is an accomplished saddle maker as well as retired rodeo competitor, and can tool leather like most old-time saddle makers only dreamed about. She asked me if I wanted to see her boots. I told her, "Sure." Her husband carried them into my living room and dumped them out on the floor from a huge plastic bag. There lay some of the most colorful old handmade boots I'd ever seen! She had spent a lot of good American dollars for them at the time they were purchased, many years ago. I hope you enjoy seeing Ethel's boots, and if I told you how old she is, you wouldn't believe me. What a lady!

Neckties

When it comes to neckties for a cowboy, there is only one true style, and that is the plain old fashioned neckerchief, sometimes tied behind and other times tied in front, like a neck scarf. However, when a cowboy had to dress up, especially in later years, the choice of tie was bolos and string ties.

String ties

String ties would have been more appropriately dubbed "ribbon ties," for that is just what they were. Most often made from a strip of black satin ribbon about one or two inches wide, they were simply tied into a loose hanging bow under his collar and around his neck, or into a tight wide bow (bow tie). Ribbon was fairly available in all of the general stores, and in every lady's sewing basket.

Bolo ties

The bolo is another matter entirely. Bolo ties were named after the piece of equipment that South American Gauchos (cowboys) used at the time of Spanish settlement in the American West and still use. A *bola* is a piece of strong leather strap with two heavy weights at each end. It is used to throw at the feet of a cow or animal in order to trip and throw him to the ground. As the Gaucho rides swiftly by the animal to be brought down, he swings the *bola* round and round above his head and, with a solid aim, turns it loose in time for it to wind around and tangle up the feet of the animal. It is a very effective method in capturing a wild cow or critter.

The word "bolo" has derived from *bola*, and resembles the actual item with one continuous long or two short leather (generally braided) strips with decorations at each end. In the middle is the clasp ornament, often the most expensive part of the bolo tie. The clasp ornaments have been fashioned of every conceivable material, from Black

Hills gold, silver, and ivory to simple wood, etc. While it has remained a very popular item in the modern-day cowboy's dress, the bolo tie has its roots in a very ancient art. Old ones are interesting to look for and collect.

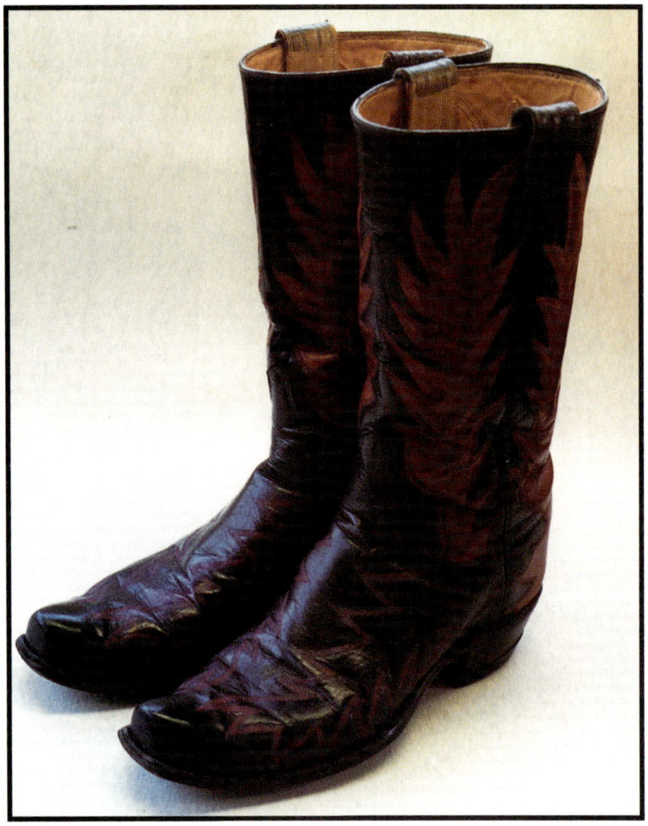

Flame stitched with red thread on supple black leather, these boots are one-of-a-kind and very beautifully made. *Courtesy Pat and Ethel Patterson. $400 to 650*

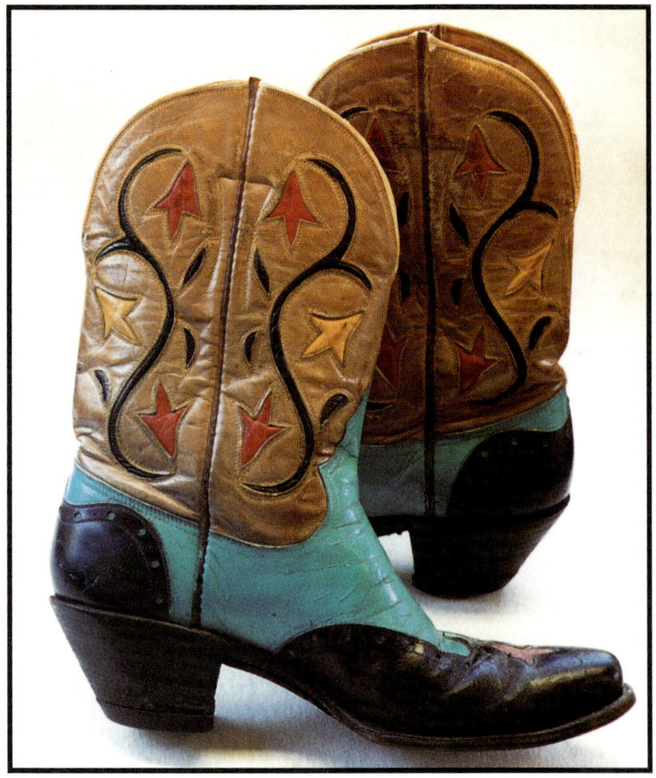

This pair of colorful hand-made boots are exquisite with overlays and stitching, highly unusual details in the world of boots. *Courtesy Pat and Ethel Patterson. $800 to 1000*

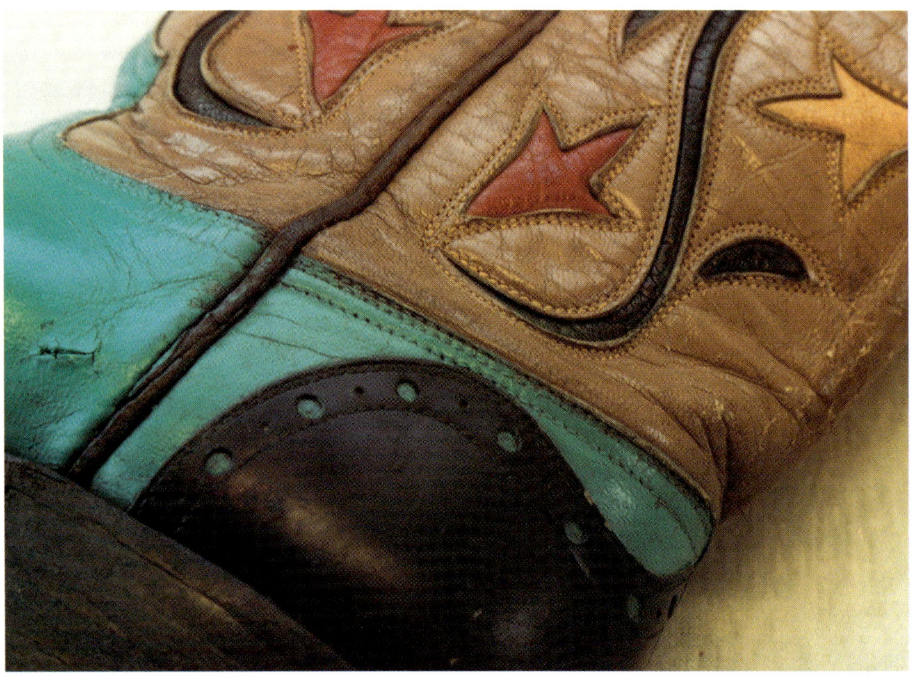

Detail of stitching and leather overlays. The tiny "barbed wire" mark adds interest and desirability.

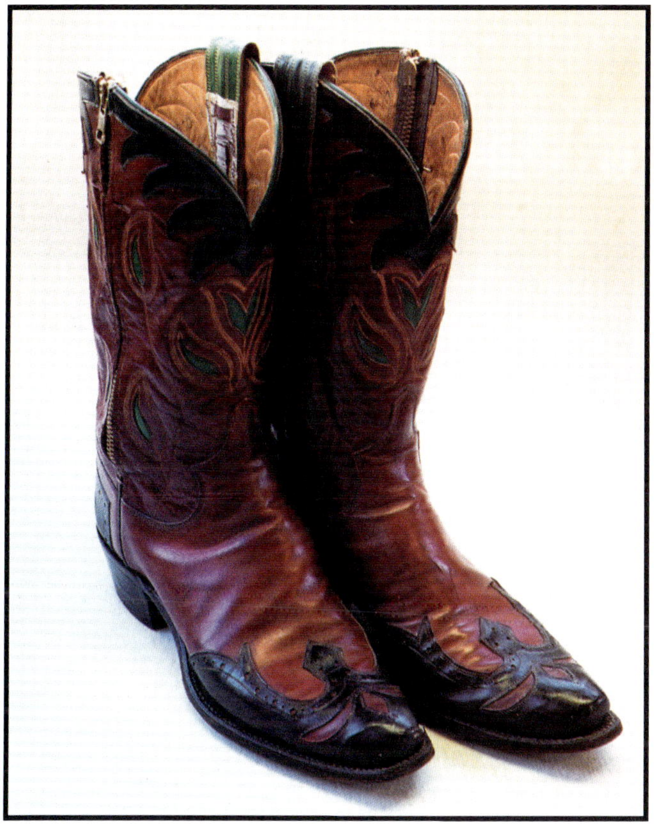

Elegant red leather boots with black overlays. The zippers are contemporary additions. *Courtesy Pat and Ethel Patterson. $750 to 900*

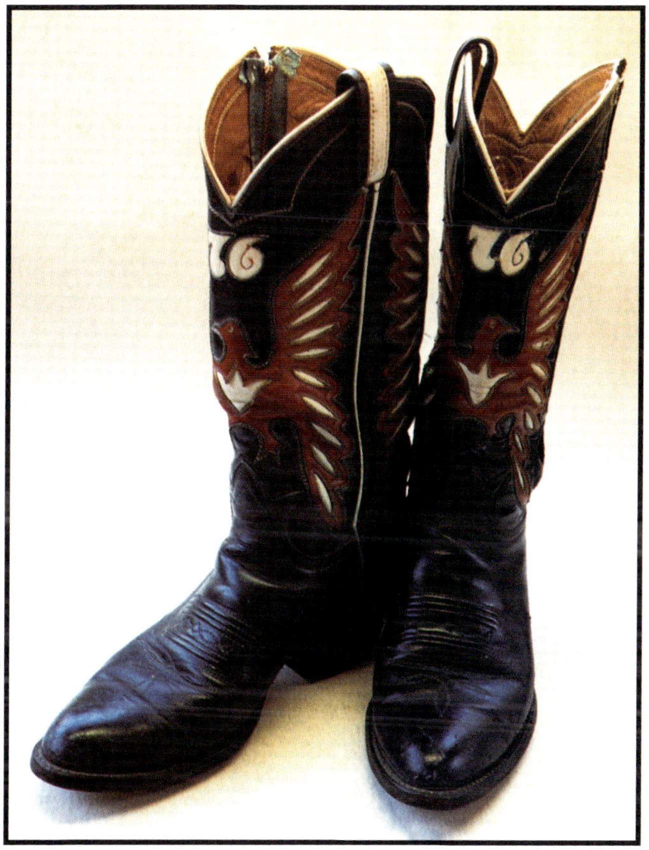

Commemorating the centennial, 1876 to 1976, these handmade boots with full winged eagles on them are distinctly and yet simply beautiful. When being worn, the only part showing would be the simple black foot. *Courtesy Pat and Ethel Patterson. $650 to 800*

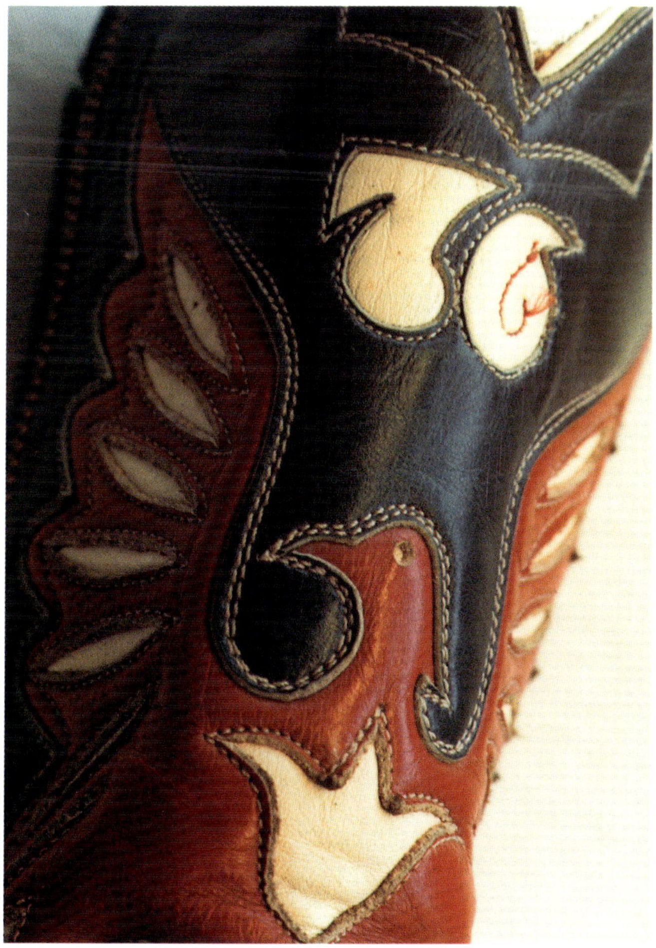

Detail. The number 76 is visible above the eagle's head.

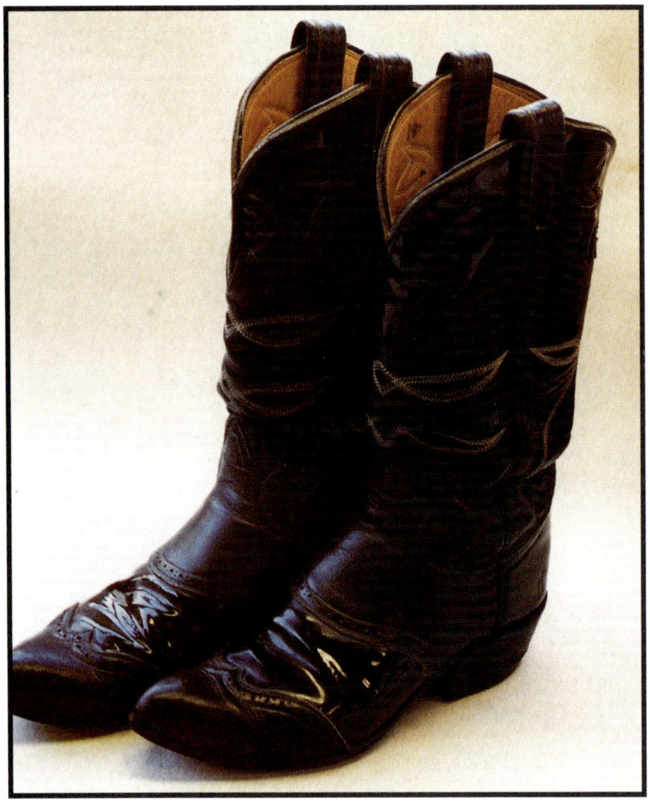

Beautiful in their simplicity, these black leather boots have patent leather inlays, giving them an elegant "tuxedo" dress-up look. Made by Tony Lama Boot Co. *Courtesy Pat and Ethel Patterson. $600 to 750*

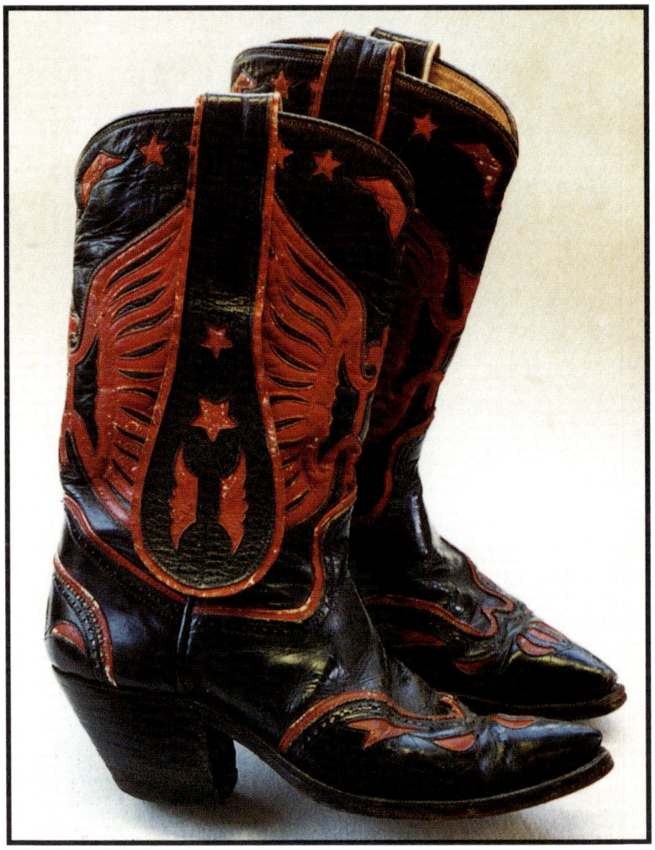

Made by Stuart Romero, Los Angeles, California, these boots are completely hand constructed and made to order to fit the buyer, c. 1940. *Courtesy Pat and Ethel Patterson. $1000 to 1500*

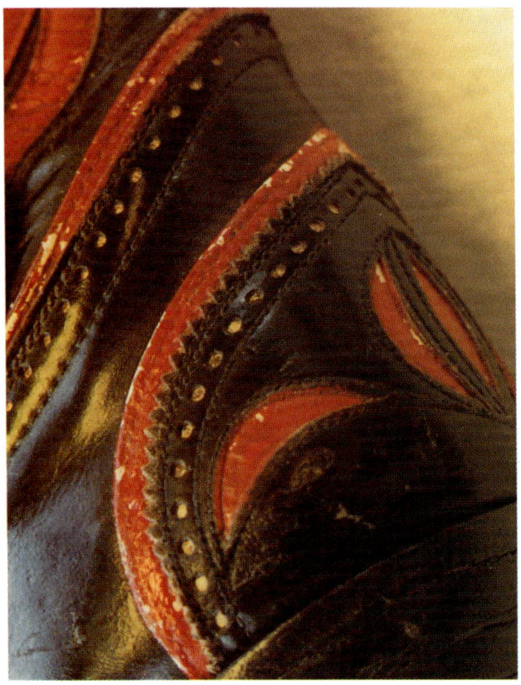

Detail of intricate overlay on heel.

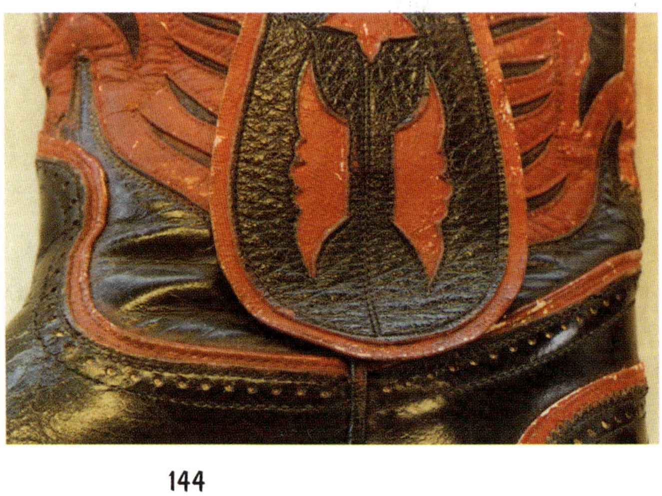

Detail of the lower side of the Romero boots.

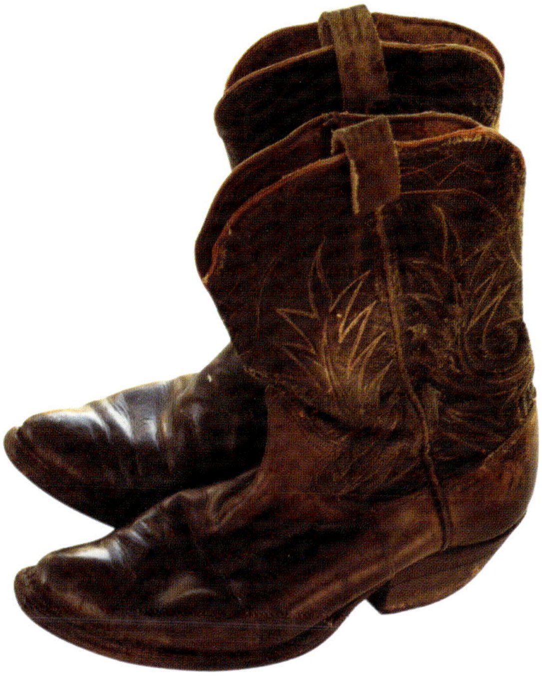

Boots are old; the low-cut tops are often indicative of age, c.1940s. *Courtesy R.C. and Marvin Bales. $150 to 200*

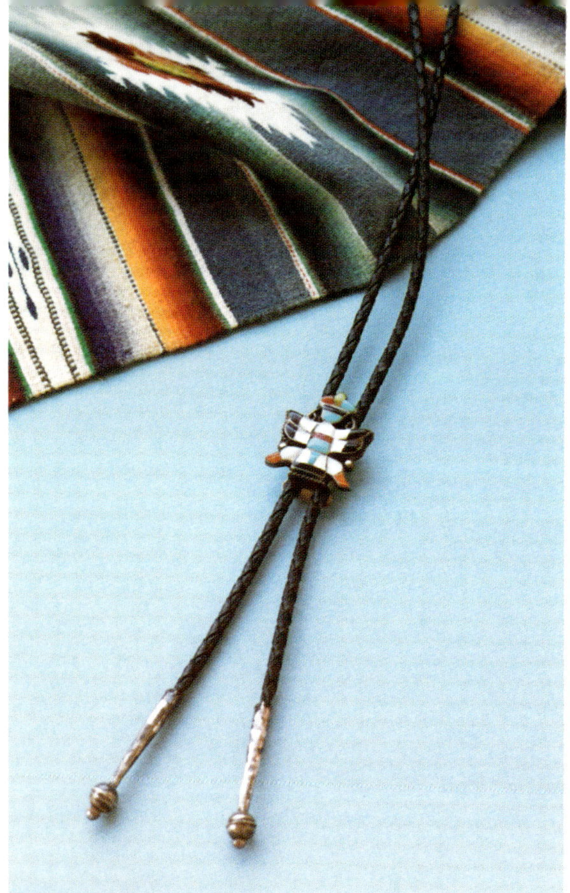

Southwestern style bolo necktie with inlaid semi-precious stones. The figure is a Kachina, the bolo tips are sterling silver, and the tie is round braided leather. *Overton collection. $50 to 65*

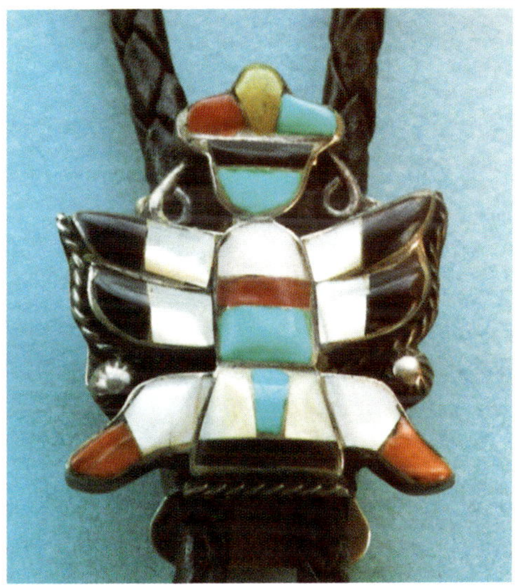

Detail of Kachina

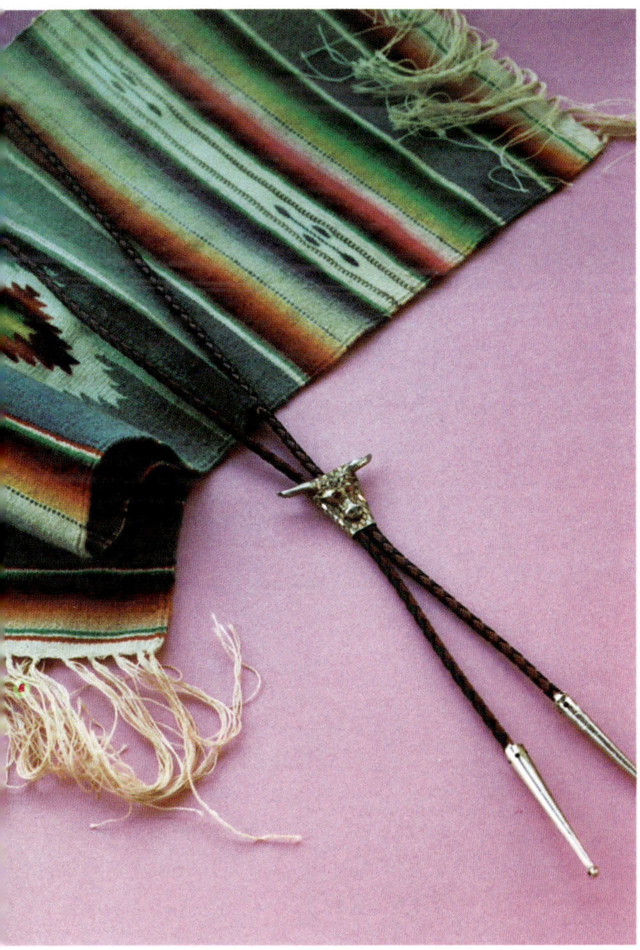

Steer-head bolo with ruby eyes and sterling silver tips. *Overton collection. $75 to 80*

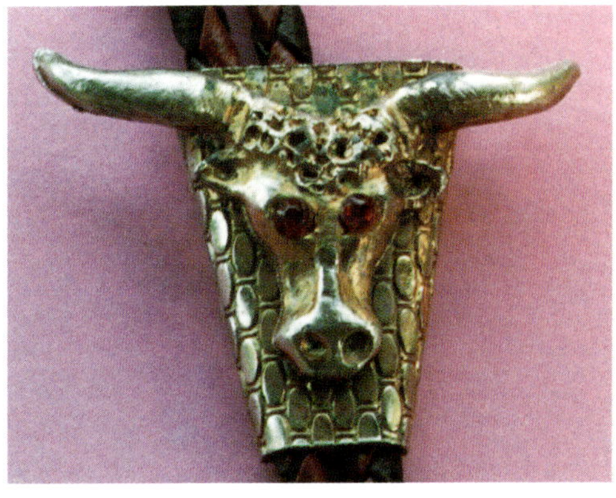

Detail of steer's head

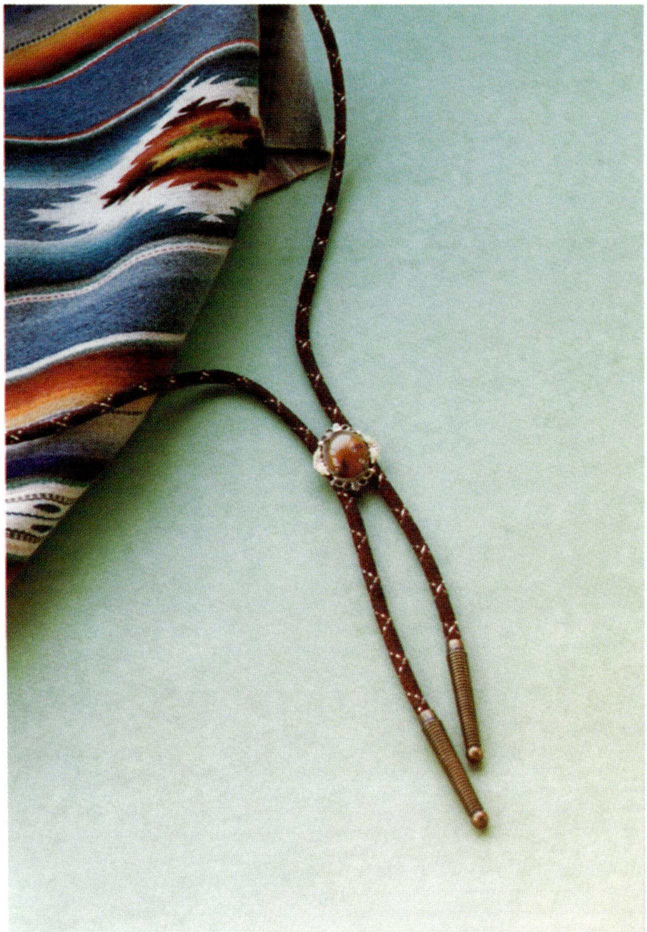

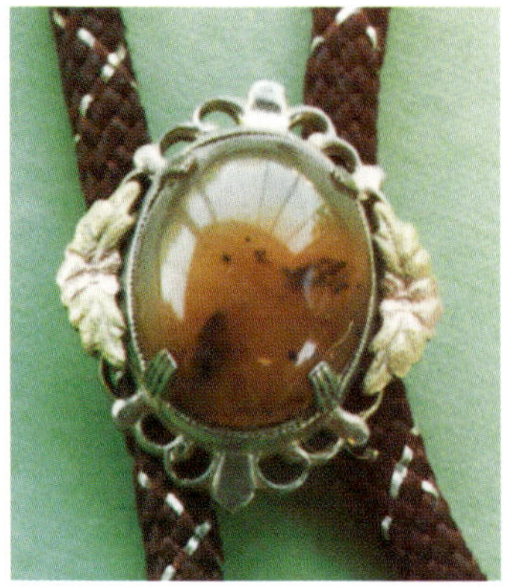

Detail of moss agate and gold frame.

Black Hills gold framing a natural moss agate. *Overton collection.* *$150 to 200*

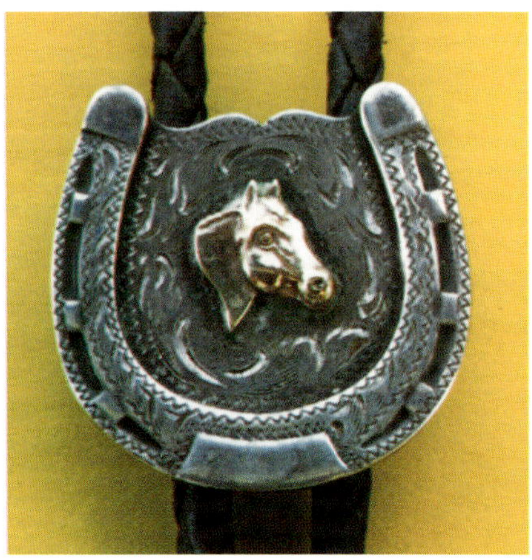

Detail of horsehead.

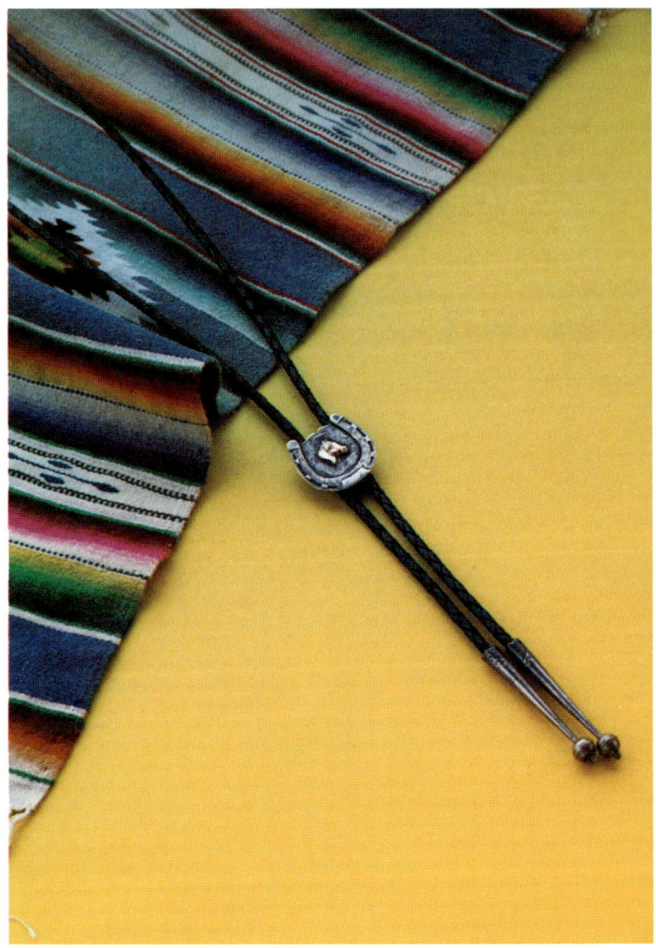

Sterling silver and gold horsehead in a horseshoe frame. The tips are sterling silver and the tie is braided leather. *Overton collection. $100 to 125*

In closing.........

Gone are the cowboys......leaving imprint of boots
weary banners falling.........
and empty chutes.

Clifford P. Westermeir, *Man, Beast, Dust, The Story of Rodeo*

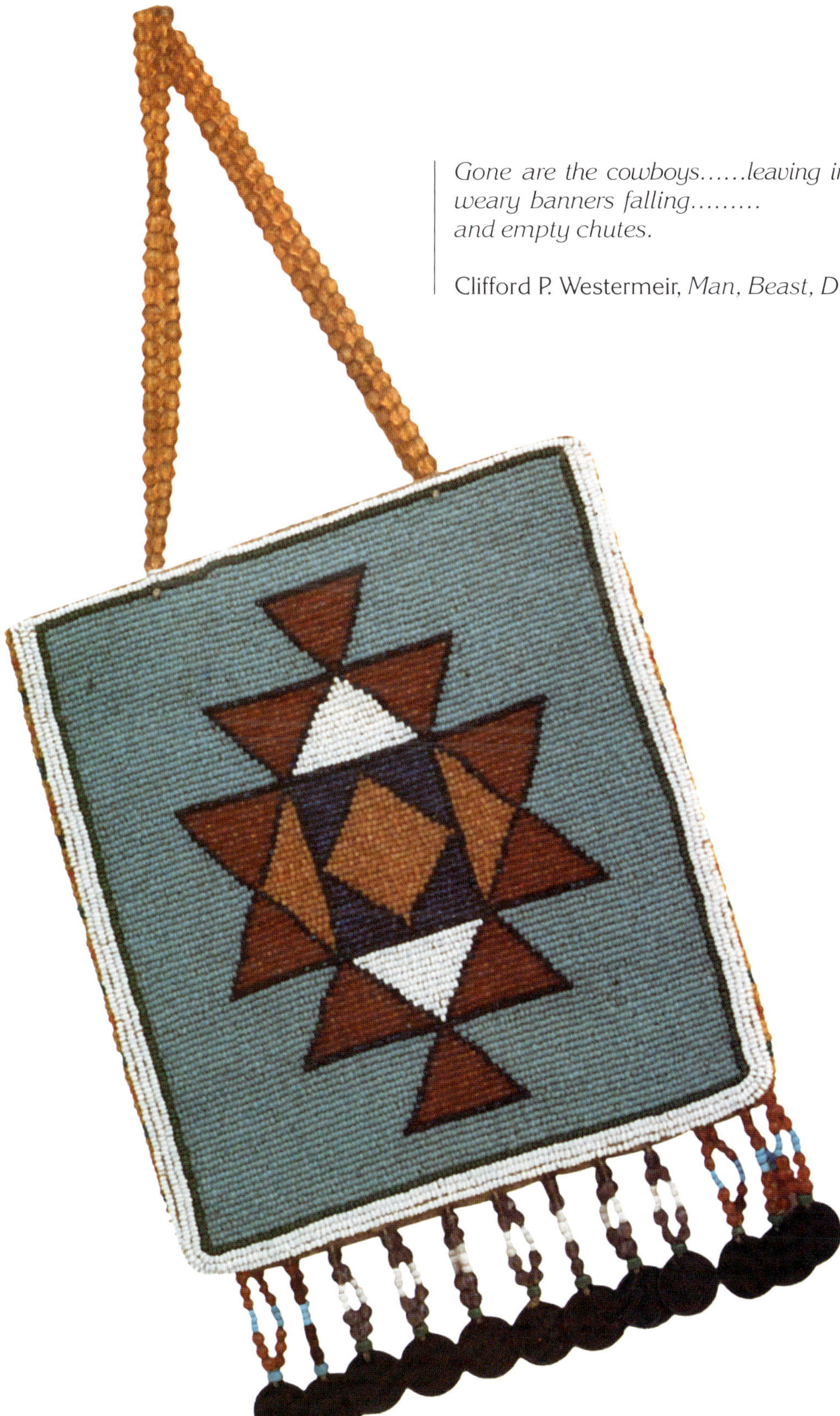

Index